A

CRITICAL INQUIRY

INTO

ANTIENT ARMOUR.

Sir Samuel Rush Meyrick

A

CRITICAL INQUIRY

INTO

ANTIENT ARMOUR,

AS IT EXISTED IN EUROPE, BUT PARTICULARLY IN

ENGLAND,

FROM THE NORMAN CONQUEST TO THE REIGN OF

KING CHARLES II.

WITH

A GLOSSARY OF MILITARY TERMS OF THE MIDDLE AGES.

IN THREE VOLUMES.

BY

SIR SAMUEL RUSH MEYRICK, LL.D. AND F.S.A.

VOL. I.

This Edition Originally Published :
London : Robert Jennings. No 2, Poultry: 1824

This Edition :
Barrie : RNU Press : 2018

Re-Typset in: Garamond Premier Pro®

Book Design & Layout: © David Edwards (RNU Press)
Cover Art: © David Edwards

Republished by RNU Press
111 Widgeon St.
Barrie, ON, L4N 8W2
www.rnupress.com

RNU PRESS

ISBN: 978-1-989434-00-0

This book is printed on acid-free paper.

Vol. 1. ISBN 978-1-989434-00-0
Vol. 2. ISBN 978-1-989434-01-7
Vol. 3. ISBN 978-1-989434-02-4

CONTENTS

LIST OF PLATES

𝕿𝕺 𝕿𝕳𝕰 𝕶𝕴𝕹𝕲

SIRE,

MAY IT PLEASE YOUR MAJESTY,

YOUR gracious permission to dedicate this Work to **YOUR MAJESTY**, proves that, while **YOUR** munificence rescues from devouring time the inhumated excellence of Greece and Rome, the humble gleanings of an individual are not considered unworthy **YOUR** Royal encouragement. Feeling grateful, as a member of that University on which has been conferred **YOUR** princely donation, my obligations increase when I thus find myself singly and ostensibly the object of **YOUR** fostering care.

While **YOUR MAJESTY** is this way pleased to demonstrate that whatever researches tend to benefit literature or the arts are not debarred **YOUR** powerful patronage, I am consequently called on to declare myself,

With all due respect,

YOUR MAJESTY'S

Most dutiful and obliged Subject,

SAMUEL R. MEYRICK.

PREFACE.

The History of Antient Armour presents a wide field of attractive research, almost entirely unexplored. With the history of the wars of mankind, it is obviously, and from the remotest periods, connected; with the mythology and sacred rites of almost all nations and religions; with the rise and progress of a large portion of the arts; with questions of jurisprudence and civil polity; and with some of the most favorite amusements of all ranks in antient, as well as modern times.

Although, therefore, in adventuring forth to the discussion of this subject, we have restrained our pursuits, we trust, within the just limits of a literary knighthood, some portion of the antient ardor in these pursuits must be expected from us by the reader: we may have deviated with great freedom into collateral questions; and we have found it generally impossible to confine our attention to what a lexicographer would teach us to understand, by Antient Armour, i.e. *Defensive Arms*. The consideration of their origin and uses will, of necessity, include some statement of the weapons to which they were opposed, the military architecture of the period, &c. The war-mat of the South-Sea islanders, and the wicker shields of the Japanese, are specimens of armour adapted to the equally barbarous offensive weapons of those tribes; and in modern Europe, with the revival of the antient demi-lance as a weapon, has appeared the cuirass of antiquity for the protection of cavalry. Defensive arms clearly *follow* the character of the instruments of assault: hence our work and its plates, are, perhaps, fully as much occupied with the one as with the other.

Particular battles of antient times, and some of the most celebrated in our own history, have been decided by the service of certain weapons, or the use of particular armour. The falling arrow, which, in a direction that no ball would take, dealt his death-wound on King Harold, and transferred the splendid laurel of the battle of Hastings to William I; the triumphs of the English bow in the battles of Cressy, of Poictiers, and of Agincourt; and the artifice of digging and covering trenches, which would not sustain the weight of the English knights, by which Bruce won the battle of Bannockburn, are instances in point. We have, therefore, felt, that an occasional sketch of these actual conflicts would afford the best illustration of our subject, and exhibit the true spirit and features of that "iron race in iron clad," which Englishmen have been.

In tracing the origin of armour, and throughout the work, we have been guided rather by the sure lights of history, than by philosophical speculation, yet is it an obvious conjecture of reason that around "the human form divine" it would be amongst the first efforts of art to throw every possible protection, both in the chase and in the field of war: the same train of reflection could lead us to expect a primary care of the most important parts of the body, the sources of life and of sensation—the head, and the chest.

And these conjectures are realized by the historic date of our subject. The earliest authentic history in the world (Gen. IV. 22) gives us a father, or "instructor of every artificer in brass and iron," inTubal-cain, (the Vulcan of the Greeks and Romans)[1], before the flood; and the helmet and the breastplate were always principal pieces of armour. Herodotus describes the battles of the antient Egyptians as having been fought in armour; Assyria, Persia, all the Asiatic empires of early date, thus exhibit their strength and their magnificence; and while our great poet mythologizes, clothing alike in the armour, and attributes of the heathen divinities those rebel hosts who

> With ambitious aim,
> Against the throne and monarchy of God,
> Raised impious war in heaven:

And gives to their celestial opponents,

> Arms
> Of golden panoply—

Mythology, in all its earlier details, is historical, and dimly shadows forth

1 Vossius de Idol. L. i, c. 16.

the first invention and slow progress of armorial defence. The Pantheon clothes all its nobler deities in armour; Vulcan, the humble fabricator, has his claim to divinity allowed with that of Mars, the inventor, of defensive arms, or the first conqueror by means of them. The exploits of Hercules invest him with the skins of the monsters he slew: and the ægis, or goat skin, furnishes to Jupiter both a breast-plate and a shield. Thus have we, upon this as upon every other topic of early historical research, that combination of fact and fable which it is frequently impossible to separate.

What may be called the mythological contributions to our subject go to establish the early prevalence of war, the importance attached from its first introduction to the personal defence of the soldier, and some few facts in regard to the early methods of defence.

The pleasures and dangers of the chase were, perhaps, among the first of human pursuits that suggested the use of armour. In the fair fields of that beautiful creation which never taught man war, he would find, when inflamed by his own passions, suggestions both of offensive and defensive warfare, upon which he has rarely improved. The mailed tortoise, the scaly shields of fish, even the beautiful lapping-over of feathers in the plumes of birds, afforded hiiu specimens of well contrived protection: while from the boar, the bull, the ram, or the sagacious and tenacious cat he might obtain lessons, not to be despised, of powerful and skilful assault. We know, in fact, that a certain disposition of the shields in imitation of the folds of tortoise-shell was in use among the Greeks; and is alluded to in a curious Treatise on the duties of the foot soldier in the fourteenth century.[2] A floating "boar" armed with iron and "pushed forward with oars," is recommended in the same Treatise in sea-fights: the battering-ram long retained a name and figure indicative of his origin, and has transferred, in modern times, no small portion of his merits, with its etymon, to the ram-rod; and the "prickly cat (*felis echinata*)" we are told, was "one of the best kind of arms and most useful for the defenders of castles." She could even be set upon *her* prey with success; being armed with "oaken teeth" and "curved nails", which, when the enemy approached, might be thrown upon him, and serve to "bring up one or more" into the walls.

The classics are full of allusions to the origin of armour in the sports of the field; and the poetical epithets of ἰκτιδέη, κυνέη, ταυρέιη, λεοντεη, αἰγείη, the weasel, the dog, the bull, and the lion-skin helmet were continued in later times when those feebler coverings were superseded by the use of brass or

2 See Vol. I, page 248 of this work.

iron. It is well known that some of the Mexican tribes made a similar use of the skins of beasts taken in the chage, and wore them, as the antient Greeks did, with the hair on, and frequently with the teeth. The Roman lorica, or body armour, like the more modern cuirass, owes its name, in like manner, to its being originally formed of leather, or prepared skins. In Virgil we have a splendid combination of these ideas (Æneid, lib. XI. v. 770) in the foaming horse of "brazen skin, like a gilt, scaly plume."

The ornaments, and several prominent parts of armour designed for display or to strike terror into the enemy, are to be traced to a similar origin. Thus the ridge of the περικεφαλ had its (λοφος) horse-hair ornament, composed sometimes of the hair but always meant to imitate the noble mane of that animal. The cock also yielded his feathers to mark the honors of a chieftain, and plumes and crests are clearly ornaments transferred from the feathered tribes to man.

The numerous *arts* that were exercised in the structure of antient arms and armour atoned, in some measure, for their connexion with the purposes of ambition and the "game of blood." The skins of animals, at first worn rough from the body, were afterwards dressed to considerable perfection, even by the early εὐκνήμιδες Ἀχαιοί, the well-booted Greeks, and the best resistance of which leather is capable was seen, perhaps in the antient shields. The history of the sling, the earliest and simplest weapon of antiquity, is connected with the art of dressing flax, and hair, as well as leather, in the first of which the Egyptians attained a very early eminence we know; while all the chief weapons of assault and defence owe their perfection to the progressive improvements in metallurgy, the modern science of chemistry, &c. As many of the arts were stimulated in their progress, others were doubtless preserved to the world, by their connection with warlike pursuits. Amongst our Anglo-Saxon ancestors the important labors of the smithery were duly appreciated. "For the gem-bearing belts and diadems of kings," says Aldhelm[3] "and various instruments of glory, were made from the tools of iron." The smiths of some districts were exempt from all the usual services to the state. It is remarkable, that an inferior kind of brass, or mixed metal, as more easily fused, long preceded the general use of iron, in the manufacture of armour, as well as of offensive arms. The art of tempering steel, we know, was carried to the greatest perfection in the swords of the Ferrara family and by the artists of Milan, centuries ago.

Chivalry in its most polished forms, inspired by gallantry, and sanc-

---

3 Quoted by Mr. Turner, Hist. Anglo-Saxon, V. II, p. 110

tioned by religion, connects itself with the topics of this work. This enthusiastic spirit may be said, like Minerva, to have been born into the world in
armour, as in armour, and superseded by steadier principles, let us hope, it
died. Mr. Turner considers it to have been first exhibited in this country
in its more refined and complete character in the reign of William II, and
to have flourished in its maturity under the auspices of Edward the Black
Prince. The knight was devoted by religious vows to the service of the wid-
ow, the orphan; the oppressed of every class; to resent the injuries of the
church in particular, and maintain the honor of the fair sex.

If not uniformly a person of high birth, he was, in the better times of
this institution, a person of distinguished valor and merit, from whose society and highsouled pursuits, persons who had lost their shields in battle, all blasphemers, traitors, adulterers, the perjured, the coward, and the
homicide were uniformly expelled. Ladies, leading forth the knights into
the tournament, and becoming the dispensers of honor and of mercy, there
present us with the softening influence of Christianity, even in its most
imperfect forms, on the condition and happiness of women, and through
them on all the strongest impulses of man. Armour was frequently the prize
of these combats; a valuable sword rewarding the victorious challenger, and
a helmet of equal value, the challenged.

The *wager of battle*, a legal appeal in this country, within the last ten
years,[4] may be said to have been our final relic of chivalrous justice. It was
the right of persons of all degrees thus to terminate certain suits, and particularly that of the near relative of a slain man, to challenge a supposed mur-
derer, although a jury should acquit him. The fullest form of directions for
the duel in this judicial combat will be found v. ii, p. 65. In the memorable
combat-scene of *Ivanhoe*, our great historical novelist has forcibly depicted
the sincere and solemn feelings of our forefathers on many of these occasions;[5] and Shakspeare alludes to the custom both as practised among the
higher and lower ranks. The royal championship of England still rests on
the foundation of this antient appeal, and conveys the fair manor of Scriv-
elsby "by grand serjeanty; to wit, by the service of finding, on the day of
coronation, an armed knight who shall prove *by his body*, if need be, that the
king is true and lawful heir to the kingdom." So that this splendid exhibition
of the antient feudal service is not likely to be soon abolished.

The joust and the tournament, while exercises of personal strength and

4 It was abolished during the regency of his present Majesty, (59 George III, cap. 46.)
5 Ivanhoe, V. III, p- 328, 345.

schools of military discipline, were also *amusements* of the privileged orders of society. Froissart preserves a singular challenge to "a deed of arms," sent by Louis, Duke of Orleans, to our Henry IV, in which he says: "Considering *idleness* to be the bane of lords of high birth which do not employ themselves in arms," he thought he could in "no way better seek renown," than in proposing to meet Henry at an appointed place with one hundred knights and esquires, "and with the usual arms;" that is to say, "lance, battle-axe, sword and dagger, each to employ them as he shall think most to his advantage, without aiding himself by any bodkins, hooks, bearded darts, poisoned needles, or razors, as may be done, (this is a singular admission,) by persons unless they be positively ordered to the contrary." Several of the varieties that are found in antient helmets, in the structure of the lance, &c. owe their origin to their being used in the amusements of the tilt or tournament-field, as distinguishable from those designed for serious combat in war.

But these occupations for "idleness" being confined, by the rules of chivalry, to the great; burgesses and yeomen established certain imitations of them: thus we have the Troy-game of the Roman youths performed among "great crowds of young Londoners," in the reigns of our Stephen and Henry II, both on land and water. A species of wooden shields was tilted against in boats on the bosom of father Thames, or suspended from a stake fixed on the ground. Similar sports are traced in Oxfordshire and throughout the country. It was particularly an Easter holiday amusement.[6]

Some of the customs which had their origin in those military atchievements, of which the following pages treat, establish the varying fashions and moods of the world, in attempting the same general object of personal defence, from age to age, others the permanency of some national habits and manners; others again are curiously connected with the etymology of modern languages. In the significant but sometimes humble wrapping of crape round the left arm of the military, for mourning, who would recognize the kercheff of plesaunce, presented antiently, by his "sovereign lady" to her chosen knight, which bound him to her service, and with which he must not part but with his life? yet such is its origin: see our Glossary. On the other hand, the scull-cap, and shield of the Turks and Saracens, in the first crusade (1146), an expedition which diverted the eldest son of the Conqueror from asserting his right to the throne of England, are precisely those of the military among the Georgian and Circassian tribes at this day. Nor, it is hoped, will

6 Brand's Pop. Antiq. 279.

the etymologist despise our aid when we instance dag as signifying a pistol, while pistolese implies a dagger, and semi-targe a corruption of scymitar, as showing conclusions should not be too readily formed from sounds; when we exhibit our DRAGOONS, as "being in all languages called so, because a musketeer on horseback, with his burning match, riding a gallop, as many times he doth, may something resemble that beast which *naturalists* call a fiery dragon;" and when we shew that the tales of knights encountering fiery dragons in the Holy-land, took their origin from the dread inspired by the Greek-fire ejected from tubes with mouths made to resemble those of that fabulous animal. To those who are interested in more modern warfare it will probably excite some interest that our researches have enabled us to fix the first use of small fire arms to the year 1430, and that in 1446 we find them in the county of Durham.

But a main object of this work is to establish that *chronology of costume*, with respect to antient arms and armour, which has hitherto been so imperfectly regarded alike by writers, painters and dramatists of modern times. Zeal for the truth of history, requires us to remind modern writers and artists that the barons of King John were not habited, as they are commonly painted, in the knightly accoutrements of Edward I; and that a sepulchral effigy, cloathed in armour of Richard the Second's time cannot represent Rhys, Prince of Wales a cotemporary of Henry II, although it is confidently made to wear his name in the frontispiece of a respectable historical work.

The full feeling and effect of historical anecdotes and incidents sometimes depend, essentially on our acquaintance with antient armour. An example or two will suffice. William the Conqueror, to crush the rebellion of his son, besieged the castle of Gerberoy, on the borders of Normandy. During the siege Robert, in a vigorous sally, engaged a knight enveloped in armour, wounded him in the arm, and unhorsed him. At the moment of his fall his helmet moved back, and he discovered that his antagonist was his father. With a true chivalrous feeling he dismounted with precipitation, respectfully assisted William to regain his horse, and permitted him to depart. The armour of that day covered the throat and head, leaving the face exposed: the helmet was a mere scull-cap. How then are we to understand this interesting scene? A circumstance apparently trifling is all that is wanting. This scull-cap was furnished with a broad piece of steel which covered the nose, and was termed a nasal, so that, the instant it was put on, the features were too partially seen to be recognised. In the fall it might be thrown back, and thus discover the wearer.

In the reign of Stephen another incident occured which will prove the necessity of some accurate knowledge of the various parts of antient armour, and probably led to the disuse of the nasal-piece. That prince, in 1141, suddenly attacked the castle of Leicester, then held by the Earl of Gloucester for the Empress Maud. When Stephen had set down before it, the earl endeavoured to surprize him by a rapid movement across the Trent, which forced the king to a battle. Always ready for deeds of valour, Stephen and his knights attempted to convert the attack into a succession of single combats or jousts; but their adversaries threw away their lances, and advanced with irresistable impetuosity to decide the contest sword in hand: the king was seen dealing death on every side of him with the battle-axe: until, at last, a stone struck him on the head and he fell to the ground: a knight sprung upon him, while stunned, and "seizing him by the helmet," according to Malmsbury, called out: "Hither! hither! I have got the kinga circumstance that decided the encounter, and, for a time, the fate of the kingdom. The fact was, the conical helmet of that day would not easily afford hand-hold; the victor had, in this instance, seized the nasalpiece by which he could command the entire person of a prostrate knight.

Our greatest poets have felt the necessity of some extensive acquaintance with these topics, and have been aided, beyond calculation, in some of their grander scenes by the splendid machinery of antient armour. How would the high debates, the terrific array, the giant shapes of Milton's Pandemonium, stripped of their armour, be denuded of their impression! In the case of the 'superior fiend:

> With atlantoean shoulders fit to bear
> The weight of mightiest monarchies,

What substitute could be found for:

> His ponderous shield,
> Etherial temper, massy, large and round
> Behind him cast; whose broad circumference
> Hung on his shoulders like the moon whose orb
> Thro' optic glass the Tuscan artist views
> At evening from the top of Fesoll
> Or in Valdamor, to descry new lands,
> Rivers or mountains in her spotty globe,

Or for that:

> —Spear to equal which the tallest pine
> Hewn on Norwegian hills, to be the mast
> Of some great ammiral, were but a wand,

What other terms could express the fallen glories of Hell as when:

> All in a moment thro' the gloom wer e seen
> Ten thousand banners rise into the air,
> With orient colours waving: and with them
> A forest of huge spears and thronging helms,
> And serried shields in thick array,
> Of depth immeasurable.

Or the battle-scene in Heaven, when:

> The madding wheels
> Of brazen chariots raged , dire was the noise
> Of conflict; over head the dismal hiss
> Of fiery darts in floating vollies flew
> And flying vaulted' either host with fire.

> —Likest gods they seemed
> Stood they or moved, in nature, motion, arms,
> Fit to decide the empire of great heaven.

Milton caught all the striking details of our subject at a period when they were just beginning to lose their importance in actual war, through the invention of fire-arms.

In the poet's eye it can never be lost. Shakspeare is scarcely inferior to Milton in his knowledge and skilful adaptation of its resources for poetic illustration. What can exceed, in happy point, the exclamation:

> O majesty!
> Whenthou dost pinch thy' bearer, thou dost sit
> Like a rich armour worn in heat of day,
> That scalds with safety.

Or the fine moral lesson in our mouths from childhood:

What stronger breast-plate than a heart untainted!
Thrice is he armed that. hath his quarrel just,
And he but naked tho' locked up in steel,
Whose conscience with injustice is corrupted.

The refined taste which, with regard to other matters of costume, has been so happily cultivated in this country, during the present reign, has not only given a general stimulus to the arts, but introduced into paintings and scenic representations of all kinds, an historical correctness with which our ancestors were unacquainted. Good drawing and correct colouring, fine acting with well delivered sentences, are now considered as insufficient without chronological accuracy. Though, in every other respect, claiming our applause, Alexander and Statira in brocade and velvet[7] are as offensive on the canvass as that conqueror in a gold lace coat and wig, and his favourite in a corresponding habit at the theatre. In the reigns of Charles II and William III, the judicious and critical antiquary did not in vain lay open the stores of the classic world. Their captivating elegance made them the general models of sculpture and painting; though they could not at once rescue the heroes of antiquity from the addition of a high flowing periwig.

Such absurdities, however, are now banished: in matter of ordinary habiliment, or antient civic costume, whether we regard the productions of our historical artists, or view a theatrical representation, we feel transported to the very era of the event we witness. And why, in respect to armour, should a similar accuracy be deemed unworthy of regard! In all the paintings since the time of Charles I the warriors of whatever age, are represented in the military costume of that period;[8] and yet, as great a variety has existed in armour and it is as characteristic of successive eras, as other habiliments. The truth is, artists have neither understood the subject themselves, nor been able to find sources of information elsewhere. The modern practice is to draw from the collection in the Tower, and yet, notwithstanding the pretence, there is not a suit there older than the time of Henry VII. Some, indeed, have possessed themselves of detached pieces in order to be more correct; but this has enabled them only to imitate more faithfully the appearance of steel: there has been no modern attempt at an historical classification of armour. It is known that chain-armour was antiently used, and

---

7 Paul Veronese has actually committed this error.

8 The late Mr. West was an exception to this remark, as appears in his picture of the Battle of Hastings, engraved for Hùme's History of England; and yet I have a painting of his in which Paris is in the armour of Julius Coesar.

although there is little now in existence, Asiatic suits are being constantly palmed upon the public as of undoubted European antiquity.[9]

There is a Treatise on Antient Armour by Captain Gi'ose, occupying half a volume of his work on Military Antiquities, and founded on Pere Daniel's Milice Françoise. These are referred to as text-books, because they are the only works of the kind extant. Much praise is due to Captain Grose for this collection, formed during his researches respecting antient castles; but there is no critical arrangement, no correct illustration to be found throughout the work. A mass of crude materials are presented to the reader accompanied with incorrect and absurd traditions, and with some representations of military usages which could only be taken from the imagination of the author.[10]

Under these circumstances the present volumes have been compiled—with a view, in some measure, of supplying the general deficiency of information on the subject: to throw a glimpse of light over the rugged paths of the historian, to furnish dates to the antiquary, and to give the vividness of truth to the efforts of painting, sculpture, and the drama.

After some introductory remarks, it commences with the Norman Conquest and is intended to display all the variations in armour from that period till its entire disuse in the time of Charles II.

The materials for the undertaking have been copies (accurate as far as possible to obtain them) of antient seals, illuminations, painted glass, and monuments, which, when chronologically arranged, have been compared with extracts from historians and poets, from wills, inventories of armour, and royal ordinances; and here the author would acknowledge the kindness of his friend Major Smith, his coadjutor in the Costume of the Original Inhabitants of the British Isles, in the loan of his memoranda and drawings; the useful hints of his much esteemed friend, that most able and critical antiquary, Francis Douce, Esq., and the valuable communications on all that relates to Scotch armour from one no less to be admired for his private vir-

---

9 The suit in Mr. Gwennap's collection, though it came from Tong Castle, is from the Mogul country. The king has one similar. Lord Clive has two mounted on an elephant, my son has two more, three others are now in the hands of dealers, and there is another in Paris. The armour on the horse is Persian. Mr. Bullock, of whom the whole was purchased by Mr. Gwennap, bought the man's armour at the sale of Mr. Green, of Lichfield's Museum, the horse-armour he procured afterwards. This will account for the former only being engraved in Mr. Grose's book, and the omission of the chain-work on the feet, which was wrapped on after the horse-armour was procured.

10 It is, however, but justice to allow, that all the plates which represent what actually exists are extremely correct.

tues than his boundless talents, his good friend Sir Walter Scott, Bart.

Lastly, as he has no pecuniary interest in this work, but is animated with warm feelings on the topics discussed, and a desire to see them respectably introduced to the public, he may probably be permitted to express his sentiments on the manner of its execution. To Mr. Schulze then, he would return thanks for the handsome type and attentive manner in which it has been printed; while it is but justice to the present proprietor and publisher, to add, that he has cheerfully, and with a noble spirit, adopted every suggestion of the author and the artists, in order to produce the whole in a style *non impar sibi.*

INTRODUCTION.

––––––––––

Armour had its origin in Asia. The warlike tribes of Europe at first contemned all protection but their innate courage, and considered any defence except the shield as a mark of effeminacy. The warm climate of Asia, however, together With its temptations to luxury, had too great a tendency to enervate its inhabitants, so that, to be on an equality with their neighbours, they were obliged to have recourse to artificial protection. As all the European armour, except the plate, which was introduced at the close of the fourteenth century, was borrowed from the Asiatics, it becomes necessary, towards its thorough elucidation, to give some introductory account of antient.

ASIATIC ARMOUR.

In considering this subject, I must be allowed to bring under that head the armour of the Egyptians; for though their country is not precisely in Asia, yet their habits were so different from those of the Africans, and their intercourse with Asia so frequent and early, that I should think it a useless distinction to separate them.

EGYPTIANS.

Notwithstanding the effeminate character given to the Egyptians by Herodotus, we have reason to conclude, that, in the earliest periods of their history, they had obtained some renown for their martial achievements. The battles of Sesostris, Asymanduas, and Xamolxis, though merely mythological, and referring to the propagation of particular religious tenets, would not have been represented under a military character, had not that at the time most suited the genius of the people. Herodotus, indeed, tells us what were the arms and armour of the Egyptians. The helmet of Psammeticus was of brass: but metal was confined to kings and nobles, for the soldiery wore them of linen, strongly quilted, a fashion continued by the sailors so late as the time of Xerxes, who employed them in his expedition into Greece. The only body armour was the pectoral, which hung over the breast and shoulders like a tippet: this was made of linen several times folded, and quilted in such a manner as to resist the point of a weapon: it was of various colours; and one, presented by Amasis, the king of Egypt, to the Lacedemonians, is said to have been adorned with many figures of animals, and enriched with gold. The chain was of admirable structure, fine and slender, although consisting of 360 distinct threads, that being a mystical number, viz., the number of days in the antient year, and, consequently, supposed to contain a charm. Such another, presented by the same king, was to be seen at Lindus, dedicated to Minerva. The warriors had likewise shields, which, in the time of Xerxes, were convex; and, as weapons, a short sword and a javelin. The troops who fought in the ships had merely large daggers, while their commanders had javelins and immense double-axes. The ornaments of the warrior were torques and bracelets. From the Old Testament we further learn, that war-chariots were used in great numbers by the kings of Egypt.

On the walls of the temple of Carnac are several representations of conquests, in which we have the armour, weapons, standards, and chariots of the Egyptians: but these bear so very strong a resemblance to Grecian workmanship, that there is no doubt of their having been painted during the Ptolomean dynasty.[1] They are engraved in Plate LXXIII of Denon's Egypt. There is, too, a military triumph at a temple near Medinet-Abou, represented in Plate LXXIV of Denon; and several paintings of arms and armour, on the walls of a chamber in the tombs of the kings at Thebes. The Greek helmet, the shield, which, from its resemblance to a gate, being oblong and curved at top, they called Θυρὲοσ, and the Grecian chariot, strike us at once; but the only body armour is the Egyptian pectoral. The colours of this last we learn from a painting discovered at Herculaneum, and published in the Antichite d'Ercolano, as we do those of the helmet, which appears to have had a kind of tiara, or ornamental frontlet. We learn, moreover, from Denon's engraving, that this thureos ivas carried by putting the spear through the aperture made for looking at their enemies; and also, that the quiver for lances, and the quiver for arrows, were put on each side the car, or across

---

[1] It has, however, been suggested to me, by my learned friend, Mr. Douce, that this may merely indicate that which the Greeks borrowed, for both they and the Romans left the Egyptians so much to themselves, as never to have erected a temple for their own forms of worship.

each other on one side, the warrior not only using his bow, but driving the horses, the reins being fastened round his waist. But the most curious painting on these walls, if correctly delineated, is a tunic of rings, set edgewise, or single mail, as it was afterwards called in Europe, as this is the earliest specimen of that species of hauberk. Mr. Hope also, from Denon, has given the figure of what he calls a priest, habited in a cuirass of scales, which comes up to the armpits, and is there held by shoulder-straps.

Plate I contains specimens of these Graeco-Egyptian arms and armour. Fig. 1. A cutting sword, with cord and tassel at the hilt, a practice still in fashion among the Persians. Fig. 2. A scymitar, with double cord to the hilt. Fig. 3. A long dagger in its sheath, with double cords: its general resemblance, particularly in the hilt, to the Moorish and Turkish daggers of the present day is strikingly curious. Fig. 4. A mace, with a guard for the hand. Fig. 5. The shield called Thureos. Fig. 6. A military pectoral. Fig. 7 and 8. Helmets. Fig. 9. The padded linen cap worn by the soldiery. Fig. 10 and 11. Helmets. Fig. 12. Military cap of a charioteer. Fig. 13. A quiver containing javelins, with a throwing stick. Fig. 14. The throwing stick taken out of the quiver. Pig. 15. A quiver for arrows, with its covering. Fig. 16. An arrow. Fig. 17. A spear. Fig. 18. A battle-axe, rendered heavier by a weight on the back of the blade. Fig. 19. Another battle-axe. Fig. 20 and 21. Standards.

LYBIANS.

I should not have noticed these savages of Africa, who merely carried wooden lances, pointed and hardened at the end by fire, and daubed their bodies with vermilion, had not Herodotus told us,[2] that from them the Greeks received the apparel and aegis of Minerva, as represented upon her images: he, however, observes that there was this difference, viz., that instead of a pectoral of scale armour, in Lybia, it was merely a skin, and that the fringe was of leather instead of serpents. In all other respects, he observes, the resemblance is perfect, and that even the name testifies that it came from Lybia, for the women of that country wear a mantle of tanned goat-skin, dyed red, and fringed,[3] over the rest of their garments. On a fictile vase, in Sir Wm. Hamilton's collection,[4] the figure of Minerva has not

[2] Polymnia.
[3] Ægis signifies goat-skin.
[4] Vol. III, Pl. 49, of the Etruscan Antiquitles.

PLATE I

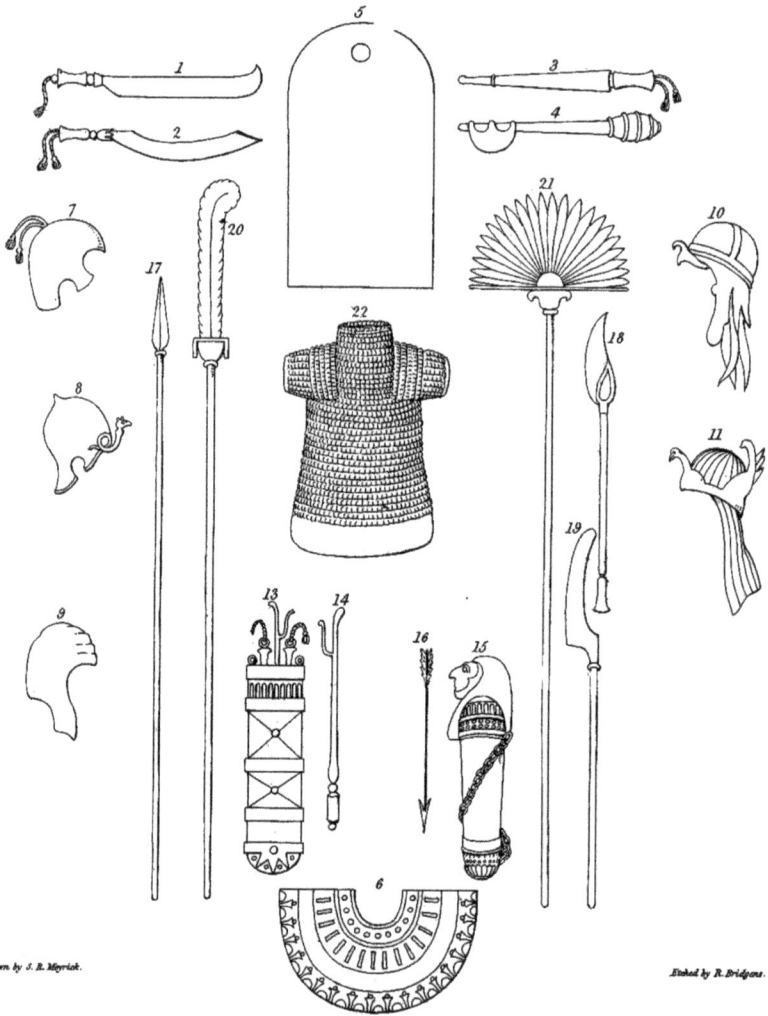

Drawn by S. R. Meyrick.

Etched by R. Bridgens.

GRÆCO EGYPTIAN ARMS AND ARMOUR.

only this pectoral of scales, but it has flap sleeves of the same; and on another[5] the aegis is similarly formed, but apparently of quilted instead of scaled work.

The Lybians, Numidians, and Getulians, according to Strabo,[6] and the Massylians, according to Lucan,[7] rode without saddles.

ETHIOPIANS.

Mr. Hope says, that the antient Egyptians are evidently descended from the Ethiopians, and gives many physiological reasons for this assertion, I ought not, therefore, wholly to pass over this people. Herodotus tells us, that the manners and habits of the Eastern Ethiopians were greatly analagous to those of the Egyptians; but the western parts of Ethiopia were inhabited by a people much less cultivated. Their shields were often made of the raw hides of oxen. Those who inhabited the parts above Egypt were clothed in the skins of lions or leopards, and, previous to their engagement in battle, they daubed one half of their bodies over with a kind of white plaster, γυψῷ, and painted the other half with vermilion, μίλτῳ. They had bows four cubits long, with arrows proportionate, and pointed with sharp stones instead of iron; and the heads of their javelins were made of goat's horns sharpened: they had also maces armed with iron. The women of this country, moreover, bore arms until they arrived at a certain age.

The dress of the Asiatic Ethiopians had some resemblance to that of the Indians, who used a species of armour made of wood;[8] but instead of a helmet they substituted the skin of a horse's head, stripped from the carcase, together with the ears and mane, and so contrived that the mane served for a crest, while the ears appeared erect upon the head of the wearer.[9] Their shields, unlike those in common use, were composed of the skins of cranes. The people who lived west of the Garamantes wore the skins of ostriches instead of armour. Those who inhabited the isles of the Red Sea were armed like the Modes.

---

[5] Vol. IV, Pl. 12, of the Etruscan Antiquities.

[6] Lib. xvii.

[7] Lib. iv.

[8] Armour of this material is still worn by the Tchutski, See a plate, representing one, in Sauer's, Account of Billing's Voyage.

[9] This will lead us to the origin of crests and tufts on helmets.

JEWS.

We have little more than mere names to assist our researches respecting the military habits of the Israelites. Their knowledge of tactics was probably derived from the Egyptians; and, it must be confessed, that they do not appear to have been by any means deficient in military skill at the time they resided in the wilderness. In the latter part of their history they probably adopted many customs of the Syrians. The thorax or pectoral, the plaited girdles for the body; the military sagum or cloak, called an habergeon in our translation of the Pentateuch; together with the helmet; and the shields, which are of two kinds, the one larger than the other; formed the chief part, if not the whole, of their defensive armour. Their offensive arms consisted of swords, some of which had two edges; daggers, spears, javelins, bows, arrows, and slings. Axes or maces, as מפץ should perhaps be translated, were also used as weapons of war. The Jewish slingers, indeed, are said to have been so expert, that seven hundred of them in one army could sling stones at a hair's breadth, and not miss.[10] Their weapons appear to have been made of brass, and of iron or steel, for the original word admits of both interpretations, ברזל, a weapon of iron or steel.[11] קשת נחושה, a bow of brass.[12] We also read of shields of gold, that is, probably, plated with gold, for we may easily conceive they would have been much too rich for common use if they had been made entirely of that metal. Although the shields and targets which Solomon caused to be made and hung up in his palace, were of massy gold, yet they appear to have been merely ornamental.[13] The Hebrew word for the thorax, or pectoral, is שדין, or שדיון, from שדה, to be strong; and, probably, the same kind of armour is meant by Jeremiah, who uses the word שדין, or in the plural, סריכוח, from the verb סד, to turn aside, as the armour does the point of the weapon.[14] The pectoral is a part of body armour, exceedingly antient, and probably originated in Egypt: it is not unlikely, therefore, that the Israelites derived its usage from that country. It is usually called, in the English translation of the Old Testament, a coat of mail, and probably, in remote times, it was attached to a short tunic, in the same manner that

---

[10] Judges, eh. xx, v. 16.
[11] Job, ch. xx, v.24.
[12] Ibid., and Psalm xviii, v.34.
[13] 1 Kings, chvx, v. 16, 17.
[14] Jeremiah, ch xlvi, v. 4 i and eh, xl, v. 3.

the sacred breast-plate was fastened upon the ephod, resembling, in Strutt's idea, χιΊων χαλκεος, or brazen vest, mentioned by Homer.[15] Beneath the pectorals were belts plated with brass or other metal, and the uppermost of them was bound upon the bottom of the tunic, which connected the pectoral with the belts, and all of them together formed a tolerably perfect armour for the front of the whole body. These belts, in the Hebrew, are called ובוה, and were generally two, one above the other, and appear similar to what are represented in antient Greek sculpture, though in some degree higher upon the breast. This mode of arming perfectly explains the passages in Scripture, where Ahab is said to have been smitten with an arrow ביןהדבקים between the openings, or joints, that is, of the belts; ובין השדין and between the thorax, or pectoral.[16] The pectorals of the Egyptians were made of linen; and perhaps, antiently, those of the Jews were the same. In after times they seem to have been covered with plates of metal; and, in the New Testament, we meet with the words θωραχας σιδηρους, or pectorals of iron.[17]

The military sagum, or cloak, is called, in our translation, an habergeon, but the original word חחדא is of doubtful signification, and occurs only twice: "And there shall be a hole in the top in midst thereof;" that is, the robe of the ephod: "it shall have a binding of woven work round about the hole of it, as it were the hole of an *habergeon*, that it be not rent."[18] But of whatever kind the garment may have been, it appears that it had an aperture at the upper part of it, through which the head was passed when it was put upon the body. Mr. Strutt conjectures, that it was the tunic upon which the thorax was fastened, and bore the same relation to the thorax that the ephod did to the sacred pectoral.

There were two sorts of helmets in use among the Jewish warriors, at least the helmets are distinguished by two different names: בובע and קיבצ. They are both said to have been made of brass,[19] but their form is totally unknown: the helmet belonging to the Israelitish monarch was distinguished from those of his subjects by the crown which was placed upon it.[20]

There are four kinds of shields specified in holy writ: their form is no where described, but it is certain that they differed in their size. "And King

[15] Iliad, I. xiii, line 439.
[16] 1 Kings, eh, xxii v. 34; 2 Chrono eh. xviii, V. 33.
[17] Revelations, eh. ix, V. 9.
[18] Exod. eh. xxviii, V. 32; and eh. xxxix, v.23.
[19] 1 Sam. eh. vii, V. 5, 38, &c.
[20] 2 Sam. eh. I, V. 10.

Solomon made two hundred צבה targets of beaten gold; six hundred shekels of gold went to one target: and three hundred מגנים shields of beaten gold; three pounds of gold went to one shield," &c.[21] Hence, it is evident, that the צבה was larger than the מגן, the שלטים in one passage seems to have been the same as the מגנים, "there hang a thousand חמנן bucklers, all שלטי shields of mighty men."[22] The סחדה is a small shield or buckler: "His truth shall be thy צ·גה shield and סחדה buckler."[23] From the expression of Isaiah, "Arise ye princes, and *anoint* the shields,some have thought that the Israelites possessed the art of making their shields with leather, or raw hides; but the use of oil would be equally proper if they were covered with brass, to keep them from rusting, and to make them bright.

The offensive weapons, which are only mentioned by name in the sacred writings, did not probably differ from those in use among other Asiatic nations. The sword was usually girded upon the thigh, as we learn from the expression frequently used in Scripture—"Gird every man his sword upon his thigh," whence, it appears, that they did not wear the sword continually, but only when the exigency of the times required the use of such weapons, and that they were suspended in front in the Asiatic style.

PHILISTINES.

From the description of the arms belonging to Goliath, the giant of Gath, we learn what were those of the Philistines. They consisted of a helmet, a coat of mail, greaves, a small and large shield, a spear, and a sword. The helmet was made of brass כובע נחשת,[24] and no otherwise particularized; but the cuirass consisted of plates of brass, laid over each other in the form of scales, which is expressed by a word in the original Hebrew, that is totally omitted in our translation: this is קשקשים, scales; which, with the word שדיון, is properly rendered by Espenius, Lorica Squamarum. In the Vulgate, this is called Lorica hamata, a cuirass of rings hooked into each other: but the former interpretation agrees best with the original word. The weight of this coat of armour was 5,000 shekels of brass, or about 189 lbs.

---

[21] 1 Kings, ch. x, v. 16 and 17.
[22] Canticles, c. iv, c. 4.
[23] Psalm xci, v. 4.
[24] 1 Sam, eh. xvii, v.5.

troy weight. Shining plates of brass מצחחנחשׁת[25] are expressly said to have been upon his feet על־דגליו but whether these extended over any part of the leg does not appear. He was provided with two shields, the smaller of which he bore between his shoulders, that is, slung probably at his back by a strap, whence he could easily take it, if required, in time of action: the larger one was carried before him by his armour-bearer. His spear was headed with iron, and seems to have been remarkable only for its size, the head weighing 600 shekels, or about 22 lbs. troy weight. The materials from which his sword, and the sheath belonging to it, were fabricated, are not specified; the sword, indeed, appears to have been of excellent workmanship, for, it is said, there was none like it: but its size was hardly in proportion to the rest of his arms, because David, at a future period, made use of it instead of his own.

In the time of the Emperor Aurelianus, several of the inhabitants of Palestine served as horse soldiers in the pay of the Romans; and Zosimus tells us, that the Palestinian cavalry, besides other arms, wielded clubs and maces, which they used so effectually on the brass and iron armour of the Palmyrenes, that they broke it in pieces.

PHOENICIANS.

Such of this nation as accompanied Xerxes, we learn from Herodotus, had helmets upon their heads, nearly resembling those worn by the Greeks; and pectorals of quilted linen upon their breasts,[26] which they probably derived from the Egyptians, and if so, this people may be considered as the connecting link, in point of military costume, between those nations. Their roving habits, which made them the best sailors of their time, was doubtless the occasion of this; and as they peopled Carthage and some of the ports of Spain, they probably carried thither their antient armour and weapons. Herodotus adds, that they were armed with javelins, and carried round shields without any protuberance at the centre. He does not, however, tell of what metal their arms were fabricated, but from the great trade in tin, which they carried on with Britain, we can have little doubt that they were of a compound metal made from that and copper. This is further confirmed by the Carthaginian swords dug up from the plains of Cannæ, and now in

---

[25] Ibid. v, 6.
[26] In Polymnia.

the British Museum; and from the fact, that they introduced this manufacture into Britain, Ireland, and, indeed, wherever they had any dealings.

CARTHAGINIANS.

The Carthaginians, though a warlike nation, raised but few troops from among their own citizens. By means of their riches they drew from various countries soldiers ready disciplined, and of the greatest merit and reputation. From Numidia they derived an active, bold, impetuous, and indefatigable cavalry, which formed the principal strength of their armies; from the Balearian isles the most expert slingers; from Spain a strong and determined infantry; from the coasts of Genoa and Gaul troops of known valour; and from Greece itself soldiers fit for all the various operations of war, for the field or garrisons, for besieging or defending cities.

It is difficult, therefore, to assign any armour as peculiar to the Carthaginians, and in no author of antiquity, as far as my researches go, is any such described. In Mr. Bullock's Museum was a helmet, said to have been found at Carthage, greatly resembling the morions antiently worn in Europe: it was, therefore, much like one in the Hamilton collection of the British Museum, which appears to have been formed by being cast in a mould, and is given Pl. vi, Fig. 4.*[27] There are, in the same collection, several brass swords, which General Vallancey says, were found in the plains of Cannae, and greatly resemble those dug up in Ireland; he, therefore, concludes they are Carthaginian; and, it is probable, that the helmet may have been found with them. In the Thesaurus Graecorum Antiquitatum of Gronovius, Vol. Ill, is a silver coin exhibiting a head of Amilcar Barcas, and another of Hannibal, both of which are quite in the Greek style.

ARABIANS.

Herodotus observes, that the Arabs carried large bows, made with a handle and two curved horns.

---

[27] I have since learnt that it was an iron morion, such as was used in the time of the emperor Charles Vth, and, therefore, probably lost in some of the expeditions against the Tunisian pirates.

SYRIANS.

The Syrians who inhabited Palestine, at least such of them as went in the expedition of Xerxes, by sea, in order to invade Greece, were, according to Herodotus, armed precisely like the Phœnicians who accompanied them. Mr. Hope has given a representation of a Syrian helmet, the resemblance of which to those of the modern Chinese is very great. They have alike a high ornamented spike on their tops: that which terminates the Syrian one is a lily. This, according to Herodotus, was the ornament which the Assyrians had carved on the tops of their walkingsticks. It may be seen Pl. II, Fig. 8.

Herodotus says further, that their casques were woven; that they carried small bucklers, with lances of a moderate length, darts, and poignards, and adds, that the Paphlagonians, the Ligyans, the Malions, and the Mariandynes, were armed in the same manner.

ASSYRIANS.

Those who lived in the time of Xerxes, we learn from Herodotus, had helmets of brass, a short sword, a buckler, and a javelin, after the manner of the Egyptians; a pectoral made of linen, and a mace of wood headed with iron.[28]

The Chaldeans were armed in the same manner.

MEDES AND PERSIANS.

The military dress of the Persians, previous to the reign of Cyrus the Great, was a cuirass of leather, girt about the body with a belt of the same material.[29] Herodotus also mentions, that they wore pectorals of linen, several times folded and stitched; and from Plutarch[30] we learn, that, among the spoils taken at the battle of Issus, there was one which so much pleased Alexander the Great, that he wore it himself as part of his martial habit.

[28] Several brass mace-heads, which have wooden handles fixedin them, may be seen in the British Museum.

[29] Herod. in Clio.

[30] In Vit. Alex.

The Median dress superseded this more simple attire of the Persians, being introduced by Cyrus. His soldiers were consequently adorned with a cloak, fastened with a buckle, and called Candys, the colour of which was a particularly high-prized purple,[31] and not permitted to the common people.

The Median and Persian soldiers belonging to the army of Xerxes, according to Herodotus, had each a tiara for his head that was impenetrable; a tunic, covered with plates of steel like the scales of a fish, and adorned with sleeves of various colours; an Egyptian pectoral on his breast, with the anaxyrides, or trowsers, which covered his legs and thighs, and, as we see on the Parthians, in Hope's Costume, drawn in round the ankles. Herodotus adds, that they carried a target of cane, strongly compacted, which served as a shield, and was called Γέρρα. This covered the quiver, in which were long arrows made of cane, and a short bow. They bore in their hands javelins, and had a sword suspended from a belt upon the right side. Some of the cavalry, however, wore helmets of brass.

In the sculptures at Persopolis[32] there are two rows of Persian soldiers wearing this tiara, which thence appears to have been cylindrical; and there is another row in helmets, which are the same hemispherical scull-caps worn by the cavalry in Persia at this day. Each soldier of one of the rows with the tiara has a bow on his left side, placed perpendicularly, so that one end passes over his shoulder, while the other goes down to his thigh: he has a quiver at his back, and a short spear or javelin in his hand. Polyænus[33] says, that in Persia, Alexander the Great had at his court 500 Persian archers, in different dresses of yellow, blue, and scarlet, before whom stood 500 Macedonians, with silver shields. This same author tells us, that the quiver was worn at the shoulder by the Persians.[34] The other row of the sculptures has its soldiers with the same kind of javelin, but, as Herodotus describes, the target obscures his quiver. That this target was the gerra we learn from its resemblance to that carried by Theban warriors on the Greek fictile vases, knowing, as we do, that the Greeks borrowed the gerra from the Persians. It is fiddle-shaped, and has an ornament in the centre. Both these are in flowing garments; but the other row, in which the figures wear the helmet, has each of them a tunic, apparently of leather, girted round the waist, as was

---

[31] Called by Strabo ἁλιπόρφυρος.

[32] See Chardin's Persopolis; Montfaucon Antiq. expliq. Vol. II, p. 402; and the sculptures now in the British Museum.

[33] Lib. IV, c. 3.

[34] Lib. XIII, c. 6.

the custom of the most antient Persians. Each carries a javelin in his hand, has a sword suspended from the belt on the right side, and on his left his bow in a half case, such as is still used. The chariots sculptured at Persopolis have a great resemblance to those of the Greeks.

Xenophon tells us, the Persians had arms for close combat, a pectoral upon their breast, and a shield in the left hand; and, speaking of the army of Cyrus, says, many of them had handsome tunics and elegant pectorals, with helmets. Their horses for the chariots were armed with forehead-pieces, and had plates upon their flanks, so that the whole army glittered with brass, and appeared beautifully decked in scarlet robes. In another passage he tells us, that the arms of Cyrus and those of his companions, which formed a royal guard, were gilt, and differed in no one particular, excepting that his were brighter, having been more highly polished,[35] shining like a mirror. They had scarlet or purple tunics,[36] (which, as we have seen, they adopted from the Medes); a pectoral of brass; brazen helmets with white crests; swords and spears, the shafts of which were made of the cornel tree. Their horses were armed with forehead-pieces, breast-plates, and side-pieces, which last served to protect the thighs of the riders.[37] Thus we see that the brazen thorax was derived from the linen pectoral, and that this change was first effected by the Persians. From this description we further learn, that the chamfrein, as it was called in Europe, or forehead-plate for the horse;[38] the poitrine, or breastplate for that animal; and plates to protect his flanks and the thighs of his rider, as were adopted in Europe in the fifteenth century, had all their origin in Persia. Perhaps the armour to protect the flanks of the horses, and the thighs of the riders at the same time, were something like what are still worn in Persia, in the form of large triangular projecting flaps, attached to the side-plates of the horseman, which answer the same purpose. As these are composed of scales of iron, covered over with embroidered velvet, they seem of greater antiquity than the coat of mail worn with them.

In the time of Alexander the Great this splendour in military equip-

---

[35] Ὡσπρ κα'Ιοπ'Ιρον εξελαμπει, are the words of the author.

[36] χιτωσι φοινικοις Phœnician tunics. The Phœnician or Tyrian dye was famous in antient times, and was produced from the shell-fish found on that coast, called murex purpura.

[37] Julius Pollux, lib. I, c. 10, seems to refer to this passage.

[38] In Asia, however, it does not appear to have enveloped the horse's head like a mask, but was merely a protection for the forehead-probably, a circular plate, with a spike in the centre: and yet Julius Pollux seems to allude to coverings for the ears and' cheeks of gold.

ments was carried to the highest degree of extravagance. Charidemus, a Persian nobleman, observed to this monarch, that the soldiers of his country were clothed in coloured garments, and glittered in armour of gold, far exceeding in brilliancy and riches any pomp that had preceded.[39]

Quintus Curtius, moreover, describes the manner in which Darius appeared with his army: "The guards of the Persian monarch were called immortal, because as fast as one of them died his place was filled up by another. The richness of their dress far exceeded that of any other corps: they all had torques of gold round their necks; their tunics embroidered with gold, with sleeves adorned with pearls. The sword-belt of Darius was of gold, and from it was suspended his scyinitar, the scabbard of which was composed of one entire pearl." The torques were a military ornament, common to many countries, and often at this day dug up in Britain and Ireland,[40] but were derived originally from Egypt. In the earliest periods of Egyptian history, its warriors were generally ornamented with a torque and bracelets. While Joseph, the Jewish patriarch, was in renown in that country, the principal men, we learn from the Pentateuch, wore דבר a wreathed necklace or torque of gold, rings, and bracelets: and Cambyses, the Persian conqueror of Egypt, sent a wreathed neck-bracelet, with bracelets for the arms, of gold, to the king of Ethiopia.[41]

Ammianus Marcellinus[42] speaks of a multitude of horses rode by the Persian cavalry, entirely defended, operimentis scorteis, with leathern housings. Heliodorus[43] observes again, that the heavy armour worn by the Persian horses rendered them immovable when they lost their conductors. The Persians called their armed steeds clibanarii.

The method of inlaying the blades and hilts of the scymitars with gold, still practised by the Persians, seems very antient, for when we read in Herodotus,[44] that among those taken as spoils by the Greeks, were many golden swords, we must understand the expression in this way. Plate II, Fig. 1, is the bow and quiver carried by the soldiers who wore the cap, Fig. 5. Fig 3, the bow, bow-case, and spear, which armed the soldiers who wore the scullcap, Fig. 4, and carried the gerra, Fig. 2.

---

[39] Quintus Curtius.

[40] Several specimens of these may be seen engraved ill the Archreologia, published by the Society of Antiquaries; and in the Transactions of the Royal Irish Academy.

[41] Herodotus Thalia.

[42] Lib. xxiv.

[43] Lib. ix, Æthiopicorum.

[44] In Calliope.

PLATE II

Drawn by S. R. Meyrick.

Etched by R. B.

ASIATIC ARMS and ARMOUR.

The Hyrcanians and Bactrians, according to Herodotus, were armed precisely like the Persians; and the Cissians likewise, except that, instead of tiaras, they wore mitres.

SAGARTIANS.

These were a people of Persian extraction, that accompanied Xerxes in his expedition against Greece. They are described, by Herodotus, as retiarii, for he tells us,[45] they had no other weapon than a short sword, and a net made of cord, which they threw over their opponents, and when they had the good fortune to entangle them, they immediately destroyed them with their swords.[46] It is much more probable, that from this people the Greeks first heard of the retiarii, than the story of Diogenes Laertius, who says, that Pittacns, one of the seven sages of Greece, in a war between the Athenians and inhabitants of Mitylene, challenged the enemy's general to single combat, and then with a net, which he secretly brought, entangled and overcame him. The contest of the retiarii and mirmillones must, however, have been instituted some time after.

PARTHIANS.

Mr. Hope, PI. xm, of his Costume of the Antients, has given the figure of a Parthian monarch, with his bow and javelin, the former of which is made of two pieces, fitted into a handle; and the latter has a large ball at the but-end, and a lozenge-shaped blade at the other. Justin[47] gives the following description of the Parthians: "Their speech is a medium between the Scythian and Median languages, containing a mixture of both. In antient times their costume was peculiar to their country, but on their acquisition of wealth it was composed of transparent and flowing garments like that of the Medes. Their mode of arming is a trifling deviation from that of the Scythians. Their army is not raised from freemen, as is practised by other

[45] Polymnia,

[46] It is a curious fact, that Cortez met with retiarii among the Mexicans, and afterwards made some .use of them.

[47] Lib. XLI. His words are: Munimentum (Parthis) equisque loricæ plumatæ sunt, quæ utrumque toto corpore tegunt. They must, therefore, have greatly resembled the Dacians on the Trajan column:"

nations, but for the most part of slaves. The power of manumission is withheld from the common class of them, and therefore their progeny are born in servitude. With equal care these and their children are taught to ride and shoot with the utmost attention. The richest persons provide the king with the greatest number of horsemen. Hence, when Anthony undertook his campaign against the Parthians, out of 50,000 cavalry, only 400 were freemen. They know not how to fight in .close quarters, or drive away a besieging army: but they fight while their horses are in pursuit, or while in retreat; often, indeed, feigning flight, that their adversaries may incautiously be more effectually wounded. The signal is given to them in battle not by a trumpet, but a kettle-drum.[48] They arc unable to keep up a long contest, not being capable of adding perseverance to impetuosity. Indeed, in the heat of the battle they often take to flight, and from that flight renew the attack. They make no use of gold except in adorning their arms." Their horses were covered with plumated loricse, which completely enveloped their bodies. Suidas undertakes to explain this more fully. He says, the lorica of the Parthian cavalry is after this manner: the prior part covers the breast, outside of the thighs, and external part of the hands and legs; the posterior part the back, neck, and whole of the head; hut there are fibulae at the sides with which both parts are united, and in this manner the horsemen have the appearance of being wholly covered with steel. Yet it by no means interferes with or hinders the contraction of their limbs, so curiously is it manufactured, notwithstanding it fits quite close. They also arm their horses in a similar manner wholly in iron, and even to their hoofs. Plate II, Fig. 6 and 7, show the Parthian bow and javelin.

SARACENS.

The Saracens, in the time of Valentinian, says Zozimus, had fleet horses, and well managed the lance, which they wielded with great strength.

---

[48] Tympano, the nacaise of the modern Asiatics. The tympanum was of metal, and sometimes covered with a skin. Indeed, the drum as well as tabour was known to the antients, as Montfaucon has satisfactorily proved.

ARMENIANS.

The helmet of the Armenians was cylindrical, with a flap hanging down behind, which was slit so as to form ear-pieces, as well as a protection for the head and shoulders. Herodotus says, they were armed like the Phrygians, from whom they were a colony. In the time of Con-stantius, according to Zozimus, the Armenians served as mounted archers in the Roman armies. Plate II, Fig. 9, exhibits an Armenian helmet.

INDIANS.

The Indians, says Herodotus,[49] who inhabit Asia, clothe themselves with garments made of rushes, which they cut from the river, and interlaying them together like mats, work them into the form of the thorax. They use bows and arrows, both made of cane, but the latter headed with iron. This military costume greatly resembles that of the antient Peruvians, and the modern inhabitants of the South Seas.

SCYTHIANS.

Many of the Scythians, according to Herodotus, clothed themselves with the skins of men, as other nations did with those of beasts; and with the skins of the right hands of their enemies they made, coverings[50] for their quivers. They likewise made cups of the sculls of those they had slain; a fact which is corroborated by the practice having been retained by their gothic descendants.[51] The poorer sort, adds the historian, clothed themselves, however, with leather' to which the more wealthy added ornaments of gold. As he speaks of their quivers, they had doubtless bows; and, indeed, archery was their constant practice, war and the chase supplying frequent opportunities. Isidorus attributes this art to the progenitors of the Scythians; and we read of the Greeks, in their earliest times, sending their nobility to be instructed by this people in the art of shooting. Thus Hercules was taught

---

[49] Thalia.

[50] Perhaps only the caps to them. The human skin has been tried merely for experiment, and found to make most beautiful leather.

[51] To drink nectar from the sculls of their enemies, in the hall of their god Odin, was declared to be the privilege of all who fell in battle.

by Teutarus, a Scythian swain, from whom he received a bow and arrows of that country. Hence Lycophron,[52] speaking of them, says:

Τοῖς Τέυταρέιοις βουκόλου πτερώμασι.

"With arrows which he had from Teutarus."

Lycophron also, arms Minerva with a Mseotian bow; and, in the same place, speaks of that which Hercules bequeathed to Philoctetes, calling it a Scythian dragon. Theocritus, as well as Lycophron, particularly distinguishes between the shape of the Scythian bows and that of the Greeks, the former resembling a crescent, or the letter C.[53]

On the column of Theodosius, at Constantinople, are sculptured some arms and armour of the Scythians in his time. They consist of a tunic, apparently wadded, with a girdle and crossbelts of leather studded; the sleeves very short, but secured with two bands like the belts; a conical helmet of leather, secured with iron bands, and surmounted by a spike; an oval shield; a mace and a club, both spiked. These are copied on Plate ii, Fig 10, 11, 12, and 13.

According to Herodotus, the Saeae, a Scythian nation, had conical helmets, bows, and arrows, according to the custom of Scythia; axes, and sagares, which, Xenophon tells us, were double-axes.

SARMATIANS.

A figure on Trajan's column exhibits a Sarmatian as wearing loose trowsers drawn round the ankle, and with a high cap, greatly resembling that worn at the present day by the Persians; and we learn from Pausanius what was the body-armour of that people. He saw a Sarmatian cuirass in the temple of Esculapius, suspended there as a trophy; and further informs us, that "the Sarmatians neither possess iron themselves, nor derive it by importation, as these barbarians keep themselves more than all others free from communication with foreign countries. In consequence, therefore, of the

---

[52] Cassandra, v. 56.

[53] There is a figure with the Moeotian bow, ona fictile vase, in Hamilton's Etruscan Antiquities, Vol: IV, PI. CXVI, and copied PI. cxvi, Fig. 14. The modern Tartar bow is of this form when unstrung, as appears by two specimens in the armoury of Llewelyn Meyrick, Esq.

want of this metal, they have devised wicker instead of iron tops for their spears. Their bows and arrows are of cornel wood, the piles of the latter being of wicker. They likewise, in battle, throw chains about every enemy they meet, and at the same time making their horses wheel about, throw down the person thus entangled. In order to make their body-armour, they collect the hoofs of horses, and, after purifying, cut them into slices, and polish the pieces so as to resemble the scales of a dragon, or pine cone when green. This scale-like composition they perforate and sew together with the nerves of horses and oxen, and the body-armour thus manufactured is not inferior to that of the Greeks, either in regard to elegance or strength, as it will sustain a blow given from a distance, or at close quarters."

In Mr. Gwennap's collection of armour there was a cuirass exactly answering this description, and brought from some part of Asia.[54] It is composed of the hoofs of some animal, which are stitched together, supporting one another without being fastened on any under garment, and formed in perpendicular rows overlapping each other. It is figured in Plate III, Fig 1. Ammianus confirms the account of Pausanius, by saying that the Sarmati and Quadi armed themselves with loricse made with shavings of horn,[55] polished into the form of feathers, and sewn upon a linen tunic. In the time of Augustus Caesar, Valerius Flaccus seems to imply, that the Sarmatians wore chain-mail, and covered their horses with the same.[56] His words are:

"...........Riget his molli lorica catena,
Id quoque tcgmen equis."

"These are confined by the lorica of yielding chain,
And such also is the covering for their horses."

Whether this poetical language does in reality designate that ingenious armour, undoubtedly of Asiatic origin, and termed double chain-mail, and how far the writer may be relied on in attributing it to the Sarmatians, may be fairly doubted,[57] as Pausanius before, and Tacitus and Ammianus after him, assign to them the plumated or scaled species. Tacitus thus speaks: "The weapons of the Rhoxalani, a people of Sarmatia, are long spears or swords, of an enormous size, which they wield with both hands. They have

---

[54] Japan has been said of late, but I am inclined to doubt it.
[55] Ex cornibus rasis.
[56] Lib. vi.
[57] See a paper on this subject in the 19th volume of the Arcbreologia.

neither shields nor bucklers, but their chiefs wear armour formed of small plates, or hardened hides, sewn together. Although impenetrable to the thrust, it is still a great impediment to any that have been thrown down by the charge of an enemy, preventing their being able to rise again: not having the power, therefore, to retreat, they are cut to pieces, more like men bound in fetters than soldiers armed for the field of battle." Mr. Gwennap's cuirass justifies the term fetters." The Roman historian, nevertheless, acknowledges that their cavalry are impetuous, fierce, and irresistible in their onset, although that cannot be said of the infantry.[58]

SUSIANS.

Xenophon describes[59] the military dress of Abradates, king of the Susians, as consisting of a linen pectoral, a golden helmet with a crest of violet colour, arm-pieces, broad bracelets, and a purple tunic reaching to the feet.

MOSYNCECIANS.

This people, we learn from Xenophon,[60] wore double tunics as a defence, with leathern helmets like those of the Paphlagonians, from the middle of which there arose a tuft of hair, braided to a point, resembling a tiara. Their shields were made in the shape of an ivy-leaf, composed of the hides of white oxen, with the hair on.

In antient times the shape of the shield had much to do with the mythology of the people, and therefore were circular to represent the sun, crescent-like to imitate the moon, &,c. The ivy-leaf was sacred to Bacchus, and it might be from this people that the Greeks derived the pelta, which Xenophon describes as of the same form.

THRACIANS.

Those Thracians who accompanied Xerxes into Greece covered their heads with a cap or helmet made of foxes' skins, and their bodies with a

[58] Tacit. Hist. Lib. I.
[59] Lib. IV.
[60] Anabasis, Lib. V.

tunic, and mantle of various colours: their shoes were bound above the ankles, and they carried small bucklers in the form of a half-moon; every one had a javelin and a short dagger.[61] The Thracians, who retained their original name in Asia, came into the field with small bucklers composed of untanned hides, two Lycian javelins for each man, with a helmet of brass, having ears and horns like an ox of the same metal; and their legs were covered with Phœnician cloth.[62] These helmets were worn also by the Phrygians, though but rarely: they were, however, adopted by the Greeks; and, according to Diodorus Siculus, by the Belgic Gauls. Being formed as typical of the religion of the country, the horns of the ox or cow being emblematic of the moon, they were a fit accompaniment for the crescent-like shields. Plate III, Fig. 19, exhibits a Thracian helmet; and Fig. 20, a Thracian shield, impressed with the representation of a serpent, the symbol of the sun.

From Roman sculptures,[63] made by the Thracian cohorts in the service of that empire, we find them armed witli a curious kind of javelin or lance, the shaft of which appears composed of little bands, perhaps of cane, and becoming larger towards the head, where it terminates in a round ball; on this is affixed either a pyramidal-shaped spear-head, or a short or long spike. Plate III, Fig. 4 and 5, are these Thracian weapons; Fig. 6, a Mysian one; and Fig. 7, a Macedonian; all having some resemblance to each other. Fig. 3, is the Mysian shield, which was used with Fig. 6, and seen inside, to shew that it was held by the hand, and not put on the arm. A weapon, much resembling the strange one above noticed, Fig. 4, is still used in part of the Persian dominions.[64]

The retiarii of the Roman games were generally Thracians,[65] and these were matched with the mirmillones, or secutores. They bore in their left hands a three-pointed lance, called a trident, and a dagger; and in their right a net, by which they tried to entangle their adversary, and then with the dagger to dispatch him: if they missed their aim they protected themselves with the trident, and then instantly took to flight to prepare for a second cast of the net. Juvenal[66] thus alludes to this practice:—

---

[61] Herod. in Polymnia.

[62] Ibid.

[63] See Montfaucon's Antiq. expl.

[64] One in the armoury of Llewelyn Meyrick, Esq., has its blade made to cut and thrust.

[65] Cie. Phil. VII, 6; Liv. XLI, 20. Horat. Sat. II, 6,44. Suet. Calig. 32. Juv. VIII 201. Anson. in Monosyll. 102..

[66] Sat. VIII, v. 208.

PLATE III

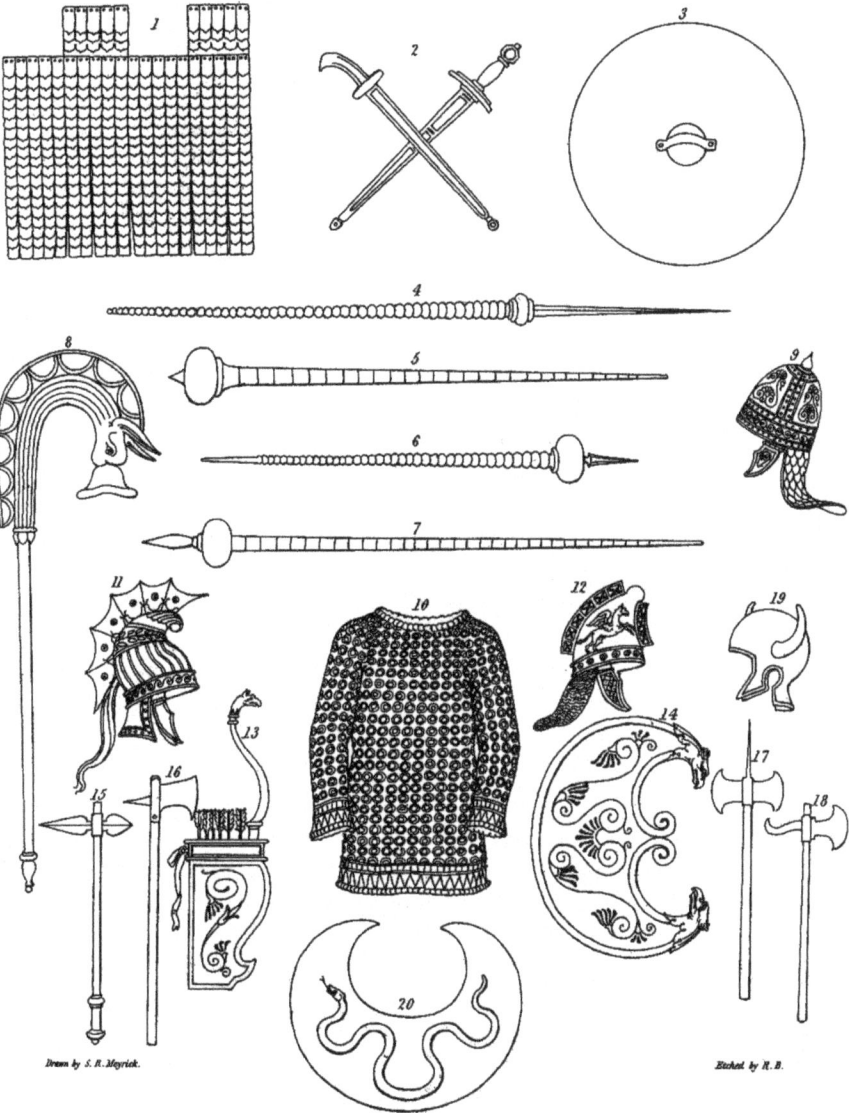

ASIATIC ARMS AND ARMOUR.

"............movet ecce tridentcra,
Postquam vibrata pcndcnta rctia dextra,
Ne quicquam effudit."

"............Lo! he moves his trident,
Having, after the net thrown by the right hand, fallen back,
Lest any one should rush upon him—"

But the antagonist as swiftly pursuing to prevent this design taking effect, was called a secutor or pursuer.

The retiarii were clad in a short tunic, or cuirass, which came up to their breasts, and reached nearly half way of their thighs: their left arms were protected by padded linen twisted round them, out of which issued a shoulder-shield high enough to guard the face. This shoulder-shield was called galerus, as we are told by the Scholiast on Juvenal, who says it was thus affixed to the shoulder, to leave the hands free for the management of the net. It was of different shapes: in the marble dug up at Chester, and in the tessellated pavement, both engraved in the Vetusta Monumenta, published by the Society of Antiquaries of London, it is square; on a lamp, engraved by Montfaucon, Vol. V, Pl. cxcvi, curved at top like the thureos; and in the pavement at Bignor, in Sussex, where the figures are in colours, semicircular. From the representation on the lamp, it appears that the Thracians fought sometimes on their knees.

The arms of the secutores were a helmet, a shield, and a sword or leaden mace.

DACIANS.

In the early periods of the Dacian history their warriors were very much habited after the Phrygian manner, and the large Cossack trowsers were common to them and the Sarmatians. They wore the Phrygian bonnet, but their helmets were high scullcaps, differently shaped from the Phrygian, with a spike at top, moveable cheek-pieces, and a flap of scale-work to cover the neck. On the Trajan column not only many of the Dacian soldiers themselves, but several of their horses, appear entirely enveloped in a covering of small scales, in close contact with the body and limbs: they are armed with bows and arrows, and a sword of the sickle kind, having its edge on the inner curve.[67]

[67] Similar to these were the seaxes of the Saxons, and such are still used by the Albanians of Turkey, several varieties of which are in the collection of Llewelyn Meyrick, Esq.

Herodotus says, the Dacians, Parthians, Chorasmians, Sogdians, Gandarians, and Arions, were all armed in the time of Xerxes like the Bactrians, except that the bows of the last resembled those of the Medes. He farther tells us, that the Pactyes, the Uians, the Myces, and the Paricanians, all carried bows; that the Sarangi had bows and pikes like those of the Medes; and that the Caspians had bows of cane which grew in their country, and swords. In Plate III, Fig. 2, the uppermost sword is that of a Dacian soldier; and the under one, such as used in the Isle of Cos, very closely resembling those of the Thracians. Fig. 8 is a Dacian standard, representing the serpent, an object of Pagan worship, and terminating in what appears to have been a bell. Fig. 9, a Dacian helmet: its similarity to the scullcaps so generally worn in Asia at the present time must be obvious.

SASPIRIANS.

Those of this nation who were in the army of Xerxes, Herodotus tells us, had helmets of wood. The Allarodians were armed in the same manner.

COLCHIANS.

Like the Saspirians, wooden helmets were the distinguishing armour of this nation when under the command of Xerxes.

MYSIANS.

These people, according to Herodotus, wore a casque, had little bucklers, and used javelins hardened at their ends with fire. It has been already observed, that Plate III, Fig. 3 and 6, exhibit a Mysian shield and javelin as used in the time of the Romans.

LYCIANS.

The Lycians had a covering of goat-skins upon their shoulders, they wore pectorals upon their breasts, and their legs were defended with greaves: they had also caps adorned with crests, stuck round with feathers.[68] In the column of Trajan some of the warriors appear with caps of this kind, and they have been supposed to be Moors of Africa; but whether the Lycians preserved this fashion to so late a period we have no means to determine. Every one of the Lycians, Herodotus further informs us[69] carried a bow of cornel, with arrows of cane unfledged, a dart, a faulchion, and a short sword.

The Milyans, according to the same author, carried short lances, or had Lycian bows; their helmets were of skins. The Moschi had wooden helmets, little bucklers, short darts, but long lances. The Tibarenians and the Macroni were armed like the Moschi. The Mares had woven casques, little bucklers of leather, and darts.

PHRYGIANS.

The prevailing helmet of the Asiatics, bordering on the Euxine and the Archipelago, appears to have been that which is generally known by the name of the Phrygian, and of which the characteristic features are, its point at top bent down forward, and its long flaps descending on the shoulders: it was of leather or metal, and enriched with embossed ornaments. To many the flaps appear four in number, and probably were cut out of the legs of the animals whose hide or skin formed the body of the casque.[70] In the figures of the Amazons, which may be considered as fabulous representations of the inhabitants of Asia Minor, bordering on the Phrygians, we often see the beak of the helmet terminate in the bill of a griffin, and on the spine or back of the casque rise the jagged crest of that fabulous animal. Minerva appears on fictile vases, sometimes in a Phrygian helmet of this species, probably as worshipped at Troy; and Roma on many Latin coins also wears it, in order, no doubt, to indicate the kindred which the Romans claimed with the Trojans. Mr. Hope has represented one Phrygian helmet, the neck-flap of which is composed of double chain-mail, or interlaced rings.[71] I cannot help regretting that he has not given his authority for this, as, if correct, it

---

[68] Πιλους ω'Ιεροισι ϖεριεσ'Ιεφανωμένους.

[69] Polymnia.

[70] In imitation of this the hoods of mail attached to the modern Asiatic scullcaps terminate in four vandykes, or pointed pieces.

[71] This, with the expression of Valerius Flaccus, "molli lorica catenâ," seems as if the chain-mail was in reality known to the antients. It may be seen pl. III, Fig. 12.

is the oldest specimen extant, and raises a wonder that such an ingenious contrivance should not have been copied before the 13th century.[72] The body-armour of the Phrygians was a tunic, with tight sleeves reaching to the wrists, and covered with flat rings, as appears from a bronze in the possession of I. Hawkins, Esq., of Bignor Park, Sussex.

The chief defensive weapon was the lunated shield, with a rise in the centre of the crescent; and the offensive ones were the bipennis, or double-bladed axe, the club, and the bow and arrow, generally carried in two different partitions of the same quiver.

Many of the Asiatic nations were celebrated for their constant use and skilful management of horses; and are often represented as fighting on horseback against the Greeks on foot. In Plate III, Fig. 11 and 12, are Phrygian helmets. Fig. 10, a tunic of flat contiguous rings. Fig. 13, the quiver, bows, and arrows. Fig. 14, the shield. And Fig. 15, 16, 17, and 18, Phrygian battle-axes.[73] Among the Herculaneum paintings is a Phrygian archer in his proper costume and colours.

CARIANS.

Those Carians who arrived in Egypt in the reign of Psammetichus appeared in brazen armour.[74] We further learn, from the same author, that they were the first who added crests to their helmets, and ornaments to their shields. They were the first, too, who gave the shield its handle. Before their time such as bore shields had no other means of managing them but by a piece of leather, suspended from the neck over the left shoulder. J Alluding to their addition to the helmet, Alcaeus says:

Λόφον τε σέιων Καρικὸν.

"Shaking his Carian crest."

They were the first who served for pay, which was at that time reckoned

---

[72] On an application to that gentleman I find that, as his authority is not now discoverable, it is probably an error of his engraver. See a paper of mine, on the lorica catenâ, in the 19th vol. of the Archeeologia.

[73] A Phrygian gladiator on a Roman lamp, with an oblong shield, may be seen in Montfaucon's Antiq. expl, Vol. V, Pl.CXCVI.

[74] Herod. in Buterpe.

so great a mark of servility, that, Strabo informs us, they rendered their name infamous.

IONIANS.

These, like the Carions at the same period, wore brazen armour.[75]

LYDIANS.

The Lydians, Herodotus tells us, were armed just like the Greeks.

CILICIANS.

The Cilicians had casques according to the fashion of their country, small bucklers of untanned ox-hide, swords like the Egyptians, and each carried two javelins in the time of Xerxes.

PAMPHYLIANS.

The Pamphylians, says Herodotus, were armed in the Grecian manner.

ÆOLIANS.

These were armed like the Greeks, as were also the Peloponesians.

CYPRIANS.

Those of Cyprus, according· to Herodotus, were armed like the Greeks.

GRECIANS.

---

[75] Ὁπλισθειτας χαλκω.

The Grecians had their share of military glory in an eminent degree, and of these the Lacedemonians were considered as the most warlike. They were soldiers by profession, the laws of their country laying them under that obligation. They were accustomed from their childhood to undergo the severest trials both of fatigue and danger, and taught to be always prepared to live or die as emergencies required.

"Οι δὲ θάνον, x ζῆν θέμενοι καλὸν, xδὲ τό θνήσκειν,
Ἀλλὰ τὸ ταῦτα καλῶς ἀμφότερ ἐκτελέσαι.[76]

"They died, not giving the preference to life or death,
But, as valour required, were prepared for both."

Next to the Lacedemonians the Athenians were considered the best troops, and there are not Avanting instances in which they disputed the Spartan superiority. The Grecian soldiers, before the age of Pericles, maintained themselves at their own expense, and for fear they should desert were marked σ'Ιίγματα ἐν ταῖς χεροί with characters punctured on their hands.[77] The profession of a soldier, as in all primitive nations, was rendered more honourable by being confined to free citizens, slaves never being permitted to bear arms except in cases of the most extreme danger.

The Grecian armies were composed of various sorts of soldiers: the principal part were infantry; but they had cavalry, some who fought in chariots and some on elephants. The foot soldiers were distinguished by the terms ὁπλιται, "those who wore armour," and carried broad shields and long spears; and ψιλοὶ, the light troops, who, with no other protection than a helmet, were armed with darts, bows and arrows, or slings. The πέλτασ'Ιαι, who carried the πέλτα, or narrow-pointed shields,[78] and spears, though a species of light troops, were considered as an intermediate kind. The heavy-armed foot were at all times the strength of the Grecian armies.

The light-armed troops were formed of the poorer citizens, hence they do not appear in the sculptured frieze of the Parthenon. Their mode of fighting was desultory, and having thrown their weapons they frequently

---

[76] Plutarch. Pelopida.

[77] Ælian's Tactics..

[78] The companion of Ajax is represented as one of those on a vase in Sir William Hamilton's Etruscan Antiquities, Vol. III, Pl. LVII. Xenophon says, the πέλτα, was in tbe form of an ivy-leaf and first used by the Amazons.

retired behind the protecting shields[79] of the heavy-armed infantry. As was the case with our Norman ancestors, the cavalry of the Grecians were composed of such only as were possessed of estates, which enabled them to provide horses at their own charge: those, therefore, were not very numerous. Their horses had bridles, with, bits called λύκοι, from their resemblance to the teeth of wolves, which, from being jagged,[80] rendered them very powerful; and though on the Elgin marbles there is no appearance of saddles, the ἐφίππια, or horse-coverings, made of cloth, leather, or the skins of wild beasts, were certainly used at a later period. According to Julius Pollux,[81] the Greeks taught their horses to stoop when they wanted to mount them. The chariots were probably used only by the nobles, being richly embossed with gold and silver ornaments. Thus Homer:

Ἄρμα δὲ ὁι χρυσῷ τε κὰι ἀργύρῳ εὖ ἤσκηται.[82]

"Silver and gold his chariot did adorn."

And again,

Ἄρμα Ἰά τε χρυσῳ πεπυκασμένα, κασσιτέρῳτε.[83]

"Chariots richly adorned with gold and tin."

They were likewise furnished with curious hangings:

.... ἀμφὶ δὲ πέπλοι
Πέπ'ΙανΙας.[84]

"..........Round about hangings
Expanded wide."

These hangings do not appear on the sculptured frieze of the Parthenon: the chariots there are about sixteen inches above the ground, with two wheels each, having four spokes. They are mounted from behind, being there open;

---

[79] Iliad, 9. v. 266.
[80] Such bave been dug up in Italy.
[81] Lib. I, c. ix.
[82] Iliad, x.
[83] Iliad, v'.
[84] Iliad, έ.

but on the sides and in front enclosed. These sides are furnished with handles, very conveniently placed for those who would get up into them. The chariots, mentioned by Homer, are for the most part drawn by two horses abreast:

.... παρὰ δὲ σφιν ἑκάσΊῳ διζυγες ἵπποι
῎ΕσΊασαν.[85]

"........... To every chariot two yoked horses
Stand."

To these a third was sometimes added, but not like the other two, which were fastened to the pole; he ran by the side, attached only by traces. They were sometimes drawn by four, as when Hector, in the Iliad, calls to his four harnessed steeds; and Homer, in another place, says:

.... ὡς ἐν πεδίῳ τεΊράορες ἵπποι.[86]

"......... As in he field the four reined steeds."

On the Elgin marbles they appear sometimes drawn by two, sometimes by three, sometimes by four horses. Every chariot carried two men, whence it was termed δίφρος, and this occurs perpetually in the Elgin marbles. One of these holds the reins, and we find he was thence called ἡνίοχος; and although this office was sometimes performed by persons of quality, it was considered as inferior to that of the παραβάτης, warrior, who commanded him where to drive. These warriors, on the frieze before mentioned, and which is referred to as of fixed date,[87] are all heavy armed, that is, they have on a leathern cuirass, much resembling that worn by the Roman generals,[88] and a helmet, and are armed with a spear and large circular shield. When

---

[85] Iliad, έ.
[86] Odyss. ί.
[87] The time of Pericles. See the originals in the British Museum.
[88] Pausanias says: "In one of the pictures of Poiygnotus there is painted, on an altar, a brazen cuirass. At present he shape of such cuirasses is very rare, but they were used in former times, It consists of two pieces of brass, one of wbich covers tbe breast and abdomen, the other tbe back: the anterior part they call gualon, and the hinder prosegon. It appears to be a sufficient protection for the body without a shield. On tbis account Homer so represents the Phrygian Phorcys, because he used a gualothorax. In the temple of the Ephesian Diana, Caliphon, the Samian, bas painted certain women adapting the parts of such a cuirass to Patroclus." Such a cuirass may be seen on a vase in Hamilton's Etruscan Antiquities. Vol. I, Pl. LV.

the chariots were driven close to the enemy, the warriors frequently:

.... ἐυπλεκέων δίφρων θίρον αἶψ' ἐπὶ γαῖαν[89]

"........ Leapt from their chariots on the ground"—

and when weary from the weight of their armour, retired into their chariots, and thence annoyed their enemies with darts and missive weapons. The chariots, however, on the Elgin marbles, are not furnished with these latter, like those of the Græco-Egyptians, sculptured on the walls of the tombs of the kings at Thebes. It is said, that the Greeks in very antient times had chariots, δρεπανοφόροι, armed with scythes, but I have never met with any in antient sculpture, and they were contemned in the better days of Greece as inconvenient, and not likely, when used by an enemy, to do them much damage: indeed, the chariot altogether became disused long before the time of Dionysius of Halicarnassus, though continued in his days by the Romans; and the Greeks gave their attention more fully to their cavalry.

Philomeenes, the master of the Achæan horse, according to Plutarch,[90] corrected the errors in the cavalry. "He obliged them to carry a shield which, from its lightness, could be more expeditiously managed, and not wider than absolutely necessary to cover their bodies; to use lances considerably shorter than the usual sarissee, and which, by being lighter, might be thrown at the enemy while at a distance, and yet sufficiently strong for close fight. lie therefore induced them to adopt, instead of the long shield and lance, the round one with the sarissa, so that, being at the same time protected with helmets, cuirasses, and greaves, they might either skirmish as light cavalry, or sustain a charge as heavy horse."

Philopæman, in like manner, according to Pausanias, changed the armour of the infantry under his command, for previous to this they used small spears, and oblong shields like the Celtic thureos, or the Persian gerra, but he persuaded them to cover their bodies with thoraxes, and their legs with greaves, and to use Argolic shields and long spears.

Greece being, however, in general hilly, will account for the preference at first given to foot soldiers for the main body of its armies; but when the Spartans carried their arms into other countries the want of cavalry was sensibly felt. Thessaly, of all the Grecian states, produced most horses, and

---

[89] Hesiod. Scuto.
[90] In Vitâ.

hence they had a superiority of cavalry; but the Spartans procured their's from the neighbouring town of Sciros, the inhabitants of which claimed, as their proper post, the left wing of the Lacedemonian armies.[91]

Of the Greek cavalry, some were ἱπποτοξόταί, or mounted archers; some ἀκροβολισται, or mounted slingers; both which may be considered as light cavalry: while the heavy horse were distinguished into regiments by their armour, as δορατοφόρόι, lancers; ξυσʹΙοφόροι, armed with sabres; κοντοφὸροι, bearers of the contus;[92] θυρεοφόροι, armed with thureos; and υπακοντισʹΙαὶ, javelin-men. Some of those who fought on horseback had a spare horse, which they led, to supply the place of that which might be fatigued or killed; they were thence called αμφιπποι, and ἱππαγωγοὶ. There was also a species of troops, introduced by Alexander the Great, who, from being heavy armed, could dismount, give their horses to their attendants, and fight with the infantry; they were thence known by the name of διμάχοι.[93] The κατάφρακτοι, or heavy-armed horse, in later times had their horses protected by armour, made of little plates, sometimes in the shape of scales, and sometimes as flat rings placed contiguously: these were at first of brass, and then of other metals, and the armour made of them took its name from the part it covered, being called προμετωπιδια, frontlets; παρώτια, ear-pieces; παρήΐα, cheek-coverings; προσʹΙερνιδια, chest-pieces; παραπλευρίδια, side-pieces: παραμηρίδια, thigh-pieces; παρακνημδια, leg-pieces, &c. This custom they probably derived from the Asiatics. Elephants have been mentioned, but these were first introduced by Alexander the Great: the tractability of these animals, however, being outweighed by their ungovernable fury when wounded, soon occasioned their disuse.

The arms of the Greeks, in Homer's time, were of brass, as indeed, with many primitive nations, copper and tin, for such was the composition, being more easily fused than iron. Tin was sometimes used by itself; thus the greaves of Achilles, the breastplate of Agamemnon, and the shield of Æneas, were composed of this metal;[94] and gold and silver formed the ornaments of armour. The armour of the early Greeks was not much, its increase was borrowed from the Asiatics;[95] after this we find it very various. The helmet was called περικεφαλαία, when it enveloped the whole head, such as those in

---

[91] Xenophon Cyropœd. Lib. IV; Thucydides, Lib. v,

[92] The contus was a long stout pike, used generally by sailors.

[93] Pollux, Lib. I, cap. x. One of the attendants is engraved in Hope's Costume, PL. LXXXI.

[94] Iliad, ί and vʹ.

[95] Euripidis Scholiastes.

the British Museum, and leaving only an opening for the sight and breath; κράνος, when a mere scullcap, and κόρυς. This, as in the case of those in the British Museum,[96] was generally of brass; hence, Homer says,

> .... ἀυτὰρ ἐπὶ σ'Ιεφάνην κεφάληφιν ἀέιρας
> Θήκατο χαλκέιην.

> "......... But upon the stephane,[97] the moveable headpiece,
> He placed of brass."

In the very early period they had been composed of the skins of quadrupeds, of which none were more common than the dog, because that animal was more readily procured, though Eustathius tells us, it was ποτάμος κύων, a water-dog: hence we have κυνέη, the dog's-skin helmet; ίκτιδεη, that of weasel's skin; ταυρέιη, the bull's-hide helmet; ἀλωπεκέη, the fox-skin; λεοντεη αίγεὶη, that covered with the lion's skin: but these in later times all became poetic appellations of the helmet, though made of brass. These skins were always worn with the hair on; and to render their appearance more terrible, the teeth of the animal were frequently placed grinning on their enemies, a custom that had been retained by the Mexicans. The περικεφαλή was slit up the front, in order to leave a covering for the nose, and when thrown back so as to uncover the face, necessarily left a great space between its own crown and the scull of the wearer, and generally had, in order to protect the cheeks, two leather flaps, which, when not used, were tucked up inwards. There are two in the British Museum, figured by Strutt and Grose. The κράνος merely covered the back part of the head, but was furnished with cheek-pieces,[98] called ὄχους, which tied under the chin, and were concave metal plates suspended from hinges, which, when not wanted, turned up outwards. The κόρυς had either a frontlet, termed ὀφρύες or a projecting piece, over the brow, called by the metaphorical term γεῖσον, the pent-house.[99] The first of these helmets was worn by the heavy-armed forces; the second by the light troops, whether cavalry or infantry; and the third by the heavy horse. The κόρυς was the most splendidly ornamented of any, quadrigae, sphinxes, griffins, sea-horses, and other insignia, richly embossed, often covered the surface; the περικεφαλή had a ridge, on which was a quantity of horse-hair

---

[96] See the engraving of them in Grose's Antient Armour.
[97] See this explained afterwards.
[98] This may be seen in Ham. Etrus. Antiq. Vol. III, Pl. LVII, before cited.
[99] In European armour termed umbril.

from the mane, cut square at the edges; the κρανος sometimes had a cock's
feather stuck on each side,[100] but the κορς had feathers, ridges, and horse-
hair. of mane and tail, the ridge was called φάλος, the horsehair ornament
λόφς.[101] Homer speaks of a golden crest:

> Τοῦξε δε οἱ κορυϑα βριαρὴν κροτάφοις ἀραρυῖαν
> Καλὴν, δαιδαλέην, ἐπὶ δε χρύσεον λόφον ἧκε.

> "But the strong helmet on his temples, well adapted,
> Beautiful, variegated, and surmounted by a golden crest, he placed."

And that by λόφον he meant the hair we learn from another passage, when
speaking of this same helmet, which Vulcan made for Achilles, he changes the expression to εθειραι χρυσεαι, golden hair: perhaps, therefore, it was
composed of wires of gold instead of hair, or of hair gilt.

A helmet is said by Homer to have been given by Meriones to Ulysses,
strengthened within with many thongs strongly interwoven, and without
ornamented profusely with boar's teeth, quite white, and placed in curious
order; in the middle was inserted a pileus, or cap of wool, to answer the
purpose, probably, of a lining.

The ridge was composed of various metals, but generally such as
were conceived ornamental to the helmet; and the crest was adorned
with divers sorts of paint, whence Pollux gives it the epithets of εὐανϑὴς
ὑακινϑοϑινοβαφης.[102] This crest was formed of the manes of the horses,
which will account for so many in the Elgin marbles appearing hog-maned;
at the bottom was sometimes added the tail of the horse, whence we read
of λόφος ἱπποχαίτης, κόρυς ἱπποδάσεια, ἵππχρις, and on each side the crest
were sometimes feathers.[103] Plumes of feathers in after ages often supplied
the place of hair, and this seems to have been occasioned by Alexander the
Great, who, we are told,[104] at the battle of the Granicus, was remarkable for
a large plume of white feathers on his helmet. This same author tells us, that
the helmet of Alexander was of steel, polished as bright as silver, and made

---

[100] Two soldiers wearing them may be seen on a lamp in Montf. Antiq. expl. Vol. V, PI.
CXCVI, which further shews the practice of a front rank kneeling being far earlier than the
use of fire-arms. See further in the account of the Romans.
[101] Suidas justly makes this distinction, though others have supposed no difference
between them,
[102] Lib. 1, cap. x,
[103] See Hope's Costume of the Antients, fl. LXXV, CLXXVII, &c.
[104] Plut. in Vit. Alex.

by Theophilus. He adds, to it was affixed a gorget of the same metal set with precious stones. The common soldiers had only small crests; the chieftains were distinguished by plumes of a larger size, and frequently took a pride in wearing, two, three, or four crests together. Sometimes the hair was gilt; hence, Homer says,[105]

.........ἠδ ἀσίηρ ὡς ἀπέλαμπεν
Ἱππχροις τρυφάλεια, περισσέιοντο δ᾽ ἔθειραι
Χρὺσεαι, ἃς Ηφαισ᾽Ιος ἵει λόφον ἀμφί θαμειάς.

".........Like a star, so shone around
The horse-haired helmet, having round its summit hair
Gilded, which Vulcan had placed about the ridge."

Thus we find the helmet was called, when surmounted with crests, αμφιαλος; when with three, τρυφάλεια; and when with four, τετράφαλος. So Apollonius:[106]

Τετράφαλος φοίνικει λόφῳ ἐπελάμπετο πήληξ.

"With a four-fold crest to the Phoenician ridge dazzled the helmet."

The design is said to have been to strike terror into their enemies.[107] For the same reason Pyrrhus, king of Epirus, beside a lofty crest, had goat's-horns upon his helmet. We are told by Suidas, that the τρίχωσις, or crest itself, was called sometimes χέρας, and cows' as well as goats' horns seem to have been worn by some of the Greeks; many of them are observable in Hope's Costume of the Antients,[108] and were probably adopted from their Mythology. Other sorts of ornaments were used, as on that called στεφάνη, which name signifies the ridge of a mountain, and on that account is applied to helmets, having several ἐξοχαῖ, eminences, such as may be seen in Hope's Costume.[109]

---

[105] Iliad, τ′. v. 382.

[106] Lib. III,

[107] Homer, Iliad, III. SO likewise Polybius, Lib. VI, in Castrametatione, says: "Besides all these they were adorned on the top with a plume and three feathers placed erect, of purple or black, almost a cubit in length, which, when other ornaments were added, made a man appear twice his natural height; very handsome indeed, but terrible to his enemies."

[108] See Pl. CXXX.

[109] Pl. LXXXVI.

But of all the Grecian helmets, the Bœotian is said to have been the best.[110] The Macedonians had a peculiar one, termed κκυσίη, which was composed of hides, and served instead of a cap to defend them from cold. It appears to have resembled the petasus, being broad brimmed.[111] A leathern scullcap, without any ridge or crest, Homer[112] speaks of as having been worn by Diomed:

.... ἀμφι δε οἱ κυνίην κεφαλῆφιν ἔθηκε
Τακρέιην, ἄφαλόν τε, κὰι ἄλφον, ἤ τε καταιτυξ
Κεκλητα.

".......... His helmet on his head he placed
Of bull's-skin, without ridge, without crest, kataityx
Called."

A small bronze antique bust of him, in my son's possession, represents it as slit open at the ears, and terminating in thongs to tie under the chin.[113]

In the earliest ages of Greece the warriors prided themselves on wearing the skins of the wild beasts which they had slain, at once the mark of their prowess and a tolerable protection to their bodies. Instances of this kind are to be met with in most of the antient poets, but Theocritus has described in what manner they were put on:

Ἀὐτὰρ ὑπὲρ νώτοιο καὶ αὐχένος ἠωρεῖτο
Ἀκροων δέρμα λέοντος ἀφημμένον ἐκ ποδεώνων.

"But o'er his neck and back was thrown
A lion's skin, held up by its feet."

But they afterwards adopted armour of a less dubious nature, confining it to the heavy-armed troops, both cavalry and infantry: it consisted of a cuirass, named μίτρη; a gorget, called θώραξ; and a girdle, ζωςΊηρ, to which was attached a petticoat, called ζῶμα. The initree was padded with wool, covered either with flat rings, or square pieces of brass,[114] and fastened at the sides: in this state it was cut round at the loins; but that in the time

[110] Pollux, Lib. I, cap. x.
[111] The petasus is frequently sculptured in the Elgin marbles. Indeed, those on the lamp in Montf. Antiq, expl, Vol. V,. Pl. cxcvi, are of this kind, and probably the καυσίη.
[112] Iliad, x,
[113] A similar, but larger one, in the possession of R. P. Knight, Esq., has been sculptured in Strutt's Dress and Habits' of the People of England.
[114] See Hope's Costume, Pl. xlvi, cii.

of Pericles followed the line of the abdomen, and was probably of leather, without metal plates.[115] Sometimes in front of it was placed another breast-piece,[116] but this only when the thorax did not wholly cover the chest. The thorax varied in its form: sometimes as a gorget it entirely covered the chest, folding over the upper part of the mitree, and covering each shoulder-blade behind;[117] sometimes it covered the upper part of the back, and passing over both shoulders terminated below each breast;[118] and sometimes it covered the upper part of the back and the whole of the chest.[119] The middle part was called γύαλα, and the extreme part πΊέρυγες,[120] and these were cither fastened by a cord from each to a ring below,[121] or put on a kind of button.[122] The complete thorax was the most antient, and borrowed from the Persians or Egyptians; but the ημιθωράκιον, or half thorax, Pollux tells us, was invented by Jason. Alexander esteemed it most soldier-like; and, according to Polyænus,[123] considering the entire thorax might be a temptation to his troops to turn their backs upon their enemies, commanded them to use instead the half thorax, which, though it covered the chest, was open between the shoulder-blades. Sometimes, though rarely, the most antient thoraces of linen were worn, which were of several folds and padded. Pausanias says, he saw one of these in the temple of Grynæus Apollo, as well as in others. These, he observes, are not so useful to warriors, because they are pervious to the vehement percussions of iron. Homer[124] gives one to Ajax, son of Oileus:

.... ὀλίγος μὲν ἔην λινοθώρηξ.

"Ajax the Less a linen thorax had."

Alexander, we are told by Plutarch, had θώρακα λινχν διπχν, a two-fold linen thorax; and Iphicrates ordered his troops to lay aside their thoraces of

---

[115] This kind of cuirass may be seen in Hamilton's Etruscan Antiquities, Vol. I, Pl. LV.

[116] See Hope's Costume, Pl. CII.

[117] Ibid. Pl. LXXV.

[118] Ibid. Pl. LXXXXIV.

[119] Ibid, PI. LXX. But these distinctions may be easily seen in the Etruscan Armour, PI. IV, of this work.

[120] Pollux; Pausanias' Atticis.

[121] See Hope's Costume, Pl. CII.

[122] Pausanias' Atticis.

[123] Strateg. Lib. IV, c. iii.

[124] Iliad, Ϭ.

steel for such as were made of hemp.[125] Brass, iron, and other metals were, however, the ordinary materials of which the thoraces were manufactured. In the British Museum is a fragment of a brass one, being the part which lay on the chest: it is covered with embossed ornaments in the shape of rings, &c. Strutt says: "Homer, speaking; of the Greeks, frequently calls them the *brazen tunic-wearers*, Αχαιων χαλκοχιτωνων;[126] it is, however, very extraordinary, that, where he speaks at large concerning the warlike habits of his heroes, he has not specified this tunic, nor given us the least hint respecting its form. In the long description of Agamemnon arming himself for the battle,[127] we do not find it mentioned, unless the words by which this description is introduced may be thought applicable to it: "He also clothed himself in splendid brass"—first about his legs he placed the handsome greaves, neatly joined with clasps of silver; then the thorax, on which Homer bestows ten lines. There is no mention of the tunic of brass in the request made by Thetis to Vulcan, for a new suit of armour to equip her son; neither is it noticed in the description of the arms as they were made by that deity; nor in a subsequent passage, where Achilles is described putting them on. But let us suppose that the thorax and the chalcochiton were only two denominations for the same armour, and we shall meet with no further difficulty. The Fig. PI. VII,[128] has the thorax large enough to cover not only the breast but all the front, at least, of the body, down to the navel; and probably it extended over the back in the same manner: the shoulder parts are fastened in the front with thongs, or cords, to the bottom of the thorax, and might, I presume, when those ligatures were unloosed, be thrown back at pleasure, so that the arms might easily be withdrawn, and the armour put off over the head of the wearer, and there are several passages in the antient poets that justify this opinion. In this example we observe appended to this breastplate several straps of leather, perhaps plated with metal, (lambrequins,) reaching nearly to the bottom of the inner garment. In fact, I conceive the thorax to have been a large breastplate of brass affixed to a short sleeveless tunic, made of leather, or some other appropriate material, to which the shoulder-guards were connected at the back. Hes-

---

[125] Cornelius Nepos in Vità Iphic. The Latin word, however, being lorica, the mitree, and not the thorax, may be implied. The passage is as follows: "Idem genus loricarum mutavit and pro ferreis atque æneis lineas dedit. Quo facto expeditiones milites reddidit: nam pondere detracto, quod æquè corpus tegeret et bene esset curavit."

[126] Iliad, Lib. III, v. 127, 131, et alibi.

[127] At the beginning of the 11th book of the Iliad.

[128] In Strutt's Dress and Habits of the English.

iod, describing the arms of Hercules, says, he placed on his shoulders αρης αλκ'Ιηα σιδρον, the harm-repelling iron;[129] or the thorax might be laced on behind. That of Agamemnon, according to Homer, wras splendidly ornamented, having upon it ten rows of black cyanus, μελανος κυανιο,[130] twelve of gold, twenty of tin, enclosed by three azure dragons, κυανεοι δρακον'Ιες τρεις, rising from either side to the summit of the pectoral, in the form of a rainbow. The thorax of Menelaus is said to have been διπλοος, or two-fold, having a girdle plated with brass beneath it, ηδ ὑπενερθεν ζωμα, τε και μἱ'Ιρη.[131] Agamemnon also had a variegated belt, strengthened with plates of silver under his pectoral, which repelled the point of a weapon that had passed through the latter ζωνην θωρηχος ενέρθε."[132] Plutarch speaks of one that may be considered as of the mixed kind: he tells us,[133] that Zoilus, an armourer, having made a present of a thorax to Demetrius Poliorcetes, for an experiment of its hardness, had it placed about twenty-six paces from a catapulta, from which was discharged an arrow; this, so far from piercing the iron, scarcely made the slightest impression on it. We are further told that it consisted of two parts, one of which being of iron and inflexible, was called θώραξ σ'Ιάδιὸς, or σ'Ιαδὸς, the stiff-standing thorax; the other was of a beast's hide, and, according to the poet,

.... τῷ δε θώακος σκύτει.

".........the skin of the thorax."

The iron part was probably a collar to the thorax, for such appears represented on a warrior crouching behind his shield, in Hope's Costume of the Antients.[134] The thoraces were, however, sometimes of linen covered with little scales of metal, and this kind always appears on that worn by Minerva; or they were covered with flat rings, a custom that prevailed even in the Graeco-Roman soldiers of Justinian, as appears by a Mosaic at Ravenna. In these cases they were called θώρακές ἁλυσιδωτοὶ, thoraces of chain-work; λεπιδωτοὶ, scaled; φολιδωτοὶ, plumated, &c.; and occur in Hope's

---

[129] V. 128.
[130] Iliaù, Lib. XI v. 2L
[131] Iliad, Lib. IV, v. 156,.187; compare also 215 and 216.
[132] Ibid. XI, 235; and in 237 it is called ζωσ'Ιης, ὥαναιολος.
[133] In Demetrio,
[134] Pl. LXVI.

Costume.[135] Ἀλσιδωτοὶ, therefore, which literally means indissoluble, and thence expresses chain-work, probably consisted of several rows of rings fastened into each other, and stitched upon linen. Two such, of the size of large curtain rings, may be seen of brass in the British Museum. The lorica hamata too, of the Romans, appears to have been of rings cut through in one part, and hooked into linen cuirasses: that Greek one, Pl. IV, Fig. 19, seems to have been of this kind, and the rings are placed like rustred armour of the 12th century. Pausanias says, the brazen thorax of Cleostratus he saw, and it was thick set with hooks turned upwards. The only way to understand this passage, appears to me, is by imagining the rings in Fig. 19 to be reversed.

The warrior completed the equipments for his body by putting on the girdle to which was attached the drapery, at once the appendage of decency and elegance. Thus, Homer says:

> Αὖσε δέ οἱ ζωσ'Ιηρα παναίολήν, ἥδ ἐπένερθε
> Ζῶμά τε καὶ μίτρην ἥν χαλκῆε κάμον ἄνδρς.

"He then embraced his rich embroidered belt, and underneath it placed
His zoma, and his mitree, which had been made by skilful armourers."

From the specimens Mr. Hope has given from Greek vases, the embroidery, ornaments, or studs, on these girdles, were varied with considerable taste. As this act made the armour secure, ζώννσθαι, to gird, became a general word to imply putting on armour. Hence, when Agamemnon commands the Greeks to arm, Homer says:[136]

> Ατρέιδης δε βόησεν ἰδὲ ζώννυσθαι ἄνωγεν.

"Atrides then commands them all to gird."

The same poet, when he makes that hero resemble the god of war, in his ζωνη, or military belt, is supposed, according to, Pausanias, to mean his whole armour, In the following passage,[137] we have all these several parts of the armour enumerated:

---

[135] Pl. XLVII, L, &c.
[136] Iliad, λ'.
[137] Iliad, δ.

Ἀύτή δ' αὖτ' ἴϑυνεν ὄϑι ζωσ'Ιῆρος ὄχηες
Χρύσιοι σύνεχον, καὶ διπλόος ἤντετο ϑώρηξ,
Ἔν δ ἔπεσε ζωσ'Ιῆ ἁρηὸτι πικρός ὄϊσ'Ιός
Δίὰ μὲν ἀρ ζωσ'Ιῆρος ἐλήλατο δαιδαλέοιο,
Καὶ δία ϑώρηκος πολυδαιδάλου ἡρήρειστο,
Μίτρης ϑ', ἢν ἐφόρει ἔρυμα χροός, ἔρκος ἀκόντων
Ἡ οἱ πλεῖστον ἔρυτο.

"But she directed it to that part where the belt
To golden rings is bound, and to which the two-fold thorax is stretched.
On his belt, well fitted, fell the piercing arrow,
And through the belt it passed, made of smith's work,
And in the thorax, curiously wrought, infixed it stands;
And in the mitree, which he wore as the surest safeguard to his body,
And in which he most delighted."

The belt in this case was not worn just above the loins, but just below the chest, as in Hamilton's Etruscan Antiqulties.[138] But besides this body-armour the Greeks[139] had protections for their legs, which rose in front to the top of their knees, nearly met behind at the calves, and terminated just above thé ankle: these were called κνημίδες, greaves, and were of metal, as brass, tin, &c. Thus Hesiod:[140]

.... κνημῖδας ὀρει χάλκοιο φαεινx
Ηφαίσ'Ιx καυτα δῶρα, περὶ κνήμησιν ἔϑηκεν.

.... The greaves of shining brass,
The famous gift of Vulcan, he round above his ankles placed."

And Homer:[141]

Τεῦξε δε κνημῖδας ἑανx καοσστεροιο

"He made his greaves of beaten tin."

---

[138] Vol. IV, PI. xxx.

[139] All the figures in armour which appear on the Elgin marbles are in cuirasses exactly resembling; those worn by the Romans, but without lambrequins; they are, therefore, probably of leather. A figure of Mars, PI. xlviii, of Hope's Costume, in the old or severe style, is thus accoutred.

[140] Scuto.

[141] Iliad, π. v. 612.

But Laërtes, the father of Ulysses, is described[142] as wearing them of hull's hide. When put on they were closed behind, being elastic, with pieces of metal terminating in buttons.[143] To this also Homer refers:

Κνημῖδας μὲν πρῶτα περὶ κνήμησιν ἔθηκ
Καλάς, ἀργυρέοισιν ἐπιοφυρίοις ἀραρύιας.

"But first round above his ankles the greaves he put,
Which were beautiful,[144] closed with silver buttons."

So general was the use of this piece of armour, that Homer perpetually calls the Greeks—

.... ἐῦκνήμιδες Αχαιοί.

".........Well-greaved Greeks."

We read of χείρεις, or guards for the hands; but though these were partially used, I have not met with any representation of them.

The original Greek shield was the ἀσπις, a word which literally implies covering; and their form was εὔκυκλοι πάντοτε ἴσαι, perfect circles, equal in every direction. They were convex, which part was termed χυτυξ, and edged witli a broad flat rim, called περιφέρεια, or κύκλος, the circumference or circle, and the edge of this was denominated ἴτυς, the extremity. The centre had on it a projecting convex part, called ομφάλος, and μεσομφάλιον, from its resemblance to the navel: upon this was sometimes placed another projection, termed ἐπομφάλιον, which is said to have been of great service in repelling missive weapons, by occasioning them to glance off, and also for bearing down their enemies.[145] Across, within side the shield, was placed a band of metal, under which passed the arm, forming with it the letter χ,[146] said to have been invented by the Carians, and called ὄχανον, or ὄχανη while the hand grasped one of the χανόνες, which were festooned all round the edge of the concave circumference; or at other times these were omitted for cords attached to little rings, and called πόρπακες, two of which crossed

---

[142] Hom. Odys. Lib. xxv, v. 228.

[143] See Hope's Costume of the Antients, PI. LXX.

[144] Several of the specimens in Hope's Costume fully justify this epithet, and it is to be recollected, that Homer only applies it to those of the commanders.

[145] These several parts are fully shewn in the specimens given by Mr. Hope.

[146] See Hope's Costume, PI. LXVII; and Eustathius' Iliad. β. p. 184, edit. Basil.

the arm, while a handle was held in the hand.[147] Such handles, when the wars were ended, and the shields, as was the custom, hung up in the temples of the Gods, were removed to render them unfit for sudden insurrection: hence Aristophanes introduces a person affrighted, when he sees the shields hanging up with the handles:

Όἵ μοι τάλας ἔχϰσι γὰρ πόπραϰας

"Oh! woe is me; for the shields have handles on."

Sometimes the shield was furnished with a thong of leather, by which it was hung on the shoulder; but though I do not recollect its application any where illustrated, I think it appears on that of Theseus, where he is represented in a contest with the Amazons, on a fictile vase.[148] Ilomer, however, thus mentions it:[149]

.... αὐτὰρ ἀπ' ὤμων
Ασπὶς σὺν τεαμῶνι χαμαὶ τερμιοεσσα.

"......... But from his shoulders
The huge shield, with its thong, fell 'on -the ground."

Æschylus speaks of little bells hung from the shields to strike terror into an enemy:

.... ἀπ' ἀσπίδος δε τῷ
Χαλϰήλατοι πλάζϰσι ϰώδωνες φοβῳ.

"......... From the shields
The brazen bells put them to flight through fear."

But of this kind I have seen no representation.

These shields were most tastefully ornamented with tripods, serpents, scorpions, and other mythological subjects, surrounded by elegant borders, as may be seen in Hope's Costume of the Antients. This custom, according to Herodotus, was first introduced by the Carians, and from them communicated to the other Grecian states, the Romans, and the Barbarians.

---

[147] Ibid. Pl. CIV.
[148] Ibid. PI. XXII; and Hamilton's Etruscan Antiquities, Vol II, PI. CXXVI. The warrior appears in a quilted tunic.
[149] Iliad, ρ'.

According to Polynoeus, the Lacedemonians on a particular occasion had their names engraven on their shields.[150]

Pausanias tells us, that "he saw in the treasury of Olympia a shield covered with laminae of brass, and adorned inside with various pictures, together with a helmet and greaves. The inscription on these arms implied, that they were spoils dedicated by the Myones. On the tomb of Epaminondas is his shield, on which is embossed a dragon, which implied that he was descended from those called Sparti, who are said to have originated from the teeth of a dragon."

All these remarks have been confined to the large round buckler, called aspis, which was made of several folds of leather, whence it was called ἀπίς βόεια. It was covered with plates of metal, which were laid one over the other: hence, Achilles' buckler is thus described:[151]

>.......... πέν'Ιε π'Ιύχας ἤλασε Κυλλοποδίων,
> Τὰς δύο χαλκείας, δύο δ' ἔνδοθι κασσιτέροιο,
> Τήν δε μίαν χρυσν.

> ".......... With five plates Vulcan fortified it:
> With two of brass, two upon those of tin,
> And one of gold."[152]

And that of Ajax as—[153]

>.......... — σάκος αἰόλν, ἐπ'Ιαβόειον
> Ταύρων ζατρεφέω, ἐπὶ δ' ὄγδοον ηασε χαλκον.

> ".......... Made of the hides of seven
> Well-fatted bulls, and covered with a plate of brass."

There appears in several representations, on fictile vases, a piece of drapery suspended from the shield, the intention of which seems to have been, to break the force of any cut made at the legs, and was probably used before the invention of greaves; though it does not occur in the Elgin marbles, where none of the figures wear greaves, while it is depicted on vases as held by warriors which often have those protections[154] It occurs generally with

---

[150] Lib. I, c. 17.
[151] Iliad, v. 270.
[152] These may bave extended beyond each other so as to display the whole.
[153] Iliad, ή. 222.
[154] It is singular that the Mexicans are the only people who had a similar custom.

the evil eye painted on it, under the superstitious idea, that it would work mischief to those it beheld.

he aspis appears to have been about three feet in diameter, for in the specimens given by Mr. Hope,[155] they reach from the neck to the calf of the leg; hence, Tyrtseus says:

Μηρχσ τε, κάμκο τε κάτω κὰι σʹIeύνα, καί ώμχς,
Άσπιδος ἐυρειης γαςτρὶ καλυψκμενος.

"Thighs, legs, aud breast, belly and shoulders too,
The mighty buckler covered."

On this account Homer calls them ἀμφιβρστς, and ποδηνηχείς, the warriors often, by kneeling down and bending their heads, concealing themselves behind them.[156] Pollux[157] mentions an aspis κοίλ,η ἐτερο μηχης, with an edge or keel longer in one place than another; but unless this refers to the flat part being prolonged at the top and bottom, to make the shield an oval,[158] while the central part was circular, I am unable to comprehend it.

The aspis was generally carried by the heavy-armed infantry, and by those who fought in chariots. The cavalry had a much lighter and smaller round shield,[159] composed of a hide with the hair on, and called λαιοῆίον, from λάσιος, hairy. Homer notices their lightness:

.... βοέιας
Ασπίδας εὐκυκλος, λαισῆία τε πτεροεντα.

".......... The bull's-hide
Well-rounded aspida, and the light laiseia,"

Polyeenus[160] mentions an iron shield in the time of the Seleucidse in Persia, as having been thrown up as a signal for the Macedonian and Thra-

---

[155] See Costume of the Antients, PI. LXVI. LXVIII, and LXX.

[156] Ibid. PI. LXVI; and Polyoenus mentions, that under cover of their shields they sometimes dug trenches to ensnare the cavalry: Lib. II, c. iii.

[157] Lib I, c. x.

[158] There is an oval shield, however, in Hamilton's Etruscan Antiquities, Vol. Ill, Pl. CVIII, where two prize-fighters are represented on a stage.

[159] See one of these placed on three cavalry lances on a frieze engraved at the top of p. 47, Vol. III, of Stuart's Antiquities of Athens. From this the diameter appears to have been rather less than two feet.

[160] Lib. VII, c. xxxix.

cian horse to massacre the Persians. A small convex bronze shield is among the Hamilton Antiquities in the British Museum.

The light infantry were armed with the πελτη, according to Xenophon; a shield resembling an ivy-leaf, and borrowed from the Amazons. The companion of Ajax, the son of Oileus, is depicted with one of these on a fictile vase in Sir William Hamilton's collection, and now in the British Museum.[161] The γερρον, or γερρα, was a fiddle-shaped shield, borrowed from the Persians, as we are told by Strabo,[162] a fact that sufficiently appeal's by comparing those sculptured at Persepolis with those represented in Hope's Costume.[163] They were adopted by the Thebans. The Greeks also used an oblong shield, called θυςεὸς, from its resemblance to a gate, being curved ou its upper line, and pierced to look through or to carry on the spear. I have not seen any one of these in Grecian representations, but it occurs in the Græco-Egyptian paintings on the walls of the tombs of the kings at Thebes.[164]

To lose the shield was accounted the greatest disgrace: hence Epaminondas, in the agonies of death, inquired for the safety of his; and the Spartan mothers desired their sons either to bring back their bucklers, or be brought upon them.

For close fight the arms of the Greeks were clubs, φαλχγγες; the maces, χορύνη; the spear, ἔγχος; the lance, Up; the pole-axe, αξίνη; the battle-axe, πέλεκυς; the sword, ξίφος; and the dagger, μάχαιρα. As the clubs were used in close fight, compact bodies of troops, called phalanxes, are thence supposed to have derived that denomination. Polyænus tells us, that Pisistratus, the tyrant of Athens, had a guard of 300 men armed with clubs.[165] This primitive weapon soon, however, gave way to the mace, which had its name from the little horns or spikes by which its head was surrounded. Periphetes, slain by Theseus, was named κορυνήτης, from using this weapon;[166] and the same appellation is given by Homer, to Areithous, for the same reason.[167]

Δίχ Αρηίθοχ τὸν ἐπ ιχπησιν κορυνήτην
Ανδρες χίχλεοχον χαλλίζωνί τε γυναῖχες,
Ὁύνεχ ἄρ χ' τοξοισι μαγέοχετο, δχρί τε μαχρῷ

[161] See Vol. III, PI, LVII, of the Etruscan Antiquities.
[162] Lib. xv.
[163] PI. LXXXVI, CIV, and CXXXVI.
[164] See Denon's Egypt, PI. LV; and PI. I, of this work.
[165] Strat. Lib. I, c. xxi.
[166] Plutarch in Theseo; and Diod. Sic. Lib. IV.
[167] Iliad, ἡ. v. 136.

Ἀλλὰ σιδηρέῃ κορύνῃ ῥνγυοκε φαλαγγας.

"God-like Areithous, called mace-bearer,
Men talk of, and women celebrate: him
Who never used bows, nor long lance,
But with his iron mace whole squadrons routed."

One of these maces in a horseman's hand occurs on an old Greek coin, engraved in Stuart's Antiquities of Athens;[168] and several brazen mace-heads, which prove that the handle was generally of wood, may be seen in the British Museum.[169]

The spear was generally of ash, with a leaf-shaped head of metal, and furnished with a pointed ferrule at the but, called σαυρωτὴρ, with which it was stuck in the ground, a method adopted, according to Homer, when the troops rested on their arms, or when sleeping on their shields.[170] Pausanias saw in the temple of Minerva a spear, attributed to Achilles, the blade and ferrule of which were of brass. It was the custom to put the spears against a column when not used, whence originated fluted pillars; hence, Homer says:

Ἔγχος ὁμὲυ ἔσʹΙηοε φέρων μακρὸν
Δχροδόκης ἔντοσθεν ἑῦξόν.

"His spear he placed leaning against a high column,
And filling the fluting made to hold pikes:"

The Macedonians had a particularly long spear, called σάρισσα, which was fourteen or sixteen cubits in length. Polyænus says, the people of Edessa had the same; but that, at the siege of that city, Cleonymus, who led them, ordered his front line to use no arms, but with both hands to seize the spears of their enemy, and hold them fast while the next rank advanced within and closed upon them: their spears thus seized the men retreated; but the next rank pressing on them gained the victory. By this manoeuvre the long and formidable spear was rendered useless, and was considered an encumbrance

[168] Vol. III, p. 53.

[169] With these are many that were not thus used, but placed on the striker of a flail, several in succession, madeto fit its increasing diameter towards its end, to prevent their flying off. Such a military weapon was used by the Portuguese till the conclusion of the 16th century.

[170] Iliad, κ'. v, 151. Aristotle de Arte Poetica. This ferrule is perceptible in the examples given in Hope's Costume.

rather than a weapon of offence.[171]

The doru, or lance, was probably that used by the cavalry, and furnished with a loop of leather, which served the warrior for a support when he chose to let it hang from his arm, and to twist round his hand for the firmer grasp when charging: this strap was called μεσάγκύλη, being put on about the middle. Three of these lances, with the laiseia, or small shield, may be seen in Stuart's Antiquities of Athens.[172]

The axine was a staff, on the end of which was a spike, with an axe-blade on one side, and another spike on the other.[173] With this weapon Agamemnon is said to have encountered Pisander.[174]

.........ὁ δ' ὑπ' ἀοπίδος εἵλετο καήν
Αξίνην εὔχαλον ἐλαῖνῳ αμφι πελέκκῳ
Μακρῷ ἐΰξεοΊῳ

".........But he from under his shield drew forth a beautiful
Axine, of well-tempered brass, and in its blade a shaft of olive,
Long and beautifully worked."

The pelekus had a short handle, and at its top an axe-blade, with a pike opposite.[175] Homer mentions it as indiscriminately used with the axine.[176]

Ἀλλ' οἵ γ' ἐΓγύθεν ἱΊοάμενοι, ἓνα θυμὸν εχονθες
Οξέσι δη πελεκεοσι, και ἀξίνηοι μάχοντο

"Both parties close together stood, and with determined courage
Wielded their pelekus, and with axines fought,"

The xiphos, or sword, was worn at the left hip, suspended from a leathern strap that passed over ,the right shoulder, and thus it appears, on several fictile vases[177] Hence, Hesiod says:[178]

Ωμοισιν δεμιν ἀμρὶ μελάνδετον ἆορ εκειτο
Χάλκεον ἐκ τεαμῶνος.

---

[171] Strat. Lib. ii, c. xxix.
[172] Vol. III, p. 47.
[173] See it in Hope's Costume, PI. LII, Fig.. 3.
[174] Iliad, γ'. 611.
[175] See Hope's Costume, PI. xx.
[176] Iliad, ό. 7l0.
[177] See Hope's Costume, PI. LXX, LXXXI, and CII.
[178] Scuto Herculis.

"From round about his shoulder hung
A brazen sword from a belt."[179]

And Homer.[180]

Ἀμφὶ δ' ἄρ ὤμοισιν βαλετο ξιφος ἀργυρόηλον

"About bis shoulder hung his silver-hilted sword."

The xiphos was straight, intended for cutting and thrusting, with a leaf-shaped blade, and not above twenty inches in length, it therefore reached only to the thigh, a circumstance noticed by the accurate Homer.[181]

.... φάσγανων ὀξὺ ἐρυσσάμενος παρὰ μηρχ.

".........Straight from his thigh the sword he draws."

It had no guard, but a cross bar, which, with the χολὲος, or scabbard, was beautifully ornamented.[182]

The makaira, or dagger, was more frequently used as a knife, but worn in the scabbard of the sword. Homer thus describes it.[183]

Ἀτρέιδης δὲ ἐρυσσὰ μενος χέιρεσσι μάχαιραν,
Η οἱ πὰρ ξίφεος μέγα κχλεὸν αἰὲν ἄορτο.

"Atrides drew the dagger with his hands,
Which in the wide scabbard of his sword was held."

The sword used by the Argives was called κοπὶς, and, from its name, seems to have been principally used for cutting;[184] those of the Lacedemoni-ans, according to Pollux, ξυίναι, or, as Xenophon has it, ξυήσΊιες; and those

---

[179] Pausanias saw in the temple of Æsculapius the sword of Memnon among the Nico-medenses, and it was wholly of brass.

[180] Iliad, ß.

[181] Odyss. λ'.

[182] Pausanias says: in the treasury of Olympia was preserved the sword of Pelops, the hilt of which was of ivory and gold.

[183] Iliad, γ.

[184] There is a figure in Hamilton's Etruscan Antiquities with a cutting sword like a hanger: this figure has the belt at the bottom of the thorax. Vol. IV, Pl. xxx.

of the Athenians, κνήσΊιες; all of which were of the short cutting kind.[185] At a later period of the Grecian history, the akinakes, or long curved dagger, with its edge on the inner curve, was borrowed from the Persians.[186]

Besides what have been enumerated, the Greeks had several missile weapons: these were slings, javelins, and bows.

The σφενδενη, or sling, was especially the weapon of the Acarnanians,[187] the Ætolians,[188] and the Achaeans,[189] who inhabited Ægium, Dyma, and Patræ; but the last of these so far excelled, that when any thing was directly levelled at a mark, it was usual to call it Αχαϊκον βελος.[190] It was sometimes made of wool,[191] and sometimes of leather, and is described by Dionysius [192] as having its cup not exactly hemispherical, but hemispheroidical, decreasing to two thongs at its ends. Out of it were cast stones or plummets of lead, called μολυβδίεςς, or μολυβδιδες σφαῖραι, some of which are engraved by Stuart, on the upper part of page 27, in the third volume of his Antiquities of Athens: they are spheroidical, having an ornament on one side, and the word δεξας on the other. We are told, some of these weighed no less than an Attic pound, i.e. an hundred drachms.[193] According to the size of them the slings were managed by one, two, or three cords. At a later period the Greeks had a method of casting from their slings, πυροβόλοι λιθοι, or fire-balls, and from their machines, σκυτάλια, made of combustibles, fitted to an iron head, which, being armed with a pike, stuck fast into its object, while it set the same on fire.[194]

The different sorts of javelins were the γρόσφος, the αίγανέν, and the ψσσὸςί, and the form of their heads may be seen in the Vignette, page 27, Vol. Ill, of Stuart's Antiquities of Athens. Several of these were loose upon their shafts, in all probability having attached to them a cord, which was held by the side of the wood, so that when the weapon once entered the

---

[185] Plutarch tells us, that the shortness of the sword was ridiculed to Agesilaus by a person who said a juggler would make nothing of swallowing it; from which, it appears, that this trick of the Indian jugglers, lately exhibited in London, is of great antiquity.

[186] Moschopulus in voc. Att. Pollux, &c. It may be seen in the hands of some Græco-Roman gladiators, on a lamp, in Montf. Antiq. expl. Vol. V, Pl. cxcvii.

[187] Pollux, Lib. J, cap. x.

[188] Strabo.

[189] Livy, Lib. xxxviii.

[190] Suidas.

[191] Homer's Iliad, v'. 599.

[192] Περιηγής, v. 5.

[193] Small ones may be seen in the British Museum.

[194] Suidas.

body the head could not be extracted without the greatest difficulty. I am led to this conclusion from an Asiatic javelin, in my son's collection, on this principle, and which, like them, has, just below the blade, a hook turned backward, to prevent its being withdrawn, and because some of the Greek javelins, according to their writers, are said to have been furnished with a cord, called αγυλη.

The τόξον, or bow, was the favourite weapon of the Cretans.[195] Lyco-phron[196] and Theocritus[197] speak of the Mæotian, or Scythian bow, which, we learn from Athenæus, was in the form of the letter C, like that now used by the Tartars. The Greek bow, on the other hand, was made of two long goat's-horns, fitted into a handle:[198] hence, Lycophron says:

.... ἐν χάρμαισι ῥαιβώσας κερας.

".......... In battles bent his horns."

The original bow-strings were thongs of leather, whence, Homer tells us,

Ἕλκε δ' ὁμχ γλανφίδας τε λαβών καὶ τόξα βόεια.

"He drew the arrow by the leathern string."

But afterwards horse-hair was substituted, which occasioned their being called ἱππέια;[199] and they were formed of three plaits, whence they were also named τρίκωσις. The knocks were termed κορωνη, and were generally of gold; and, indeed, the bows were ornamented with gold and silver also on other parts. The arrow-heads were sometimes pyramidal, whence the epithet τετράγονα; and the shafts were furnished with feathers. They were carried in a quiver, which, with the bow, was slung behind the shoulders: thus Apollo, in Homer, is represented as

Τόξ ὤμοσν ἔχων, ἀμφηρεφία τε φαρέτρην.

"Carrying his bow and quiver on his shoulders."

---

[195] Diodorus Sic. and Isidorus.

[196] Cassandra, v. 914.

[197] Idyll. XIII, v. 56. One may be seen on a vase in Hamilton's Etruscan Antiquities, Vol. IV, Pl. CXVI.

[198] Homeri, Iliad, δ. v. 105.

[199] Hesychius.

Some of these were square, some round: many had a cover to protect the arrows from dust and rain, and many appear on fictile vases to have been lined with skins. As the Greek bows were small they were drawn not to the ear but to the right breast, which Homer thus describes:

Νευρὴν μεν μαζῷ πέλασεν, τοξῳ δε σίδήρον.

"Up to his breast he drew the string, till the iron head touched the bow."

I have not found any passage in the antient writers, nor discovered any representation, to authorize the conclusion that the Greek archers, like those of Mexico and many modern American tribes, made use of the shield, though sculptures on the Trajan column shew that that was not an unusual custom with slingers. There is, however, in the British Museum, a sculpture in marble, of a collection of arms, which appear to have been merely for one man, and are of the same size as the originals: this consists of a pair of greaves, made exactly to fit the legs and projecting bones of the knees, above them a helmet, and on the right side a bow, and an oval shield, rather more than two feet in its greatest diameter, and having a boss in the centre.[200]

Plate iv consists of Greek arms and armour. Fig. 1, is the Theban shield, copied from the Persian gerra. Fig. 2, a Theban bow-case and quiver united. Fig. 3, a Greek bow in its case. Fig. 4, the double-headed lance of the cavalry, taken from an equestrian figure on a lamp in Montfaucon's Antiq. expl.[201] Fig. 8, the laiseion, or equestrian shield, from the frieze of an Athenian temple. Across Fig. 4 is the long spear of the infantry. Fig. 5, the inside and outside of a greave for the right leg. Fig. 6, the aspis. Fig. 7, the inside of ditto, exhibiting the liockanon and the canones. Fig. 9, 10, 11, and 12, various Greek helmets. Fig. 10, one with three crests, or eminences, seen in front. Fig. 14, the xiphos, or straight sword. Fig. 21, the kopis, having its edge on the inner curve of the blade. Fig. 10, the xiphos without the scabbard. Fig. 20, the sheath of the kopis. Fig. 15, a Greek quiver. Fig. 17, a Greek bow. Fig. 18, a cuirass, worn by the warrior who uses the kopis, and which exhibits the girdle as passing over the ends of the shoulder-pieces. Fig. 19, a cuirass of quilted linen, covered with a mitree of rustres, above which is the complete thorax of two pieces, and below the zone, or girdle.

---

[200] This curious antique relic was found in the plains of Marathon, and forms the centre of the Vignette in the title page of this work.

[201] Tom. V, Pl. cxcviii.

PLATE IV

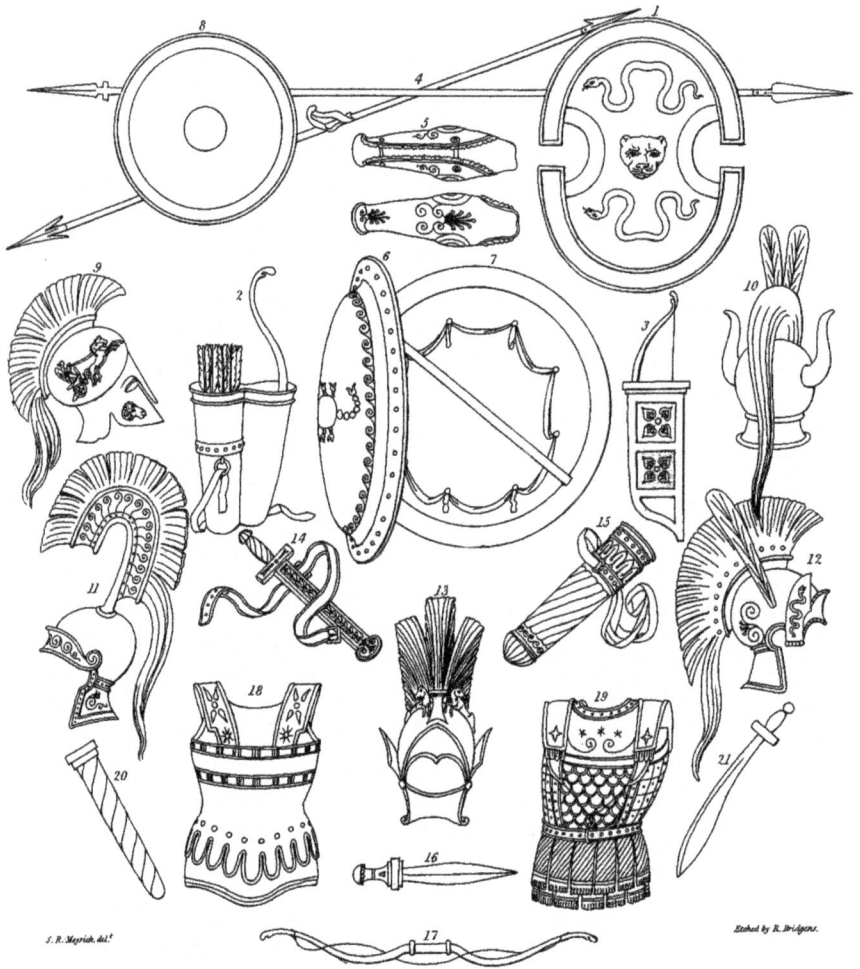

S. R. Meyrick, del.ᵗ

Etched by R. Bridgens.

GRECIAN ARMOUR.

ETRUSCANS.

As the Etruscans were colonies from Greece we could not expect to find much difference in regard to their armour. But we derive the confirmation of such a curious fact from the bronzes and fictile vases discovered in that part of Italy which they inhabited: and we may perceive among them not only the remains of the antient Grecian style of armour, but subsequent changes unlike those of the parent country, and to which we may trace the origin of the Roman warlike habits.[202] The body-armour of the Etruscans consisted of a helmet resembling those of the Greeks; a cuirass, plain, scaled, ringed, laminated, or quilted; and a thorax. They sometimes wore greaves,[203] which subsequently gave way to buskins, or sometimes had their legs quite unprotected.

Their shields were circular, and much smaller than the aspis of the Greeks, and held by one handle in the centre, or else octagonal, but of that form that might be described in an acute angle subtended by a curve.[204] Their swords much resemble those of the Greeks, being short, with leaf-shaped blades, but the hilt had sometimes a guard, which encircled the hand, of a single bar. Dependent from their cuirasses were straps, sometimes merely of leather, at others with pieces of metal on them, and these appendages, termed by the French lambrequins, were, together with their plain and laminated cuirasses, adopted by the Romans. Some of their spearmen had a cap, probably of linen, which protected the throat, leaving their face only visible, like the capuchon of the Normans; and these, for armour, wore a quilted tunic with short sleeves.[205] Their archers had a cap and tunic

---

[202] Strutt gives a representation of an Etruscan warrior in bronze, and notices a peculiar protection of grating, or network, for his face, attached to his helmet, adding, that this is not the only specimen he has met with.

[203] In the small Etruscan bronze, figured by Strutt, that author observes, they are exceedingly rough, and to all appearance made of the hides of some animal, being fastened behind by a single ligature over the middle of the calf."

[204] In my son's possession is a little bronze figure, between three and four inches high, with a shield, of the kite shape, extending from his shoulder to his feet. Another, very similar, but with the shield only half its height, is also in my son's collection. These came from Naples. Qu. Were they Etruscan? They greatly resemble a figure in Montf. Antiq. expl. Vol. IV, Pl. xv, the shield of which, though not of the kite form, might be mathematically inscribed in it. It is likewise impressed with the figure of a griffin.

[205] See Hope's Costume, Pl. XL.

of leat her, and had twisted woollen cords round their legs, similar to those worn by the early Saxons.

Strutt thus describes his bronze Etruscan warrior: "He is clothed with a short tunic, having no skirts on the sides below the girdle. It is remarkable that the sleeve of the right arm is full of folds, and seems clearly not to belong to the tunic, while that of the left arm as evidently forms a part of it. The tunic, I presume, was made of leather, too thick and rigid to admit of sufficient liberty for the sword arm; and for that reason the sleeve, probably, which belonged to the inner garment, was made of some more flexible material. These observations will also apply to a similar bronze in the possession of 11. P. Knight, Esq." In reading this one cannot help being struck with the resemblance to the Thracian retiarii.

Plate v, Fig. 5 and 6, are the cap and bow of an Etruscan archer. Fig. 7, an Etruscan shield seen on the inside. Fig. 8 and 9, two Etruscan helmets, the last five-crested, with the horse-tail besides. Fig. 10, a cuirass, with the thorax. Fig. 11, a ditto, covered with rings. These two shew the shape of the single thorax. Fig. 12, a scaled cuirass, on which the thorax assumes the shape of merely two shoulder-pieces. Fig. 13, a banded cuirass, with singular thorax. Fig. 14, a cuirass apparently quilted.

SAMNITES.

Count Caylu, in the third volume of his Antiquities, has given, among the Etruscan warriors, an armed Samnite. The helmet is something like the Greek pericephalaia, but instead of the visor forming' a part of it, it is put on the face like a mask, perforated merely for the eyes, and comes down to the collar-bones: it is also furnished with a ridge. Beneath the helmet the warrior wears a gorget, and a breast and back piece of leather terminating at the shoulders, reaching to the hips with an indented edge, and strapped round the abdomen with two broad bands. Round his arms he wears bracelets, and his legs are defended by boots which reach nearly to his knees. His sword is of the Greek fashion, leaf-shaped; and his shield, in shape, a portion of a cylinder.

This shield was afterwards adopted by the Romans, when the Samnites became incorporated with that people. At a later period, therefore, the Samnite equipments were used only by the gladiators, such, perhaps, as may have been of that nation.[206] In one of the tessellated pavements discovered at Bignor, in Sussex, is represented a combat between one of these and a retiarius. The helmet appears devoid of its ridge, and may have been only of leather, for the face-guard is of the colour of steel, while that is red and brown.

But we have another most interesting representation in the monument which the Emperor Caracalla erected to Bato. Dion Cassius, quoting Xiphilin, tells us, that that tyrant, having filled Rome with blood and murder, turned his thoughts to the public games, where, besides other cruelties, he took pleasure in the number of gladiators he caused to perish. He obliged one, named Bato, to fight successively three others on the same day. Bato was killed, and Caracalla had a fine monument erected to his memory. This monument was discovered in the Villa Pamphilia, bearing the simple but comprehensive inscription "BATONI." His helmet is on a tree, having a small ridge, and the perforations in the visor circular: instead of a gorget, if Fabretti's engraving be correct, be wears two straps of leather as necklaces, fastened in front with fibulae: his body-armour is of the antient kind at first described: his shield a heini-cylinder, but rounded at the lower end, approaching to a point, the handles subtending its edges: on his legs are ornamented boots, reaching to the ankle and covering the instep; and over that on the left leg, is placed a plate of iron fixed upon a wadded wrapper: his sword is straight. Livy mentions this shield of the Samnite gladiators thus[207] "Its form was broad in the upper part, the better to guard the breast and shoulders, and from this part towards the lower end of equal width: at the bottom, however, its form was wedge-like for the convenience of movement." He adds, "the covering for the chest was of sponge, a greave was bound on the left leg, and the helmet was crested."

Plate v, Fig. 1, is a Samnite cuirass and gorget. Fig. 2, a ditto helmet. Fig. 3, a ditto, from Montf. Antiq. expl.[208] Fig. 4, a Samnite shield seen inside.

SICILIANS.

The people of Sicily being of Greek and Carthaginian origin, their ar-

---

[206] Livy says, (Lib. IX, c. xI,) that, through hatred of the Samnites, the Campanians armed their gladiators after their manner.

[207] Ibid.

[208] Suppl. Vol. III, Pl. LXVII.

PLATE V

ETRUSCAN ARMOUR

Drawn by J. R. Meyrick.

Etched by R. B.

mour partakes of the characters of both. There is a shield, helmet, and cuirass, with a figure of Perseus, in Montf. Antiq. expl.[209]The shield is octagonal, with a boss in the centre, but the sides are by no means equal: indeed, it might be mathematically inscribed in the long kite shape. The helmet is a mere scullcap, with a bird's wing on each side; and the cuirass is like that of the antient Greeks, consisting of back and breast pieces, with lambrequins. In Vol. IV, of Montf. Pl. xv, Fig. 2, is a bronze figure, with a shield greatly similar, on which is engraved a griffin: and in my son's possession, two much resembling this, with the shield absolutely kite-shaped. These came from Naples, as has been already observed.

ROMANS.

The Latin people, according to tradition, were composed of those wandering Trojans that had survived the destruction of their city, and the subjection of their country to the Greeks: from these, and the original Celtic inhabitants of Latium, Romulus collected and combined those predatory bands, which became the parents of the Roman people. As the hardy Celtic race were without body-armour, we should look in the earliest specimens of this new people for some traces of that which distinguished the Trojans. Our search is not without the expected result, for we find the head of Roma in the Phrygian helmet. But the Romans, once formed into a regular yet ambitious society, would naturally in time adopt the arts and characteristics of their more polished neighbours; hence we find the Etruscan to be the principal style followed in Roman armies.[210]

The Romans were a nation of warriors. Every citizen was obliged to enlist when the public service required, nor could any one enjoy an office who had not served ten campaigns.[211] Various alterations were subsequently made. In the purer times of the republic the cavalry were chosen from the equites or knights,[212]and the infantry from the next class, slaves and the lowest order being excluded. But Marius made a great alteration in the military system. After that period the cavalry was composed, not merely of Roman equites, but of horsemen raised from Italy and the other provinces;

[209] Vol. I, p. 146.
[210] Florus indeed, Lib. I, c. v, tells us, that Tarquin first introduced the Tuscan usages among the Romans.
[211] Polyb. Lib. VI, 17.
[212] Liv. Lib. v, 7.

and the infantry consisted for the most part of the poorer citizens, or mercenary soldiers, which is justly reckoned one of the principal causes of the ruin of the republic. Under the Emperors indeed, the Roman armies were chiefly formed of foreigners, the Celtiberians of Spain having been the first hired for pay.[213]

The Roman army was organized into legions, consisting of ten cohorts of infantry and ten troops of cavalry.

The foot were distinguished into heavy and light infantry: the former composed of the hastati, principes, and triarii; and the latter of the velites, funditores, and sagittarii. The cavalry into the equites, and the equites cataphracti. The hastati were so called, because at their origin they fought with hastte, or long spears; and they probably formed the centre rank, because they were able to reach beyond those of the front; but as they consisted of young men in the flower of life, they were afterwards appointed to the front rank:[214] when this alteration took place their long spears were laid aside as inconvenient.[215] In all the monuments, from the time of Titus to that of Theodosius, we meet with only one kind of spear, which appears little more than six feet long: it is carried both by the officers and soldiers. The Roman lance received an improvement while in Britain; and this being patronized by Lucullus, at that time governor of the island, who permitted them to be called "Lucullean lances," after his own name, afforded Domitian a pretext for putting him to death.[216]

The principes were men of middle age, and derived their name from having originally been posted first:[217] they afterwards, however, occupied the second rank.

The triarii were old soldiers of approved valour, who formed the third line. They were also sometimes called pilani, from the pilum, or javelin, which they used; whence the hastati and principes, who stood before them, were termed antepilani; and sometimes postsignani, from being placed in the rear of the principes, who carried the standard of the legion.

The arms of these three classes, composing the heavy infantry, were both, offensive and defensive, much the same. The scutum, or shield, which was a hollow hemi-cylinder, a convex hexagon, or that shape with its side angles rounded off, protected the hastati and principes. It was generally

---

[213] Ibid. xxiv, 49. This was A.U.C. 537.
[214] Livy, Lib. VIII, c. viii.
[215] Varro de Ling. Lat. IV, 16.
[216] Suet. in vit. Dom. s. 8.
[217] Varro de Ling. Lat. iv, 16.

four feet long by two and a half broad,[218] and made of wood joined together with little plates of iron, and the whole covered with a broad piece of linen, upon which was put a sheep's skin or bull's hide, having an iron boss jutting out in the centre. This contrivance was of great service in close fighting, whence, Martial says:

In turbam incideris, cunctos umbone repellat.

"If you should get in a crowd, let all be repelled by the boss."

The shields in more antient times were .made of wicker, whence, Virgil ob-serves:[219]

.... Flectuntquè salignas
Umbonem crates.

".......... And they bind the willows,
Putting a, boss on the wicker."

The principes seem, however, sometimes to have used the clypeus, or round buckler. The triarii generally used it, though sometimes of a peculiar form, for in a drawing from thé antique, in my possession, is one with a half pike in his right hand, and a shield on his left arm, apparently of leather, of a square form, but crimped into undulations. That he is a triarius is clear from his kneeling on his right knee, for, as Montfaucon observes, they waited the signal of attack in this posture. They were all armed with a headpiece, called galea or cassis, of brass or iron, with a flap behind which reached to the shoulders, but without any covering for the face:[220] hence, Cæsar, at the battle of Pharsalia, directed his men faciem fieri, to strike at the face, Pompey's cavalry being principally composed of young men of rank, who prided themselves on their appearance.[221]

Originally the galea and cassis were two distinct headpieces, the for-mer, like the lorica, being of leather, and the latter of metal; but after this the terms were applied indifferently. The leathern cap seems to have fallen

---

[218] The longest about four feet nine inches.
[219] Æneid, VII, 632.
[220] Florus, IV, 2. A curious one, with a broad plate in front, is given by Montfaucon, in his Snpplement to his Antiq. expl. Tom, IV, PI. IX. In the same plate is a soldier with a cap like the Phrygian reversed.
[221] Florus, IV, 2.

into disrepute in the time of Camillus, for, according to Polysenus, in his Stratagems, "as the Gauls aimed the blows of their broad swords at the head, he made his men wear light helmets, by which their swords were blunted and broken; and the Roman shield being of wood, for the same reason he directed them to border it with a thin plate of brass. He also taught the use of the long spear, with which they engaged in close fight, and, receiving the blow of the sword with their shields, made a thrust with the spear."

Upon the top of the helmet was sometimes merely a round knob, particularly that of the common soldiers, and sometimes the crista, or crest, ornamented with plumes of feathers of various colours. Hence, Virgil has:[222]

..........Cristâque tegit galea aurea rubrâ.

"..........And covers the golden helmet with a red crest."

The body-armour was the lorica, which, like the French cuirass, was so called from having been originally made of leather,[223] and afterwards, like that, applied to metal: it followed the line of the abdomen at bottom, and seems to have been impressed while wet with marks corresponding to those of the human body; at top the square aperture for the throat was guarded by the pectorale, or plate of brass, and the shoulders were in like manner protected by pieces made to slip over each other. Livy, speaking of Servius Tullius, says, "he armed the Romans with the galea, the clypeus, the ocreae or greaves, and the lorica, all of brass."[224] This was the Etruscan attire, but several changes took place afterwards; and from the time of the republic greaves were not used, but the word ocrese applied to the boots which succeeded them. On the Trajan column we find the lorica of the hastati and principes, consisting of several bands, each wrapping half round the body, and therefore fastening before and behind on a leathern or quilted tunic. In the British Museum some of these bands may be seen, and we thence learn that they were of brass, and about three inches wide. At a later period this was not the case, as Silius Italicus[225] has the expression:

.... ferro oircumdare pectus.

".......... To surround the breast with steel."

---

[222] Æn. IX, v, 49
[223] Varro says, "de corio crudo pectoralia faciebant."
[224] Omnia ex oere.
[225] Lib. VIII.

This laminated lorica was very heavy, and Tacitus informs us,[226] its weight was made a subject of complaint by some of the soldiers in the time of Galba; and even the emperor himself, in his old age, found the weight of his cuirass too much for his feeble frame. It, however, was probably of the compact kind, for that writer further observes, that, when he was put to death, his murderers, finding his breast impenetrable from the armour which covered it, dissevered his legs and arms.[227] The Roman lorica was frequently enriched on the abdomen with embossed figures, on the breast with a gorgon's head by way of amulet, on the shoulder-plates with scrolls of thunder-bolts, and on the leather border which covered the top of the lambrequins with lions' heads: and these were formed of the precious metals, as the last quoted author tells us,[228] that some of the auxiliaries of Vitellius sold "their belts, accoutrements, and the silver ornaments of their armour." The compact cuirass was made to open at the sides, where the breast and back plates joined by means of clasps and hinges. The boots of the Roman officers were laced, before, and lined with the skin of some animal, of which the muzzle and claws were displayed as an ornamental finish. Each different legion had its peculiar device marked on its shields, and Tacitus[229] alludes to this, when, describing the rebellion of Otho, and the effects of his inflammatory speech, he says, "having closed his harangue he ordered the magazine of arms to be thrown open. The soldiers seized their weapons; they paid no regard to military rules; no distinction was observed; the praetorians, the legions, and the auxiliaries crowded together, and shields and helmets were snatched up in a tumultuous manner."[230]

The loricae of the triarii appear to have been of leather only. From the column of Antonine we learn that, in the time of Marcus Aurelius, the oblong shield had almost altogether given way to the clypeus, while the triarii were clad in a cuirass of scales, or leaves of iron, called squammata. This had been first adopted from the Dacians, or Sarmatians, by the Emperor Domitian, who, according to Martial,[231] had a lorica made of boars' hoofs stitched together. Speaking of it, he says:

> Quam vel ad Ætolæ securum cuspidis ictum.
> Texuit innumeri Iubricus unguis apri.

---

[226] Hist Lib. 1.
[227] Hist. Lib. 1.
[228] Ibid.
[229] Ibid.
[230] Lib. 1 Hist,
[231] Lib. VII.

"Which either secure from the thrust of the Etolian spear,
He has covered with the polished hoofs of innumerable boars."

Virgil alludes to this scaled armour:[232]

.... Rutilem thoraca indutus, ahenis
Horrebat squammis.

"Having put on the shining thorax, with brazen
Scales, he looked horrible."

and Plutarch tells us, that Lucullus wore θώρακα σιδηρουν φολιδωτον, "a lorica made with pieces of iron shaped like the scales of a fish."

The clypeus again was laid aside in the time of Constantine, when the hexangular shields above mentioned were used by the hastati.

The troops of the empire were clad in pantaloons that reached to the calves of their legs, though, in the time of the republic, they were bare-legged, like the modern Highlanders. Polybius, who wrote about 130 years before the Christian sera, thus speaks of these various troops: "The hastati were appointed to carry the arms, which they kept in their houses. Their shields were four feet, or four and a half, long, by two and a half broad, bending round the bearer; they were made of two boards glued together, covered with a thick cloth glued in like manner, and over this a calfs skin; round it was a border of iron to defend it against all cutting strokes, and keep it in shape; in the midst an iron boss to sustain the blow of a stone, or the push of a lance or other weapon.[233] They had also a Spanish sword, which they wore on the right side, fit either for thrusting or cutting, with a strong well-tempered blade edged on both sides. Moreover, they carry two great spears, some of which are thicker, others more slender; of the largest sort, the round ones are four fingers in diameter, and the others as much from side to side: the less sort resembles the ordinary Roman javelin; the shaft is three yards long, with an iron blade in the form of a hook, and pointed at the end,[234] of an equal length with the shaft; this iron, which reaches as far as the middle of the shaft, is firmly secured and rivetted with nails, to prevent its being loosened or breaking by any accident where it is

---

232 Æn. XI, 487.

[233] This alludes more particularly to the iron plate, in the centre of which the boss was fixed.

[234] This description makes the Roman like a Persian weapon in my son's armoury.

joined. These soldiers wear a brass helmet, on the top of which is fastened a small coronet, or circle of iron, with three feathers, red and black in the middle, a foot and a half in length, which, towering so far above the head, make those who wear them appear big and terrible to their enemies: they have, moreover, protections for their legs and thighs. The ordinary soldiers wear on their breasts a plate twelve inches each way; but those who are worth 10,000 drachmae (or £150) estate have, instead of this, a lorica. The principes and triarii have the same weapons, except that the latter, instead of javelins, used a kind of half pike."

Their sandals were called caliga, being set with nails, or rather spikes, underneath, and from the wearing of which the Emperor Caligula had that name.[235] The centre and rear ranks had invariably swords, the long or short gladius, or ensis; and the triarii two pila, or javelins, each man: the swords were almost constantly worn on the right side, the principes wearing them at the hip, the triarii above it. In the time of the Emperor Theodosius the sword was so short that the blade was not above twice the length of the hilt; they were all of the stabbing kind, or rather cut and thrust: that carried by the generals was called parazonium, because worn near the girdle that surrounded the lorica just above the hips: it greatly resembled the Lacedemonian sword, from whom, with its name, it was probably borrowed.

When the lorica was of one piece, whether of leather or metal, and reached to the abdomen, it had pendent from it several flaps, borrowed from the Etruscans, and these have been called by the French, lambrequins: they were of leather, fringed at the bottom, and sometimes highly ornamented. At the time of Trajan, the lorica was shortened, being cut straight round above the hips, and the bronze breast and back plates in the British Museum are of this style and period:[236] when this was the case there were two or three overlapping sets of lambrequins to supply the deficiency in length, and generals thus habited may be observed on the Trajan column.[237]

The light-armed troops were called by the general name of ferentarii, or

---

[235] Suet. in Vita Tacit. Ann. I, 41; Cic. Att. Lib. II, 3. See an engraving of them in Montf, Antiq. expl,

[236] It has been conjectured, that these were merely the shapes on which the moistened leather was stretched to give it the form of the human body; but as a person could have a free motion of his body in them, and as one of the buttons to which the shoulder-plates were fastened to hold the back and breast together still remains, it is put beyond any doubt that they formed the lorica actually worn. An engraving of these may be seen in Grose's Antient Armour. Besides, Pausanias, Lib. I, says: "There were two pieces of brass, one which covered the chest and abdomen, the other the back."

[237] See Pl. ccxxv, of Hope's Costume of the Antients.

rorarii,[238] and were, as before observed, of three kinds. The velites, so called from their agility, or the velocity with which they moved, were first instituted in the second Punic war.[239] They had no other protecting armour than a helmet and round shield, called parma,[240] about three feet in diameter, made of wood, and covered with leather; had no particular post assigned them, but fought in scattered parties as occasion required, usually before the lines. They each carried seven javelins, with points so slender that when thrown they bent, and could not easily be returned by the enemy,[241] by no means an unusual case; and a Spanish cæsim et punctim, "cut and thrust" sword. Polybius is particular in describing their javelin. He tells us, "it had a wooden shaft, about two cubits long and a finger thick; to this was affixed a blade of steel, about half a foot long, so fine at the point as to bend at the first hit, so that when thrown against an enemy it could not be used again, otherwise it would serve both parties, and he that lanceth would find weapons for his adversary to annoy him."

The funditores, or slingers, were generally from the Balearic isles, or Achæns.[242] Several of these may be seen on the Trajan column, and there appear in tunics with only a helmet and shield to protect them: the shape of the sling seems in those specimens of the ordinary kind; and Mezentius, on the 9th Æneid[243] of Virgil, has observed, that, before it was loosened from the hand, it was whirled three times round the head:

Ipse ter adducta circum caput eget habéna.

"Thrice round his head the loaded sling he whirled."

And Ovid:[244]

.... Quara cum Balearica plumbum
Funda jacit: volat illud, ct incandescit eundo.

".......... Just like the lead the Balearic sling
Hurls out: it flies, and gathers heat while going."

---

[238] Varro de Ling. Lat. Lib. VI, 3.
[239] Liv. Lib. XXXVI, c. iv.
[240] Because é medio in omnes partes sit par.
[241] Liv. XXIV, 34.
[242] Ibid. Lib. XXI c. 21; XXVIII, c. 37; XXXVIII, 21,29.
[243] V.587.
[244] Metam. Lib. II, v. 727.

From which we further learn, that these people introduced the leaden bullet into the Roman army.[245]

The sagittarii, or archers, attached to the legion, were of various nations, but chiefly from Crete and Arabia.[246] The arrows that they used had not only their piles barbed, but were furnished with little hooks just above, which easily entered the flesh, hut tore it when attempted to be withdrawn. Hence, Ovid[247] says:

> Et manus hamatis utraque est armata sagittis.

> "And his hand is armed with arrows hooked on both sides."

And Statius:

> Aspera tergeminis acies se condidit uncis.

> "The sharp head, with three twin-hooks armed, buried itself in his body."

Accius speaks of the bow-string, as made of horse-intestines, thus:

> Reciproca tendens nervo equino concita
> Tela.

> "Drawing the arrow's with a horse's nerve,
> They reciprocally spring forward."

The mode of drawing the bow-string was with the fore-finger and the thumb, as depicted in representations of Amazons, on fictile vases; for Seneca, in his Hippolytus, has:

> Amentum digitis tende prioribus
> Et totis jaculum dirige viribus.

> "The thong with your fore-finger draw,
> Then shoot with all your strength."

These light troops sometimes, instead of the Galea, wore on their heads the galerus, which was made of the skin of a wild beast, to appear more terrible.

---

[245] This passage, and what has been said in the description of the Greek weapons, shews the high antiquity of the bullet. In the middle ages it was used for the cross-bow, and in later times for the musket..

[246] Livy, XXXVIII, 40; XLII,35.

[247] De Amore.

The musicians and standard-bearers are represented with such on the Tra-jan column, from which we learn, that it consisted of the head and mane of the animal. Polybius, however, says, that the velites had, on the tops of their casques, merely a wolf's paw, that their leaders might distinguish them.

The cavalry at first used only their ordinary clothing for the sake of agil-ity, that they might more easily mount their horses, stirrups being neither mentioned by the classic writers, nor appearing on antient coins and stat-ues. When these were first used is uncertain; but their Latin name is stape-dae, or stapise, "stations for the feet." Neither the Greeks nor Romans had what may properly be called saddles, but either the skins of wild animals, or some drapery termed by the former ephippia, and by the latter vestis stragula, were put on the horse's back[248] these were kept in their places by a breast-band and a breeching, and from whence they issued were little loops, to which the warrior, when dismounted, affixed his shield.[249] The saddle, however, had been adopted in the time of Theodosius, as may be observed on the column of that emperor, and its form is delineated in Pl. LXXX, Fig. 1, of this work.

Polybius, describing the Roman cavalry near a century and a half before the Christian fera, says: "Their armour is now the same as that used by the Greeks. Formerly, however, they did not wear loricae, but only had cover-ings for their thighs, which rendered them lighter, and more readily able to dismount, though fighting thus without armour they were more exposed to danger. Their javelins were useless weapons for two reasons; first, because they were so slender as to bend with their own weight, and hence some-times broken by the motion of the horse; and next, because being armed with iron at one end only, they were merely suited for one thrust, which broke and rendered them unserviceable. They carried too, a buckler made of the hide of an ox, which resembled loaves indented,[250] such as are used at sacrifices; and these not being firm enough to make any resistance were of little use at best, but when thoroughly wet with rain quite unserviceable. It was on this account that, after the submission of Greece, they laid aside all those things, and adopted the Greek arms instead, by which they are now able to secure the blow, the javelin being firm, and capable of being used at either end."[251]

[248] Horat. Epist. r, 14,44; Liv. xxi, 54.
[249] Several specimens occur on the Trajan column.
[250] Concave,
[251] Polyb. Lib. VI. The Stradiots, or Greek troops antiently in the pay of France, used similar javelins. For one of these see Plate IV, Fig. 4.

In consequence of this change of the armour and weapons Pliny, at a later period, wrote a book dejaculatione equestri,[252] or the art of using the javelin on horseback, but which, unfortunately, has not come down to us. When the cavalry, like the Greek, wore armour similar to the infantry,[253] they were called loricati; but long after this period the major part consisted of light troops. So early, however, as the days of Livy, there was a body of heavy horse, termed equites cataphracti, which seem to have been borrowed of the eastern nations through the medium of the Greeks.[254]

Sallust, in a fragment preserved by Servius, an antient scholiast on Virgil, explains the equites cataphracti, by telling us, that ferrea omni specie, equis paria operimenta, quæ linteo ferreis laminis in modum plumse adnexuerunt. "They were clad in steel; their horses are in similar armour, made of linen, with laminae of iron fastened on them in the manner that feathers overlap each other in a plume:" on which, Servius observes, Pluma est in armaturâ, ubi lamina in laminam se indit. "The plume in armour is where one layer is placed over the other." This similitude to plumes of feathers, Justin and others consider as resembling the scales of fish, whence they were denominated squammata loricte. The appearance differs but slightly, the mode ol attaching them not at all. Virgil, in the passage commented on by Servius, towards the end of the 11th book[255] of the Æneid, unites the similitude of both, but making the material brass, and instead of linen having them fastened on leather:

Spumantemque agitabat equem, quem pellis ahenis
In plumam squammis auro conserta tegebat.

"And drove on the foaming horse, whom a brazen skin,
Like a gilt scaly plume, covered."

Quintus Curtius speaks of this kind of armour, though he does not distinguish whether the pieces of iron were shaped like scales, or quadrangular laminæ. He says:[256] "Equitibus, equisque tegumenta erant ex ferreis laminis serié inter se connexis. "The armour of the (Asiatic) horses and their riders was of iron laminæ, connected in rows within each other." Ammianus Mar-

---

[252] Plin. Ep. III, 4.
[253] Josephus, Lib. III, Excidii Ierosolym. says: Galeas et loricas omnes habeant, uti pedites.
[254] Lib. xxxv, 48; xxxvII. 40.
[255] V. 770.
[256] Lib. IV.

cellinus[257] tells us, that in the time of Constantine the Great the cataphractes equites composed part of the Roman army; and adds, they were the same as the Persians called clibanarii. He says: Thoracum muniti tegminibus, et limbis ferreis cincti, ut Praxitelis manu polita crederes simulacra, non viros, quos laminarum circuli tenues apti corporis flexibus ambiebant per omnia membra deducti, ut quocunque artus necessitas commovisset, vestitus congrueret junctura cohærenter, aptata. "They were so fortified with flexible armour, in the form of thoraces, and so girt with covering work of iron, that you might have supposed them statues formed by the masterly hand of Praxiteles, than men who had the rings in layers,[258] so delicately fitted to their bodies as to allow all its motion while surrounding it, and brought over all their members, that whatever limb necessity required to move the garment, while it followed the bending, adhered firm to its place, so well was it fitted."

Lampridius also says, they were the same as the Persian clibanarii. From Nazarius we learn, that armour made after this fashion was called operimentum ferri.[259] In his Panegyric he asks, "What is said to have been that species so dreadful to behold, so terrible? Horses and men covered in steel work. It is called in the army clibanarium. Above the breasts of the horses, which are entirely covered, the lorica[260] hangs down and reaches as far as the thighs: they can proceed without impediment: it protects them from the hurt of wounds." These, Trebellius, in Claudio and in Alexandro Severo, says, were commonly called cataphracti, or cataphractarii. Claudian, in the sixth consulship of Honorius, elegantly speaks of steel armour, and probably the scaled. His words are:

> Ut chalybe indutos equites, et in ære latentes,
> Vidit cornipedes. Quanam de gente rogabat
> Ferrati venêre viri? Quæ terra metallo
> Nascentes informat equos? Num Lemnius auctor
> Addidit hinnitum ferro, simulacraque bellis
> Viva dedit?

> "As in steel put on horses, and concealed in brass
> Are seen the hoofed feet. From what nation, he asked,

---

[257] Lib. xvi.

[258] This seems to refer to the flat ringed or the rustred armour; or rather, that the scales were held by little rings. See this subject amply, discussed in a paper printed in the 19th volume of the Archoeologia.

[259] Or munimenta, tegumenta, and tegmina loricæ.

[260] It here implies the armour for the horse.

Have these steel-clad men come? What land gives birth
To horses clothed in metal? Whether Lemnius,[261] the inventor,
Has given the neighing power to iron, and to warlike images
Hath given life?"

Here, though the material is named, the form of the armour is by no means specified: but its fashion may be gathered from what he says elsewhere,[262] where he speaks of little plates sewn together:

Flexilis inductis hamatur lamina,[263] membris—
Horribilis visu: credat simulacra moveri
Ferrea, cognatoque, viros spirare metallo.
Par vestitus equis.

"The flexible lamina is hooked on, being put on his limbs—
Horrible to the sight: you might believe him to be a moving
Image of iron, and that men breathed from the kindred metal.
The horse is clad in the same manner."

Vegetins does not seem to approve of this kind of heavy cavalry. He says: "the equites cataphracti, on account of the armour which they wear, are secure from wounds, but its inconvenience and weight render them liable to be easily taken prisoners." The troops, however, thus accoutred, were not Romans, but foreigners levied in the subdued provinces, which were armed in their national manner: hence, we find that the equites cataphracti have always attached to them, in the Notitia, the epithets Persae, Palmirenorum, Parthi, Ambianenses, &c.

Cæsar[264] says: "Almost all the knights (in his time) had tunics or armour (tegmenta), either of stuffed and quilted work (subcoactis), or tanned garments (centonibus), by which they secured themselves from the weapons aimed at them." Pliny[265] explains this more particularly by saying, that the garment thus made was stuffed with wool only.

In all this there is nothing like plate armour, except the breast and back plates in the British Museum: but the antients, nevertheless, used a plate for the horse's forehead, called a frontal. Euripides describes this as solid when

---

[261] Vulcan.
[262] Lib. II, in Rufinum.
[263] The hamatur lamina in this sentence seems to be the same as the Laminarum circuli of Ammianus.
[264] Lib. III, of his History of the Civil Wars.
[265] Lib. VIII, c. xlviii.

he speaks of Rhæsus and his horses:

> "A shield on his shoulder shone, with
> Golden figures united. But the gorgon,
> Such as is on the shield of Pallas, was of iron,
> And strapped to the foreheads of the horses."

At a later period the Emperor Leo says:[266] "The horses, especially those of the prefects, should have pectorals and frontals, either made of iron, of prepared hides, or of sinews, on their breasts and necks, if that can be done; and their bodies should be protected by small pieces suspended from the feletra of their saddles, which would liberate from the greatest dangers both horses and riders. The antients armed their horses with laterals and frontals." In the next section he says "Others of the equites cataphracti had contaria, that is, spears, which were formerly called lonchte, but now inenaula: and these are of service in a charge. Others, who throw their weapons from a distance, are called acrobolistse, velitares, &c. Others, thureoi, because they have shields, while some again fight without, having merely lances." These thureoi are called, in the Notitia Imperii, equites scutati. In section 33, Leo says: acrobolistse use rhictarii, (peculiar kind of javelins,) others bows. Of this class too, some throw their spears from a distance, some ride up at once to attack, and others gallop round the enemy: these last are called hippocontistsæ, arquites, (probably from arcus and equites,) or hippotoxotæ. Some of these are so expert in the use of their darts, that they return to the fight again and again. Of the rest they enter the conflict with spears, swift-flying darts, or swords; and these are the velites, or light cavalry: of them some carry small battle-axes, and in such manner the antients organized their bodies of cavalry." In confirmation of this, it may here be mentioned, that Cæsar de Bell Civ.[267] and Hirtius de Bello Africano speak of mounted archers, whom they call hippotoxotæ.

From various passages of the classic authors we may collect, that the antients not only greatly esteemed white or grey horses, but preferred them from an idea that they excelled in swiftness those of a different colour.

> Qui candore nives anteirunt cursibus auras.

> "Those with the whiteness of snow will outstrip the wind in their course."

---

[266] In his Tactics, c. vi, s. 8, and s. 31.
[267] Lib.III.

It has been observed, that the Roman cavalry were distinguished into light and heavy horse: hence Ælian, in his Tactics, says: Equestres copiee modo armaturm inter se distant: pars enim tota obsepta est; et hinc cataphracti; pars non tota armis tegitur. Cataphractos igitur eos intelligi volo, qui non solum sua corpora, sed etiam equos lorica undique muniunt. "The light cavalry wore leathern loricae, or tunics stuffed with wool," &c.: hence, Varro says, "they make their pectorals de 'corio crudo,' of raw hidesand Pliny,[268] "they make a garment which they stuff with wool, and if to this vinegar be added, it will even resist steel." Such cuirasses, however, were edged with iron round the neck, and sometimes round the line of the abdomen. Hence, Silius Italicus[269] says:

.... Ferro circumdarc pectus.

".......... To surround the chest with iron."

The Greek cavalry, in the service of Rome, at the destruction of Jerusalem, are described by Josephus, as having a long sword suspended at their right side, a long contum in their hand, three or four javelins with broad heads in a quiver, and a ponderous spear. In the light cavalry were included equites sagittarii, as well as jaculatores equites.

That the Romans used spurs is evident from the discovery of two at Woodchester, of the spear kind, but without a neck.[270] They are of iron, which was frequently the case, as appears from many passages in the Roman writers. Virgil has:[271]

Quadrupedemque citum ferratâ calce fatigat.

"And he fatigues the swift quadruped with the iron spur."

Silius Italicus has the same expression.[272] But they have been found of brass. A particular sharp bit was sometimes used, said to be wolfed, but from what

---

[268] Lib. VIII, c. 48.
[269] Lib. VIII.
[270] See Lysons's Woodchester .Antiq. Pl. XXXIV.
[271] Æn. XI, v, 714.
[272] Lib. VIII, 696.

cause the learned are not agreed.[273] Hence, Horace[274] says:

> .... Gallica nec lupatis
> Temperet ora frænis.

> ".......... Nor with wolfed bits
> Manage the mouth of the Gallic horse."

The ordinary bit, however, was merely a thin bar of iron, with large rings at its extremities. Such an one, found near Froome, in Somersetshire, was presented to my son by B. E. Willoughby, Esq.

It was not only the practice of the Greeks and Spaniards to have their horses taught submissively to stoop and take their riders on their backs, but that of the Romans in their early history. Hence, Silius Italicus,[275] speaking of the horse of Clselius, a Roman knight, says:

> Inde inclinatus collum, submissus et armos
> De more, inflexis prædebat scandere terga
> Cruribus

> "Downwards the horse his head and shoulders bent,
> To give his rider a more free ascent."

The Romans at one time used elephants in their armies; and Caesar sent one into Britain, which, we are told by Polyænus,[276] was mailed in scales of iron, with a tower on its back, in which were archers and slingers. This quadruped easily put the terrified Britons to flight.

These animals had their foreheads protected by a large plate, in which was fixed a spike,[277] a fashion retained in India at the present time. On a Roman coin[278] the armour of the elephants appears to consist of a trellis-work, probably of leather, and this occurs again on one of the tessellated pave-

---

[273] In Mr. Douce's possession is what I conceive to be the centre part of one of these bits, of bronze. It consists of three spikes, about an inch long, placed upright, two in front and one behind, upon a base, to each end of which is a fixed ring, to which was attached the remainder of the bit. It would Îie flat in the horse's mouth until checked, when, rising up, it would instantly take effect.

[274] Lib. I, Ode viii.

[275] Lib. x.

[276] In his Stratagems.

[277] Livy, Lib. XXXVII.

[278] Superscribed Æternitas Augg. in Montfaucon's Antiq. expl, Vol. I, p. 334. They appear the same on a dyptic of the Consul Basilius, given by Montf. Sup. Vol. III, Pl. LXXX.

ments, discovered at Woodchester, in Gloucestershire:[279] only that part of the head from the eyes to the tip of the trunk being without it. In the coin alluded to, a naked man, with three darts in his hand, is represented sitting on the elephant's back.

In this review of the Roman armour we have seen nothing like interlaced rings, or double chain-mail: still hooks and chains are mentioned, and it therefore remains to inquire what was meant by these words. Statius, in his Thebaid,[280] has:

> .... Ter insuto servant ingentia ferro
> Pectora.

> ".......... With triple plates of iron they defend

And from another part of this work,[281] we learn in what manner these plates were kept together:

> Multiplicem tenues iterant thoraca catenæ.

> "The little chains join the many-folded thorax."

Hence the chain-work does not appear to have of itself made the armour, but merely to have been instrumental to it: the hooks were for the same purpose. Virgil has:[282]

> Loricam consertam hamis, auroque trilicem.

> "The three-fold lorica held together with golden hooks."

Which is still more clearly explained by Silius Italicus.[283] Speaking of the Consul Flaminius, he says:

> Loricam induitur tortos huic nexilis hamos
> Ferro squamma rudi, perraistoque asperat auro.

> "He puts on the lorica—it looks terrible:
> scales Of plain iron and gold intermixed,

---

[279] See Lysons's publication on that subject.
[280] Lib. VII.
[281] Theb. XXI.
[282] Æn. III, v. 467.
[283] Lib: v.

Being knitted together with the twisted hooks."[284]

From all these quotations it appears, that the hooks and chains were merely employed as auxiliary.

As the Roman armour was generally of brass, so were their weapons of steel.[285] They had, indeed, in their infant state, used brazen weapons, and many discoveries in Italy seem to prove this, but from their arrival in Britain, the writings of their authors and repeated exhumations prove iron to have been the general material.[286] The hilts of the swords were of brass or copper, even when the blades came to be made of steel.[287]

French bayonet-blade, the ferrule of a scabbard, a barbed arrow-head, and a sword-blade, resembling a large broad knife, all of iron, and of undoubted Roman origin.[288] Mr. Douglas, in his Nenia Britannica,[289] gives an engraving of a Roman gladius of iron, found with a fibula of brass, the blade of which is nineteen inches and a half. Cæsar encouraged his men, according to Polyamus,[290] to have their arms richly ornamented with gold and silver, in order to make their owners more reluctantly part with them.

The Roman officers wore a military cloak, which was called paludamentum,[291] and very similar to the chlamys of the Greeks. It was of a scarlet colour, bordered with purple. Under this they sometimes wore a tunic, called sagum, said to have been borrowed from the Gauls. This, Polyænus[292] tells us, was introduced by Scipio, who used himself to wear one of black.

From Vegetius[293] we learn, that a centurion was chosen, whose office it was to see that all the arms of the infantry were in proper order, sharpened, and kept bright; in the same manner a decurion, who commanded a troop of cavalry, had to attend to his men, that they took care of and frequently

---

[284] The hooks, or rather, as we have seen, the rings, divided in one place, were used for holding together the scales, and, therefore, might have helped to compose a garment wholly of metal. But if the interlaced ringed armour was known to the antients, bow came it forgotten in Europe till the 13th century?

[285] Yet Tacitus, Hist. Lib. II, mentions Otho as wearing an iron breastplate to shew his humility.

[286] General Melyill was also of this opinion. See Archoeologiaca Vol. VII, p. 374.

[287] Brazen swords or daggers, with hilts and sheaths of the-same material, may be seen in the British Museum.

[288] See Lysons's Woodcbester Antiquities, Pl. xxxv.

[289] Pl. xxvi. The same as noticed in Archoeologia, Vol. VII; p. 376.

[290] Lib. viii, c. 23.

[291] Liv, I, c. 26; Plin. xvi, 3; Tacit, Aim. Lib. xii, c. 66; and Juvenal's Sat. vi, 399.

[292] Lib. viii, C. xv.

[293] Lib. ii, c. xxiv.

cleaned their armour, whether loricated or cataphracti, as well as their conti and helmets; observing, "for the splendour of arms adds considerably to the terror of an enemy."

There were certain soldiers appointed under a prefect, to act as city watch-guards, of which there were seven cohorts, one for every two wards. They were composed chiefly of manumitted slaves, and wore over their tunics three leathern straps, which were crossed longitudinally by three in front and three behind, and where these intersected was hung a bell.[294]

Each century, or, at least, each maniple of troops, had its proper standard and standard-bearer.[295] This was originally merely a bundle of hay on the top of a pole; afterwards a spear, with a cross piece of wood on the top, sometimes the figure of a hand above, probably in allusion to the word manipulus, and below a small round or oval shield, generally of silver[296] or of gold.[297] On this metal plate were antiently represented the warlike deities, Mars or Minerva; but after the extinction of the commonwealth the effigies of the emperors or their favourites[298] it was on this account that the standards were called numina legionuin, and held in religious veneration. The standards of different divisions had certain letters inscribed on them to distinguish the one from the other.[299] The standard of a legion, according to Dio,[300] was a silver eagle, with expanded wings, on the top of a spear, sometimes holding a thunder-bolt in its claws; hence, the word aquila was used to signify a legion.[301] The place for this standard was near the general, almost in the centre. Before the time of Marius figures of other animals were used, and it was then carried in front of the first maniple of the triarii.[302] The vexillum, or flag of the cavalry, was, according to Livy, a square piece of cloth, fixed to a cross-bar, on the end of a spear. The labarum, borrowed by the Greek emperors from the Celtic tribes, by whom it was called llab, was

---

[294] Suet. Aug. 25 and 30. Dio, LIV, 4. See one in Hope's Costume of the Antients.

[295] Varro de Lat. Ling. IV, 16; Liv. Lib. VIII, c. viii; Veget. Lib. II, c, xxiii.

[296] Plin. Lib. XXXIII, C. iii.

[297] Herodian, Lib. iv; c. vii.

[298] Tacit. Ann. Lib. I, c. xliii; Suet. Tib. XLVIII; Cal. XIV.

[299] Veget. Lib. ii, c. xiii.

[300] Lib. XL, c. xviii.

[301] Cæs. Hisp. xxx

[302] Plin. Lib. X, c. iv, s. 5; SaUust Cat. c. LIX. Mr. Lysons, in his Reliq, Brit. Romanæ, has represented several silver laminæ and other antiquities, which he calis parts of Roman standards; but Mr. Douce agrees with me in thinking that he was quite mistaken, and that some of the inscriptions on them refer to quite a different subject. They were found at Stoney Stratford, Bucks.

PLATE VI

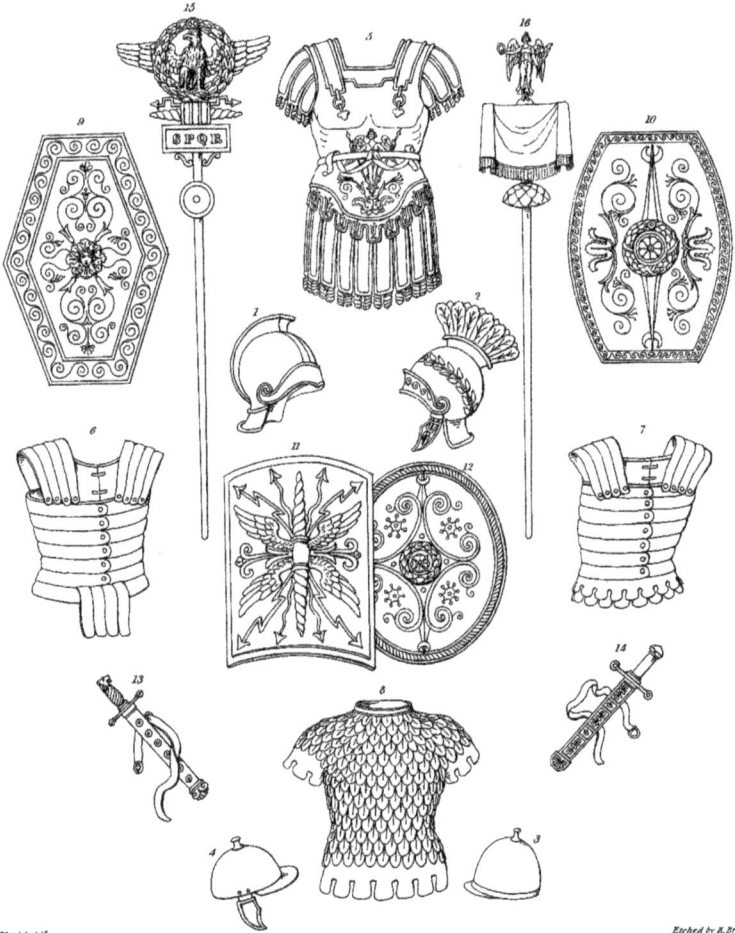

ROMAN ARMOUR.

similar to this, but with the monogram of Christ worked upon it.

Vegetius[303] wonders by what fatality it happened that the Romans, after having experienced the advantage of their armour during a space of 1,200 years, from the foundation of Rome to the reign of Gratian, should at length abandon their antient discipline, and, by laying aside their breast-plates and helmets, put themselves on a level with the barbarians.

Plate VI, Fig. 1, is the helmet used in the time of the republic. Fig. 2, that in the time of the emperors. Fig. 3, is a Roman-British helmet, found in Hertfordshire, and now in the British Museum: it is of bronze. Fig. 5, is a general's lorica, with the zone tied round it. Fig. 6, a laminated cuirass worn by the private soldiers in the time of the emperors, seen in front. Fig. 7, a ditto, seen behind. Fig. 8, a plumated lorica of the time of Trajan. Fig. 9, 10, and 11, various shaped scuta, or shields. Fig. 12, a clypeus, or buckler. Fig. 13 and 14, Roman swords. Fig. 15, the principal signum, or standard of the infantry. Fig. 16, the vexillum, or colours of the cavalry.

The Roman mode of attack and defence is very fully described by Tacitus,[304] where he relates the particulars of the siege of Cremona, in the war between Vitellius and Otho. "Antonius, the Othonian general, invested the fortified camp of the German legions, and began his attack at a distance with a volley of stones and darts. The advantage was on the side of the besieged: they possessed the heights, and with surer aim annoyed the enemy at the foot of the ramparts. Antonius saw the necessity of dividing his operations: to some of the legions he assigned distinct parts of the works, and ordered others to advance against the gates. By this mode of attack in different quarters he knew that valour as well as cowardice would be conspicuous, and a spirit of emulation would animate the whole army. The third and seventh legions took their stations opposite to the road that leads to Bedriacum: the seventh and eighth C'laudian legions carried on the siege on the right hand of the town; and the thirteenth invested the gate that looked towards Brixia. In this position the troops rested on their arms till they were supplied, from the neighbouring villages, with pickaxes, spades, hooks, and scaling-ladders. Being at length provided, they formed a military shell with their shields; and under that cover advanced to the ramparts. The Roman art of war was seen on both sides. The Vitellians rolled down massy stones, and wherever they saw an opening, inserting their long poles and spears, rent asunder the whole frame and texture formed by the shields, while the

---

[303] Lib. I, c. xi, s. 12.
[304] Hist. Lib III.

assailants, deprived of shelter, suffered a terrible slaughter. Cremona being devoted to plunder, nothing could restrain the ardour of the soldiers. Braving wounds, danger, and death itself, they began to sap the foundation of the walls: they battered the gates; they joined their shields over their heads, and mounting on the shoulders of their comrades grappled with the besieged, and dragged them headlong from the ramparts. The most vigorous assault was made by the third and seventh legions: to support them, Antonius in person led on a select body of auxiliaries. The Vitellians were no longer able to sustain the shock: they saw their darts fall on the military shell, and glide off without effect. Enraged at this disappointment, and in a fit of despair, they hurled down their missile battering engine on the heads of the besiegers: numbers were crushed by the fall of such a ponderous mass. It happened, however, that the machine drew after it the parapet and part of the rampart; an adjoining tower, which had been incessantly battered, fell at the same time, and left a breach for the troops to enter: the seventh legion, in the form of a wedge, endeavoured to force their way, while the third hewed down the gates, and the camp was taken.

"The whole space between the camp and the walls of Cremona was one continued scene of blood. The town itself presented new difficulties—high walls and towers of stone, the gates secured by iron bars, and the works well manned with troops. Antonius ordered his men to advance with missive combustibles, and set fire to the pleasant villas that lay round the city, in hopes that the inhabitants, seeing their mansions destroyed, would more readily submit to a capitulation. In the houses that stood near the walls he placed the bravest of his troops, and from those stations large rafts of timber, stones, and firebrands, were thrown in upon the garrison. The Vitellians were no longer able to sustain their post. The legions under Antonius were now preparing for a general assault: they formed their military shell, and advanced to the works, while the rest of the army poured in a volley of stones and darts. The besieged began to despair, and finally capitulated."

The same author thus[305] speaks of the military machines of the Romans: "Some Roman deserters taught the Germans to make a kind of pluteus;" or what, in subsequent ages, was called a chatfaulx. He describes it as being "a platform made of rude materials in the shape of a bridge, and constructed to move forward on wheels. From the top of the arch, as from a rampart, some were able to annoy the besieged, while others, under its cover, endeav-

[305] Hist. Lib. IV.

oured to sap the walls. They then began to prepare pent-houses,[306] and to form a covered way with hurdles. The besieged attacked them with a volley of flaming javelins, and poured such an incessant fire, that the assailants were on every side enveloped by the flames."

He also tells us, that "the Romans used poles, pointed with iron, which were darted at random; nor did they discharge their massy stones without being sure of their effect. They, moreover, by hurling strong beams and other instruments crushed a strong tower, of two floors, made by the Germans, and the soldiers posted therein lay buried under the ruins. The legionary soldiers, in the mean time, framed with skill a number of new machines: one in particular struck the enemy with terror and amazement. This was so constructed, that an arm projecting from the top waved over the heads of the barbarians, till being suddenly let down, it caught hold of the combatants, and, springing back with sudden elasticity, carried them up in the air in view of the astonished Germans, and, turning round with rapidity, threw them headlong into the camp."

We learn, however, from Polybius,[307] that this extraordinary engine had been invented by Archimedes, and used at the siege of Syracuse.

LIGURIANS.

"These," says Diodorus,[308] "are a hardy race, but lighter armed than the Romans, for they defend themselves with along shield,[309] made after the fashion of the Gauls. Their tunics are girt about them with a belt, over which they throw the skin of some wild beast: their swords are of ordinary length. From tlieir intercourse with the Romans, however, they have mostly changed their antient mode of arming."

BALEARES.

It was not possible to speak of the Greeks, Carthaginians, and Romans, without noticing the skill of the Baleares in the use of the sling, but nothing

---

[306] Called, in subsequent ages, "cats."
[307] Lib. VIII.
[308] Lib, v, c. ii,
[309] Παραμήκη θρεὸς.

was then said about their manner of using it. Diodorus, the Sicilian,[310] describes them more particularly. He says, their arms are three slings: one they wind about their heads, another they tie about their loins, and the third they carry in their hands. In time of war they throw much greater stones than any other people, and tvith as much violence as if shot from a catapulta: on this account they are called Baleares, from the Greek work, βάλλειν "to cast." Hence, when they assault a town, they grievously gall those on the bulwarks; and, in the field, break in pieces shields, helmets, and all the defensive armour of their enemies: indeed, they are such expert marksmen as scarce ever to miss their object. They are taught from their childhood; and as an incitement, their mothers place their daily food on a pole for them to aim at, and keep them fasting until they succeed in hitting it.

GAULS.

Diodorus gives us[311] the following account of the Gauls: "In their fights they use chariots with a pair of horses, each holding a charioteer and a warrior, and when they engage cavalry they attack them with their barbaric weapons, called saunians, and then, quitting their cars, fall to with their swords. Several of them so despise death as to fight naked, with merely something round their loins. When a Gallic army is drawn up in order of battle, it is usual for the chiefs to step out before the line and challenge the stoutest of their enemies to single combat, brandishing their arms to terrify their adversary. They deliver their spoils to their attendants, all besmeared with blood, to be carried before them in triumph, they themselves singing the song of victory.

"Their defensive arms are, a shield proportionable to the height of a man, garnished with his own ensigns."[312] These, Pausanias also calls thureoi, adding, that they were introduced into Greece by Brennus. He tells us, "the Gauls had no other defence, and used them as rafts on crossing a river." This kind of shield is depicted PI. i, Fig. 5. That carried, however, by the Parisian boat-men, in the time of Tiberius Caesar, and found sculptured at Notre Dame, in 1711, appears to be hexagonal and convex, though long and nar-

---

[310] Lib. v, c. i.
[311] Lib. v, c. ii.
[312] Θυρεοῖς υμέν ανρομήεσι πεποικιλ ἰδιοτρόπως.

row.[313] Diodorus says further: "Some of the Gauls carry the shapes of beasts in brass, artificially wrought, as well for defence as ornament.[314] Upon their heads they wear helmets of brass, with large appendages for the sake of ostentation; for they have either horns of the same metal joined to them, or the shapes of birds and beasts. They have trumpets[315] after the barbarian manner, which, on being· sounded, make a dreadful noise. Some of them wear iron thoraces, and hooked;[316] but others, content with what nature affords them, fight naked. They wear bracelets on their arms and wrists of pure gold, torques round their necks of the same, and rings of gold on their fingers: golden thoraces are sometimes worn." As Diodorus does not mention these latter when enumerating the arms and armour of the Gauls, they were probably used as ornaments by the judges, and the same as the jodhain moran of gold, frequently found in Ireland. Those with the hooked cuirasses are probably the same as Tacitus calls[317] crupellarii, "whose armour," he says, "rendered them less able for inflicting wounds, but impenetrable to receiving them." "For swords," Diodorus adds, "they used a long and broad weapon, called spatha, which they suspended by iron or brazen chains on their right thigh;" and Posidonius adds, "they carried a dagger which served the purpose of a knife."[318] Diodorus says, "for darts they cast those called lankia, whose iron blades are a cubit or more in length, and almost two hands in breadth." Propertius attributes to them one of a particular kind, which he calls gesum. Hence, speaking of Viridu-marus, he says:

Nobilis é tectis fundere gesa rota.

"Nobly .standing on the roofs to hurl down the whirling gesa."

"Though their swords are as large as the saunians of other nations, the points of their saunians are larger than those of their swords: some of them are straight, others bowed or bending backwards, so that they not only cut but break the flesh, and when the dart is drawn out, it tears and rends the wound most exceedingly."

---

[313] See Montfaucon's Antiq. expl. Vol. II, p. 423.
[314] Whether these were used as shields or body-armour does not appear from the context.
[315] See an Irish one, of a similar kind, called buadh-vail, or the mouth-piece of Victory, in the Costume of the original inhabitants of the "British Isles.
[316] Θώρακας σιδηεους ἀλυσιδωτοὺς.
[317] Lib. III.
[318] In Athenæus, Lib. XIV.

Some of the Gauls were exhibited in the games at Rome as gladiators; and from the shapes of animals, which Diodorus notices, on their helmets, derived their naine.[319] The first who exhibited had chosen a fish for their crest, whence they were called mirmillones, from the Greek μορμυρος, a fish: and this designation was probably given by their adversaries, who were Thracians. The mirmillo was armed with a small circular shield, and a curved sword, whose edge was inside.[320]

CELTIBERIANS.

"These people," says Diodorus, the Sicilian,[321] "bring into the field not only stout and valiant horsemen, but brave infantry, strong, hardy, and able to undergo all kind of labour and toil. Some of them are armed with shields resembling the light ones of the Gauls; others with curtiæ, or bucklers, as large as shields.[322] They wore ou their legs greaves made of rough hair, and on their heads helmets of brass adorned with red plumes. They carry two-edged swords of well-tempered steel, and have besides daggers a span long, of which they make use in close fights. They make weapons and darts in an admirable manner, for they bury plates of iron so long under ground as necessary for the rust to consume the weaker part, and therefore use only that which is strong and firm. Swords and other weapons are made of this prepared steel, and these arms are so powerful in cutting, that neither shield, helmet, nor bone can withstand them. As they are furnished with two swords, the cavalry, when they have routed their antagonists, dismount, and, joining the infantry, fight as auxiliaries." Strabo tells us,[323] that it was the practice of the Spaniards to teach their horses to stoop and take their riders on their backs.

---

[319] Hence, according to Festus, a retiarius called out, "Non te peto, piscem puto quid me fugis Galle!"

[320] Gladio incurvo et falcato. On a lamp, engraved by Montf. Antiq. expl, Tom. V, PI. CXCVII, is such a combat, in which the curved sword, with the device of a snake on the helmet, are fully visible: the shield, however, used by the mirmillo is oblong.

[321] Lib. v, c. ii.

[322] Κυρτίαις κυκλοτέρεσιν ἀσπίδων ἐχούσαις τὰ μεγέθη. Lucan, Lib. I,. says: the Spaniards used a small shield, called Cerra, which a part of the Roman cavalry afterwards-adopting, were termed, in the Notitia Imperii, cetrati equites.

[323] Lib. III.

LUSITANIANS.

Diodorus says:[324] "Those called Lusitanians are the most valiant of all the Cimbri. In time of war they carry little targets[325] made of bowel-strings, so strong and firm as completely to guard and defend their bodies: they manage them with such dexterity, that by whirling them about here and there with skill they avoid or repel every dart thrown at them. They use hooked[326] saunians made all of iron, and wear swords and helmets like those of the Celtiberians. They throw their darts at a great distance, and yet are sure to hit their mark anti wound deeply. Being active and nimble they easily pursue or retreat from an enemy; but they cannot bear hardships so well as the Celtiberians."

GERMANS.

Tacitus describes[327] the Germans who lived near the Weser as "wearing' neither helmets nor breastplates, but armed with a spear of enormous length, and an unwieldly buckler, not rivetted with iron, nor covered with hides, but formed of osier twigs intertwined, or slight boards daubed over with glaring colours. The foremost ranks were provided with pikes and javelins, but the remainder had merely stakes hardened in the fire, or weapons too short for execution." In his account of the manners of the Germans[328] generally, he says: "Iron does not abound in Germany, if we may judge from the weapons in general use. Seldom are seen swords or the greater kind of lances, but they carry spears, which, in their language, are called framea, with short and narrow blades of iron, yet they use these with so much dexterity, that they can fight with them from a distance as well as hand to hand. The infantry use missile weapons, of which each man carries a considerable number, but have neither helmet nor cap. Being naked, or at least not encumbered by bis light mantle, he throws his weapon to a distance almost incredible. Their cavalry use the framea and a large shield, and these shields

---

[324] Lib. v, c. ii.
[325] Πέλτας μικρὰς.
[326] Ἀγκιοτρῶδεσι.
[327] Ann. Lib. II.
[328] Ch. vi,

are distinguished by splendid colours: they are, indeed, the only objects of their care, as a German pays no attention to the ornament of his person. The infantry likewise used these shields."

"Breastplates are uncommon: in the whole army you will not see more than one or two helmets. According to the best estimate, the infantry form the national strength, and for that reason always fight intermixed with the cavalry. Their order of battle is generally in the form of a wedge. They make it a point to carry off their slain, and hold it a flagitious crime to abandon their shields. The tribe called Cattians never rush to battle, but march to war. Each soldier carries, besides his arms, his provisions and military tools. The Arians study to make themselves horrible by every addition art can devise: their shields are black, their bodies painted of a deep colour, and the darkest night is the time for rushing to battle. The sudden surprise and funereal gloom of such a band of sable warriors are sure to strike a panic through the adverse army, who fly the field as if a legion of demons had broken loose to attack them, so true is it, that in every engagement the eye is first conquered. The Rugians and Lemovians (who lived on the Baltic, near Dantzic,) used round shields and short swords. The Æstians (who inhabited Prussia) have a club as their general weapon . The Venedians know the use of shields, hut the Fennians point their arrows simply with bone."

In 1053 the German infantry fought with two-handed swords, (retained for four hundred years after by the Switzers,) and were considered so strong and impenetrable a phalanx, that neither man, steed, nor armour could resist their blows. The Germans were not, however, at that time skilful in the management of the horse and lance, but this remark is only applicable to the Frankish settlers in that country.

HUNS.

The Huns, in the time of Valentinian, according to Zozimus, were mounted archers and very expert horsemen. Their costume may be seen on the· sculptures engraved in Professor Pallas's Travels,[329] from which they appear to have resembled the modern Tartars.

---

[329] Vol. I, p.445.

VANDALS.

Pliny[330] and Procopius[331] coincide in opinion, that the Vandals and Goths were originally one people, and this seems countenanced by a. similarity of manners, &e. They were, however, distinguished into Heruli, Burgundians, Lombards, and other petty states. They used, like the Goths, round bucklers and short swords, which rendered them formidable in a close engagement, and consisted of infantry and cavalry.

SCANDINAVIANS.

Under this title are comprehended all the nations on the Western coasts of the Baltic, whom the Britons called Llychlynwys, viz., the Cimbri, with the Goths and Saxons, the descendants of the Sacæ and Massa-Getiæ of the Caspian, and the Danes.

The Cimbri were the most antient of these as settlers on the Baltic, and while they continued independent and distinct, seem to have worn armour, for they are represented on their invasion of Gaul as wearing iron breastplates, and carrying white shields.[332] They bore, as offensive weapons, maces, darts and swords of unusual forms, and, according to Plutarch, had long swords, but were ignorant of the use of the helmet. The sword which Plutarch mentions seems to have been the degan, or spad, so highly prized, as to be sometimes, on account of its cruciform shape, the symbol of the deity. It was sharp, and often inscribed with Rhunic characters; and in order to create greater terror, those of the chiefs had proper names.[333] Their women, as was the case with their Gaulish and British consanguinei, fought with lances.[334]

The Gothic and Sclavonian nations, who had intermixed on the western coasts of the Baltic, fought, in remote periods, almost destitute of armour, a practice which they retained from prejudice long after they became familiarized with the warlike manners of their more polished neighbours.

---

[330] Hist. Nat Lib. IV, c. 14.
[331] Bell. Vandal, Lib. I, c. i.
[332] Freinshemii Sup. in Livii, Lib. LXVIII, c. lxii.
[333] Mallet's Introd. to Hist. of Denmark.
[334] Freinshemius ut supra

At a later period the Saxons and Danes made use of battle-axes, bows, and arrows, and were distinguished by short curved swords slung in a belt across the right shoulder. This distinctive weapon was called saex, and its form was that of a scythe.[335] It seems to have been peculiar to the Saxons, and possibly, because fighting more constantly on horseback than the Danes, they made this weapon serve both for action and procuring fodder. The battle-axe was double-edged, that is, a bipennis, and denominated byl: when these were affixed to long staves, which was generally the case for the infantry, they were termed alle-bardes, or cleave-alls.

n the most antient chronicles, the Scandinavians are represented as excellent archers, a quality for which the Anglo-Saxons do not appear to have been conspicuous. All the Northern nations made occasional use of the dart, the sling, the mace armed with points, the hammer, (often of flint, called Miölner,)[336] the lance, and the poignard. For defence they had shields, some of which were of a long oval form, so as entirely to cover the bearer, and called skiold, whence our English word shield; others were round, but not so large, convex, and often furnished with a boss of iron and other metal.[337] The larger sort were invariably of wood, bark, or leather; the others, and particularly those of the chiefs, were of iron or brass, and engraved, painted, or gilt, and sometimes covered with a plate of gold. The large shield served as a bier for the wounded, or, in the manner of the Gauls, to enable its owner to swim across a river: they were white until the bearer, by some exploit, obtained permission to bear some distinctive mark. The helmet, though often disregarded, from their intercourse with the Romans, was known to the Scandinavian and Gothic tribes, the inferior warriors wearing them of leather, and the chiefs of iron or metal gilt.[338] The lorica they also acquired from the Romans, and if the scale-armour was not likewise borrowed of them, it might have been derived from the Sarmatians, who settled near the Baltic after the Vandals had departed. As Sweden produced the best iron in Europe, and in the greatest abundance, it will account for the arms of

---

[335] It was also called sais, which, in the modern dialect of Lower Saxony, still signifies that implement of husbandry.

[336] One of these, of compact stone, is in the armoury of Llewelyn Meyrick, Esq.

[337] Many of these, as well as iron bow braces or grasps, have been found in barrows in England. See Douglas'sNenia Brit. Pl. III and VII. One discovered in Lincolnshire is in the collection of Llewelyn Meyrick, Esq.

[338] The helmet, as worn by the warriors on a, golden horn found at Galhuus, in Denmark, is of the basin kind, with a nasal, and having two long feathers rising from it in the modern Tartar fashion.

the northern nations being of that metal, and also so broad and heavy. The torque was an ornament of the northern warrior.

ANGLO-SAXONS.

The Anglo-Saxons, under Ilengist and other followers, wore many of them the loricse of leather, and four-cornered helmets.[339] This armour was probably acquired through the alliance of their fathers with the Romans, under Carausius and his successors. Subsequent intercourse with the Greek Emperors[340] induced them to adopt the Phrygian tunic covered with flat rings.[341] This, however, does not occur till the middle of the eighth century, about 300 years after their arrival in England. According to Aneurin, Hengist wore scale armour, and, it seems, a mantle of fur; and was armed with a large piercing weapon, and a shield made of split wood. A very early illuminated MS. in the British Museum,[342] represents a warrior exactly answering this description: his four-cornered helmet has a serrated crest,[343] his spear is broad bladed, and his shield convex, with an iron boss terminating in a button, exactly like those found in the tumuli opened by the Rev. Mr. Douglas, and which are generally accompanied with a sword and dagger of steel of moderate size.

The lorica seems to have fallen into disuse after the conquest of England, for the drawings of the eighth century represent the Anglo-Saxon soldier without any other defensive armour than the shield and helmet, which latter seems in general to have been nothing more than leather, and is often omitted even in representations of battles. His offensive arms are the sword and the spear.

The form of the shield at this period is constantly oval: it is usually surrounded by a broad rim on the outside, and has a sharp boss protuberating from the middle, both of metal: the materials were wood, covered with leather. One of the laws of Æthelstan[344] prohibits the making of shields of

---

[339] Aneurin, the British bard, in his Gododins, asserts this frequently.

[340] Douglas's Nenia Brit.; Gibbon's Dec. of Rom. Emp.; and Turner's Angl. Saxons.

[341] Compare an illumination in a MS. in the Cotton library, marked Cleopatra, C. VIII, with the Phrygian warrior of bronze, in Hope's Costume of the Antients, before noticed.

[342] In the Hari. library, No. 603.

[343] Called by the Saxons Camb, or Comb.

[344] Leges Æthelstani apud Wilkins.

sheep-skin, under the penalty of thirty shillings.

The helmet, as It is commonly represented in the drawings of this æra, appears to have been nothing more than a cap of leather, with the fur turned outwards; but personages of rank had one of a conical form of metal and gilt.

The sword appears so large and long that it seems ill calculated for close fighting: the chief dependence of the warrior was, probably, in the vigour of his attack, or by keeping his opponent at bay with the shield, while he struck at him with his sword. The blade of the sword was iron or steel, and its hilt ornamented or gilt. The head of the lance was sometimes barbed.

When the tunic supplanted the lorica, the Roman pectoral was still retained, and called, balſ-beaſh, or beoꞃꞅ, "neck-guard;" bꞃeoꞃꞇ-beꝺen, "defence for the breast;" and bꞃeoꞃꞇ-ꞃocc, "breastplate." It may be seen on a warrior in an illumination, marked Tiberius, B. v, in the Cotton library, in which the resemblance to the Roman pectoral is quite manifest. The Saxon authors are by no means explicit with respect to the form or materials of the breast-guards, but the epithet applied to such as were of metal is "rigid." Others are mentioned which are said to have been "rough or shaggy," so that we may suppose these to have been formed of wool or hair.

Notwithstanding these remarks, the word lorica frequently occurs in the writings of the most antient Saxon authors, and as composed some-times of metal. Such seems intimated by Aldhelm, bishop of Sherborne, who lived in the latter part of the seventh century. His ænigina is contained in the following lines:

> Roscida me genuit gelido de viscere teilus:
> Non sum setigero lanarum vellere facta;
> Licia nulla trabunt, nec garrula fila resultant;
> Nec croceit seres texunt lanugine vermes;
> Nec radiis carpor, duro nec pcctinc pulsor;
> Et tamcn en! vestis vulgi sermone vocabor:
> Spicula non vereor longis exempta pbaretris.

> "The dewy earth produced me from its congealed bowels:
> I am not made from the rough fleeces of wool;
> No woofs drewr me, nor did the tremulous thread resound;
> Nor did the yellow down of silk-worms form me:
> I passed not through the shuttle, nor was I stricken with the wool-comb;
> And yet, behold 1 a vesture am I commonly called:
> I fear not the darts that are drawn forth from the long quivers."

Whether this was the scaled armour, such as worn by Hengist, or that made of flat rings in the Phrygian style, is not quite clear; but there is, in an illumination of the eighth century, a king habited in a tunic covered with flat rings: and in another MS. of that period, similar armour occurs.[345] The Saxon authors call this Lehᵖynᵹeb bÿᵖn, or "ringed byrne." Some illuminations seem to shew, that the rings were worn edgewise,[346] and in either case the name is equally applicable. Still, the rarity of these specimens, and their being confined to kings or principal chieftains, favours the idea that the manufacture was expensive. The Britons, however, in their frequent skirmishes with the Saxons, saw the utility of this armour, and their princes soon adopted it. They called it mael, i. e. steel, whence, probably, the word mail,[347] afterwards so generally used as contradistinguished from plate-armour. It is applied as an epithet to the Welsh chieftains so early as the sixth century: hence, a celebrated leader of cavalry was termed, from his wearing this armour, Mael the Tall[348] another, Maelgwyn, or "Shining-Mail Cynvael, "Mailed Chief;" and so on: all which, while it proves its existence, tends to shew its rarity.

Towards the conclusion of the ninth century the coriurn, or corietum, was the armour generally used, and appears frequently in the drawings of that period. It was formed of hides cut into the resemblance of leaves, and covering one another; sometimes all of one colour, as blue, &c.: and sometimes of two, as brown and orange; the upper part as far as the abdomen being of the one, while that, which covers the thighs is of the other.

It should be observed, that the Saxon byrne, originally in shape like a tunic, became in form afterwards a complete cuirass, sitting close to the body, and generally terminating with it.

Alcuin[349] speaks of the Anglo-Saxon military tunics of linen in the following terms: "The soldiers are accustomed to wear linen tunics, so well fitted to their limbs as to enable them, with the utmost expedition, to direct the dart, poise the shield, and wield the sword," &c.

The weight of the ringed byrne seems, however, to have been found a great impediment to activity. Hence, when Earl Harold, in 1063, obtained

---

[345] See an illumination in the Cotton library in the British Museum, marked Claudius, B. IV, written about the time of Coedmon; and another marked Cleopatra, C. VIII.

[346] See an illumination marked Cleopatra, C. VIII.

[347] Some have derived this word from mascle, or macle, but it is 'of more antient use than the mascled armour.

[348] His monumental stone with its epitaph is now in the possession of Llewlyn Meyrick, Esq. It is in the antient British language and the old orthography.

[349] De Offic. Divin.

immediate and decisive success over the Welsh, it was owing to the change
of armour among his soldiers. He had observed that these mountaineers
could not be pursued to their fastnesses by his troops when clad in ringed
tunics, and, therefore, commanded them to use their antient leathern suits,
which would not impede their agility.[350]

The Saxon artists made no distinction between the cyne-beaLm, or
royal helmet, and the crown. The monarch is depicted by them, in his court
and in the field of battle, with the same kind of head-covering, even when
every other part of his dress is marked with decisive variation; but upon the
figure of Edward the Confessor, in his great seal, the diadem is evidently
put on a helmet. The casque of the nobility is usually pointed in the form
of a cone, and made of brass or some other metal. In the two succeeding
centuries its shape is the same, but it is ornamented with gold and precious
stones, and is improved by the addition of a small piece to protect the nose,
called a nasal.[351]

Leg-guards are decidedly mentioned by the early Saxon writers, but
they uniformly appear to have been made of twisted pieces of woollen cloth,
coming from within the shoe, and wound round the legs to the top of the
calves, in imitation of the hay-bands used by their rude ancestors.

The cavalry had also spurs, but do not seem ever to have adopted boots.
The spur was formed on the model of the Roman, but with a much longer
neck, and was called the spear-spur.

A mantle was generally worn, which fastened on the right shoulder
with a buckle; but in every contest this was laid aside.

The shield still continued oval, and, indeed, until the Norman conquest, but it differed from time to time greatly in dimensions, especially in
the tenth and eleventh centuries, in the drawings of which times it appears
of various sizes, from a magnitude sufficient to cover the head and body,
to a diameter not greater than a cubit. This variation is further supported
by historical testimony, for we find mention made of "little shields," and
"smaller shields." In the will of Æthelstan, dated 1015, the shoulder-shield
is included among the legacies, and it is distinguished from the target. It
was probably of the larger sort, and received its appellation from being usually slung upon the shoulder.

The form of the sword was not subject to much variation according to

---

[350] Ingulphus, 68; John of Salisbury de Nugis Curialium, Lib. VI, c. vi, p. 185. An
author of the twelfth century also notices this invasion of Wales.

[351] See an illumination in the Cotton library, marked Tiberius, B. v,

the illuminations of the period; but the Saxon records specify several sorts, as the shining sword, the sharp-pointed sword, the dull or pointless ditto, the two-edged ditto, and the broad sword. The saex, or curved dagger, is likewise noticed. Every man of rank possessed a number of swords, suited to different occasions; upwards of a dozen, the property of Prince Æthelstan, are bequeathed in his will: and the sword-cutler appears to have been an artist held in high estimation. In the antient records his name is frequently added to the arms he fabricated, as a mark of their superior excellence. Silver-hilted swords are particularly specified in the will before cited, and swords with hollow hilts. These last Mr. Strutt considers to be hilts ornamented with fret-work, and although I am by no means inclined to dispute this, I will merely mention, that in the 12th volume of the Archseologia, Pl. XLI, Fig. 4, is given the representation of a sword which belonged to a Bishop of Durham, on each side of the hilt of which is a bar, which, producing two holes for the fingers, may answer the denomination hollow-hilted.[352] Hilts of gold are also spoken of by the writers of this sera. Sometimes the sword was suspended from the shoulder, but the prevalent fashion was to gird it upon the side. The sword-belts were often not distinguished from the common girdle with which the tunic was usually bound; yet this was not always the case: and the Saxon writers speak of them as adorned with gold, silver, and jewels. The sword-sheath was generally black; but a variety of instances occur, in the drawings of the time, in which they appear worn without any sheath at all.

There are three sorts of spears mentioned by Saxon authors—the war-spear, the boar-spear, and the hunting-spear, but in what particulars they differed from each other cannot easily be determined. As a weapon of war it is, in drawings, given to the foot soldiers, and the cavalry are very rarely depicted without it.

To keep up the military spirit of the people their amusements were made conducive to skill in war: among these was a dance, called the sword-dance, and held in high repute, because derived from their gothic ancestors. Tacitus, in his description of the Germans,[353] says: "One public diversion was constantly exhibited at all their meetings; young men who, by frequent exercise, have attained to great perfection in that pastime, strip themselves and dance among the points of swords and spears with most wonderful agility,

---

[352] The three bars seem, however, to have been wholly covered by the wooden gripe. It belonged to Anthony Beck, Bishop of Durham, in 1283.

353 De Mor. Germ. c. XXIV.

and even with the most elegant and graceful motions. They do not perform this dance for hire, but for the entertainment of the spectators, esteeming their applause a sufficient reward." This dance continues to be practised in the Northern parts of England, about Christmas, when the foot-plough, as it is called, goes about a pageant that consists of a number of sword-dancers dragging a plough, with music. It is, however, so far altered from its original ingenuity, that the dancers of the present day, when they have formed their swords into a figure, lay them upon the ground, and dance round them.[354] In an illuminated Saxon MS., of the ninth century,[355] a military dance of a somewhat different kind occurs: Two men, equipped in martial habits, and each armed with a sword and shield, are engaged in combat; the performance is enlivened by the sound of a horn, and the musician, together with a female assistant, dances round them to the cadence of the music, which, probably, regulated the actions of the combatants. The rapier-dance of Yorkshire seems to have been derived from this. The performers are usually dressed in a white frock, or covered with a shirt, to which, as also to their hats or paper helmets, are suspended long black ribbons. They assume the names of military heroes, from Hector and Paris down to Guy Earl of Warwick. A spokesman repeats some verses in praise of each, when they begin to flourish their rapiers. On a signal given all the weapons are united or interlaced, but soon withdrawn again and brandished by the performers, who exhibit a great variety of evolutions, being usually accompanied by slow music: at last the rapiers are united round the neck of a person kneeling in the centre, and when they are suddenly withdrawn the victim falls to the ground. He is afterwards carried out, and a mock funeral performed.

Plate VII exhibits specimens of Saxon arms and armour. Fig. 1 represents the large shield used at the first arrival of the Saxons, behind which are two Anglo-Saxon spears and two swords, and above it Edward the Confessor's crown-helme. Fig. 2 and 3, two specimens of the Saxon corium. Fig. 4 and 5, two helmets. Fig. 6, the antient Saxon four-cornered helmet.

In forming their armies the following regulations were observed by the Anglo-Saxons: All such as were qualified to bear arms in one family were led to the field by the head of that family. Every ten families made a tithing, which was commanded by the borsholder, in his military capacity styled

---

[354] See Brand's Notes upon the 14th chapter of Bourne's Vulgar Antiquities. Mr. Brand has collected, from Olaüs Magnus, the various. motions and figures formed by the gothic dancers.

[355] It is a Latin MS. of Prudentius, with Saxon Notes, in the Cotton library, marked Cleopatra, C. VIII.

PLATE VII

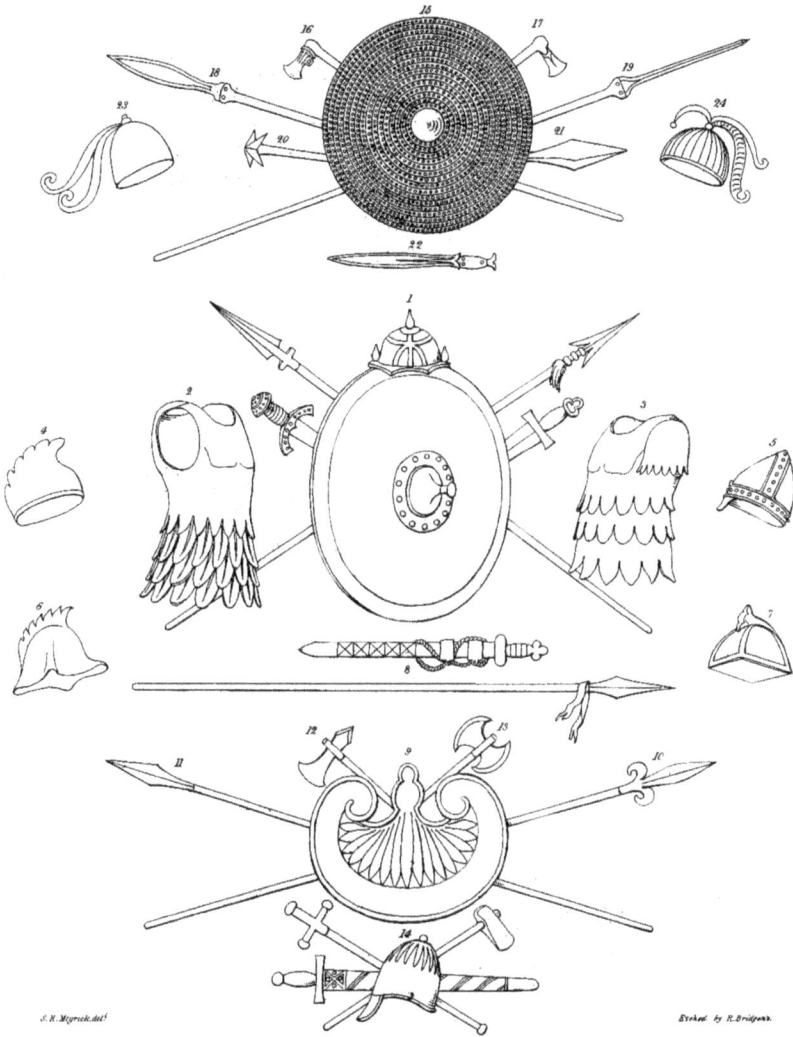

BRITISH, SAXON, AND DANISH ARMOUR.

conductor. Ten tithings constituted a hundred, the soldiers of which were led by their chief magistrate, called, sometimes, a hundredary: this officer was elected by the hundred, at their public court, where they met armed, and every member, as a token of his obedience to him, touched his weapon when chosen, whence the hundred courts, held for this especial purpose, were called wapen-takes, a name still retained in Yorkshire. Several hundreds were called a trything, corrupted into riding, and this was commanded by an officer, called a thrything-man, and the whole force of the county was placed under the command of the heretoch, or general. When the king did not command himself an officer was appointed, called the kyning's-hold, or king's lieutenant, whose office lasted only during the year.

Every landholder was obliged to keep armour and weapons according to his rank and possessions; these he might neither sell, lend, nor pledge, nor even alienate from his heirs. In order to instruct them in the use of arms, they had their stated times for performing their military exercise; and once in a year, usually in the spring, there was a general review of arms throughout each county.

The military affairs of Wales were regulated much in the same manner.

FRANKS.

About the year 240 a new confederacy was formed against the Romans, under the name of Franks, or Freemen, by the old inhabitants of the Lower Rhine and the Weser. Part of them were the Chauci, who, in their inaccessible morasses, defied the Roman arms; another tribe was composed of the Cherusci, whose equipments under Arminius have been before noticed; and another class were the Catti, formidable by their firm and intrepid infantry; together with several other tribes of inferior power and renown. These united people invaded and established themselves in Gaul, and laid the foundation of the French monarchy. As they not only spread themselves over Gaul, which they called France, but likewise great part of Germany and Italy, their name was afterwards applied, by the Greeks and Arabians, to all the Christians of the Latin church. The vast body that had been united by Charlemagne, and his wonderful victory, seems to have been the cause. A French writer of the ninth century[356] has given us a complete description of the dress of Charlemagne, who, he says, adhered strictly to all

---

[356] Eginhart de vità Caroli Magni. c. xxiii.

the antient manners of his country, as well in dress as every thing else. From this, we learn, that he had a military tunic of linen, exactly like those of the Anglo-Saxons, and never appeared without his sword and sword-belt: in these last he took particular pride. The belt was composed of gold or silver, and the hilt of the sword corresponded with the belt, except upon solemn court-days, when he wore a sword, the hilt of which was embellished vrith jewels. He is said, further, to have had a thorax, and in the representation given of him, from a mosaic of the time, by Montfaucon,[357] this appears to have been composed of several metal plates. Excepting this thorax, there is no part of the dress of Charlemagne but what may be traced in the drawings of the Anglo-Saxons. The spurs were of the same kind, for one, in my son's collection of steel, and brought from Paris, though somewhat corroded, appears exactly like those in the AngloSaxon illuminations. But the spur shewn in Paris, as that of Charlemagne, is a pryck-spun and nailed to the leather, whence there is reason to refer it to the 12th century. They seem, however, latterly, to have imitated the Norman military habits, for in a MS. of Prudentius, illuminated by the Franks, occurs the haubergeon, consisting of breeches and jacket in one, like those in the Baveux tapestry. Some of the figures too, have, with this hauberk of the tapestry, a Saxon-crested helmet, and kite-shaped shield, while others are with Saxon shields and spurs. Lu-itprand tells us,[358] that "the Franks were rude and unskilful in the service of cavalry; and in all perilous emergencies their warriors were so conscious of their ignorance, that they chose to dismount from their horses and fight on foot. Unpractised in the use of spears or of missile weapons, they were encumbered by the length of their swords, the weight of their armour, and by the magnitude of their shields."

Plate vn, Fig. 7, represents a Frankish helmet as worn by the guards of Lothaire. Fig. 8, a sword and spear of ditto. See Montfaucon's Monarchie Françoise, Tom. I, PI. xxvi, where is also a convex oval shield, with a spike in the centre, exactly resembling those used by the Saxons.

ALLEMANNI.

This nation of warriors, as their name imports,[359] were also composed

---

[357] Monarchie Française, Tom. I, Pl. xxii.
[358] In Legat, p. 480.
[359] All-men.

of various tribes of Suevi, who united in the time of Caracalla. They fought chiefly on horseback, but their cavalry was rendered still more formidable by a mixture of light infantry, selected from the bravest and most active of their youth, whom frequent exercise had inured to accompany the horsemen in the longest march, the most rapid charge, or the most precipitate retreat.

TUNGRIANS.

A Roman inscribed stone, ornamented with sculpture, and found in Northumberland, gives us the costume of a Tungrian and a Gaul. One is so much defaced that, with the exception of the lorica, nothing can be discerned but two belts, one of which merely crosses the body from over the right shoulder, and the other placed round the neck passes under the right arm. The first of these is a broad belt, and the other a kind of cord, to which is suspended, by a ring on its handle, a curved dagger, with its edge inside. The other is an archer much resembling the figure which Montfaucon[360] calls a Gaul, and round which is a forged Greek inscription: he appears in a helmet with a high ridge on its top, a lorica, long tight sleeves on his arms, a short petticoat, and apparently pantaloons; besides his bow, and a quiver of arrows, which he wears at his right hip, he has a sword and dagger; and what doubtfully appears to be a mallet, is seen just above his right shoulder as if at his back. This costume in a great measure agrees with the following description which Procopius[361] gives of the Roman auxiliaries: "But ou-rarchers now go into the field armed with loricæ, and greaves that reach up to their knees; they have, besides, their quiver of arrows on the right side, a sword on their left, and some a javelin fastened about them; a kind of small buckler, without any handle, made fast to their shoulder, which serves to defend their head and neck." This shoulder-shield may be that which in the sculptures resembles a mallet.

ANGLO-DANES.

When the Danes made their first appearance in England they seem to have had no other armour than a broad collar, which encircled their chest

---

[360] In his Antiq, expl, Vol. IV, Part 1, p. 37,
[361] Lib. 1, de Bell. Pers.

and lower part of their neck, or a small thorax of flat rings, with greaves, or rather shin-pieces, of stout leather. There is still in existence a curious reliquary, which represents the murder of Theodore, abbot of Croyland, and his attendant monks, by the Danes. This event took place in the year 890, and there is no doubt of its having been fabricated not long posterior to the event it commemorates, and likewise by a Saxon artist. The reliquary was formerly preserved in the abbey of Croyland, and it represents the abbot officiating at the high altar, with a figure supposed to be intended for Oscytel, the Danish king, in the act of striking off his head with a sword. The workmanship is admirable; the figures are chased in gold upon a blue ground; the heads are of silver, and in high relief.[362]

The Danish swords were made in the same manner as those of the Anglo-Saxons, but the scabbard is more ornamented. They had more particularly as their weapon the battle-axe and the bipennis, the former having, in the reliquary before noticed, a broad flat spike on the opposite side to the blade. The shields are lunated, but rising in the centre of the inner curve, and, therefore, greatly resembling those of the Phrygians.

About Canute's time the Anglo-Danes adopted a new species of armour, which they probably derived from their consanguinei, the Normans. This consisted of a tunic, with a hood for the head, and long sleeves, and what were afterwards called chauses, i. e. pantaloons, covering also the feet, all of which were coated with perforated lozenges of steel, called, from their resemblance to the meshes of a net, macles, or mascles.[363] They wore, too, a helmet, or scullcap in the shape of a curvilinear cone, having on its apex a round knob, under which was painted the rays of a star. This helmet had a large broad nasal to protect the nose, and the hood was drawn up over the mouth and attached to it, so that the only exposed parts were the eyes.[364] Spears, swords, and battle-axes, or bipennes, were the offensive arms, and the shield remained as before.

In Plate vii, Fig. 9, is an Anglo-Danish shield. Fig. 10, the spear of Canute on his coin. Fig. 11, that of the soldiers in his prayer-book. Fig. 12 and 13, battle-axes. Fig. 14, a sword, with a helmet in front; a stone miolner, in my son's collection, and one from an antient coin.

---

[362] See an engraving of it in Strutt's Habits orthe Bngfish, Pl. xxiv.

[363] Johannes De J anua says, the word is derived from the Latin macula; and the manufacture was probably brought with its name by the Normans, from Italy, who introduced it to the Danes.

[364] The authority for these observations is the prayer-book of Canute, in the British Museum.

NORWEGIANS.

It was probably the flat-ringed armour, or that with the ring set edgewise, that was worn by the Norwegians, thougli we have no where any definite description of it. Snorre Sturlson, in his Edda,[365] accounts for the victory which Harold the Second gained over Hardrada, by saying, the Norwegians not having expected a battle on that day had not put on their coats of mail. In that battle the king of Norway formed his men in a long but not dense line, and bending hack the wings, he drew them into a circle everywhere of the same depth, with shield touching shield· The first line were ordered to fix their lances obliquely in the ground, with the points inclining towards the enemy, who had so great a superiority of cavalry. The second line were to plunge their spears into the breasts of the horses when near, while the archers, who were within with the king and his standard, were to annoy them at a distance.[366] When the enemy had not such advantage of cavalry, the Norwegian troops were generally drawn up in a straight line, with one wing flanked by a river, and the other by a ditch, marsh, or whatever might form a kind of protection.[367] The Norwegian forces were, however, generally infantry, and they found that the mode of attack of the Saxon horse was by charging in a promiscuous mass, then to fly off, and to return either at the same or some other point.

The Norwegians being sea-rovers will account for their strength lying principally in their infantry; and from what is before stated their arms appear to have been spears, swords, bows and arrows, with shields and body-armour.

From an old chronicle of Norway, quoted by Pontoppidan, we learn that the warriors were previously practised in such exercises as might contribute to their success in war. Thus Olaff Trygvason, a king of that country, is said to have been stronger and more nimble than any man in his dominions. He could climb up the rock of Smalserhorn, and fix his shield upon its top: he could walk round the outside of a boat upon the oars while the men were rowing; he could play with three darts, alternately throwing them in the air, and always kept two of them up while he held the third in one of

[365] P.163.
[366] Snorre Sturlson, 159.
[367] Ibid. 155. Orkneyinga Saga, p. 95.

his hands: he was ambidexter, and could cast two darts at once; he excelled all men of his time in shooting with the bow, and he had no equal in the certainty of his aim.

With respect to the helmet, we meet with the following curious fact in Snorre Sturlson's Norwegian Chronicle: "The sons of Erik Blodoexe having attacked Norway unexpectedly. King Hagen Adelsteen collected a few troops hastily, and boldly defied the enemy. A desperate engagement ensued, in which the enemy impetuously rushed towards the king, he being particularly distinguished by a gilt helmet. Meanwhile Hagen, supported by Thorleif and others of his bravest warriors, maintained the unequal conflict with determined heroism. At length it was discovered, that the splendid helmet was the occasion of so much peril to the king's person, upon which one of the Norwegians threw a covering over it. Evind Skreia, an undaunted warrior of the opposite party, had forced his passage to the king, but losing sight of the helmet he exclaimed, 'Does the king of Norway hide himself, or is he fallen or fled?' Hagen Adelsteen, indignant at this scornful language, boldly answered, 'No! behold in me the king of Norway.' Evind recognized his voice, and pressed forward."

BRITONS.

The inhabitants of Britain and Ireland, previous to their intercourse with the Phœnicians, had merely bows, with arrows of reed headed with flint or pointed with bones, sharpened to an acute edge.[368] The arrows were carried in a quiver formed of ozier twigs; and besides these weapons they had spears and javelins made of long bones, ground to a point, inserted in oaken shafts, and held in them by pegs;[369] a battle-axe, called Bwyellt-arv, of flint;[370] and a club of four points or four edges, denominated Cat, and made of oak.

No sooner did the Phœnicians effect an amicable interchange with these islanders, than they communicated to them the art of manufacturing their warlike implements of metal. The composition was copper and tin, the proportions of which were varied according to the object that was intend-

---

[368] Costume of the Original Inhabitants of the British Isles, with its authorities, p. 2.

[369] Such have been found in tumuli. See Archoeologia, Vol. XV, Pl. II.

[370] One found in Suffolk, at an immense depth below the .surface of the earth, is in the possession of Llewelyn Meyrick, Esq.j and others are engraved in the Archreologia, Vol. XV.

ed. At first they exactly imitated the weapons of bone, and spear and javelin heads, as well as those for battle-axes, were made to be inserted in their respective handles.[371] The javelin, called gwaew-fon, or fonwayw, had its blade generally about a foot in length, which was nailed in a slit made in the ashen shaft: the flat bladed one, introduced by the Phœnicians, was called paled. After a time, in imitation of the weapons of this maritime nation, the British spear had its shaft fitted into the blade, and the battle-axe was formed in the same manner. Instead of the shield merely of wicker, it was made of this compound metal, but retained its circular form, being flat, rather more than two feet in diameter, with a flattened conical boss in the middle: it was ornamented with concentric circles and intermediate knobs, and was held by the hand in the centre.[372] The Britons as well as the Gauls and other Cimbri used dogs in battle.[373] The spathse, or two-handed swords, were used by the Britons and Irish as well as the Gauls, and called cheddyv-hir deuddwrn by the former, and dolaimghen by the latter, but I am not aware of any having been discovered. Both straight and curved swords formed part of the Irish weapons, and straight ones, less than two feet in length, were used by the Britons: these have been found in great quantities in Ireland, and frequently in England, but always of bronze.[374] There was also a broad-edged lance, called by the Irish lagean, and by the Britons llavnawr.[375] Tlie sword was suspended by a chain, and though we are told, by Herodian and Xiphilin, that the Britons did not wear helmets, yet the antient British coins represent the warrior mounted, and with a scullcap, from which fall the prolix appendages noticed by Diodorus, in his account of the Gauls. The hilts of the British swords seem to have been of horn, from the adage, "He that has got the horn has got the blade." The Caledonians had a ball filled with pieces of metal at the end of their lances, in order to make a noise when engaged with cavalry,[376] which was called cnopstara; and the general

---

[371] See particularly Archreologia, Vol. XVI, PI. LXX; and CoUect. de Reb. Hib. Vol. IV, Pl. XI.

[372] One of these, found in a turbary, is engraved in my History of Cardiganshire. It is now in the possession of Llewelyn Meyrick, Esq., to whom it was presented by Miss Probert, of Shrewsbury.

[373] Plin. Lib. VIII, c. xl. Strabo Geog.

[374] One of these; in the collection of Llewelyn Meyrick, Esq., has its edge remarkably sharp.

[375] All these are more particularly described, and the authorities given, in Major Smith's and my Costume of the Originell Inhabitants of the British Isles.

[376] Xiphilin ex Di-one Nicæo.

INTRODUCTION. ciii

ornament of the warriors of the British isles was the torque of gold, silver, [377]
There is also reason to suppose the Britons used wooden slings.

All the British and Irish youths were trained to the use of arms from their infancy, and their very diversions were of a martial cast. The infantry were the most numerous; the cavalry rode on small but mettlesome horses, without saddles; and the chiefs fought from chariots, of which the essedum was the most renowned: it was drawn by a pair of horses, while the covinus, with its axles armed with brazen blades, somewhat of the scythe shape, was hurried on merely by one. Hence, Silius Italicus says:

Agmina falcifero circumvenit arcta covino.

"He gallops round the compact band with the scythe-armed covinus."

One of these scythe-blades of bronze, thirteen inches long, was found in Ireland, and engraved in the Collectanea de Rebus Hibernicis.[378]

When the Romans had obtained a firm footing in Britain, they formed, from the strong and active of its inhabitants, several military corps, which they attached to their legions as auxiliaries: the brazen weapons were exchanged for steel, and the skins of wild beasts for the well-tempered leathern cuirass. This costume, so readily adopted, as Tacitus has observed,[379] was continued by the Britons after their conquerors had returned to them their antient territory. Aneurin,[380] the bard of the fifth century, therefore, particularizes the troops of Vortigern as llurigawg, or loricated.

Tacitus describes[381] the army of Galgacus as having long swords, and targets of small dimensions.[382] He says, they had the address to elude the

---

[377] Archæologia, Vol. XIV. Pliny, in his Natural History, xxxiii, 2, in the time of Vespasian, says: "The golden torque was presented exclusively to auxiliaries and allies; none but the silver torque to citizens." Silver not being flexible like gold, the torque of that metal, instead of being formed of twisted bars, was generally a chain, ex annulis singulis, "of single rings;" vel binis, or " in pairs;" inter se cohoerentibus, "linked within each other." One of this kind, taken probably by a Pict, from some Brito-Roman, in an incursion of that people into Britannia Prima, was found, in the year 1808, in a large cairn, near Torvaine, and is now in the possession of the Society of Antiquaries, at Edinburgh.

[378] Vol. IV, Pl. xi.

[379] In Vit. Agricolæ.

[380] In his Poems, called the Gododins.

[381] Vit. Agrie.

[382] The claymores and targets of the present Highlanders are derived from them. At that time the latter was composed of ozier twigs, or boards as now, and covered with leather.

missive weapons of the Romans, and, at the same time, to discharge a thick volley of their own. In close conflict these small targets afforded no protection, and the unwieldly sword not sharpened to a point would do but little execution. They, however, made use of armed chariots.

Plate VII, Fig 15, is the British shield, found in Cardiganshire, of bronze. Fig. 16 and 17, two bwyellt-arvau, or battle-axes. Fig. 18, the Llavnawr, or blade-weapon. Fig. 19, the Gwaew-fon, or spear. Fig. 20 and 21, two specimens of the cat, or club. Fig. 22, a sword. Fig. 23, a helmet. Fig. 24, a Gaulish ditto.

In order to enable the reader to form a clear geographical idea of the various nations of antiquity, whose warlike peculiarities have been noticed in this Introduction, the following Comparative Table is added:—

ANTIENT AFRICA.	MODERN AFRICA.
Ægyptus.	Egypt.
Libya.	Bildulgerid.
Æthopia.	Ethiopia.
Numidia, containing Carthage.	Tunis.

ANTIENT ASIA.

Asia Minor. {
1. Mysia, Lydia, Caria, Phrygia, Bithynia, Galatia, Paphlagonia.
2. Pontus.
3. Armenia.
4. Cappadocia, Cilicia, &c.
5. Babylonia, Chaldea.
6. Mesopotamia.
7. Assyria.
8. } Armenia.
9. }
10. } Syria, Palmyrene. Phoenicia, Judea.

Arabia. {
Arabia Patræa
Arabia Deserta.
Arabia Felix.

India. {
1. Palibothra.
2. Agora.
3. Regna Pori et Taxilis.
5. Dachanos.
6. Prasil vel Gangaridæ.
8. Male
} Intra Gangem.

Taprobanæ Ins. vel Salice

MODERN ASIA.

1. Natotia.

Turkey in Asia. {
2. Amasia, or Siwas.
3. Aladulia.
4. Caramania.
5. Irak.
6. Diarbek.
7. Curdistan.
8. Turcomania.
9. Georgia.
10. Syria and Palestine.

Arabia. {
Arabia Patræa
Arabia Deserta.
Arabia Felix.

India. {
1. Delhi.
2. Agra.
3. Cambaia.
4. Bengal.
5. Decan.
} Mogul Empire.
6. Golconda.
7. Bisnagar.
8. Malabar.
} Within the Ganges.

Island of Ceylon.

ANTIENT ASIA.	MODERN ASIA.

Persia.
1. Heroaniss et Sogdianre Pars.
2. Bactriana.
3. Drangiana.
4.
5. Gedrosia.
6. Persis.
7. Susiana,
8. Parthia.
9. Assyriæ Pars.
10. Media.
11.
12. Iberia, Colchis, et Albania.
13.
15. Hyrcanioe Pars
16. Albanise Pars.

Persia.
1. Chorassan.
2. Balk, Sablustan, and Candahar
3. Sigistan.
4. Makeran,
5. Kerman.
6. Farsistan.
7. Chusestan.
8. Irak Agem,
9. Curdcstan.
10. Aderbeitzen.
11. Georgia.
12. Gangea.
13. Dagestan.
14. Mazanderam,
15. Gilan Taberistan.
16. Chirvan.

Sinarum Regio. } Extra Gangem.

China. — Beyond the Gangees.

Scythia in-tra Miaum.
1. Sarmatia Asiatica.
2.
3.

Russia in Asia.
1. Astracan.
2. Oremburg.
3. Casan.

1. Bactriana.
2. Sogdiana.
3. Aria.

Independant Tartary.
1. Great Bucharia.
2
3. Karasam.

Scythia extra Imaurs.
1.
2.
3.
4.
5.
6.

Aluth Tartars.
1. Little Bucharia,
2. Casgar.
3. Turkestan.
4. Kalmuc Tartars.
5. Thibet.
6, Little Thibet.

ANTIENT EUROPE.

Scandinavia, Scadia, vel Baltia.
1. Nerigon.
2. Sitones.
3. Scritofinni,
4.. Suiones.
5. Gutæ et Hilleviones.
6. Finnigia.
7. Insulæ Sinus Codani.

Chersonesus Cimbriea.
1. Cimbri.
2.
3. Harudes.
4. Phundusii, Sigulones.
5. Saablingii.

Insula Sinus Codani.
{1. / 2.} Teutones.

Sarmatia Europæa.
1. Hirri et Æsthi vel Ostiones.
2.
3.
4. Budinorum Pars.
5.
6. Busilici.
7. Cariones.
8.
9.
10. Budinorum Pars.
11. Roxolani.
12. Iazyges.

Saxones.
1.
2.
3.
4. Cauci vel Chauci.
5. Franci.
6. Brutcteri, Catti, Siambri.
7. Batavi.

MODERN EUROPE.

Part of Norway.
1. Drontheim.
2. Bergen.

Sweden.
3. Lapland and West Bothnia.
4. Sweden Proper.
5. Gothland.
6. Finland.
7. Islands of Gothland, Oeland, Aland, and Ruges.

Jutland.
1. Alburg.
2. Wyburg.
3. Aarhusen.
4. Rypen.
5. Sleswick.

Danish Isles.
1. Zealand.
2. Funen.

Russia in Europe.
1. Livo?ia and Esthonia.
2. Ingria.
3. Carelia.
4. Novogrod,
5. Archangel, Samoieda.
6. Moscow.
7. Nishnei Novogrod.
8. Smolenski,
9. Kiew.
10. Bielgorod..
11. Woronesk.
12. Azoff.

United Netherlands.
1. Holland,
2. Friesland.
3. Zealand.
4. Gronigen.
5. Overyssell.
6, Guelderland & Zuphen.
7. Utrecht.

ANTIENT EUROPE.		MODERN EUROPE.	
Belgæ, &c.	1. Menapii, Tungrii. 2. Toxandri. 3. 4. } Allemanni. 5. } 6. Treveri. 7. Remi. 8. 9. Atrebates, Veromandui. 10. Belgoe, Morini.	Austrian, French, and Dutch Nether- lands.	1. Brabant. 2. Antwerp. 3. Mechlin, or Malmes. 4. Limburgh. 5. Luxemburgh. 6. Namur. 7. Hainault. 8. Cambresis. 9. Artois. 10. Flanders.
Nationes Germaniæ.	Saxones. { 1. Suevi, Lingoe, &c. 2. Saxones, Longobardi, Gambrivii. 3. Cherusci, Chamavi, Cauci, et Germania Inferior. 4. Germania Superior. 5. Marci, Tinteri. 6. Marcomanm, Hermonduri. 7. Noricum. 8. Rhætia. 9. Vindelicia. 10. Boiohæmum. 11. Corconti. 12. Quadi,	Germany. Bohemia.	1. Upper Saxony. 2. Lower Saxony. 3. Westphalia. 4. Upprer Rhine. 5. Lower Rhine. 6, Franconia. 7. Austria. 8. Bavaria. 9. Suabia. 10. Bohemia Proper. 11. Silesia. 12. Moravia.
Germano Sarmate.	1. Peucini. 2. Lugii. 3. } Burgundiones. Rugii, Guthones. 4. } 5. Ombroges. 6. Scyri. 7. } Germanæ Sarmatia. 8. } 9. 10. 11. } 12. } Bastarnæ 13.	Poland.	1. Greater Poland. 2. Less Poland. 3. Prussia Royal. 4. Prussia Ducal. 5. Samogitia. 6. Courland. 7. Lithuania. 8. Warsoyia. 9. PolachIa. 10. Polesia. 11. Red Russia. 12. Podolia. 13. Volhinia,

ANTIENT EUROPE.		MODERN EUROPE.	

ANTIENT EUROPE.

1. Ambiani.
2. Bellovaci, Parisii, Suessones.
3. Remi, Catalauni, Tricasses, Lingones.
4. Unelli vel Veneti, Saii, Lexovii, Veliocasses.
5. Osismii, Veneti, Namnetes, Andes, Redones.
6. Aureliani, Carnutes, Senones, Yurones, Pictones, Bituriges.
7. Ædui, Segusiani.
8. Salyes, Cavares.
9. Volcæ, Arecomièi, Helvii, Tolosates.
10. Petrocorii, Bituriges, Cadurci, Ruteni.
11. Aquitani.
12. Attobroges, Centrones.
13. Lingones, Ædui, Sequani.
14. Leuci, Mediomatrici, Triboci, Nemetes.

Celtæ.

1. ⎫
2. ⎬ Ambrones.
3. ⎪
4. ⎭
5.
6. ⎫
7. ⎬ Tigurini.
8. ⎪
9. ⎭
10.
11.
12
13.
14. Nantuates.
15. Veragri, Vallis Pennina, Lepontii.

...ia.

Insulæ Italicæ.
1. Sicilia, Sicania, vel Trinacria.
2. Sardo vel Sardinia.
3. Cyrnus vel Corsica.
4. Mehta.
5. Liparioe Insulte.
6. Caproe, Ischia, &c

MODERN EUROPE.

France.
1. Picardy.
2. Isle of France.
3. Champagne.
4. Normandy.
5. Britany.
6. Orleannois.
7. Lionnois.
8. Provence.
9. Languedoc.
10. Guienne.
11. Gascoine.
12. Dauphiné.
13. Burgundy and Franchecomté.
14. Lorraine and Alsace.

Switzerland.
1. Bern.
2. Friburg.
3. Basil, or Bâle.
4. Lucern,
5. Soluturn,
6. Schaffhausen.
7. Zurick.
8. Appenzel,
9. Zug.
10. Sehweitz,
11. Glaris.
12. Uri.
13. Underwald.
14. Geneva.
15. Grisons, &c.

Italian Islands.
1. Sicily.
2. Sardinia.
3. Corsica.
4. Malta.
5. Lipari Islands.
6. Capri, Ischia, &c.

ANTIENT EUROPE.

MODERN EUROPE.

ANTIENT EUROPE	MODERN EUROPE
Italia. 1. Leponti, Segusiui, Taurini.	**Italy.** 1. Savoy.
2. Orobi.	2. Piedmont.
3.	3. Montserrat.
4. Insubres. (Liguria.)	4. Milan.
5. (Gallia Cisalpina vel Togata.)	5. Genoa.
6. Anamani.	6. Parma.
7. Boii.	7. Modena.
8. Cenomani.	8. Mantua.
9. Venetia.	9. Venice.
10. Tridentini.	10. Trent.
11. Lingones, Senones, Picenum, Umbria, Sabini, Latii Pars.	11. The Popedom.
12. Tuscia vel Etruria.	12. Tuscany.
13. Tusciæ Pars.	13. Lucca.
14. Umbriæ Pars.	14. San Marino.
15. Samnium, Latii Pars, Apulia, Campania, Lucania, Bruttium.	15. Kingdom of Naples.

ANTIENT EUROPE	MODERN EUROPE
Græcia. 1. Dalmatia.	**Turkey in Europe.** 1. Dalmatia.
2. Moesia Superior.	2. Bosnia.
3. Dacia Ripensis.	3. Servia.
4. Getæ.	4. Wallachia.
5. Daciæ Pars.	5. Moldavia and Bessarabia,
6. Moesia Inferior.	6. Bulgaria.
7. Epirus.	7. Albania.
8. Macedonia.	8. Macedonia.
9. Thracia.	9. Romania.
10. Thessalia.	10. Li vadia.
11. Peloponnesus.	11. Morea.
12. Scythia et Daciæ Pars.	12. Budziac Tartary, or Bessarabia.
13. Scythia Parva.	13. Little Tartary. ,
14. Taurica Chersonesus.	14. Crimea.

ANTIENT EUROPE	MODERN EUROPE
Insulæ Martis Inonii. 1. Corcyra.	**Greek Islands.** 1. Corfu.
2. Cephalenia.	2. Cephalonia,
3. Zacynthus.	3. Zante.
4.-Ithaca, &c.	4. Ithace, Thiace, &c.

ANTIENT EUROPE	MODERN EUROPE
Insulæ Maris Ægæi. 1. Creta.	**In The Archipeligo.** 1. Candia.
2. Euboea.	2. Negropont.
3. Lemnos .	3. Stalimene.
4. Scyros, &c.	4. Scyro, &c.

ANTIENT EUROPE.	MODERN EUROPE.

Spania / Iberia.
1. Galloecia, Cantabri.
2. Astures.
3. Varduli.
4. Vascones.
5. Tarraconensis.
6. Valetani.
7. Carthaginensi, Æditani,
8. Contestani.
9. Bœtica, Bastiani, Bastuli,
10. Turdetani, &c.
11. Gallæciæ Pars-Accæi, Arevaci.
12. Tarracone,nsis Pars-Carpetàni, Oretani.
13. Galleeciæeæ Pars-Vettones.
14. Lusitaniæ Pars-Boeturia.

Spain.
1. Gallicia.
2. Asturia.
3. Biscay.
4. Navarre.
5. Arragon.
6. Catalonia.
7. Valentia.
8. Murcia.
9. Granada.
10. Andalusia.
11. Old Castile.
12. New Castile.
13. Leon.
14. Estremadura.

Baleares.

Ivica, Majorica, Minorica.

Lusitania.
1. Calliaci.
2. Lusitani.
3. Celtici.

Potugal.
1. Entre Minho e Douro, Tralos Montes.
2. Beira, Estremadura, Etre Tajo.
3. Alentajo, Algarva.

Britanniæ Insula.
1. Britannia Prima.
2. Britannia Secunda.
3. Caledonia.

Great Britain.
1. England.
2. Wales.
3, Scotland.

Hibernia.

Ireland.

A CRITICAL INQUIRY

INTO

ANTIENT ARMOUR.

A CRITICAL INQUIRY
INTO
ANTIENT ARMOUR.

William The Conqueor.

1066.

UCH had been the state of Armour in Britain when William led his army of Normans and Flemings to the victory at Hastings. His warriors had relaxed in no respect from the martial sentiments of their ancestors, but to their native courage added the improved science and discipline they had acquired from the Græco-Romans.

In the age of Rollo, the founder of the Norman dukedom, the love of personal distinction and public admiration had been the great actuating principle. In order to attain glory, it was pursued by an assiduous cultivation of bodily strength, agility, and manual dexterity, combining, with the most daring intrepidity, savage and warlike fortitude.[1] To hew well with the sword, to wrestle, to cast heavy weights, to run in skates, to sit firmly on horseback, to swim with vigour, to dart the lance with skill, and to manage dexterously the oar, were the Norman warriors' boast. Vigour in archery was an emulation of excellence, and they proved their strength by sending a blunted spear through a raw bull's hide.[2]

---

[1] Turner's History of England, Vol. 1.
[2] Snorre, Vol. II, p. 19; and the Lodbrog Quida, or Death Song of Regnar Lodbrog,

In an examination into what was their armour at the time of their conquest of England, the engraving which purports to represent the seal of the Conqueror[3] is that to which our attention would be primarily directed. If this be authentic it may have been the work of a Greek artist, which, from the Norman intercourse with that country, is by no means improbable: the helmet, indeed, which he wears, is in no respect like any other specimen of the time, but exactly resembles one on a GræcoRoman trophy, copied by Montfaucon.[4] To afford ocular demonstration, they are both represented at the bottom of Plate vm, that without the ear-pieces being taken from the seal. From this it will be further perceived, that it cannot represent his king-helmet,[5] "which," says the Saxon Chronicle, "he wore thrice every year when he was in England: at Easter he wore it at Winchester, on Pentecost at Westminster, and in mid-winter at Gloucester."

The seal exhibits the king bare-legged, but booted, which was also perhaps a Greek fashion, and not adopted by the Anglo-Normans till the next century. He is in a hauberk apparently of rings set edgewise, which kind of armour had been used by the Anglo-Saxons: yet we learn from William of Poitou, and also from an anonymous author of the time, that, when he was preparing for the battle of Hastings, he accidentally inverted his hauberk, which is much more likely to have happened with one of rings or máseles sewn flat on the vesture, as in the Bayeux tapestry, than with the former projecting.

His lance with its gonfanon is in his right hand. It differs from a banner in this respect: that, instead of being square and fastened to a transverse bar, the gonfanon, though of the same figure, was fixed in a frame made to turn like a modern ship's-vane, with two or three streamers, or tails. Notwithstanding this distinction the terms were often indiscriminately used, as will be found as we proceed. The object of the gonfanon was principally to render great people more conspicuous to their followers; and, secondly, to terrify the horses of their adversaries: hence the gonfanon became a mark of dignity, which is the cause of its being generally represented on the seals of

---

[3] See it in Sandford, Speed, &c. Whether the original wax impress still exists is not very certain, as this engraving itself has been copied for the new edition of the Fœdera, while, generally speaking, the editors have had the seals reengraved from the originals.

[4] Antiq. expl. Sup. Tom. IV, Pl. xxv.

[5] This was used instead of a crown, probably having some regal ornament in the Anglo-Saxon style. Abbot Suger, in his Life of Louis VI, says, that. the head-dress of the Emperor Lothaire was composed of a mitre, surrounded at the top by a circle of gold in the form of a casqué, beginning. at the front and .ending- at the back part of the head.

our early kings. In the left hand of the Conqueror is his shield, but from the situation in which it is viewed its shape is not wholly defined.

The arguments of Mr. Stothard[6] seem to have placed it beyond a doubt, that the manufacture of the Bayeux tapestry is coeval with the reign of William the First. To this source, therefore, we may freely recur for a correct representation of the armour of this period. It is of two kinds, leather and steel, with the conical nasal helmet: the former seems to be an improvement of the Anglo-Saxon; and the latter, in one of its forms, together with the helmet, to bear a strong resemblance to that of the Danes in the time of Canute. The leather, which consists of a tunic with many overlapping flaps, has close sleeves which reach to the wrists, and was called corium and corietum. It is so termed in the Leges Nonnannicæ,[7] in the following passage:[8] Ad diem autem duelli assignatam, debent se pugiles in curia justiciario offerre ante-quam bora meridiei sit transacta, apparati in corietis vel tunicis consuetis, et cum scutis et baculis cornutis annati. "On the day appointed for the duel, the champions should present themselves in the court of justice before the hour of twelve o'clock, clad in corieta, or tunics, made of pieces sewn over each other, and armed with shields and cornuted staffs." This cornuted staff was the besague, or bisacutum, being double pointed like a pickaxe, with a short, handle. Although it was subsequently much used, at the time of the conquest it was not considered a military weapon, but seems then to have been a double adze, and used by the carpenters. Thus, in the Roman de Rou, we read:

> Li charpentiers qui cmpres vindrent
> Grans coignies en lcurs couls tindrent,
> Dolouerres et besagues
> Ourent & leur cotez pendues.

> "The carpenters, who came on purpose,
> Had great hatchets suspended from their necks;
> Planes and double-adzes
> Hung at their sides."

Guillaume le Breton, in his Life of Philippe Auguste, calls this dress corium, for it continued till the time of Henry III.

---

[6] See Archreologia, Vol. XIX, p. 187.

[7] Apud Ludewig.

[8] On the trial by wager of battle.

Pectora tot coriis, tot gambesonibus armant.

"So many arm their breasts with coria, so many with gambesons."

The steel armour consists of the flat rings placed contiguously, or the mascles; the former such as had been worn by the Saxons, the latter such as had been adopted by the Danes. It appears to have been extremely heavy, if we may judge from the following anecdote, recorded by William of Poitou, a cotemporary. The Duke of Normandy, after landing at Hastings, went with twenty-five companions to explore the country, but so deep and rugged was the road, that William is praised for having burthened himself with the armour of one of the party, who was unable to reach the camp without putting it off.

The Saxons wore their armour either as a tunic or a cuirass; the Danes as a tunic, which hung over pantaloons, or, more technically speaking, chausses: but the Normans, as depicted in the tapestry, are, for the most part, habited in armour, which forms both breeches and jacket at the same time. This I take to be the liaubergeon, as there are some few specimens of the tunic, or hauberk, and both being mentioned in the Roman de Rou. This opinion is further strengthened by a specimen of this curiously shaped armour existing on a monument in Ireland as late as the time of Edward III. It appears to have been put on by first drawing it on the thighs, where it sits wide, and then putting the arms into the sleeves, which hang loosely, reaching not much below the elbow, as was the case with the Saxon flat-ringed tunic: the hood attached to it was then brought up over the head, and the opening on the chest covered by a square piece, through which were passed straps that fastened behind, hanging down with tasselled terminations, as did also the strap which drew the hood, or capuchon as it was called, tight round the forehead. This is evident in several figures in the tapestry, but the manner in which the armour was put on and fastened, is best shewn where William is arming Harold. The Duke of Normandy is there represented as placing the helmet on the head of the Saxon earl with his left hand, while his right is busied making tight a strap, which is drawn through the rings on the breast of the latter. This circumstance is thus noticed by Robert Wace,[9] in his Roman de Rou, or History of Rollo and his Descendants:

> Quant il fu au Due communez
> Qui ii Aurences done estoit,

---

[9] Wace's father was at the battle of Hastings.

Et en Bretaigne aler vouloit,
Là le fist le Due chevalier
Armes et dras li fist baillier
A lui et k ses compaignons
Puis l'envoya sus les Bretons.

"When Harold was conducted to the Duke's presence,
Who at that time was at Avranches,
And wished to go into Britanny,
The Duke created him in that place a knight:
Arms and clothing he caused to be distributed
To him and his companions,
And then sent him among the Bretons."

No examples of such shaped armour in England occur previously, or in any subsequent reign; but it appears to have been introduced into Ireland, and worn in that country as late as the time of Edward III: nor does any distinguishing name seem to have been applied to it; hence, I conclude, that it is what Waee calls the haubergeon. Describing the conduct and appearance, at the battle of Hastings, of Bishop Odo, the Conqueror's half-brother, he says:

Forment y a ce jour valu
Un haubergeon avoit vestu
Desouz une chemise blanche
Lé en fu le cors et la manche,
Sor un cheval tout blauc seoit
Toute la gent le congnoisscnt
Un baston tenoit en son poing
Faisoit les chevaliers torner
Et la bataille arrester
Souvent les faisoit assaillir
Et souvent les fesoit ferir, &c.

"Acting on that memorable day,
A haubergeon had he put on.
Under a white frock,
Which covered his body and sleeve.
Seated on a milk-white steed,
Every one recognised him.
He held a. baton in his clenched hand;
He made the knights wheel about,
And the line to halt;
Often too he made them attack,

Often he made them strike," &c.

The seal of this prelate is still extant, but the armour on it is not sufficiently distinct to warrant any conclusions.[10]

The Normans probably derived their armour from the Sicilians, as, when they first entered Apulia, a chieftain, who wished for their services, supplied them with arms;[11] and though they no doubt communicated it to the Danes, it does not occur in their delineations before the time of Canute. The Normans, however, had been constantly in the habit of sending for fresh succours from Denmark ever since their settlement in Normandy: these augmented their military population, and, by increasing their warlike energies, made them renowned for their splendid achievements. Wace, in his Metrical History of Normandy,[12] did not let this circumstance escape him. Speaking of Duke Richard, in 1030, he says:

> Richart, ki volt sun dreit tenir
> De Danemarche fist venir
> Dancls, e bons combatturs
> Ki lui firent si grant sucurs.

> "Richard, who was determined to maintain his right,
> Induced Danes to come from
> Denmark, who were good warriors,
> And who afforded him great succours."

The legs of the figures in the tapestry are, generally speaking, bound with bands of different colours, rising out of the shoe in the antient Saxon manner; but in some instances, and where the hauberk is worn, they appear covered with mail to the ankles. Such, however, is the case only with the most distinguished characters, as William, Odo, Eustace, &c. This covering for the legs, according to William of Mahnsbury, was called lieuse, or hose; whence Robert of Normandy, being rather short-legged, we are told by Ordericus Yitalis, his cotemporary,[13] was often called by his father, Court-hose.

The Saxons are depicted as using their long javelins, battle-axes, and swords; while the principal weapon of the Normans is a lance, to which is

---

[10] He is bare-headed, with a mantle at his back, a sword in his hand, and pryck-spurs on his heels. See Archreologia, Vol. I, p. 336.

[11] Gibbon's Decline of thé Roman Empire.

[12] MS. in the Royal library, marked 4, c. 11.

[13] P. 664.

sometimes attached the gonfanon, and sometimes the penon.

These ensigns distinguished the rank of those who bore them, and are thus noticed by Wace:

> Li barons ourcnt gonfanons
> Li chevaliers ourent penons.

> "The barons had gonfanons,
> The knights had penons."

This last-mentioned was a simple streamer, of which the pennoncel, or pennon-ceau is the diminutive. It has been said, indeed, that it is owing to the right of the chief lords to carry the first kind of banner, when they joined their vassals to the armies of their kings, that they derived the title of baron; and that the knights, from their penons, for the same reason were termed bannerets. The bannerets, however, were those knights who were created on the field of battle, while the others were termed bas-clievaliers, inferior knights, corruptedly bachelors.

But besides these, the commander-in-chief had a particular standard generally borne near his person, which was often alluded to under the word gonfanon. This standard occurs several times in the tapestry, but is invariably argent, a cross or, in a bordure azure;[14] but there is neither hint nor trace of the later invention of the Norman leopards. As this banner had been a present from the Pope, who had given the expedition his blessing, the colours were peculiarly applicable to its religious character. The cross, perhaps, was gilt, to convey an idea of its splendour; and put on a white ground, to denote that it had been raised in purity: this, in that superstitious age, might have been contrived in the hope of exciting such an enthusiastic feeling as the revival of the miracle of Constantine: In hoc signo vinces; a relic, however, was added, to give greater efficacy. Thus, Wace observes:

> L'Apostolle li ottria,
> Un gonfanon Ii envoia
> Moult précieux, et chier et bel
> ....anel.
> Si, come il dit, dessus la pierre
> Avoit un des clieveuls Saint Pierre.

> "The Apostolic father worked for him overmuch,
> And sent him a gonfanon,

---

[14] See it represented in the initial letter of this reign.

> Very precious, high-prized, and handsome.
> . . . .
> So, as he said, under the jewel
> Was placed one of the hairs of St. Peter."

The carrying of this standard was considered a high honour, and confided only to a trusty and valiant person of rank. The office, however, seems to have been at this early time hereditary, for the same author thus speaks of William:

> Portez, dit-il, mon gonfanon
> Ne vous veil faire le droit non
> Par droit et par ancessorie
> Devez estre de Normandie
> Et vos parenz gonfanongnier
> Mont furent tint bon chevalier.

> "Bear, said he, my gonfanon:
> I could not deprive you of your due.
> By right and by ancestry
> You should be standard-bearer in Normandy:
> And your parents, as gonfanoniers,
> Were always accounted valiant knights."

Acknowledging this right is a circumstance for which the knight thinks proper thus to thank him:

> Grant merchi, dit-il
> Que nostre droit recongnoissez
> Mes le gonfanon, par ma foy
> Ne sera hui porté par moy.

> "Many thanks, replied he,
> For acknowledging our right:
> But the gonfanon, by my faith,
> Will not this day be borne by me."

He then states his reasons for the refusal; upon which William—

> Donc apela un chevalier
> Que mont avoit oi proisier
> Toustainz Fiz-Rou le Blanc, ont nom
> Au Bec au chans avoit maison;

Le gonfanon li a livrez
Et cil l'en a sceu bon crez
Volontiers la et bel et bien portez
Parfondmcnt l'en a clinez.

"Then called a knight
Who had great prowess,
Toustainz Fitz-Rou the Fair was his name;
In the fields near Bee was his house;
To him he delivered the gonfanon,
And he knew how most suitably
To carry it willingly, well, and handsomely.
Bowing most profoundly."

Harold had his standard also near his person, and on it, according to-Malms-bury, was the figure of a man in combat, woven sumptuously with gold and jewels;[15] though in the tapestry it appears charged with a dragon merely.

Heralt à l'estendart estoit
A son poer se deffendoit
Mez mout estoit de l'œil grevez
Pour ceu qu'il li estoit crevez
A la douleur qu'il sentoit
Du cop de l'œil qui li doloit
Vint un armé par la bataille
Heralt feri sor la ventaille
A terre le fist treshuchier;
A ceu qu'il se vout condrecier
Un chevalier le rabati
Qui en la cuisse le feri
En la cuisse parmi le gros
La plaie fu disi qu'a l'os.
"Harold was at his standard;

He defended himself with all his might,
But much was he pained in the eye,
Because it had been put out."
From the smart which he felt
At a blow in the eye which pained him,
There came a man armed for battle.
And struck Harold on his ventaille;
This made him tumble on the ground,
Though he w'ould have recovered himself;

---

[15] P.I01.

> A knight beat him hack, however,
> Who struck him on the thigh,
> On the fleshy part of the thigh,
> The wound was made down to the bone."

By the ventaille is here meant merely the open part below his helmet, and in front of his hood, by which he received the air. The ventacuhim, or ventaille, strictly speaking, was not at this time invented, but was in full use when Wace lived: he adopts it, therefore, merely for the sake of the rhyme, and as familiar to his countrymen.

The other weapons used by the Normans are maces and long cutting swords, bows and arrows, their main body appearing to be flanked by archers. All those circumstances are noticed in the Roman de Rou. Thus, in describing the preparations for assembling the army, the author tells us, that William—

> Par la contree fist mander.
> Et as vilains dire et crier
> Que o tiex armes corn il ont
> Viengnent à luy ains qu'il porront
> Lors voissiez haster vilains
> Pilx et Machues en lor mains.

> "Throughout the country sent his orders,
> To call upon and proclaim to the villains,
> That with their arms, such as they had,
> They should come to him as speedily as possible:
> Then you might have seen the villains hastening
> With piles and maces in their hands."

And afterwards, recounting the battle, he exclaims:

> La voissiez here assemblée
> Maint coup de lance, et maint d'épée
> Des lances fièrent chevaliers,
> Et o les arz traient archiers
> Et o les pilz vilains lour donnent.

> "There you might have seen a proud assemblage,
> Many thrusts of lances, and many cuts of swords;
> Of lances made by the knights,
> And shots from the bows drawn by the archers,
> And blows from the piles given by the villains."

The pilx et machues were clubs and maces; pil, or pile, being a piece of wood cut smaller at one end than the other, resembling the Irish shillelah:[16] the inachue was something of the same kind, but with a large head. A superior one, probably of iron, appears in the hand of Odo, in the tapestry, and some other equestrian figures,[17] but its adoption by the knights generally was later than the Conquest. The piles and maces were the weapons of the serfs, who were not permitted to make use of the lance and sword,[18] which, in the Conqueror's laws,[19] are expressly called anna libera, "the arms of freemen."

The archers appear variously habited, some with their quivers at the left hip, and others at the left shoulder. The bow as a weapon of war was certainly introduced by the Normans; the Saxons, like the people of Taheite at the present day, using it merely for killing birds. On this account, in the speech which Henry of Huntingdon puts into the Conqueror's mouth before the battle, he makes him stigmatize the Saxons as "a nation not even having arrows." William himself was skilful in archery; and such was his strength, according to Malmsbury,[20] that no one could bend his bow: and others affirm, that, sitting on horseback, he could draw the string of a bow which no other man could bend even on foot.

As Harold fell by an arrow, and the firm phalanx of the Saxons was chiefly broken by this weapon, the bow ever after became a favourite weapon in England. The laws of the Conqueror do not rank it, however, among the arms of a nobleman. All that are required are the following: De relief al cunte, pie al rei afeist: vin chivalz selez e enfrenez, les IIII halbers, et IIII hammes et IIII escuz et IIII lances et IIII espes.[21] "Of the assistance which a count must bring to the king—eight horses saddled and bridled, four hauberks, and four helmets, four shields, four lances, and four swords." This ordinance would mount and equip four knights, and leave four spare horses for light cavalry, for sumpter horses, or to supply the place of such as might be killed. The archers in the tapestry are habited in haubergeons, as it were, of cloth, or in tunics: one appears in the same armour as the cavalry, from

---

[16] It is used as a charge in heraldry, and is there depicted as an inverted obelisk.

[17] It seems to have been derived from the Græco-Romans in Italy, where antient heads of maces are frequently dug up,

[18] The sword was attached by a small belt too short to form a girdle, as may be seen in the initial letter of this reign.

[19] Cap. lxv, de Manumissione Servorum.

[20] P. 112.

[21] Leges Gul. I, c. xxii.

which it may probably be inferred, that he is a knight, or son of some rich baron.

Plate VIII represents the different costumes of the archers and that of a knight on horseback. The mounted figure is in the mascled, and one of the bowmen in the flat-ringed armour.

The Normans placed their chief reliance on their cavalry, while the Saxons depended on the compact masses of their infantry. Normandy indeed furnished, as it still does, most excellent spirited little horses, capable of great fatigue; but William, we are told, preferred the Spanish breed. Thus, on the eve of battle:

> Son bon cheval fist demander
> Ne peust l'en meilleur trouver
> Des Espaigne li ont envée
> Un roi par moult grant amistié
> Armes ne presses ne doubtast
> Se si sires n'esperonnast
> Gautier Gif Tart lour amené
> Qui à Saint Jame avoit esté.

> "He gave orders for his good horse,
> A better than which could not he found.
> From Spain had it been sent
> By a king, who had for him the greatest friendship:
> It feared neither arms nor the press of battle,
> If its riders merely spurred it.
> Walter Giffard brought it with him,
> Who had been at Sant Jago."

From this description it appears to have been an Arabian, or a cross from one. Indeed, we know that breed was in high esteem with the Normans, as Robert Duke of Gloucester, in Stephen's reign, first improved the English horse by the importations of Arabians, with which he stocked his park at Powis Castle.

Not only did the Normans pay attention to their cavalry, but they introduced the art of shoeing horses, as at present practised, into England; for though the Britons had been taught the use of them by the Romans, their pedolau were probably considered too clumsy to be adopted by the Saxons. The Roman horse-shoe, or pedillum, lapped over, and was tied round

PLATE VIII

NORMAN KNIGHT AND ARCHERS.

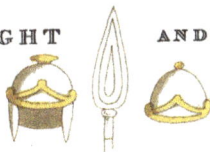

A.D. 1066.

the hoof of the horse, and, therefore, occasioned a rattling sound.[22] All the horses in the tapestry appear shod, but the want of correct drawing in this respect will not allow us thence to determine, whether they were in the Roman or modern fashion.

Henry de Ferrers, or de Ferrariis, who accompanied the Conqueror, took his name, it seems, from having been appointed to superintend the shoeing of the horses, as prsefectus fabrorum, a circumstance which his posterity commemorated in their armorial bearings. William also gave to Simon St. Liz the town of Northampton, with the hundred of Falkley, then valued at £40 per annum, on condition of providing shoes for his horse. We see the infancy of the art in the great value put on the production; and, indeed, so late as the time of Edward I, the rarity of horse-shoes is evident from their being demanded besides the horse. Thus, in the Plac. Cor. 13, Edw. I, we read: Henricus de Averyng tenuit manerium de Morton in com. Essex in capite de dom; rege per serjantium inveniendi unurn hominem cum uno equo precii x *s.* et quatuor ferris equoruin, et uno sacco de coreo, et una brochea ferrea, quotiescunque contigerit dominum regem ire in Walliam cum exercitu sumptibus suis propriis per quadraginta dies. "Henry de Averyng held the manor of Morton, in the county of Essex, in capite of our lord the king, by the sergeantry of finding a man with a horse, value ten shillings, and four horse-shoes, one sack of barley, and one iron buckle, as often as it may happen that our lord the king should go with his army into Wales, at his own proper expense, for forty days."

The Franks in the ninth centuiy used only to shoe their horses in winter, and it is probable that the Normans, in like manner, did not keep their steeds constantly shod. That the mode of fastening the shoes in France was, however, with nails, we learn from the discoveiy of one which belonged to the horse of Childeric, and was found, with many other things, in his grave. This would intimate, that the practice had been continued for about five centuries before the landing of the Normans in England.[23]

The saddles, too, are worthy of remark, being somewhat in the Asiatic style, rising very high before and behind, so as to form curves, differing in this respect from those of the Saxons, which seem to have been little more than a cushion on the horse.[24] The high bow of the saddle occasioned the

---

[22] See the subject amply discussed in the Archoeologia, Vol. III. I have seen one of this kind of horse-shoe, which was found, about eight years ago, at Amblcside, in Cumberland, together with a Roman sword.

[23] See it represented by Montfaucon, Mon. Fran. Tom. I.

[24] See examples of both these kinds in Pl. LXXX.

Conqueror's death; for having burnt the town of Mante, while directing his troops where to spread the conflagration, his horse stepped on some hot ashes, suddenly plunged, and he, having become very corpulent, was struck on the belly; this produced a rupture or an inflammation, which, from the heat of the season and of the fire, was followed by a fever that soon exhibited mortal appearances.[25]

The Norman spurs differed but little from those of the Franks and Saxons: the neck was rather shorter, the pyramidal head rather concave on every side, which afterwards suggested the ring arid spike of the pryck-spur; and the shanks, instead of being straight, curved.[26]

The shield, as depicted in the tapestry[27] and introduced by the Normans, was of a very peculiar form. It has been called heater-shield and kite-shield by modern antiquaries, from its supposed resemblance to those familiar objects, but by the Normans themselves it was merely termed escu, from the Latin scutum. It appears to have been derived, as well as its name, from the Romans, the Danish origin of the Normans seeming to imply that their more antient shield was lunated. This supposition is countenanced by two figures, intended to represent Roulant and Olivier, the paladins of Charlemagne, sculptured on the cathedral church of Verona, which, from other details of costume, there is reason to conclude are rather older than the Conquest.[28] Their shields, however, are not quite so round at top as the Norman. Livy[29] says, that "the shield used by the Samnites was long, and at the lower part cut off towards an acute point." This did not, however, resemble the Norman shield,[30] nor have we any thing to show that it was retained by the Romans after the days of that historian.

In Montfaucon's Antiq. expl.[31] is a representation of Perseus, with his armour lying by him. It appears to be Etruscan; and if the angles of the

---

[25] Malms. 112; Ordo Vit. 656; and Wace.

[26] Original specimens of both kinds are in the armoury of Llewelyn Meyrick, Esq.

[27] See it represented in the initial letter of this reign.

[28] See an engraving of them, inMaffei's Verona Illustrata. One of them has only one leg covered with armour, and wears a hauberk; the other is without any body-armour. There is however, one circumstance which seems to militate against the date I have assigned to them, viz., that Olivier is represented cross-legged: but it is still a question whether that custom originated with the crusades; or, if appropriated to the champions in holy wars, whether that of Charlemagne against the Mahomedans may not come under this denomination.

[29] Lib. IX.

[30] See Pl. VII, and its description in the Introduction.

[31] Vol. I, p. 146.

shield were rounded off we should exactly have the form of the Norman one, though not so large. This leads us to the Greeks,[32] and we find in Sir Wm. Hamilton's collection of Greek and Etruscan vases,[33] one on which is painted the rape of Cassandra, from the temple of Pallas. The companion of Ajax is here represented with one of these heater-shields, but as the top is obscured by the position in which it is held, whether it was curved or straight there are no means to determine. This, however, is the only instance in those four large folio volumes that contain the collection. It appears to have been the original pelta, and if so it would necessarily be rounded at top, for, according to Xenophon, that was in the form of an ivy-leaf, and first used by the Amazons. Thus, like every part of early armour, we find it had an Asiatic origin.

From two Sicilian bronzes, in the museum of Llewelyn Meyriek, Esq., it appears that the kite-shaped shields were used by the inhabitants of the kingdoms of Naples and Sicily, and had, therefore, been retained from their ancestors, the Greek colonists. Now fifty years before the conquest of England the Normans had penetrated those territories; and Melo, the chief of Bari, according to Gibbon, furnished many of them with arms and horses: thirteen years after they founded the city of Aversa, and in about a dozen more they conquered Apulia. The constant intercourse between the Normans in France and their brethren in Italy and Sicily will account for the adoption of similar weapons, whether offensive or defensive. In the tapestry the shields appear to have been at least four feet in length, and not quite two in their greatest breadth. Upon them are seen various devices, but none which may properly be termed heraldic: on no one can a lion, fess, chevron, or other charge of blazonry be found; all that appear are dragons, crosses, and spots: nor do we perceive any particular or distinguished individual twice bearing the same device. The gonfanons and penons attached to the lances are similarly ornamented, with this exception only, that they bear no animals. On a shield held by a Sicilian bronze figure, engraved in Montfaucon's Antiq. expl.,[34] precisely like one of those with the kite-shaped shield already noticed, is a griffin, which seems to indicate that the Normans not only borrowed the form, but also the monsters, for decoration, from the

---

[32] And yet the later Greeks of Constantinople were quite unacquainted with them, for Cinnamus informs us, that the Emperor Manuel Comnenus, on his succession to the throne, taught bis people a new mode of fighting, ordering them in future to use long shields instead of round ones, and to learn the management of long lances like the French.

[33] Neapolitan edition, Vol. III, Pl.LVII.

[34] Tom. IV, Pl. xv.

same source.

While in the tapestry most of the Saxon shields are represented round or oval, with a central boss, as in the illuminations of that people, there is no instance of a Norman with any other than the long kite-shaped one just described.

It was the custom at this period, when a town or castle surrendered, for the principal person to bring and present to the conqueror the keys on the point of a spear. This is depicted in the Bayeux tapestry; and Hollinshed informs us, that when Malcolme, long of Scotland, besieged the castle of Alnwicke, and had reduced the garrison to the last necessity, a young knight, willing to undertake some hardy enterprise in its defence, took a swift horse, and without armour or weapon except a spear in his hand, upon the point of which he bore the keys of the castle, rode into the camp of the enemy, who, supposing he came to surrender them, received him with joy, and unsuspectingly led him to the king. The knight then couched his spear, as if he intended with reverence, to present to him the keys, but, watching his opportunity, he urged on his horse, and ran the point into the eye of the king, killing him on the spot: that done he clapped spurs to his horse, and by his swift flight saved his own life.[35]

With respect to fortifications, the Normans, Saxons, and Welsh used often in cases of necessity to erect forts of wood for immediate use. Verstegan informs us, that William the Conqueror, on his first arrival in England, set up "three castles of wood, which had been made and framed in Normandy," and from thence brought over with him: and Matthew Paris says, that the Saxon warrior Hereward, when he withstood the Conqueror, being in the fenny parts of Cambridgeshire, where he intended to winter, constructed a castle of wood.

But we are not from this to draw our conclusions respecting the military architecture of the Normans: Canterbury, Rochester, Lincoln, Tickell Castle, and others, with Clifford's Tower at York, evince superior skill in the art of defence and masonry during the reign of William the Conqueror. It does not come within the limits of this work to enter into an investigation of this subject, therefore it will be sufficient to notice, that the most antient part of Launceston Castle, in Cornwall, affords a clue to the British mode of fortification: Coningsborougli, Yorkshire, and Castleton, Derbyshire, that of the Saxon heptarchy; Colchester Castle, Essex, that of the reign of Edward, son of Alfred the Great, who first contrived deceptions of weak-

---

[35] History of Scotland, p. 258. He was hence called Pierce-eye, or Percy.

ness to mislead besiegers, and added chapels to fortresses; and Norwich Castle, that of Canute the Dane.

The important protection of the portcullis was introduced by William the Conqueror.

Such was the armour in this reign, and the account of it cannot be better closed than with a description of the battle of Hastings, as that will lay open the military tactics of the Normans and Saxons at this period.

Superstition had much to do with events in those days, and of this commanders, who had superior minds, did not neglect to avail themselves: William, therefore, hung round his neck the relics on which Harold had sworn, and proceeded, in the following manner, to arrange his troops.[36] He drew up his army, which was stationed on an eminence, in three lines, then called batailles: in the front he placed his light infantry, armed with arrows and balista;[37] behind these were the heavy-armed foot; his last division was composed of his cavalry, among whom he stationed himself.

The Saxons had possessed themselves of the hilly ground, which was flanked by a wood. They were chiefly infantry, and drawn up by Harold into an impenetrable wedge. Their large oval shields covered their bodies, while their hands wielded the death-dealing battle-axe. Harold, whose courage was equal to his dignity, quitted his horse to share the danger and the glory on foot; and his brothers, following the example, accompanied him: indeed, the cavalry dismounted, and added to the firm mass of Harold's array. The javelin-men and slingers were in the midst.

Previous to the engagement the Saxon monarch dispatched his spies to reconnoitre, who brought him word that the Normans were an army of priests, a circumstance thus related by Wace:

> Un des Engleiz qui ont veu
> Les Normans tous reis tondus
> Cuida que tous provoires fussent
> Et que messes chanter peussent
> Que tuit erent tondus ct reiz

---

[36] This account is taken principally from William of Poitou, Ordericus Vitalis, and the spirited language in Turner's History of the Anglo-Saxons.

[37] These were probably slings at the end of staves, similar to that in Pl. XVIII. But under this title was comprised the cross-bow, which the Normans derived, with its name, from Italy; for in Domesday Book mention is made of Odo, the arbalester, as a tenant in capite of the king, of lands in Yorkshire. The name shews bim to have been a Norman, and this instànce is sufficient to prove the introduction of the weapon, though the few that may have been used might occasion its not being represented in the Bayeux tapestry.

Ne lour estoit guernon remciz
Cil dist it Heralt que li
Dus Avoit prevoires assez plus
Que chevaliers ni autre gent
De ceu se merveilla forment
Que tuit erent rez et tondus,
Et Heralt li a respondus
Que ce sont chevaliers vaillant
Vassourmout tiers, mout combattant
N'ont mié barbe ni guernons
Ce dist Heralt, com nos avons.

"One of the English, who had seen
The Normans all shaven and shorn,
Thought that they were all priests,
And could chaunt masses;
That all were shaven and shorn,
Not having mustachios left.
This he told to Harold, that the duke
Had far more priests
Than knights or other troops;
At which he wondered, seeing
That all were shaven and shorn.
Rut Harold answered him,
That these were valiant knights,
Vassals very fierce and warlike,
'Notwithstanding they have not beards nor mustachios,'
Says Harold, 'as we have.' "

In the tapestry, however, the Normans have mustachios, but no beards, and appear with the crowns of their heads shaven, in a manner that, in some degree, resembles the clerical tonsure. This is a circumstance which proves the antiquity of the tapestry, as, in the next age, the hair in all illuminations appears flowing. The Normans may have derived this custom from the manners of Sicily, it having been, as we learn from Polyænus, a Greek fashion. He says,[38] that Theseus, in his battles, used always to have the fore part of his head shaved, (as have the Normans in the tapestry,) to prevent the enemy's advantage of seizing him by the hair: his example was followed by all the Greeks, and that sort of tonsure was from him called theseis. But those who were particularly distin guished for this imitation of Theseus were the Abantes, whom Homer thus characterizes:

[38] In his Stratagems, Lib. I.

"......... their foreheads bare,
Down their broad shoulders flowed a length of hair."

At the time of the Norman invasion, and, indeed, in periods more remote, it was usual to commence the attack with a war song. The Britons had
their Arymes Ynys Prydain, "Armed Confederacy of Britainand the Saxons
their Song of Odin. The battle of Hastings was commenced by one Taille-
fer, who, singing the song of Roland and Charlemagne, rode forward and
killed a Saxon ensign-bearer; another likewise became his victim; a third
overpowered him, and then the armies joined.[39] The cry of the Normans
was, "God help us!" the Saxons exclaimed, "The holy Cross!" "The Cross of
God!" The Norman foot advancing dis charged their missile weapons with
effect, but the Saxons with patient valour kept their ground.

They returned to the attack with spears and lances; with their antient
weapons, the terrible battle-axes; and with stones, whose falling masses
were directed to overwhelm. The battle glowed. Distant weapons were
abandoned for a closer conflict. The clamour of the engaging soldiers was
drowned in the. clashing of their weapons and the groans of the dying.
Valour abounded on both sides, and the chieftains fought with all the desperate firmness of personal enmity and ardent ambition. Befriended by the
elevation of their ground, by the mass of their phalanx, and by their axes,
which cut through all the armour of their adversaries, the undaunted Saxons not merely sustained but repelled every attack. Intimidated by such invincible fortitude, the foot and cavalry of Bretagne, and all the other allies
of William in the left wing, gave way. The impression extended along all the
line. It was increased by a rumour that the duke had fallen. Dismay began
to unnerve his army, and a general fight seemed about to ensue. William,
observing the critical moment which threatened destruction to all his glory,
rushed among the fugitives, striking or menacing them with his spear, and
lifting up his helmet shewed them the countenance of their leader.

Having rallied he led them to another onset. His sword strewed his
path with slaughter. Their valour and their hopes revived. Their charge on
their pursuers was destruction—they rushed impetuously on the rest. But
the main body of the Saxons continued unmoved and impenetrable: all the
fury of the Normans and their allies could force no opening: an unbroken
wall of courageous soldiery was every where present.

Depressed by this resistance William's mind was roused to attempt a

---

[39] Roman de Rou; Hen. Hunt. 368; Radulp. Dicet. 480; and Brompton, 960..

stratagem. He had seen the success with which his rallied troops had turned upon those vTho pursued them. He resolved to hazard a feigned retreat to seduce the Saxons into the disorder of a confident pursuit, and to profit by their diffusion. A body of a thousand horse vrere entrusted with the execution of this manoeuvre. With a horrible outcry they rushed npon the Saxons, then suddenly checking themselves, as if intimidated, they affected a hasty flight. The Saxons were cheated. They threw themselves eagerly on the retreating Normans, and at first they prospered, for the Normans retired upon a ditch or ravine, somewhat concealed by its vegetation: driven upon this, great numbers perished, and some of the Saxons wrere dragged into the ruin.

But while this incident was occupying their attention, the duke's main body rushed between the pursuers and the rest of the army. The Saxons endeavoured to regain their position; the cavalry turned upon them, and thus enclosed they fell victims to the skilful movement of their opponents. Twice had the Norman artifice repeated, and twice had the Saxons to recover this credulous pursuit.

It appears strange that the Saxons should have been deceived by this stratagem, so frequently adopted, that even they themselves had put it in practice against the Norwegian forces not a fortnight before. Probably, it was owing to the first Norman retreat not being feigned, that they were off their guard when William adopted it as a ruse de guerre.

In the heat of the struggle twenty Normans pledged themselves to each other to attack in conjunction the great standard of Harold. Eying the expected prize, they rushed impetuously towards it. In attempting to penetrate through the hostile battalions many of the party fell, but their object not having been foreseen the survivors secured it.

The sun was departing from the western horizon, and the victory was still undecided. While Harold lived and fought, his valorous countrymen were invincible; but an order of the duke's, by occasioning his fate, gained the splendid laurel. To harass the hinder ranks of that firm mass which he could not by his front attack destroy, he directed his archers not to shoot horizontally at the Saxons, but to discharge their arrows vigorously upwards. Those fell with fatal effect on the more distant troops. The random shafts descended like impetuous hail, and one of them pierced the gallant Harold in the eye. A furious charge of the Norman horse increased the disorder which the king's wound must have occasioned; his pain disabled him, and he was mortally wounded. Panic scattered the Saxons on their leader's death. The Normans vigorously pursued, though the broken ground and frequent ditches checked their ardour. Encouraged by observing this, a part of the fugitives rallied, and, indignant at the prospect of surrendering their country to foreigners, they sought to renew the combat. William ordered Count Eustace and his soldiers to the attack. The count exposed the peril, and advised a retreat: he was at this instant vehemently struck in his neck, and his face was covered with his blood. The duke, undismayed, led on his men to the conflict. Some of his noblest Normans fell, but he completed his hard-earned victory.

William Rufus.

1087.

HE Armour of this reign remained precisely the same as in that of the Conqueror, and we have no new specimen of any part except the chapel de fer. This appears on the seal of Rufus,[1] and exactly resembles a Tartar cap, being a cone which projects beyond the head.

It is somewhat curious, that on a very antient cup, presented to the French King St. Louis, and still preserved in the castle of Vincennes, Haroun al Raschid is represented as wearing one, as well as such officers of his court as are in armour. Besides this chapel de fer, the king of England is exhibited in a corium,[2] to which there is a hood: his shield is like the Conqueror's, except that it has an ornamental border, and in his right hand is a gonfanon.

A Welsh MS. History of the Life of Grufydd ab Cynan, king of North Wales, who was cotemporary with Rufus and Henry I, and which appears to have been written but just after his death, calls Rufus Gwylim Cleddyv-hîr, or William Long-sword, which Norman peculiarity is in the tapestry, and continued during this reign. From this manuscript we learn that the people of South Wales fought with staves, to which were attached iron balls covered with spikes, while those of North M ales had only swords and shields.

---

[1] It is represented at the foot of PI. x.

[2] This kind of body-armour appears on one of the figures in PI. xxiv.

This singular weapon, afterwards termed a moming-star,[3] and continued in use till a very late period, was probably introduced by the Normans; and it may be that it is designated by Wace under the word pilx, Lacombe considering that word as nearly allied to peloton. One of the figures before leferred to, as being on the front of the cathedral church of Verona, which is intended to represent Olivier, is thus armed; and on a font, in Waiulsford church, Northamptonshire, if not of the time of Rufus, certainly not much later, there are two figures, one of which is in the Norman hauberk, has the kite-shaped shield, and is fighting with a morning-star.[4]

Weapons of this kind were, till within the last thirty years, carried hy the pioneers of the Honourable Artillery Company, and had, probably, belonged to that corps from their first establishment, as they resemble some of Henry the Eighth's time, in the armoury of Llewelyn Meyrick, Esq. Father Daniel[5] has given the engravings of two, shewn in the abbey of Roncevaux, as the arms of Roland and Olivier, not much unlike that represented on the cathedral of Verona; but as they are of a more finished kind, and the handles straight instead of curved like that, a much later date than even the time of Rufus must be assigned to them. The staves, or handles, of these are like the carving at Verona, about two feet in length, or rather more, while those in my son's collection, and those which belonged to the Honourable Artillery Company, are at least five, and their chains still more. One of those, at Roncevaux, has merely a large ball of iron without spikes, but fastened with three chains to its staff; the other one of mixed metal, in the form of a channelled melon, weighing, like the former, eight pounds, is also connected with its handle by a triple chain. In general the ball is held by a single one. At the end of both those staves are rings for affixing cords or leathers to fasten them to the hand.

The Welsh, during this reign, used arrows and javelins as missile weapons,[6] which last only were employed by the Irish.

On the brass-work of the antient cover of an Irish manuscript, apparently of the tenth century,[7] are embossed two warriors, one of which is in a tunic, with a scull-cap, and an ornament hanging down from its top: he holds in his right hand a javelin, and in his left a circular convex shield, with

---

[3] Or morgan stern, according to Monro.

[4] The other has a kite-shaped shield and a mace. See Archreologia. They are both represented in the initial letter to this reign.

[5] Milice Fran.

[6] Ord. Vital. and the Hanes Grufydd ab Cynan,

[7] Exhibited to the Society of Antiquaries about three years ago.

a boss in its centre, much like those used by the Anglo-Saxons. The other has a tunic, and over this on his breast a pectoral, a scullcap on his head, and is represented in the attitude of drawing his short sword.

We learn from the Bayeux tapestry, that crosses, at the time of the Conquest, were the principal ornaments of the Norman shields; and the success of that expedition, undertaken under the banner of the cross, no doubt principally contributed to bring that emblem into general fashion. Hence, one of his barons telling Rufus, that he had taken up the cross, that is, embarked in a crusade, added, that "he would mark it on his shield, his helmet, his saddle, and his horses, and thus become the soldier of Christ."[8]

Armorial bearings on the shields do not occur in England during this reign; and yet Snorre Sturlson, in his Edda, would have us believe that the Norwegians used them at this time. He tells us, that when Magnus Berfetta, or Barefeet, the son of Olaf-Kyrre, who succeeded his father on the Norwegian throne in 1093, invaded Ireland,[9] he was thus attired: "He put on his helmet, braced his red shield on which was a golden lion, and took his favourite sword, called leg-biter, and his battle-axe, and threw over his coat of mail his red silk vest, on which appeared a yellow lion, that the king might be conspicuous." Snorre, however, habited him according to his fancy, and therefore arrayed him in the habiliments of his own time. Surcoats in England were not worn before the reign of Henry II, did not become general till the time of John, and had not armorial bearings till that of Henry III. But there is a seal among those of the Earls of Flanders, attributed to Robert Friso, who lived in 1071, on which he is represented as habited in a surcoat,[10] and having a shield on which is his device.[11]

During this reign nothing was worn over the armour, but that continued to be formed of máseles, or flat rings, placed contiguously on cloth, stag or elk skin. Máseles, or macles, have derived their name from the latin word macula, which signifies the mesh of a net.[12] The term is heraldic, but the celebrated Du Cange[13] unites in opinion with other French writers, that the colours, furs, and many of the charges in heraldry, have derived their names from the habiliments worn by the knights. Edmondson[14] says, the másele

---

[8] Ordo Vital. p. 769.
[9] This invasion was in the time of Henry I.
[10] It is also the case in Plate IX, but this is a very rare instance.
[11] The authenticity of this is much to be doubted.
[12] Cicero 7, in Vetr. Statius, Lib. II, Theb.
[13] In his Dissertation on Joinville's History of St. Louis.
[14] In his Body of Heraldry, Vol. II.

is like the lozenge in shape, but distinguished from it by being always perforated. Johannes de Janua interprets macula, by squamma loríese, and tells
us it was a small angular piece of iron, with a hole through it, of which hauberks were made: these were so worked one on the other that there were not
any openings left between them; and from Edmondson we further learn,
that in heraldry many were borne together, and sometimes so as to cover
the field.[15] Nicholas de Braya thus notices them in his Life of Louis VIII:

> Nexilibus maclis vestis distincta notatur.

> "By its interwoven macles bis hauberk is conspicuously marked."

Guillaume le Breton, in the second book of his Philippics, speaks of it:

> .... inter
> Pectus et ora fidit maculas toracis.

> ".......... between
> His breast and moutb he cleaved the macles of his thorax—"

alluding to that part of the armour which was at first part of the hauberk,
but afterwards separate from it, and called the capuclion, or hood. He again
says:—

> Restilit uncino maculis haerente plicatis.

> "He stood his ground, although an oucin was sticking in the overlapping macles."

The oucin was a staff, with a hooked iron head, somewhat like one horn
of a pickaxe, whose use was very serviceable for striking through the apertures of the macles.

The liaubergeon, consisting of jacket and breeches attached, which had
been introduced at the Conquest, was no longer generally used, but instead, the hauberk came more into fashion. This was a tunic, or frock, with
wide sleeves reaching a little below the elbows, terminating with a broad
gilt border, and having a hood not separate. In a manuscript Life of Christ,
prefixed to a Latin and Franco-Norman version of the Psalms, in the Cotton Library,[16] there is a soldier thus habited, the hauberk having on it flat
contiguous rings; underneath it is a red tunic, the sleeves of which reach to

---

[15] In this manner they are represented in the under shield at the foot of Plate IX.
16 Marked Nero, C IV,

his wrists: there is no armour on his legs, but he wears boots that come as high as the calves. In general the hauberks were slit up before and behind for the convenience of riding, but in this figure these openings are at the sides: it seems also to have been made to fit close to the body, and the skirts afterwards added.

The sword appears worn on the right side, there being a hole made just above the hip to insert the scabbard, the lower part of which comes through the side opening: it is long and straight as during the last reign; and the figure wears the nasal helmet. There does not appear any thing like a sword-belt during the time of the first two Williams, and if such was at all used, it was completely concealed by the hauberk.[17] The hauberk, which was of German origin, was probably derived from hauen, "to hew or cutand berg, "a defence," that is, a protection against cuts and stabs.

The representations of warriors either in the tapestry or seals of this period do not exhibit them with the long pointed toe, which was curved down to prevent the foot slipping out of the stirrup; and yet those Franks who passed into Greece, according to Anna Comnena, had rendered them-selves remarkable for this fashion. She tells us,[18] that the Emperor Alexius had been taught by experience, that the formidable cavalry of the Franks, when dismounted, was unfit for action, and almost incapable of motion; he, therefore, directed his archers to aim their arrows at the horse rath-er than the man, and had a variety of spikes and snares scattered over the ground on which he might expect an attack: the knights, when unhorsed, were so encumbered by their projecting toes,[19] that they were then more readily overcome.

William II was a great encourager of military renown, for he never heard a knight praised for his prowess without enrolling him in his service. Thus, we read:

---

[17] In the Bayeux tapestry, where Harold is represented as approacbing Wido, he is depicted as having unbuckled his sword, and holding it out to be, delivered up: one of bis attendants is doing tbe same, it being a ceremony on requiring hospitality. Sbort straps ap-pear attaohed to these, such as migbt serve to fasten them to tbe side, but not such as would reach round the body. See sucb represented in the initial letter to the reign of William I.

[18] Alexias, Lib. v. p. 140.

[19] The long pointed toes she calls των πεδιλῶν προαλματα, which Du Cange rightly considers should be thus translated, while others have most thoughtlessly termed them the spurs. The spikes were the caltraps. The Greeks had the greater part of their infantry archers, great encouragement having been given to the long bow by the Emperor Leo, the Armenian, as may be seen in his Tactics.

Li Reis ros fu de grant noblesce
Proz, et de mult grant largesce
N'oist de chevalier parler,
Qui de proesse oist loer
Qui en son brief escrit ne fust
Et qui par an del soien n'eust.

"King Rufus possessed great nobleness,
Was valiant, and of great bounty:
He never heard mention made of a knight,
Whom he heard praised for his prowess,
Without having him enrolled in his muster-list,
And who was not sought without care."

Indeed, the king himself, as Mr. Turner has observed, was an example of chivalry in its rudest state, while the Black Prince exhibited it in its fullest perfection. What was considered a skilful warrior at this period we may learn from the Roman d'Alexandre.

Hardis et de fin cuer pour grant fés endurer
Et plusque nus des autres ce savoit bien borter
Couvrir de son escu, de son espie jeter.

"Bold, and stout of heart for enduring great feats;
And, almost uncovered, knows well how to thrust with others,
To cover himself with his shield, and to hurl his spear."

Knight-errantry had its origin in the reign of this king, who, as an encouragement to military prowess, had unwarrantably permitted his young knights and squires to amuse themselves with plundering persons and their estates.[20] Many of better principles, who panted for the renown of valorous exploits, undertook to redress their grievances, and as there were always tyrannical barons to be conquered, and captives to be released, they travelled in search of such adventures. Knights were the disciplined and effective soldiery of the day: they were the only part of the military that were completely armed; and their skill and power in the use of their weapons made their exertions the usual means of victory. Hence, the abbots of St. Albans gave a part of their manors to have knights engaged to watch the roads, and keep them safe from all assailants.[21]

Knights were usually persons of birth, but not always so, the lower

---

[20] Ordo Vit. 680.
[21] Mat. Paris. Abb. Alb. 45,46.

ranks being sometimes raised to the honour for extraordinary valour. Thus Rufus knighted the soldier that had unhorsed him. On that occasion the king fought bravely on foot after his horse had been killed, till his armour was pierced, and he was thrown to the ground.[22]

The constitutional military force of the kingdom consisted of the feudal troops, who owed suit or service for their different portions of land, called knights' fees, and the posse comitatus. The feudal troops were either the persons who held lands in capite, that is, immediately of the crown, or their vassals and undertenants, both of whom were obliged, by their tenures, not only to attend their lords in their own respective quarrels, but also the king to the wars at home and abroad, completely armed and mounted, for different periods, up to forty days in a year, according to the value of the fees they held. Matthew Paris tells us, that Rufus, wanting on a sudden emergency to draw together a body of forces, sent word to such as held of him in fee, that all who refused to repair to his assistance should be stigmatized with the odious name of nithing, which he says in Latin, nequam sonat; and immediately incredible numbers flocked to him from all quarters.

The posse comitatûs, or power of the county, included every freeman above the age of fifteen, and under that of sixty; and although the chief destination of this establishment was to preserve the peace, under the command of the sheriff, they were also, in case of hostile invasions, summoned to defend the country, and repel the enemy. They differed from the feudal troops in being only liable to be called out in case of internal commotions or actual invasions: on such occasions only could they be legally marched out of their respective counties, whereas the others were subject to foreign service.

Not much advance was made during this reign in the science of military architecture, but Trematon Castle, in Cornwall, and the keep of Tunbridge[23] and Rochester Castles, Kent, may be considered as specimens.

---

[22] Malmsb. 121.

[23] The castle of St. Angelo, at Rome, was probably the original from which the Normans copied their round towers, as that of Norwich was for their square ones.

Henry the First.

1100.

UTHORITIES begin to multiply during this century, so that we are able more fully to investigate the Armour of this reign than of the one preceding. An illuminated manuscript Psalter, written about this time, in the possession of F. Douce, Esq., presents to us a military figure completely armed, except his shield.[1] The hauberk in this instance, as before, is, with its hood, of the same piece, but with sleeves fitting close to the arms, terminating with gloves, manakins, or mufflers, which cover the outsides of the hands and fingers; it also reaches to the knees, and is terminated with a broad gilt border. The shoes and hose of the former reigns, it appears by this figure, were now abandoned for coverings for the feet and legs made all in one, which were called chausses, and fitted close like modern pantaloons, fastening over the soles with straps. The helmet, instead of being exactly conical, has its apex in a line with the nasal, similar in shape to that on the seal of Stephen.

The blade of the spear, which seems ornamented with fluted work somewhat in the manner of the Asiatic daggers, appears to be at least eight inches broad and twelve or fourteen long, being of the kite-shape invert-

---

[1] This has been engraved by Mr. Strutt, in his Dress and Habits of the People of England.

ed,[2] the jagged or barbed kind used by the Saxons having gone quite out of fashion. In Mr. Gwennap's collection of armour, formerly exhibited in Pall Mall, there was a leaf-shaped spear-head, twenty-two inches long and six broad, which, as the iron is extremely corroded by age, and as such large bladed lances were not used in later times, may perhaps be assigned to this reign. The hooded hauberk and chausses of this figure are covered with mascles. He is also armed with a long sword like those of the Conqueror's and Rufus's time, and like them it has a straight guard.

John, a monk of Mairemoustier, in Touraine, who was cotemporary with Geoffry Plantagenet, that married the daughter of Henry I, gives a very full description of his armour. He says: "When Geoffry Duke of Normandy was knighted, his anus were brought to him, and he was invested with an incomparable hauberk, (lorica incomparabile,) wrought with mascles (maclis)[3] of iron, so closely interwoven that it was impenetrable to the point of the lance or the arrow; the chausses, made also in like manner, with mascles,[4] were then given to him, and a pair of gilt spurs were put on his feet: this done, a shield was hung upon his neck, ornamented with lions of gold; a helmet, richly decorated with precious stones, and so well tempered that no sword could make any impression upon it, was set upon his head; a lance was then brought him, made of oak, and surmounted with a head of Poictou iron; and, lastly, a sword from the royal treasury. Thus armed he mounted a Spanish horse, which was also given him by the king; and the festival which appertained to his reception of this dignity was called festum tyrocinii, and was honoured with tournaments and masks, which lasted no less than seven days."

The shield, sword, and helmet may be seen Pl. LXVII, Tom. I, of Montfaucon's Monarchie Françoise, which represents his effigy on a beautiful enamelled copper, still existing in France. The helmet is in form something approaching to the Saxon or Phrygian cap, and on the side which is shewn it is charged with a lion: the rest of the armour appears to have been precisely like that before described on the figure in Mr. Douce's Psalter. The shape of the shield at this period was, in this as well as other instances, as long as in the Conqueror's time, but was made to curve considerably more round the body. In a MS. in the British Museum,[5] there is a warrior holding three

---

[2] See it represented at the foot of Pl. VIII, between the helmets,

[3] See my observations on this passage in a paper sent to the Society of Antiquaries, and printed ill the Archoeologia, Vol. XIX.

[4] In the Bayeux tapestry some of the mascles are square instead of lozenge-shaped.

[5] Bibl. Cotto Nero, C IV.

PLATE IX

A KNIGHT performing HOMAGE.

A.D. 1100.

spears, with a long curved shield exactly like this: he wears a nasal helmet, and a hauberk with tight sleeves, his legs bare, and cross garterings up to the calves. The curved shape, however, of Geoffry's shield prevents our accurately ascertaining the number of lions on the field, which is blue; only four appear, but in all probability there were six, and as on that of his illegitimate grandson William Longespee.[6]

This shield is, however, most interesting, as affording one of the earliest specimens of heraldic bearings, at least such as became hereditary: besides this, it is furnished with a boss in the centre, which does not occur on those in the seals of our kings till that of Richard I. About this time the practice of suspending the shield from the neck by a strap came into general use. There is great reason to think that it was introduced at the Conquest; yet in only' one figure on the tapestry can we find any thing to confirm this opinion. Where William is represented as crossing the water with an army to attack Conan, there is a knight thrown from his horse, and his shield, that is falling from him, has a belt, which seems to have been for the purpose of hanging round his neck. Whether the belt was then used for that purpose, or merely to twist round the arm, the shield being held by cross cords, as practised by the Mamelukes of the present day, is by no means reduced to a certainty. The Normans, however, undoubtedly introduced the practice, as it was wholly unknown to the Britons and Saxons, though it does not appear on the seals of the English kings till that of Stephen.

On the seal of Henry I is the first representation of a saddle-cloth, and either during that reign or the preceding one, the high peak behind the saddle was altered for a back of greater breadth.

What the real armour is on this seal is not so easily decided. In Speed's and Sandford's engravings it looks like the rustred; but in that given in the new edition of the Foedera, as a bad representation of the ringed. The form of the rustred armour seems, indeed, to have grown out of the ringed, it being nothing more than one row of flat rings, about double the usual size, laid half over the other, so that two in the upper partially covered one below. For the name we are indebted to the vocabulary of our antient heralds, who, in the exuberance of their fancy, have transmitted it to us as forming one of the charges of blazonry. The rustre may be seen in Fig. 70 and 71, of the fourteenth plate to the second volume of Edmondson's Heraldry;[7] and

---

[6] See Pl. XVI.

[7] It is also given in the upper shield at the foot of Plate IX of this work.

the term, though omitted in his Dictionary, will be found in French works on the same subject. That many bearings in blazonry arose from the adoption of the different parts of the habiliments and equipments of the knights has been observed, and that it was so in the case of the rustre is evident, by comparing that charge with a carving in ivory, represented Pl. xxxii, Fig. 1, of the first volume of the Monarchie Françoise: this is, indeed, so interesting a specimen, that it has furnished the materials for Pl. ix. The knight, who is performing his homage to his feudal lord, is habited in a rustred haubergeon, the form of which is that of the Conqueror's time, terminating as it does in breeches; the surcoat, however, which is thrown over this, and the costume of the prince or nobleman, would place it later than the reiga of Henry I, but the form of the throne is that of the Franks and Saxons: probably, therefore, by avoiding these extremes, and placing it under this reign, which is countenanced by other early examples of the surcoat,[8] we may be about right. The knight is without his helmet, but his chaperon and hose, which cover also his feet, are composed apparently of four leather bands woven cross-wise with four others, a circumstance, as far as my researches have gone, unique.[9] The chaperon, or hood, is of course separate from the liaubergeon, and from this time that continued to be the case. The warrior is kneeling on one knee, and about to kiss the foot of his liege lord, holding one hand up, and the sword, with its point downwards, in the other. This was the antient ceremony attending feudal homage. When the French king granted to Rollo the Dane the territory in his dominions, from that time called Normandy, the condition was that it should be held by feudal homage: but when the ceremony was stated, the proud warrior exclaimed, "I will never bend my knees to the knees of any man, nor kiss any man's foot and it was forced to be performed by substitute.[10]

The next species of armour which occurs during this reign is the scaled, which appears on the seal of Alexander I, king of Scotland, who ascended the throne in 1107, and seems, from similar sources, to have been worn by his two successors.

Imitations of the natural protections of fish had been early adopted in the East as coverings for defence, and had been copied by the Greeks, Etruscans, and Romans, as well as the Dacians and Sarmati, but do not seem

---

[8] Those,.for instance, of Robert Friso Earl of Flanders and Richard de Basset.

[9] On the monument of Gronw ap Iorwerth, however, in Gresford Church, Denbighshire, of the time of Bdward II, the manakin; or glove; is formed in the same manner.

[10] Dudo, p, 84; and Gemmeticensis, p. 231.

to have been followed in this island earlier than the twelfth century.[11] Johannes de Janua calls this armour lorica squammata, the name by which it was known to the antients.

The hauberk of Alexander is a tunic, with wide sleeves, the body of which has been made to fit close, and the skirt subsequently attached. The hood is not separate from the hauberk, but appears to sit loosely on the head, over which is placed a chapel de fer, with a nasal.[12]

The Scotch seals also furnish us with another species of armour during this reign, and that is the trellissed. It might be supposed that this word refers to hauberks made threefold, but the import of it being also lattice-work, and finding that kind of armour without a name, it seems identified by this title. It appears in the seal of David Earl of Huntingdon, who was afterwards king of Scotland. His armour resembles a cuirass with sleeves, such as is depicted in Saxon illuminations, instead of the Norman haubergeon with breeches attached, or the long hauberk; and below it is seen the skirt of the tunic, or under garment. The shape, however, is not so curious as the formation of it. It is made like a vest, with straps of leather laid upon it, and crossing in opposite directions; these, by passing over each other, leave large intervening squares placed angularly, in the centre of each of which appears a round knob, or stud of steel. That the straps were leather and the studs steel is determined by an illumination in the Bodleian library,[13] which has furnished the subject of a future plate.[14] The tunic was of cloth, and, in all probability, a small plate of iron was fastened within by each stud,[15] while the leather straps were intended to cover the parts at which they met.

This kind of armour seems, therefore, to be what the early Norman writers termed trellissed, and the shape of the cuirass that which they called broigne. The writers of the middle ages manifestly derived this latter word from some gothic source, as the terms brunia, brunea, bronia, brugna, and bruna, occur principally in the Latin documents relating to Charlemagne. Indeed, we may discover in it the Saxon Býɲɲ, or Býɲɳ, and this is further confirmed by the Saxon connexion of the Earl of Huntingdon.[16] The trellis

---

[11] The "scaly mail," which Aneurin attributes to Hengist, was an imitation of a Roman cuirass.

[12] See Plate x.

[13] Marked 86. Arch B.

[14] Plate xxiv.

[15] Such diamond-shaped plates, perforated in the centre, are made a charge in French blazonry, and this bearing is termed, by their heralds, "Pampelonné."

[16] He was the sun of Malcolm Canmore, king of Scotland, who married Margaret, the sister of Edgar Etheling.

PLATE X

ALEXANDER 1ST   KING of SCOTLAND.

A.D 1107.

work we find formed after the same design as the cross-gartering observable on the legs of the Saxon youths in many illuminated MSS. of that people, and which had been adopted in imitation of the protecting hay-bands worn by their rude ancestors. This light armour appears to have been also copied by the Normans, for their poets repeatedly speak of it. Thus, in the Roman de Garin we have:

En son dos vest une broigne trelice.

"On his back he wears a trellissed broigne."

Again—

L'escu li perce, s'a la broigne faussée

"The shield he pierces, and even the broigne is broken."

Again—

Et mainte broigne percier et cstroer,

"And many a broigne to pierce and cleave."

In the Roman de Rou occurs:

Des haubers, et des broignes mainte male faussée.

"Of hauberks and broignes a great number were badly broken."

And in the Roman de Gaydon:

L'escu li perce, et la broigne treslit.

"His shield was pierced, and his trellisscd broigne."

Sometimes, indeed, these broignes were highly ornamented; hence, we read in the Roman de Roncevaux:

Là veist-on tante broigne saffrée.

"There might be seen such an embroidered broigne."

Such it is that is represented in Plate XI.

Besides these various kinds of body-armour, there were introduced some novelties in the covering for the head.

In addition to the nasal chapel de fer, or wide iron conical cap, as well as the nasal heaume, or conical helmet, with its apex in a line with the nasal, antient writers speak of the chap de mailles, or cap of mail. This appears represented in a drawing of Sir Richard Basset, on a deed of his.[17]

It is a high cap, tapering towards its apex, but not pointed, and composed, like the hauberk and chausses, of rings set edgewise.[18] The shield which he holds is not only kite-shaped, but notched at top like the hearts in a pack of cards. Besides this, we have the first attempt at a moveable vizor, and it seems evidently imitated from the antient Roman sculpture. This occurs on the seal of Ranulph Earl of Chester.[19] It is perforated, and the helmet has attached to it cheek-pieces, hollowed out under the eye so that they may almost approach the nose. This seal further affords the earliest specimen of the long pointed toe used by the knights, and which Gibbon supposes is that which Anna Comnena alludes to in the expression τῶν πεδιλᾶν προαλματα His spur too has a spear-shaped head, though it is rather leaf-like than pyramidal, nor are the shanks straight,[20] as was the case with those worn by the Saxons. The monumental effigy of William of Normandy, Earl of Flanders, the nephew of Henry I, exhibits an invention for the face somewhat of this sort.[21] His helmet is of the pot kind, such as became more general under King John, but his face is guarded by a plate, which is hollowed out for his nose, eyes, and mouth. The earliest pot liehnet, however, is probably that of Charles the Good, Earl of Flanders, in 1122.[22]

There is, in Gloucester Cathedral, a wooden monument of a knight cross legged, with a coronet on his head, which is attributed to Robert Duke of Normandy, the eldest son of the Conqueror; but though he died

---

[17] See Antiquarian Repertory.
[18] See it represented at the bottom of Plate X.
[19] See Archoeologia, Vol. IV, Plate CXX; and the base of Plate XI of this work.
[20] My son has one of these early Norman spurs in his possession.
[21] See at the foot of Plate XI.
[22] See the seal in Olivarius Vredius, p. 11.

in this reign, such a period would be too early to assign for the sculpture. If, indeed, it was intended to represent this unfortunate prince, it can, nevertheless, by no means be attributed to an earlier date than the reign of his nephew Henry II.

Archery seems to have been much cultivated from the time of the Conquest, and great numbers of bowmen constantly brought into the field. To encourage its practice, a law was made during this reign, which freed from the charge of murder any one who, in practising with arrows or darts, should kill a person standing near.[23] This appears to be the first regulation to be found in our annals, and was probably founded on the old law of Rome.

The cross-bow seems to have been used principally in the chase, for Wace adds to Rufus's death[24] a strange stoiy, that Henry, going that day to the New Forest, found the string of his cross-bow broken, and taking it to a villain to be mended, met an old woman there, who told him that he would be a king.

From this same author we learn, that the infantry at this period were armed, some with sharp-headed lances and guisanns,[25] for in the Roman de Rou are the following lines:

> Et vous avez lances agues
> Et guisarmes bien emollues.

> "And you have sharp-headed lances,
> And guisarmes very destructive."

Grose[26] conceives, that the weapon termed launceguay, which is mentioned in several statutes, made during the reign of Richard II, was the same as the lance-ague, being merely a corruption of it. The gisarm has puzzled several commentators. The Rev. Mr. Lamb, who edited the poem of Flodden Field, says, "Gisarings, (halberts,) from the French guisanne, a kind of offensive long handled and long headed weapon, or as the Spanish visarma, a staff, that has within two long pikes, which, with a shoot or thrust forward, come forth." In the armoury of Llewelyn Meyrick, Esq., are two of the last described weapons, which came from Genoa, but they throw out

---

[23] Si quis Iudo sagittandi, vel alicujus exercitii jaculo, vel hujusmodi casu aliquem occidat, reddat, &c. Laws of Hen. I, eh. 88, Cambo edit. 1644.

[24] MS. in the Royal library in the British Museum.

[25] Called also guysarmes, gisarms, jaisarmes, and jusarmes.

[26] Treatise on Antient Armour.

PLATE XI

DAVID EARL OF  HUNTINGDON.

A.D. 1120.

three spikes, and are about three feet in length each. These weapons canliot, however, be the gisanne, for the passage Mr. Lamb by this note endeavours to illustrate is the following:

> "Some their grisly gisarings grind."

Grinding being rather more applicable to an edged than a pointed weapon: he seems more correct while considering it a kind of halbert.

Lacombe, in his Supplement to the Dictionnaire du Vieux Langage François, says, the gisanne is a sort of lance, or pike: and Bailey defines it to be a military weapon, with two points, or pikes. Strutt, in his Horda Angel-cynnan, represents it as a battle-axe on a long staif, with a pike projecting from the back of the axe. One thing is certain, that it had a blade, from the term "grind," in the poem of Flodden Field; and from the following passage of Gowan Duglas, that it was fixed on a staff:

> "..........Every knight
> Two javelins, spears, or their gisarm staves."

Du Cange considers it as an axe, and derives it from the geesum of the Gauls. Now it could not be simply an axe, because William Guiart, under the year 1214, says:

> Les reçoivent aus fers de lances
> Aux haches, aux espees nuës
> Et aux juisarmes esmoluës.

> "They received them with the points of their lances,
> With their axes, with their naked swords,
> And with their destructive juisarmes."

From this we also learn, that it was not a lance nor any kind of sword; and further, may gather from another passage, that it was not a bill:

> Plommées fermement tenuës
> Fauchons, juisarmes esmoluës.

> "Mells firmly held
> Bills, and destructive juisarmes."

So also Octave de St. Gelais, in Viridario Honoris, speaks of—

Lances, hastons, espees et guisarmes
Harnois complez pour bien mil hommes d'armes.

"Lances, staves, swords, and guisarmes,
Harness complete for full a thousand men at arms."

Fleta calls it sisarme, the Spanish name is visarme, and in the Consuet.
S. Severi,[27] it is called bisanne. From these words we may collect, that it was
a double weapon, or compounded of two kinds of arms, or had both a cutting blade and some sort of spike: in truth, it was either a glaive gisarme,[28]
or a bill gisarme. Of the former kind are several in my son's armoury; and
of the latter, Grose has figured one, without being aware of its name, that
was dug up at Battlefield, near Shrewsbury, which seems to have once had
bells attached to it, and was found with a staff six feet long. These are both
represented at the bottom of Plate xxvii, and have both the rising spike at
the back, the distinctive mark of the gisarme.

An antient statute of William King of Scotland, who began his reign in
the year 1165, explains it as a hand-bill. The words are, De Venientibus ad
guerram. Et qui minus liabet quam quadriginta solidos terrse, liabeat gysa-
rum, quod dicitur hand-bill, arcum et sagittam. "Concerning those present-
ing themselves to serve in war. And whosoever has less than forty shillings
worth of land, shall be armed with a gisarum, which is called a hand-bill, a
bow and arrow." Now Grose has engraved what he calls a hand-bill, from
one in the collection of Mr. Cotton, which is hung round with small bells
to frighten horses. This is also represented at the foot of Plate xxvii, for
the advantage of comparison, and the whole three will be perceived to be
gisarmes, this last having a handle like a sword-hilt. In the statute of Winchester the gisarme is appropriated to the lower order of people only, being confined, as in that of the king of Scotland, to such as have less than
forty shillings worth of land. In the manuscript statute of Arles it is called
gazarnia, and thus prohibited: Non defferatur sine licentia consulum, per
Arelatem, pergreriam accu-tam, vel gazarniam, vel falsonum longum, vel
alia anna, nisi cultellum, nisi portaret dacam exeundi civitatem. "No one
shall carry, without license from the consuls, through Arles, sharp pergre-
rias, or gazarnias, or long bills, or other arms, except a knife or dagger, on
quitting the city." The pergreria was probably some weapon in the nature of

---

[27] Tit. 18, Art. 5.
[28] An antient Latin and French Glossary has gesa, jusarme, maniere de glaive.

a glaive, but its peculiar distinction I have not been able to trace.

The word. glaive is derived from the Welsh Cleddyv, "a sword." The Gauls had their saunia, and the Britons their llavnawr, or blade-weapon, which were of the same kind: these, however, gave the idea of the glaives, which are sometimes expressly called Welsh glaives. They are cutting weapons on one edge, being much in shape like the blade of a penknife, and had generally an ornament at the back.[29] This description of the arms and armour of Henry the First's time may very well be concluded by a short account of the skirmish at Audelay, in the year 1118. Though of no great moment in itself, yet as a chivalrous achievement it procured much celebrity to the English king and his subjects. Louis VI of France, who had once challenged Henry to a personal combat, found himself near to him at Audelay, and both were accompanied by their principal knights. They were dissuaded by some of their friends from engaging, but the more chivalric spirits demanded the battle. With five hundred knights in complete armour Henry took his station. Louis came down to the field with four hundred of his best knights of France; William, the son of Robert Duke of Normandy, hoping that day to end his father's captivity, eagerly accompanied him. Crispin, a Norman knight, who had joined the French, led the conflict in a furious attack on Henry's centre with eighty knights. They were all unhorsed and taken, but not till Crispin had endangered the life of Henry I. Animated with great personal hatred, he struck the king twice on his helm with such strength and fury, that the blood gushed out. He was himself soon felled to the ground, and taken. The next charge of the French knights was as unsuccessful, and Louis was then advised to fly. The English attacked in their turn, and so fiercely, that he was forced to make a precipitate retreat into the woods.

This battle, from the rank and known individual prowess of the combatants, became much spoken of in Europe. It was a trial of the chivalry of both nations, and was fought as such on both sides with so much good temper, that they endeavoured to capture rather than kill each other. The English knights having the glory of the victoiy, and having taken a hundred and forty of their opponents, the defeat of the French was commented on with much sarcastic criticism.[30] Mr. Turner observes, that Abbot Suger but slightly mentions this battle, and takes some extenuating distinction between the Franci incoinpositi, "the French not drawn up in order," and the

---

[29] Several specimens arc in the armoury of Llewelyn Meyrick, Esq.
[30] Ordo Vital. p. 854,855; Hen. Hunting. p. 381;, Suger, p. 123.

PLATE XII

RICHARD FITZHUGH  CONST^LE OF CHESTER, &

STANDARD-BEARER OF ENGLAND.

A.D. 1141.

compositis aciebus, "the well-arranged ranks," of their opponents.

The entrance tower of Restonnel Castle exhibits a specimen of the military architecture of this reign.

From the time of Edward the Confessor to that of Henry 111 inclusive, our monarchs are represented on their thrones as holding a sword in their right hands instead of a sceptre. Henry I is thus depicted in the initial letter of this reign.

Stephen.

1135.

HE reign of Stephen was completely martial, it being throughout a continual contest for power; we should, therefore, expect some improvements in Armour. The only novelty, however, appears to be what may be called the tegulated, which consisted of several little plates, covering each other in the manner of tiles, and sewn upon a hauberk, without sleeves or hood. For, although the knights who wore this armour had also a hood and sleeves, which were tight and reached to their wrists, yet the former was detached, and the latter belonged to the under garment, and neither were covered with the laminae. Guillaume le Breton, where he relates the particulars of the skirmish at Mante, in the time of Henry II, seems to describe this armour in the following lines:

> Tot ferri sna membra plicis, tot quisque patenis
> Pectora tot coriis, tot gambesonibus armant.

"Their limbs with so much iron, each with so many little folding plates:
Their breasts with so many leathern coats, so many gambesons they arm."

That this armour was gilt appears from the figure of St. Michael in alabaster, found at Porth Sini Cran, in Monmouthshire, and now in the Ashmolean Museum, at Oxford.

The seal of Richard Fitzhugh, Earl of Chester, affords a fine specimen of this kind of hauberk, and enables us to ascertain its date.[1] As he was constable of England in 1140, he is represented, in Plate XII, with the royal standard, though in the seal he carries one resembling that at the foot of this engraving. The national flag, during the reigns of William the Conqueror and his two sons, is said to have been two leos-pardes, or lions passant guardant; one being the device of Normandy, and the other that of Poitou, and that hence arose the mistaken idea, that the antient arms of the kings of England were leopards.[2] They were not, however, regarded as hereditary, nor probably as armorial bearings earlier than Henry I, if even then. Stephen took for his device a Sagittarius, both because he entered, England when the sun was in that sign, and was greatly indebted to his archers.[3] As, however, Henry II added to the two former, the lion of Acquitaine, making three in the whole, the standard has been here depicted as containing merely two. The next singularity in this figure is the excessive long point to the toe of the shoe, which William of Malmsbury indicates came so greatly into fashion during the reign of Rufus. Indeed, he even says: Tunc usus calceorum cum arcuatis aculeis inventus. "Then was invented the use of shoes with curved sharp-pointed toes." But, as we have seen, Anna Comnena assigns a somewhat earlier period for their appearance among the Franks, as all other Europeans, than the Greeks were called. They were probably not a great deal longer than the foot, and curved downwards to keep the toes from slipping out of the stirrup; but this is the earliest specimen I have met with of any so excessively long, and which, in the subsequent reign of Richard II, were fastened by little chains to the knees.

The red tunic is very long, and the saddle-cloth ample. This last is marked somewhat in the same manner as the shield, which cannot be considered an armorial bearing, occuring, as it does, in the seal of Roger Mowbray, in the time of King John. The seal of Waleran Earl of Worcester, in 1144, represents him bearing his gonfanon, on which are his armorial

---

[1] It is published by the Society of Antiquaries in their Vetusta Monumenta, and is represented inthe initial letter to this reign.

[2] That it. was a mistake is proved by the fact of our finding no instance of the arms of England 'blazoned as having leopards, while even heralds have thus termed the lions to alate period. The French call a lion passant regardant a-lionleopardé, and a leopard rampant a leopard-lionné, a confusion of terms that will account for the error.

[3] Probably mounted ones; and if so, his reign is the first in which they occur. He migbt have obtained the idea from the Greeks and Asiatics when on the crusade.

bearings, viz. checquy az and or, terminating with three streamers: his conical nasal helmet is made particularly high, surmounted by a cross, and the
cords or ribbons, which fasten the hood, appear coming from underneath
it: his shield, like that of Geoffry Plantagenet, has a boss in the centre. The
costume of William Earl of Mellent greatly resembles this, the saddle-cloth,
however, being much more ample.

Henry Prince of Scotland, in 1148, on his seal, engraved in Anderson's
Diplomata Scotise, is exhibited in a hooded hauberk of rings set edgewise,
a conical helmet without nasal, and pryck-spurs.

The rings set edgewise had been known to the Saxons, and seem to be
represented on the seal of William the Conqueror, but, though occasionally worn, do not appear to have come into general use till the latter part of
Richard the First's reign. Such kind of armour was subject to a great evil,
as tlic rings, projecting from the buckram tunic on which they were sewn,
were liable to be cut off by the blow of a sword, and the hauberk laid bare.
This is alluded to in a French manuscript romance, called the Roman d'Au-
bery, in the following lines:

> Et le hauberc vait apres desmaillent,
> Ausis le cope come lit un bouquerant.

> "And tbe hauberk became, after they had despoiled it of its mail,
> By such a blow, as if it had been simply of buckram."

The next unusual circumstance in this seal is the helmet being without its nasal. It became in many instances disused towards the close of this
reign, as will be shortly noticed, but this is an early instance, though the
earl of Huntingdon had also appeared without it.[4] The greatest curiosity is
the shield of the prince of Scotland^ which, though kite-shaped, appears
formed of three flat boards, so placed together as to represent, as it were, so
many sides of an octagon: the top of the centre one is horizontal, the others oblique, so that, in this respect, it differs from the ordinary kite-shaped
shield, which, at top, was curved. The saddle-cloth seems, like the modern
sliabrach, to cover the saddle as well as project beyond it, and is ornamented
by an edge terminating in lambrequins.

The chief alteration in the helmet during this reign, was the moving
forward of its apex, so as to be in a line with the nasal, and subsequently to
allow it to project. The following interesting event, however, seems so much

---

[4] See Plate XI.

connected with the general disuse of the nasal, that it appears highly worthy of insertion, being as illustrative in that respect, as Robert's encounter with William the Conqueror is of its use.

In the year 1141 Stephen suddenly besieged Lincoln, then held, for the Empress Matilda and her renowned and skilful general, the earl of Gloucester, by two of the principal noblemen. The earl on his part projected to surprise the king. It was manoeuvre against manoeuvre. He hastened with his military force to the Trent, but found it unfordable from the late heavy rains. He explained to his followers the exigency of their affairs, and the opportunity they now had of ending their calamities by one blow.[5] They boldly rushed into the river, and passed it swimming. The king, ever ready for knightly deeds, received their onset with undaunted courage. At first he attempted to convert the battle into single combats of the joust, in which his friends were expert; but the assailants threw away their lances, and, unsheathing their swords, rushed on to a close and more deadly combat. Their attack was irresistible. They dispersed their antagonists, and surrounded the king and a few barons who would not leave him, but whose intrepidity was unavailing. The king fought, with all the fierceness of his native courage. Every knight pressed forward to take him. He felled them with his battle-axe till it broke with the vehemence of his blows. Undismayed by this accident he rushed on them with his sword, until that also shivered upon their bodies. He still disdained to yield, till a projectile stone struck him to the ground. A knight then sprang upon him, and seizing him by the helmet, exclaimed "Hither! hither! I have got the king!"[6] As the earl had ordered him to be taken alive no further violence was attempted. He was led away to Gloucester, and afterwards to Bristol, where, from their anxiety to secure him, they are stated to have put him in fetters. He was subsequently exchanged for the earl of Gloucester, who had also been taken, a circumstance highly creditable to the military talents of that nobleman, when it is considered that by this act they were proved to have raised him in value equal to a king.

Two circumstances are remarkable in this account—the king being seized by the helmet, and his use of the battle-axe. The figure of the helmet being that of a cone, though in this reign its apex projected a little forward, a good hold could not easily be made. It must, therefore, have been by the

---

[5] Hen. Huntingdon, p. 391.

[6] Malmsbury, 187; Hen. Hunt. 352. Both these authors lived at the time. Also the Gesta Stephani, p. 952.

nasal as Avell as the apex by which the knight held him. Subsequently to this period we find the helmets without nasals; this act, therefore, or similar ones, probably gave occasion to their disuse. The shape of the battle-axe may be seen on the seal of Adam de Hereford, in the second volume of Lobineau's Histoire de Bretagne, for though that is attributed to the commencement of the next century, the shield and helmet are such as used in the latter part of the reign of this monarch. The axe has a spike on the opposite side to the blade, and greatly resembles the Danish one in Pl. VII.

Indeed, such were still called Danish axes, and there were lands held by the tenure of attending with such weapons. Thus, in the time of Henry III, Walter de Plompton held certain lands at Plompton, in the parish of Kingsbury and county of Warwick, by a Danish axe, which, being the very charter, as Dugdale says, whereby the said land was given to one of his ancestors, hung up for a long time in the hall of the capital messuage, in testimony of the said tenure.[7] So, in the reign of Edward I, Robertus Hurding tenet unam acram terrae et unum furnum, in villa Castri de Lanceveton, nomine seijantiee essendi in castro de Lanceveton cum uno capello ferreo et uno liachet Denesli per XL dies tempore guerrse, ad custum suum proprium, et post xl dies, si dominus castri velit ipsum tenere in eodem castro, erit ad custus ipsius domini.[8] "Robert Hurding holds one acre of land and one bakehouse, in the vill[9] of Launceston Castle, by the sergeantry of being in the castle of Launceston with a chapel de fer and a Danish axe for forty days, in time of war, at his own proper cost; and after forty days, if the lord of the castle wishes it, to be there at the expense of the said lord himself."

The great seal of Stephen represents him with a flat-ringed hauberk and a conical nasal; but what is singular, the upper edge of his shield is made to curve outwards at top, a contrivance, probably, for the easier management of the bridle, and which was still more attended to in later times. The seal of his son Eustace FitzStephen is exactly the same, except a boss on the shield, and the drapery which appears from under the hauberk. But that of Milo-Fitzwalter Earl of Hereford[10] represents him in the mascled hauberk, with a somewhat projecting apex to his helmet, which is with the nasal.

On the arch of the portal of St. Margaret's Church, at York, are two figures of warriors, one with a helmet much like that of Milo-Fitzwalter,

---

[7] Dugdale's Warwickshire.
[8] Plac. Coronæ 12° Edw. I[ml] in Com. Cornubiæ.
[9] Town. Of this word village is the diminutive.
[10] See Archreoiogia, Vol. XIV, p. 271.

but without the nasal, having a convex kite-shaped shield, which he holds with his left hand in the centre, and brandishing his sword in the right; the other has a circular convex shield, with a boss in its centre, exactly like those carried by the Saxons, and which he uses in the same manner, and a club in his right hand. Both these figures are in tunics girted round the waist. These garments, however, must not be taken for surcoats, which were not as yet generally introduced. This is proved not only by the paintings and seals of this period, but greatly countenanced by the following circumstance in the escape of the Empress Matilda from Oxford to Wallingford.

The ground was covered with snow, and the waters frozen over. While the royal army were sounding their trumpets for an assault on the castle, she silently went out at a postern gate, with only three chosen knights clothed in white. Amid the general bustle their footsteps Avere unheard, their garments occasioned them to be undistinguished over the snoAv-clad ground, and the empress reached Wallingford in safety.[11]

Now these garments were white certainly, to resemble the then state of the country; but as they were put over the armour for disguise, the inference is, that by such coverings these knights rendered themselves unlike military persons.

We have some very curious representations of armour during this reign, for which Ave are indebted to Abbot Suger, prime minister of Louis VII, king of France, and cotemporary of our Henry I and Stephen.[12] They existed in ten circular pieces of painted glass, in a window behind the high altar of the abbey of St. Denis, near Paris, in that part called Le Chevet. There are other corresponding pieces, but relating to other subjects; in one of them, however, is the portrait of the abbot himself.[13] They, however, carry with them internal evidence to shew that they were executed not long subsequent to the time they are intended to represent, and might have been put up, in conformity with the national enthusiasm, when Bernard, abbot

[11] Gesta Step. p. 959; Guil. Newb. lib. I, c. 10.

[12] He wrote a Life of Louis VI, or Ie Gros, with whom he was cotemporary, as he relates that Walter Tyrrel positively assured him that he had not seen Rufus on the day he was killed.

[13] None of these are now in existence. A friend of mine inquired of M. Le Noir, and M. De Bre, the architect of the abbey, but neither could give him any account of them, Theyfnrther searched some boxes containing painted glass, but without success. He then called on all the collectors he could hear of in Paris, and acquainted me that it was his full conviction that they had been destroyed during the revolution. I am forced, therefore, to give' my descriptions from the engravings in Montfaucon's Mon. Fran., which, if we may judge from the Bayeux tapestry, may', perhaps, not be quite accurate.

of Clairvaux, preached to his countrymen a third crusade in 1146.[14] These ten pieces of glass represent the second, or rather (as it should be called) the first crusade. They are curious, not only as exhibiting the armour of Europe, but that of the Turks and Saracens; and when we consider the conspicuous part which Robert, the eldest son of the Conqueror, and Stephen, afterwards king of England, took in this crusade, they appear not an improper subject of interest to the English antiquary.

The four bodies of adventurers who composed the first crusade either never reached their destination, or disappeared almost as soon as they arrived.

The expedition, however, of the French and Italian princes, which is the subject of these paintings, was carefully planned, and n'ell executed. Besides William of Tyre, who was born at Jerusalem,[15] and Albert Aquensis,[16] who may be considered as nearly cotemporaries, we have the account of Raymond de Agiles, who accompanied Raymond Count of Provence in this expedition; and the narrative of Fulcherius Carnotensis, who attended Robert Duke of Normandy; so that authentic documents are in plenty. From these we learn, that, on the 15th of August, 109G, Godfrey de Bouillon, duke de Lorraine, a respected and experienced chief, began his progress into Germany. He was joined by bis brother Baldwin and several other nobles. In March, 1097, Godfrey having passed the Hellespont, and encamped on the Asiatic plains, was joined by Bohemund, the son of Robert Guiscard, the Norman, under whose banners followed the celebrated Tancred.

The next body that arrived was under Robert Earl of Flanders.

Then came Raymond Count of Provence with the Gascons, Spaniards, and Bishop of Adhemar.

Next followed, with the last column, Robert of Normandy, son of William the Conqueror, and Stephen Earl of Blois, attended by Breton lords, and others. On a computation of the whole collected crusaders, they were found to amount to 600,000 pedestrians of both sexes, and 100,000 mailed knights, of whom Godfrey was appointed leader,[17] and with their subsequent operations the painted glass begins.

---

[14] There are some reasons for assigning an earlier date, as 'Louis VII having determined to lead the crusade, Suger tried all he could, though ineffectually, to dissuade him from his purpose.

[15] His History of the Crusades is published in the Gesta Dei per Francos.

[16] He wrote a Hist. HierosoI.

[17] William of Tyre, 664; Fulcher, 387.

The first object of attack was Nice, the capital of the Turkish kingdom, which Solyman had extended from Syria to the Hellespont. While, however, a column of the crusaders advanced towards it, this active soldan rushed down from the mountains with 50,000 cavalry, and a severe battle took place. He was, notwithstanding, in the end defeated, and compelled to retreat.[18] This is the subject of the first piece of glass. Solyman is represented with his cavalry armed with bows, lances, and swords, charging the crusaders. These are also on horseback, and have the cross marked on their helmets and the penons of their lances. The bow was the usual destructive weapon of all the Turkish tribes. Fulcher, therefore, at the same time that he speaks of the archers who served in the crusades selling their bows to return home as pilgrims, says, that the crusaders being at first unaccustomed to the rapidity of the Turkish shooting, were destroyed in great numbers by their arrows.[19]

The crusaders are represented as on horseback, and charging the Turks. Of these, more conspicuous from their situation, three appear in hauberks of rings set edgewise, or single mail, and one in a mascled tunic. All have wide sleeves reaching not quite to the wrists, and chaperons, or hoods, attached; underneath appear the sleeves of their under garments, which are themselves seen below the hauberks. In what manner their legs were armed is not so clear, but the toes (if correctly copied) are rounded. The helmet is conical, but without the nasal. The shield, which is kite-shaped, is attached to the neck by a belt; and a military girdle, answering the purpose of a sword-belt, secures their hauberks. Besides the saddle and its girths, a kind of saddle-cloth is visible. Their spear-heads are barbed. This body all advance under one banner, on which is the cross, and which terminates in three streamers like that on the seal of William the Conqueror. The crusaders do not appear to have mustachios.

The Turks are very curiously accoutred. They have round scullcaps, such as are still worn by the Georgian and Circassian tribes, round the edges of which appear fillets, or, perhaps, turbans; and something resembling ruffs of fur round their necks. They have all mustachios. Their military tunics seem to be formed either of quilted work stitched down perpendicularly,[20] or of laminae of metal arranged in that order, and kept together by bands.

---

[18] William of Tyre, 667.

[19] 387.

[20] I should conceive this the most probable, and that the European hauketons were made after this fashion; I am further inclined to this opinion from comparing them with the gambesons as perpetually occurring in the illuminations of Henry the Third's time.

Immediately below each of these bands occur one or two rows of scales.[21] One of the Turks appears to be in a tunic completely scaled. In the figure of the soldan the scales are in two rows, and his shoulder seems to be protected by something like a pauldron; under this tunic is another of simple drapery reaching nearly to the ankles. Their stirrups are large and broad, and their swords are straight, the blades being so wide near the hilts as to act as guards for the hand. Their shields are round and convex, like those used throughout Asia at the present day. Besides these the Turks are armed with bows, as has been before observed, and lances.

The second piece of glass represents the taking of Nice, and has above the words, "Franci viotores, Parthi fugientes," and below "Nicena Civitas." Godfrey after his success, previously noticed, made his approach, and formed a regular siege round the city, each leader having his allotted part to superintend. Perpetual attacks ensued for seven weeks. Machines of strong oak-beams were raised close to the walls, within which manual labour might securely undermine them; others were made to contain battering-rams, and to hurl immense stones to bruise the walls. One tower, thought to contain Solyman's wives, was particularly attacked. The Turks defended themselves with arrows from their bows and balistæ; and threw down oil, pitch, tallow, and lighted torches, to burn, often successfully, the machines that annoyed them. Frequently they caught up the besiegers with iron hooks, stripped the body, and projected it back into the camp. Breaches were made, and were repaired by new masonry; but one large building was at last fabricated, and pushed to the walls, which neither the stones nor the fire hurled down could destroy. Within this the crusaders worked to undermine the tower selected for the chief attack, inserting wooden props to support it as fast as they excavated. When a sufficient hollow was mined they filled it with combustibles, to which they set fire.[22] In the middle of the night, the supporters being all consumed, the tower fell down with tremendous noise. The crusaders flew to arms at the sound, rushed over the ruins, and became masters of the city, with Solyman's wives, on the 20th June, 1097.

William of Tyre says, a German invented one machine, which the Turks destroyed; the count of Provence others; and a Lombard at last that which was finally successful.

---

[21] These, if the drawings be not quite correct, which is very possible, may have been rings, and then the armour would resemble thatstill put on Persian horses, made of little plates, held together by rings,

[22] William of Tyre, 667, 672; Fulcher, 387.

The crusaders are represented in the painted glass as entering one gate, and charging the Turks who are escaping by the opposite one, while one of the Christians plants the standard of the cross on the principal tower. In the body-armour the artist seems scarcely to have observed a distinction between that of the Turks and that of the crusaders, except that one of the former is in a scaled tunic. The buildings every where present the circular arch.

The capture of Nice was the conquest of Asia Minor. But the object of the crusaders was the deliverance of Jerusalem, and after a short repose they began their march onwards to effect it. On the third day of their progress they divided into two bodies: Bohemund, with Robert of Normandy, Tancred, and others, took a direction to the left; Godfrey proceeded on the right with the rest, and encamped at a few miles distance. Solyman had followed them unperceived, burning for revenge. He observed their separation, and at dawn rushed upon the weaker column with 200,000 horse. The warriors at their outposts sounded their horns, the trumpets and heralds summoned all impetuously to battle. The females, old, and sick, were hastily huddled together into a marsh, with the waggons drawn around them. The soldiers formed rapidly in array, the knights arranged themselves in cohorts of fifty, on the wings of the infantry, and, sending dispatches of the attack to the other column, awaited the Turkish charge.[23] With horrible howlings and loud clangour of drums and trumpets the Turks rushed on, sending before them such an immense shower of arrows, repeated almost before the others had fallen, that scarce one of the Christians was unwounded. The knights, seeing their horses perishing, made a furious charge with their swords and spears on the Turks, who, breaking into parts, wheeled off to elude the force of the assault, but soon returned to throw another flight of arrows, which drank deep of the blood of all the unmailed host. Tancred, in the meantime, flew into the centre of the enemy, prodigal of life, and intemperately brave. He was scarcely saved by Bohemund.

The Turks, finding their numbers prevailing, and that the crusaders began to hesitate, tossed back their bows on their shoulders, and attacked with their sabres. Their assault was intolerable. The Christians broke, but soon rallied round their baggage. The Turks pursued with new fury, when Godfrey suddenly appeared at the head of 40,000 knights, eager to partake the fray. The tide of victory then ebbed back: the Turks were in their turn discomfited, and chased beyond their own camp, and all their baggage be-

---

[23] William of Tyre, 673.

came the spoil of their conquerors. Solyman had 180,000 horse engaged in the battle, the crusaders only 50,000.[24]

The next piece of glass represents this defeat of the soldan, who had attacked the Christians on their march towards Antioch. The crusaders are clad and armed as before; but, if it be not the under tunic erroneously copied, they appear to wear loose breeches. Except their scullcaps the Turks are armed like the crusaders, with the exception of two: Solyman, who appears in a very curious and inexplicable banded tunic, but apparently of the gambeson kind, holding in his right hand a whip, consisting of three knotted lashes, and protecting himself with a large convex circular shield; and a Turk on foot, who has a mascled broigne. The inscription, which is above, is "Parthi vincuntur." Probably the designation Parthi is given to the Turks on account of their mounted archers.

After the last mentioned encounter the crusaders refreshed themselves three days on the field of battle, and then marched on to Pisidia. Having experienced many hardships they passed into Lycaonia, and reached Iconium, its capital. The Turks, taught by experience, evacuated their towns, after stripping them of supplies, and desolating the country, trusting that famine would destroy the invaders. They, however, went into Cilicia, and after some dissensions between Tancred and Baldwin, advanced towards Antioch. Hitherto they had been conflicting with Solyman and his kingdom of Roum; they now entered the Turkish kingdom of Syria, whose capital was Antioch, on the Orontes, and whose sovereign collected all the accessible force of his countrymen to preserve his dominions from the fate of that territory. At Antioch the Turks made a desperate stand. The Christians besieged it with determined bravery. For eight months it defied their power, and the length and difficulties of the siege afflicted them with severe distresses. The city was taken at last on the 3d of June, 1098,[25] and a Christian principality was established at Antioch.

The painted glass represents the city taken by escalade. The citadel is circular. Two ladders appear applied to the wall on which the Christian troops are seen fighting to gain an entrance opposed by the besieged. A Turk within the citadel is drawing his bow to shoot with great elevation; another is opposing his buckler; while one in a round tower with a horn, and another on another part of the walls with a trumpet, are sounding to

---

[24] Ibid. 674.

[25] William of Tyre, 689, 712. Albert Aquensis has noticed many interesting particulars of this siege, in his third and fourth books.

animate their combatants. Their circular shields, different from those of Solyman's troops, are of a conic form, while those of the crusaders, in all the pieces of glass, are kite-shaped, or oval. None of the Turks appear in armour, as was the case with those at Roum; and one of the crusaders is clothed with a gambeson stitched horizontally. At the bottom of the citadel is inscribed the word "Antiochia."

The crusaders had captured Antioch, but they were so exhausted by their efforts to obtain the success, that the Turkish prince and his emirs promised them selves a speedy revenge. On the 20th of the same month, with above 200,000 cavalry, they made a desperate attack on the Christian force. The fury and chief danger of the battle fell on Bohemund, and he had nearly perished. At this crisis he formed his division into a small circle of despair, resolved to die fighting to the last man. From this perilous situation Godfrey and his friends extricated him. The battle, long and ominous to the crusaders from their great numerical inferiority, became balanced, and after new exertions of valour was decided in their favour. The Turks fled in complete dismay, and abandoned their rich camp to their conquerors.[26] This victory decided the safety and superiority of the Christian forces in the Syrian territory; and Jerusalem now lay within their reach, and accessible to their progress.

The painted glass, representing this engagement, has at the bottom the words "Bellum inter Corp. Arain.[27] et Francosand represents a charge from both parties. Two of the crusaders have different hauberks from the rest, one of which is perhaps a hauketon, having diagonal bands and perpendicular lines or stitches between; the other shaggy or hairy, a singular specimen of the coriiun; in other respects they are as before. The Turks are all, but one, habited as in the last, except that their scullcaps are highly ornamented. One has a hauberk of leaf or large scale-work, with sleeves reaching nearly to bis elbows, below which appear those of his under garment; his scullcap has cheek-pieces, to tie under the chin, of platted or scaled work, while under the others are hoods.[28] The shields are smaller than what occur in the preceding pieces of glass, and may probably distinguish them as the Bedouin Arabs, because, when Richard I entered the land of Zuph, near Jaffa, the historians of that time notice this race as distinguished by their small

---

[26] William of Tyre, 725, 726; Alb. Aquensis, 255, 256.

[27] Montfaucon says, this is Corbaram, though, as all the letters are capitals, he could only make it Corparam. Was he, an emir? or might not the words Corp. Aram. signify corpus Arabum ?

[28] If Montfaucon be ,right this is probably Corbara, as he is falling from his horse.

round shields. On their right flank the infidels appear to be protected by machines, unless the bows of their archers be what are represented. Below are apparently some very singular arches, but what a friend of mine[29] has conjectured to be the vessels of the crusaders drawn up on the shore.

Godfrey having thus overthrown two Turkish kingdoms, Roum and Syria, prepared to conflict with the soldan of Egypt, whose dominions extended from the Nile to Syria. Almost a whole year however elapsed before the crusaders advanced to Jerusalem, the great object of the whole crusade, which was now additionally fortified. During this period they suffered greatly from heat, want of water, and provisions, as well as from pestilence; still, however, they were not inactive. Baldwin conquered Edessa, in Mesopotamia; and Bohemund took Tarsus and other places.[30] Godfrey, nevertheless, had now a fresh kingdom to conquer with the skeleton of an army. So many had been killed, died, returned home, or stayed with Baldwin and Bohemund, at Edessa and Antioch, that he reached Jerusalem with only 40,000 persons, the effectives of whom amounted to 20,000 foot and 1,500 horse; with these he had to attack a city defended by 40,000 combatants.

On the 7th of June, 1099, he encamped round Jerusalem, with Robert of Normandy, Tancred, the count of Flanders, and other distinguished leaders. The siege was severe. On the 15tli of July, in the same year, he stormed the city, and the catastrophe was horrible. Twenty thousand Mussuhnen were put to the sword, and Godfrey was elected king of Jerusalem.[31]

The piece of glass which represents this event has, at its lower part, the following inscription. "Irem a Francis expugnat." The citadel of Jerusalem, with its various towers and turrets, is exhibited, and in all the doors, windows, and loopholes appear the circular arch. The crusaders are exhibited as having wheeled against the walls a high wooden tower, of at least three stories, turretted at top, where it is in a line with that of the citadel:[32] its roof is covered by crusaders, Vliose helmets appear but just above the turrets. From the top of the citadel they are attacked by the Turkish archers,

---

[29] Major Smith, author of the Antient Costume.

[30] I am not quite certain whether or not the last described piece of glass may not refer to one of these, because the habits of the infidels are more splendid than before; and machines of the sling or bow kind, seem to imply the vicinity of a town. Supposing, with Montfaucon, that the inscriptions refer to a battle between Corbara and the French, or, as I do, that Corp Aram is a contraction of Corpus Arabum, this idea is, rather strengthened than invalidated. A word of great importance is contracted in the next piece of glass.

[31] Alb, Aquensis, lib. VI; William of Tyre, lib. VIiI.

[32] See it represented in PI. xxvi, Fig. 1.

one of whom is represented as in the act of drawing his bow. In a line with the projecting part of the citadel a bridge, or platform, supported by props underneath,[33] forms the means for the Christian troops to enter the city, and here a conflict is depicted, in which an infidel in scaled armour is cut down and falling over. Below, the Turks appear to have made a sally, but are received jn their charge by the Christians.

William of Tyre informs us,[34] that, after this splendid victory, the Turks took shelter in Ascalon; they are, therefore, in the next piece of glass, represented as in full flight, and taking refuge in that city. The Turkish shields, as in the last, are convex, with a boss in the centre. Three kinds of armour are visible—the scaled, the gamboised, and the mascled, reaching no further than the hips. The figure with the mascled broigne has his scullcap, or rather coif, likewise mascled.[35] They have all wide Turkish breeches; the Asiatic saddle, which peaks up behind as well as before, and embroidered saddle-cloths. Below is the inscription "Arabes victi in Ascalon fugiunt."

The next event is peculiarly interesting to the English antiquary. It represents Robert Duke of Normandy in an encounter with an Egyptian emir, into whose throat he is thrusting his lance, and consequently pushing him off his horse. Robert, having partook of almost every laurel that had been gained in the crusade, after this event returned home, but found his brother Henry possessed of the crown of England. There is nothing new in the costume of the crusaders. To their lances are attached penons as in some former instances, and on that of Robert is the sign of the cross. The principal standard has three crosses, and appears to have once had more painted on it. In this crusade these were invariably red. Behind one of the lances appears an eagle, or some bird of prey. The emir is in a gambeson, which reaches to his loins, and is double banded with the scales or rings as before; he is in the wide Turkish breeches, but, what is singular, has his arms from the elbows, and his feet, bare. The artist has not forgotten to depict the sword-strap, or ornament, as hanging from its pommel, still so generally used in Asia. Those inexplicable arches occur again at the bottom, and incline me to think they are intended for sand-hills. Below is the following inscription: "R. Dux Normannorum Parthum prostern it."

History tells us, that Robert Earl of Flanders penetrated to the middle of the enemy's squadrons. We learn from the next piece of glass, that there

---

[33] This Montfaucon calls "Un pont abattu."

[34] P. 769.

[35] This is the only specimen of the kind I have ever seen.

was a duel or single combat between him and an Egyptian emir, for the inscription is, "Duellum Parthi et Roberti Flandrensis Comitis." They are represented fighting, and although we do not see the result of the fight, the Christian earl seems to have struck the emir a blow that would sever his head from his body. The principal standard of the crusaders terminates in three streamers, and the cross is painted in the midst of four very small circles, which may have distinguished that of the Flemings. The gon-fanons, or penons, are as before, except, that like the standard, they are attached to the lances by little cords, in the antient Anglo-Saxon manner, instead of bound round them, as in the former described pieces of glass. The Turks have long gambesons reaching to their knees, wjith under garments. The emir seems to have lost his scullcap, as a knot of his hair hangs over his forehead. One of his men carries the horse-tail on the end of his lance, which, even to this day, remains a Turkish standard· Again there occur what I take to be sand-hills.

The last piece of painted glass represents a battle with the soldan of Egypt, whom some authors call the Amiravisi,[36] and which was the final one of this crusade. This Turkish prince is probably the person who appears before his troops: his hauberk with its hood is mascled as far as the hips, and from thence to half way the thigh where it terminates, is rustred. His breeches, which reach to his knees, are nearly tight. His scullcap is ornamented with radiating leaves, apparently embossed; while those of his attendants are plain. They also are in hooded hauberks of scale. In the back the soldán seems to be again represented (if he is distinguished by his scull-cap) turning his horse round for flight. The crusaders appear differently from before, being exhibited in hooded hauberks, or hauketons, stitched in diagonal wavy lines, with close stitches perpendicular to them; in other respects they are as before. They, as well as the Turks, have the sleeves of their armour terminating just below the elbow, and shewing those of the under garment below. Here again occur the sand-hills, which, in this specimen, have on them some foliage. Throughout there has been no instance of a curved sword; in this piece of glass that of the leader of the Christians has on its blade engraved ornaments. The inscription at the bottom is so much obliterated that it has become difficult to decipher. It is "Belhun Amit. E. Ascalonia ju...., probably juxta.

From these paintings in glass it would seem, that the Europeans derived the hauketon, or hoketon, from their Asiatic enemies during the crusades;

---

[36] Or great emir.

and this countenances the supposition of Perizonius, who supposes the word a corrupted pronunciation of the Greek ὁ χιτων. Boxhorn is anxious to derive it from the Welsh word actuum, which, he adds, implied a double cuirass; but though this British origin gives it an early date, unfortunately for him, neither does the Welsh language afford any word at all like actuum, nor was the armour of that people in any instance a double cuirass. A German derivation from liauen, to "hew or cut," and quittung, "a riddance,"- seems less probable than the Greek, especially as the Germans had their wambais, which answers the same purpose. Whether the Turks had adopted the Greek name and corrupted it, or the garment was originally Asiatic, and called by the Greeks, who might be ignorant of its real name, ho kiton, i. e. the tunic, when asked by the inquiring crusaders, may be matter of doubt; but the several corruptions of the word are in this order, hoketon, lioqueton, hauqueton, hauketon, haukton, auketon, aketon, actione, and acton. From the manuscript Chronicle of Bertrand du Guesclin, though compiled at the commencement of the fifteenth century, we learn that it was made of buckram, for, it is said:

> Le hauuton fut fort, qui fut de bouquerant.

> "The hoketon was strong, being made of buckram.

And from the MS. Roman du Ride et du Ladre, that it was stuffed with cotton:

> Se tu vucil nn auqueton
> Ne l'empli nie de coton
> Mais d'œuvres de miséricorde
> Afinque diables ne te morde.

> "If you wish for au hauketon,
> Don't fill it full of cotton,
> But of works of mercy,
> To the end that devils may not bite thee."

Thus it differed from the wambais, which was of linen and stuffed with wool, being evidently a coarser garment. The use of cotton, too, implies its invention in a warm country, or at least in one in which cotton was in abundance. Perhaps originally it was of cotton cloth, or faced with silk, as is the Asiatic taste. It was certainly stitched, and that in an elegant manner, sometimes, indeed, with threads of gold, for the Roman de Gaydon speaks of:

L'auqueton, qui d'or fu pointurez.

"The hauketon, which was pointed with gold."

This garment was probably not introduced into England till the time of Richard the First, after which it became, and continued for a long while, very prevalent.

An event which was deemed of much importance, and which contributed greatly to exhibit the valour and military tactics of the English, was the Battle of the Standard, fought in the year 1138. It took place between the Scots army, headed by King David, and some English troops, under the command of Sir Walter Espec.[37] The latter were drawn up on Cuton Moor, about two miles from North Allerton. As soon as they had arrived on this plain, which was about break of day on the 22d of August, they erected a standard of a very peculiar contrivance: it was the mast of a ship fixed upon a wheel carriage, at the top of which was placed a silver pix,[38] containing a consecrated wafer; and under that were hung three banners, dedicated to St. Peter, St. John of Beverley, and St. Wilfred of Rippon. "All these decorations," observes Lord Lyttleton, "were proper to strike the imagination, and probably were suggested by the Archbishop of York, to keep up that spirit of religious enthusiasm he had wisely inspired." But, though it might be suggested by that prelate, it was by no means his invention. Indeed the word standard, by which the writers of the time have denominated it, is of Asiatic origin, the historians of the crusades attributing it to the Saracens. Thus Tudebodius[39] says, "but one of our soldiers took the standard of the great emir,[40] on the top of which was a golden apple, and the spear of which was wholly covered with silver, which standard we call a banner."[41] Albert Aquensis says, it was supposed to cany with it a particular virtue. It was probably on this account that it was adopted by the Italians. William Guiart, in his manuscript History of France, assigns it to the Emperor Otho, but without any other authority than the custom of his own time. He says:

---

[37] It is described by Ailredus, p. 338-342; by Ric. Hagulstad, 318—326; and by Hoveden, 277.

[38] The pix, or pyxis, was a.oasket,

[39] Lib. v. See also Albert Aquensis.

[40] Standarum Ammiravisi.

[41] Vexillum.

Othes pour la paix despecier
Fait lors son Estendart drecier,
Fols est qui nus plus riche cerche
Un grant dragon ot sur la perche
Qui fu sus un beau char posée,
Vers France et la gueule baée
Pour le reauine chalengier,
Come s'il deust tout mangier.
Cis dragons sousting la bannière
Des connoissance l'emperiere,
Qui porte au bel et aloré
Dessus ot un aigle doré
C'est signe de guerre cuisant.

"Otho, to prevent the peace
Then, had his standard set out;
He is mad that would seek a richer:
On the top of the pole was a great dragon,
It being erected in a handsome car.
Towards France was its mouth opened
To challenge the kingdom,
As if it would eat the whole.
This dragon held the banner
With the cognizance of the emperor,
Which it carried handsomely and upright:
Beneath was a golden eagle,
Which is a sign of a sharp war."

Turpin, in his History of Charlemagne, mentions it as belonging to the Saracens. He says, "in the midst of them was a waggon drawn by eight horses, upon which was raised their red banner. Such was its influence, that while this banner remained erect no one would ever fly from the field." Bertholdus Constantiensis describes one as belonging to the King of Hungary, in 1086. Egidius the monk attributes[42] its invention to the Duke of Lovain, who had the banner, which had been beautifully worked by the Queen of England, placed in a superb chariot, drawn by four yoked oxen. The author of Manipuli Floruin ascribes the invention to Heribert, Archbishop of Milan, about the year 1124,[43] and gives of it the following pompous description: "But there is the standard-car, which, in the most admirable manner, was covered all round to its summit with scarlet; in the midst of this was

[42] Atme Vallis in Alexandre Episc, Leod. c. 24.
[43] Corius Hist. Midolan. p. 1.

the stem of a tree almost reaching to the heavens, which four people could not carry, and which, from the effects of the pressure of the crowd, was held upright by ropes: on the top of this shaft was a golden cross glittering with great splendour, and below it a white banner, having on it a red cross. This car was drawn by four oxen yoked together, covered with trappings and housings of white silk, surmounted by red crosses. The master of the standard is a most honourable man, who is retained in the service of the state by a continual salary, a sword, and hauberk. Besides this the community is held to provide a chaplain always to celebrate mass near the standard, and give absolution to the wounded; he also receives from the community a large stipend. There are, moreover, eight trumpeters, belonging to the city, with as many knights on their chargers, whom the community furnish with two tents, and a proper military parade." It was, therefore, of Asiatic origin, and first introduced in Europe in the reign of King Stephen. The Italians, who seem to have been the first to adopt it, called it carrocium,[44] or the carriage, and had it drawn by four yokes of oxen, and protected by a chosen band of knights. In fighting under this kind of standard the soldiers felt a religious enthusiasm, approaching to that which had influenced the Saracens, and considered themselves the champions of Christ, his saints, and martyrs.

When this was raised on Cuton Moor, Walter Espec mounted the carriage, and from thence harangued the army: they then drew up in order of battle with as much judgment as circumstances would permit. Being greatly outnumbered by the enemy, they formed themselves into one compact body, composed wholly of foot, for the cavalry had been commanded to dismount, except a few, who, posted in the rear, might guard the horses of the rest. Almost the same disposition had been made by Harold, at the battle of Hastings, but this differed in their being archers and spearmen intermixed with the heavy-armed troops. In the foremost ranks were all the bravest of the barons and knights; but the more aged nobles, with the young earl of Northumberland, Roger de Mowbray,[45] stood in the midst of the phalanx, about the standard, and some of them were mounted on the carriage to which it was fixed. This was according to general practice, for in the Roman de Garin we read:

> Nostre cmperere fist l'estendart venir
> Mult l'a bien fet de chevalier emplir,
> Et de serjans por le fez sostenir.

[44] Καρούχιον, carrocium; carrochio, carrosse, whence our English word coach,
[45] His effigy, when in more advanced life, as on his seal, is given at the foot of Plate xv.

"Our emperor caused the standard to approach:
Very well was it done to fill it with knights
And with sergeants, to sustain the feat."

Hoveden tells us, that the men of Lothian were the first to commence the attack, madly rushing on the English knights, discharging their missive weapons, and with spears of most extraordinary length striking at men who were so well armed, that their thrusts were made, as it were, upon a wall of impenetrable iron. The English archers and slingers in return poured a continual show er of stones and darts, which did great execution, they being very slightly armed. Finding, however, that their spears were broken against the plastrons and helmets of the English, they had valiantly thrown these away, and renewed the attack with their swords and bucklers of cow-hide; but, beat down by the missive weapons of their foe, they were forced to give way, and the Scotch army was ultimately routed. Indeed, great reliance seems to have been placed by the English on their armour, for, before the engagement, the bishop of Durham, by way of encouragement, reminded his men "that their breasts were defended by strong armour, and their heads with helmets, their legs were secured by chausses of iron, and the rest of their bodies by the shield that every one bore on his arm."[46]

This armour on the breast was in all probability the plastron de fer, an iron plate, which was placed under the hauberk to raise it from the chest, its pressure upon which had been found very injurious. This, which gave at the same time additional security, seems to have been but lately introduced. Guillaume le Breton, in relating the skirmish at Mante, where Sir William des Barres encountered with the lance Richard Earl of Poictiers, afterwards king of England, says:

Utraque per clipeos ad corpora fraxinus ibat
Gambesumque audax forat et thoraca trilicem
Disjicit ardenti minium prorumpere tandem
Vix obstat ferro fabricata patena recocto.

"On both parts the lances were thrust through the shields to the body,
Penetrating the daring gambeson and the trellissed broigncs:
Scarce were they stopped by the plastron of wrought iron which was concealed within."

Whether the helmets, of which the bishop spoke, were improved by the

---

[46] Hoveden.

addition of a visor is very doubtful; but the seal of Ranulph Earl of Chester, who took Stephen prisoner at the siege of Lincoln, and died in 1155,
represents him with one.[47] Indeed, one of the seals of Henry I, where he is
in a hauberk, covered with flat circular plates,[48] presents us with a helmet
apparently with a visor; and yet in another, more consonant to the general
custom, he is exhibited in flat-ringed armour, and a conical nasal helmet.[49]
The monument attributed to William Earl of Flanders does not appear older than the time of Richard I, and though that has got a mask for the face,
called aventaile, covering,[50] as it did the ventaile, or open space, such does
not appear to have been worn so early as the time of Stephen: I should presume, therefore, that the visor, which appears to have been moveable, was
by no means generally adopted. It was probably considered as little better
than the nasal helmet, which protected the nose, but left the eyes exposed,
as the apertures for vision in the visor did not remedy this inconvenience.
The rest of the face too was left uncovered, and hence we find, that when
the nasal was disused the helmet became again a mere scullcap. In the time
of Richard I, as we shall hereafter see, the aventaile, or mask for the face,
which was pierced for the eyes and breath, was first introduced, and it was
not till the reign of Henry III that this was made to be moveable. Ranulph
has in his hand an enormous broad sword, the cross-bar of which, as in
that of the figures on the arch of the doorway at York, before described, is
curved downwards on both sides.

The earls of Chester appointed barons under them, the tenure of one
being that he held his estate on the condition of being the first to enter
Wales in any expedition to that country, and the last to leave it; and all were
bound, in time of war with the Welsh, to find, for each knight's fee, one
horse harnessed or two unharnessed, within the divisions of Cheshire; and
that their knights and free tenants should be furnished with loricæ[51] and
haubergeons, and defend their respective fees in person.

---

[47] See foot of Plate XI. He saw the fault of the nasal, and the necessity of protecting
the nose.

[48] See that in the new edition of the Fœdera, and also a modification of it in Speed's
Chronicle.

[49] This is annexed to a deed, entitled "Libertates canonicis Sanctæ Trin London con-
cessæ, et quod habent soccam de Anglica CniEthenegild." See new edition of the Fœdera.

[50] See foot of Plate XI,

[51] Gough's Camden, Vol. II, p. 427. He calls this "breast-plates," but what the original
word is does not appear. He gives no reference, nor is the passage in the Latin edition of
Camden, in 1617.

The description which Ordericus Vitalis[52] gives of the siege of Exeter, shews a considerable knowledge of the arts of attacking and defending a town, to which, therefore, the reader is referred for such information. It cost the king three months' time and fifteen thousand marks to take it.

Some idea may be formed of the military architecture of this reign by the contemplation of Pontefract Castle, and that of Newark, Knaresborougli, Yorkshire.

---

[52] P.936.

Henrp the Second.

1154.

E find this king represented on his seal in a flat-ringed hauberk, and a conical helmet without a nasal. As he introduced the short mantle prevalent at Anjou, for the greater convenience of riding, he was surnamed Curt-mantell;[1] and such was his extreme restlessness, that if he was not on horseback he was always standing.

Very little alteration took place in the armour of this reign, notwithstanding the military character of the monarch. The principal circumstance, therefore, worthy of notice is, that, soon after its commencement, the flat-ringed hauberk was laid aside, and never afterwards revived, while that of the rings set edgewise came into general fashion.

Hereditary armorial bearings seem, however, to have been adopted about this period. Henry, on his accession, revived the lions of Normandy and Poitou, which had been the national device during the reigns of his uncles, and added to them that of Acquitaine. To his son Richard he assigned for arms two lions combattant, and to his son John two passant. The first were borne by Richard on his accession, the latter by John before he was king, as appears from their respective seals at those times; but Richard on his second one had engraved the three lions passant guardant as had been

[1] Brompton, p. 1150.

first adopted by his father.

The shape of the shield became somewhat shortened during the reign of Henry H, and often more angular on each side at the top.[2]

Armour seems still to have been very expensive, if we may judge from the account which Giraldus Cambrensis gives of the first English expedition to Ireland. He relates, that Dermod King of Leinster, having obtained authority from Henry II, went to Bristol, and invited English knights, by large promises of rewards, to assist him in the recovery of his kingdom. His oifers were long announced in vain, till Richard, surnamed Strongbow, earl of Strigul,[3] was tempted to interfere. In Wales Dermod found another adventurer, Robert Fitz-Stephens, who collected from his relations and neighbours 130 knights, 60 coats of mail, and 300 foot archers: these, after their arrival in Ireland, were joined by 10 knights and several bowmen, to which Dermod added 500 Irish partisans.

In this account we see how great was the disproportion of armour, more than every other knight being without any; and although the enemy they had to encounter was ill armed and undisciplined, yet their numbers were too disproportionate to be contemned.

The same author describes the people with whom they were about to engage. "The Irish," he says, "despised armour as burtliensome and coward-like, wearing merely black woollens. In riding they used neither saddles, boots, nor spurs, and their bridles were put through their horses' mouths so as to answer the purpose of a bit. They were dexterous in the use of the war-hatcliet and the sling."

Lord Lyttleton has remarked, that it is very extraordinary that the Irish, at this time, seem to have been altogether without archers, particularly as their neighbours, the Welsh, obtained great celebrity for their use of the bow. Giraldus,[4] speaking of those who inhabited Gwentland,[5] formerly the territory of the renowned Caractacus, says: "It seems worthy of remark, that the people of Gwentland are more accustomed to war, more famous for valour, and more expert in archery, than those of any other part of Wales. The following examples prove the truth of this assertion: In the last assault of Abergavenny Castle, which happened in our days, two soldiers, passing

---

[2] See the initial letter to this reign for its shortness.

[3] This place is in Monmouthshire, where he had a castle. It is a corruption of Ystrad Jul, or Strata Julia; being situated on the Roman road, made by Julius Frontinus, through that country.

[4] tIter Cambrioe, c. 3.

[5] Venta Silurum, comprehending Monmouthshire and Glamorganshire.

over a bridge to a tower, built on a mound of earth, in order to take the Welsh in the rear, their archers, who perceived them, penetrated with their arrows the oaken gate, which was four fingers thick; in memory of which circumstance, the force having been so great, the arrows are still preserved sticking in the gate, with their iron piles seen on the other side. Wiliam de Breos[6] also testifies, that one of his knights, in a conflict with the Welsh, a *quodam ipsorum per mediam coxam cum panno loricse ocreali ferro utrinque, vestitam, sagitta percussum esse, eadem quoque sagitta per partem illam sellec, quse alvavocatur, usque ad ipsumequum letlialiter transpenetrante,* "was wounded by an arrow, which pierced the coat of mail, greaved on both sides with iron,[7] in which he was clad, and, passing through his hip, entered the saddle in that part which is called the alva,[8] and mortally wounded the horse." *Alia quoque sagitta, militis alterius coxam ferro similiter utrinque munitam cum panno loricse usque in sellam perforavit.* "Another knight in like manner, having his hip guarded on both sides with a coat of mail,[9] had it penetrated by the pile of an arrow quite into the saddle, and on turning his horse round, received a similar wound in the opposite hip, which fixed him on both sides to his seat. What more could be expected from a balista ? Yet the bows used by this people are not made of horn, ivory,[10] or yew, but of wild elm, unpolished, rude and uncouth, but stout; not calculated to shoot an arrow to a great distance, but to inflict very severe wounds in close fight."

From the observations of a foreigner we are often led to conclude what must be the custom of his own country. Thus, when Giraldus speaks of the armour used by the Welsh, he enables us, by pointing out their deficiencies, to judge of what were possessed by the English: *Armis, says he, tamen utuntur levibus, agilitatem non impedientibus, loricis minoribus, sagittarum manipulis, et lanceis longis, galeis et clypeis, ocreisque ferreis rarius.* "They use light arms, such as may not impede their agility, the smaller lo-

---

[6] Guil. de Breusa,

[7] This seems to refer to. the trellissed armour; the studs going through the cloth of which would occasion iron on both sides, and the cross bandages making it like the coverings for the legs, authorizing the word ocreali, "greave-fashioned." It must also have been a hauberk, ami'not a broigne, as in Plate XI.

[8] Evidently the seat of the saddle, though Du Cange, who cites this passage, gives no explanation of it.

[9] This seems .to refer to the chausses which wrapped round the thigh, and therefore guarded it both inside and out.

[10] The horn and ivory would only have made the ends of the bow, as the latter especiallyhas no elasticity whatever. We may, however, infer from this, that the English made use of these materials at this time.

ricæ,[11] a handfull of arrows,[12] and long lances, helmets, and round shields, and very rarely coverings for the legs studded with iron."[13] He adds, "fleet and generous steeds, which their country produces, carry their nobility to battle; the greater part, however, of the people are obliged to march on foot over marshes and irregular ground; but those who are mounted, according to opportunity of time and place, both for the retreat or attack, easily become infantry. The foot soldiers have either bare feet, or use a shoe made of a raw hide, and sewn up in a barbarous fashion." From this account it is clear, that in England there were two kinds of armour, the hauberk and the broigne; but Giraldus does not leave us in doubt upon the point, for, in his remarks upon the best mode of carrying on a campaign in Wales, alluding to the English troops, he says, "Where the armies engage in a flat country, a heavy armour made of many folds of linen, covered with steel,[14] both protects in a superior degree and decorates the soldier; but when the engagement is in narrow defiles, &c, a light armour is far preferable."

An important use of knights, and which long continued the profession, was the feudal obligation attached to all land, that a specified number of knights should be furnished, at the call of the sovereign, for a certain number of hides. This equally held good with respect to the real possessions of heiresses and the clergy, as of lay proprietors; and they were always obliged to retain the necessary quantity of knights to perform the service for them, as they could not do it in person. Hence, we often find in the enumeration of the possessions of a church, the land let or given to knights, as the hire of their military services. The baron or his children might attend for themselves; but when their possessions were large, as a knight was to be found for every fifteen or twenty pounds a year of landed property,[15] they were under the necessity of retaining many knights to fulfil their feudal obligation. Knights also became a necessary part of both regal and baronial state: thus, Thomas a Becket had 700 knights as part of his household, besides 1,200 stipendiary retainers, and 4,000 followers, serving him forty days.[16] The le-

---

[11] Broignes,

[12] Alluding to the custom of carrying them in the bow-hand, which appears also in the Bayeux tapestry. See Pl. VIII.

[13] Probably such as are represented in Pl. XXIV.

[14] Multiplex armatura tam linea se quam ferrea.

[15] The value of twenty pounds a year was not established as a knight's fee till the 1st of Edward fI. In 1253, the 37th Henry III, every person having fifteen libratas terræ was ordered to be made a knight. Matt. Paris, 864.

[16] Stephanides, 22, 23.

gal service of a knight for the land, which he held by military tenure, was to serve forty days at his own costs, where the king went against his enemies.[17]

As society advanced, knighthood became so expensive that statutes were obliged to be made to compel the holders of adequate portions of land to assume the dignity, and hence, when offered as an honour by a sovereign wishing to confer distinction, was sometimes refused. Thus, the Emperor of Germany observing great bravery in an individual of inferior condition, at the attack of a castle, ordered him to be honoured with the military belt. Aware of the expense which would attend his acceptance of it, he answered, though a plebeian he was sufficiently contented with his situation, and preferred to remain in it.[18] Knighthood, however, being quite independent of, but additional to, nobility,[19] it was still emulously sought for by that class, and the consequence was that it embraced persons very unequal in wealth. The richer knights distinguished themselves by luxuries, and to the poorer this was a subject of complaint. John of Salisbury, who lived in this reign, found their luxurious habits so increasing, that he has left us a copious declamation against them.[20]

The author tells us how knights should qualify themselves for their duty. They must learn from the beginning to labour, run, carry weights, and bear the sun and dust; to use sparing and rustic food; sometimes to live in the open air, and sometimes in tents then to practise the use of arms. He draws a strong picture of the effeminate knight, which proves to us, that in his time this order was beginning to degenerate, and, consequently, that society was becoming, happily for its comfort, less warlike. He says, "Some think that military glory consists in this: that they shine in elegant dress, that they make their clothes tight to their body, and so bind on their linen or silken garments as to seem a skin coloured like their flesh. If they are sitting softly on their ambling horses they think themselves so many Apollos. If you make an army of them you will have the camp of Thais, not of Hannibal. Each is boldest in the banquetting-hall, but in the battle every one desires to be the last; they would rather shoot arrows at the enemy than come to close fighting. When they return home without a scar they sing triumphantly of

---

[17] An oath was taken to this effect; thus, in a parliamentary roll, 6th of Edward I, it is given in these words: "Mes tus jurs par le service de un chivaler attendirent au roi quarant jurs sur lur custages demeyne p la ou le roy deveit aler sur ses enemis."

[18] Otto. Frising. Urtizii, p. 458.

[19] Thus we frequently read of nobles not yet distinguished by knighthood, and of others attaining it. 2 Gale Script. 60, 71; Matt. Par. 323.

[20] In his Polycraticus, 181.

their battles, and boast of the thousand deaths that wandered near their temples. If diligent idleness can procure any spears, which, being brittle as hemp, should chance to be broken in the field; if a piece of gold, minium, or any colour of the rainbow, by any chance or blow should fall out of their shields;[21] their garrulous tongues would make it an everlasting memorial. They have the first places at supper. They feast every day splendidly if they can afford it, but shun labour and exercise like a dog or a snake. Whatever is surrounded with difficulty they leave to those who serve them. In the meantime they so gild their shields,[22] and so adorn their tents,[23] that you would think every one, not a scholar, but, a chieftain of war."

The true merit of a knight is correctly stated by the Troubadour Arnaud de Marveil:[24] "It is to fight well; to conduct a troop well; to do his exercise well; to be well armed; to ride his horse well; to present himself with a good grace at courts, and to render himself agreeable there. Seldom are these qualities in the same person." To unite martial habits and vigour with the courteous elegancies of polished life, could not be often accomplished in a half civilized age. Knighthood was conferred by investing the person with a belt,[25] in which a sword was inserted.[26] Heniy II made it indispensable that the candidate should be a freeman.[27] There was no limit as to age, for Henry I was made a knight at sixteen,[28] and we read of another at nineteen.[29] Abbots, after the year 1102, were forbidden to make them,[30] which they had previously done, for Hereward went to the abbot of Peterborough for that purpose.[31] But bishops, knights, and princes had this power, and it was Lanfranc who made Rufus a knight.[32] No person, however great his rank, could command knights, without having himself become a knight.

The ceremony of conferring knighthood was solemn and splendid. The AngloSaxon custom was, that the intended knights should confess

---

[21] By this we see how highly they were decorated in the reign of Henry II.
[22] This is a still further proof.
[23] Of the splendour of tents at a somewhat later period the illuminated MSS. afford many examples.
[24] St. Palaye's Hist. Troub. Vol. I, p. 81.
[25] Matt. West. 189; Duchesne's Hist. Norm. 973; Ordo Vit. 573; Matt. Par. 231.
[26] So Salisbury declares, 187.
[27] Hoveden.Bl-t.
[28] Matt. Par. ll.
[29] Chron, Mailros, 185.
[30] Eadmer, 68.
[31] Ingulp. 70.
[32] Malmsb. 120.

themselves, and watch all the preceding night in a church.[33] The Normans thought this too unwarlike, but even they admitted it to be connected in some measure with religion, by taking an oath when they were dubbed. This, Henry II, in his laws, calls Sacramentum armorum. Hence, John of Salisbury says, "Without the religion of an oath none is bound with the belt of knighthood:"[34] and on the day of creation the new knight went solemnly to the church, his sword and belt were placed upon the altar, and prayers were offered.[35] His oath declared his duty to be, "To defend the church, to attack the perfidious, to venerate the priesthood, to repel the injuries of the poor, to keep the country quiet, and to shed his blood, and, if necessary, to lose his life, for his brethren.[36]

As the creation of a duke or earl was expressed by girding on the sword, so was that of a knight by the "gift of the military girdle." Hence, Mat. Paris says, Rex Anglorum Willielmus apud Westmonasterium Henricum filium juniorem cingulo militari donavit. "William King of England, at Westminster, gave to his younger son Henry the military girdle," i. e. constituted him a knight.

As the ceremony of investiture was splendid, so was it attended with great expense. To provide the means for this purpose, it was lawful for kings and territorial lords to raise money from their tenants, when their eldest sons were to be made knights. In the Records of the Exchequer some of the expenses are state: "For clothes and horses, and other apparatus, to make two knights, £12 2s. 6d." "For three robes of scarlet, three of green, two baldekins,[37] one culcitra,[38] and other things necessary to make a knight, £33." "For three robes of silk, three of green, three wrappers, three spurs, three saddles with thongs, three vests, See, to make a knight, £21 10s. 2d."[39]

As the knights had their duties, so had they their privileges. They were free from all gelds and taxes, and from all other services and burthens, by Henry I, in order "that, being so alleviated, they may instruct themselves in the use of horses and arms, and be apt and ready for my service and the de-

---

[33] Ingulp, 70.
[34] Polycrat. 187.
[35] Polycrat. 187, 193. Peter Cosensis, who also wrote in the time of Henry II, says the same.
[36] Ibid. 186.
[37] A composition of silk and gold threads, so called from Baldack, the modern name of Babylon,
[38] Cushion.
[39] Madox's Exeh. 37-2.

fence of my kingdom.[40] Salisbury also mentions, that knighthood "rejoices in many immunities, and more eminent privileges, and has not to provide horses, carriage, and other sordid burthens."[41]

But the great inducements to the rank were the honour, the donations, they perpetually received, and the plunder they were always acquiring. Hence, the Troubadour Durand says, "War pleases me. By war I see feasts, gifts, pleasures, and songs, multiplied. War converts a villain to a courtois. War well made, therefore, pleases me. Hence, I wish the truce broken between the Sterlings (English) and the Tournois (French)."[42]

Warlike energy was certainly the first point of excellence. Rufus thought it a loss of honour, if, on a sudden alarm, any one should seize his arms earlier than himself, or if any one challenged the enemy before he did, unless he afterwards conquered the challenger.[43] They allowed their enemies safe conduct from one part to another for the purpose of battle.[44] They might, however, be degraded for misconduct; then their belt was taken away.[45]

As the manners of the age softened they attached themselves to the fair sex: but in the earlier state of chivalry they had neither leisure nor taste for the refinement of love, their gratifications were then coarse; war was their passion, and their manners partook of the fiercer spirit of the times. Even the ladies themselves were fond of war, and sometimes waged it. Ordericus Vitalis relates a curious instance of this.[46] Two Norman ladies quarrelled, Eloisa and Isabella. Each roused their friendly knights to assert their cause, and plundered and burnt each other's possessions. They were both spirited, loquacious, and beautiful, and governed their husbands; but they differed in temper. Eloisa was cunning and persuasive, fierce and penurious. Isabella was liberal and courageous, good-humoured, merry, and convivial. She rode among the knights, armed as they were, and was as dexterous in the use of their weapons. The Troubadour Rambaud de Vaqueiras men tions,[47] that through the crevice of the door he saw the Lady Beatrix one day pull off her long robe, gird on her brother's sword like a knight, draw it from the scabbard, and toss it in the air, catching it again with address, and wheeling

[40] Matt. Paris, 56; Wilkin's Leg. 234.
[41] Polycrat. 187, 188.
[42] St. Palaye's Troub. 209.
[43] Malmsb. 119.
[44] Ibid. 184.
[45] Sal. Polycr, 189.
[46] P. 687, 688.
[47] St, Palaye, Vol. I, p. 271.

about from right to left, till, having finished the exercise, she returned the sword into its sheath: hence, he named her Le bel Cavalier.

Knights travelled with their esquires, or armour-bearers, whose origin probably arose from the weight of the arms and armour, being too great together to allow of their entering the fight free from fatigue. Escuyer, from which our word esquire is derived, literally implies shield-bearer. When the knight thus travelled he was considered to do so peaceably: hence, the emperor, in an edict, dated 1158, says, "If a foreign knight comes peacefully to the camp, sitting on his palfrey, without shield or arms, then whoever hurts him shall be deemed a violator of the peace."[48] For a similar reason as the attendance of the esquire, they had also a page, namely, to lead their warhorse or charger, which, being by the right hand, occasioned those animals to be called destriers, dextrarii. The state parade of a knight was to march with his shield displayed, his lance elevated, and a banner before him.[49] If, however, he came to a camp with his shield on his neck, and his lance in his hand, it was deemed an attitude of defiance, for which, if he was attacked, he had no legal redress.[50]

It has been before observed, that their shields were highly ornamented with gold and brilliant colours: a German poet describes one fulgens auro, and a helmet vermiculated with amber.[51] Sometimes the knights, as the count of Poitou, placed on their shields the portrait of their favourite lady.[52]

It was a fashion for newly made knights to travel to other countries to prove their prowess at tournaments against foreign knights. Hence, Geoffry, the son of Henry II, by Fair Rosamund, went abroad for that purpose,[53] and unfortunately perished, by being trampled under the horse's feet, at one held at Paris.

The great appointed tournaments on purpose that knights might come both to learn and shew their martial powers, and at these ladies were frequently present. As many perished in these dangerous exercises, the clergy perpetually decried,[54] and some of our kings[55] prohibited them, yet nothing could annihilate the custom but the increased general civilization. Perhaps

---

[48] Radev. de Gestis Fred. 492.
[49] Matt. Paris, p. 444.
[50] Radevicus de Gest. Fred. Urtis. 492.
[51] Meib. Vol. I, p. 579.
[52] Malms. 170.
[53] Hoveden, 580 and .631.
[54] Hoveden, 584; Rymer's Foed. Vol. I, p. 245, 301.
[55] Especially Henry III and Edward II. SeeCalend. Rotular, 11; 12, 13, 14, &c.

what most tended to encourage them was the custom of ladies giving the prizes.[56]

The chivalry of the gothic nations began in the woods of Germany. No youth was there permitted to assume arms, at that time the great privilege of the noble and the free, at his own pleasure. It was made a social rank, to which it was necessary that the aspiring candidates should be elected in the public councils of their rude commonwealth,[57] and the emulated distinction was then solemnly conferred by the prince or a kinsman giving them a javelin and a shield.[58]

In these customs we see the origin of knighthood. The ceremony of the election and of the investiture was always continued, but in course of time the belt and the sword were substituted for the javelin and the shield. Until this period he belonged to his family, afterwards to the state; and it was a part of the dignity and power of the prince to be accompanied by a numerous train of these elected youths. Tacitus calls them comités, the companions of the prince. Their first Latin designation, in the old charters and chronicles, is milites. The Anglo-Saxon term cnıꝺhꞇ, which gave rise to their name in England, expresses in part the meaning of the comités of Tacitus; for that his word implied, like that, a service, we may infer from his remark, "nec rubor inter comités aspici." The word cnıꝺhꞇ was not, however, the only word used in the Saxon language after the Norman conquest, for in an old MS.[59] is the following account of the Conqueror's making his son a knight: ꝺubbaꝺe hıꞃ benꞃıe ꞇo ꞃıꝺene bæꞃ, "and here lie dubbed his son Henry a rider," which agrees with the French chevalier, the German ritter, and the Welsh marchog, all derived from the Roman eques. Thus also Lidgate[60] observes:

Eques ab cquo, is said of very ryght
And chevalier is said of chevalrie
In whiche a rider called is a knight,
Arogoners done also specifie
Caballiero through all that partie,
Is name of worship, and so took his ginning
Of spurs of gold and chiefly riding.

---

[56] One of these was a bear. Matt. Par. 265.
[57] Turner's History of England, Vol. I, p. 145.
[58] Tacit. de Mor. Germ. s. 13.
[59] Quoted by Dr. Hickes in his Saxon Grammar, p. 1M,
[60] In bis Tale of thé Horse, the Sheep, and the Goat,

As the Christian clergy prevailed in Europe, and became a constituent portion of the national councils of every country, they made religion a part of the ceremonial on these elections. They caused an oath to be imposed on the knight; they made the protection of the church a part of his duty; they extended this to the assistance of the weak and injured; and they gained an influence over his mind by consecrating his sword and belt on the altar.[61]

The earliest form of making a knight, after Christianity was diffused through Europe, was the girding on his sword in a belt. This custom existed in the days of Alfred, who so knighted Atlielstan; and knighthood, as a military order, invested with command, prevailed in England long before the Norman conquest.[62]

Chivalry, thus improved by its religious ceremonial and obligations, became an important agent in civilizing the fierce and predatory warriors of the gothic nations. It led their rude minds to make even the warfare they loved a subject of ethical discrimination. The actions of the base knight became marked, and were separated from the noble and applauded. One path led to fame, the other to disgrace. This distinction once arising could not fail to be permanent. It was the interest of the church to preserve and increase it; the king perceived his advantage in maintaining it; the barons found in it superior safety; and the fair sex experienced in chivalry their most effective guardian and avenger. In their presence knights delighted to prove their martial prowess, and from the hands of ladies they received their public honours. The smile of the lady he adored or professed to extol became the highest ambition of the sturdy warrior; and her excellence was the topic, not only of his praise but of his defiance. Her service, her favour, was his proudest boast.[63] Gradually in his festive hours he imitated her dress.[64] Her gentle manners diffused their magic over his own; and social courtesy, the first herald of the compassionate virtues, became the indispensable accomplishment of the preux and polished chevalier. Hue de Tabarie in his Ordene de Chevalerie, edited by Barbazan.[65]

In the days of Rufus these milder qualities began to take root, and the clergy, who did not anticipate their civilizing tendency, inculpated their ef-

---

[61] Turner'S History of England, Vol. I.
[62] Turner's History of the Anglo-Saxons, Vol. II, p. 139.
[63] Turner's History of England. Vol. I.
[64] Eadmer.
[65] Hue de Tabarie in his Ordene de Chevalerie, edited by Barbazan.

feminacy.[66] By the reign of Edward III they had established themselves in the knightly character, for though there was no code of chivalry at first, yet in this, as in most professions, the improved practice led some individuals to describe the customs which had become rules. L'Ordene de Chevalerie, by Hue de Tabarie, is of this sort. It is a poem, containing a series of instructions, supposed to have been given to Saladin, when he applied to be made a knight; and an allegorical meaning is given to most of the ceremonies.[67] Rufus was an example of chivalry in its ruder state; the Black Prince exhibited it in its last perfection. But after his time, the improvement of society having diminished its utility, it disappeared with the evils it had contributed to remove.[68]

Sometimes the king compounded with his tenants for particular services, and sometimes for those of the whole year, accepting in lieu thereof pecuniary payments, with which he hired stipendiary troops. This is generally supposed to have introduced the practice of levying scutages, first begun by Henry II. The other antient levies were in the nature of a modern land-tax, for we may trace the origin of that charge as high as the introduction of our military tenures, when every tenant of a knight's fee was bound, if called upon, to attend the king in his army a certain number of days in every year. This personal attendance becoming troublesome in many respects, the tenants found means of compounding for it, by first sending others in their stead, and, in after times, by making a pecuniary satisfaction to the crown in lieu thereof. This composition at last came to be levied by assessments, proportionate to each knight's fee, under the name of scutage, and which appears to have been first practised in the 5th of Henry II, on account of his expedition to Thoulouse. At this time, however, they appear to have been imposed only by agreement between the sovereign and the subject; but the precedent was abused, and they were levied at the command of the crown only: hence, it became one of the national complaints to King John, who, in his Magna Charta, was compelled to promise that no scutage should be imposed without the consent of the common council of the realm. This clause was omitted, indeed, in the charter of Henry III, but it was confirmed by a

---

[66] Besides John of Salisbury, St. Bernard, in some of his Crusade Sermons, attacks what be calls the degeneracy of the knights,

[67] The most complete collection of facts on chivalry bas been made by St. Palaye, in bis Mémoires sur l'ancienne Chevalerie.

[68] Turner's History of England. This elegant and indefatigable writer bas collected bis authorities from English history; but by taking the whole of Europe they would be found far more ample.

variety of statutes enacted in the reign of his son.

That the feudal troops, but particularly the posse comitatûs, might be ready, when required, to take the field, the following law was enacted in the year 1181, the 27th of this king's reign.

"Whosoever holds one knight's fee, shall have a coat of mail, a helmet, a shield, and a lance; and every knight as many coats of mail,[69] helmets, shields, and lances, as he shall have knights' fees in his domain.

"Every free layman, having in chattels or rent to the value of sixteen marks, shall keep a coat of mail, a helmet, a shield, and a lance.

"Every free layman, who shall have in chattels or rent ten marks, shall have a habergeon,[70] a chapelle de fer,[71] and a lance.

"Also all burgesses, and the whole community of freemen, shall have each a wambais, a chapelle de fer, and a lance.

"Every one of these (before-mentioned) shall swear that he will have these arms before the feast of St. Hilary, and will bear fealty to King Henry, to wit, the son of the Empress Matilda, and that he will keep these arms for his service according to his command, and with fidelity to our lord the king and his realm: and no man having these arms shall sell, pledge, or lend them, nor alienate them in any other manner; nor shall the lord take them from his vassal by forfeiture, pledge, or any other manner.

"On the death of any one having these arms, they shall remain to his heir; and if the said heir is not of such age as to be able to use arms, they shall, if necessary, be put into the custody of him who has the guardianship of his person, who shall provide a man to use them in the service of our lord the king, if required, until the heir shall be of proper age to bear arms, and then they shall be delivered to him.

"Any burgess having more arms than he is by this assize required to have, shall sell or give them, or so alienate them, that they may be retained for the service of our lord the king of England; and none of them shall keep more arms than he is by this assize bound to have.

"No Jew shall have in his custody a coat of mail or liaubergeon, but shall

---

[69] The word used is lorica, which, in this instance, probably comprehends the hauberk and chausses, or pantaloons, worn at this period.

[70] Halbergelluro. This was evidently not so expensive as the hauberk and chausses, and consequently less in size; yet it was something more than a covering for the body to the abdomen, for that was called a broigne: I therefore conceive, it to have been the body-armour, which terminated in breeches, as worn at the conquest, especially as Wace describes the warriors at that time 'Clad in haubergeons and hauberks.'

[71] The capelet ferri was a flattened conical cap. See Pl. x of this work.

sell or give it away, or in some other manner so dispose of it, that it shall remain in the king's service.

"Also, no man shall carry arms out of the kingdom unless by the command of our lord the king, nor shall any man sell arms to another who means to carry them out of the kingdom."

By other parts of this law, it was directed that juries should be appointed to discover who had chattels or rent to the value expressed therein, and the justices were enjoined to cause it to be notified over all the counties through which they were to pass, that those who had not these arms as aforesaid, the king would punish corporally in their limbs, and not in their goods, their lands, or chattels. The king further commanded, that none but a freeman should be admitted to take the oath of arms.

The wambais was originally a German garment, implying a covering for the belly.[72] Its name, however, has been corrupted by the writers of different nations by whom it was adopted, into wamines, wambeys, wambasium, gambiex, gambaison, gamboisson, gambaycho, gambocia, gambeson, gambison, gamvisum, gombeson, gaubeson, goubisson, and gobisson. Nicetas, in his first book of the Life of the Emperor Isaac, describes it as a quilted tunic, well stuffed with wool, that had been washed and beat up with vinegar, and therefore supposed to resist iron.

All anonymous writer De rebus bellicis Notitise Imperii subjectum, says it is vestimenti genus quod de coactili ad mensuram et tutelam pectoris liumani conficitur de mollibus lanis. "A kind of vestment, which was made of the shape of the human breast to be its protection, and stuffed with soft wooland the Scholiast On Thucydides states it to be πῖλον τό ἐξ ἐρία ὦηκ'Ιον ἔνδυμα θωράκίον τι, ὑπὸ τὰ σ'Ιήθη ὅ ἐυδυομεθα. "A tunic stuffed with wool, and put on like a breastplate, being placed under the other garments." And Constantine Porphyrogenitus, in his Tactics, σπολὰς ἔιχον οἱ τοιϰτοι ψιλοί ἰσχυρὰς, ϰὰι πηϰ'Ιας ἀντὶ ϰλιβανιων ϰαί λωριϰίων. "A garment like Such as are flexible, but strong, and stuffed, worn under the clibanium or lorica."

The Chronicon Colmariense relates, that Igitur Rex Adolphus contra Ducem Austi'ise cum magna multitudine venientem, in occursum currit cum liominum armata multitudine copiosa. Annati reputabantur qui galeas ferreas in capitibus liabebant, et qui wambasia, id est, tunicam spissain ex lino et stuppa, vel veteribus pannis consutam, et desuper camisiam ferream, id est vestem ex circulis ferreis contextam. "King Adolphus, therefore,

---

[72] From wamba or wambon, the abdomen; whence the Saxon wambe, and our word womb.

marched against the duke of Austria with his troops, and had with him a great multitude of men at arms. Those were called men at arms who wore iron helmets on their heads, and who had a wambais, i. e. a garment wadded with wool, tow, or old rags, stitched together, over which was placed the chemise de fer, i. e. a tunic of interwoven iron rings."

On this account it was sometimes called subarmale. William de Guilleville, in his MS. poem, entitled Le Pelerinage de l'Ame, says:

> Là sont heaumes et haubergons
> Gorgeretes et gambisons.

> "There are helmets and haubergeons,
> Gorgets and gambesons."

By which it appears that he speaks of it, not as armour of itself, but as worn with the haubergeon; and this is more evident in a subsequent line:

> Le gambison vesti Jesus
> Quant por ti en croix fu pendus.

> "The gambeson clothed Jesus
> When for thee he was crucified."

And Guillaume le Breton*[73] has:

> Gambesumque audax forat, et thoraca trilicem.

> "Boldly he pierced the gambeson and trellisscd thorax."

The wambais, however, was sometimes used instead of other armour, being found sufficiently strong to resist the ordinary force of a weapon. Thus the Roman de Gaydon MS. has:

> A ces paroles li vavasor s'arma
> D'un gambison viez enfumé qu'il a.

> "At these words the vavasor armed himself
> With an old smoky gambeson which he had."

So the Roman de Jordain MS.

---

[73] Lib. ii Pbilip.

Chascun avoit son gambison vestu.

"Each was clad in his gambeson."

The Roman de Rou et des Ducs de Normandie, by Wace, thus notices it:

Plusours ourent vestus hambeis
Cojures ont chaint et carquois.

"Many were clad in the wambais:
The conspirators had chains and quivers."

This seems, however, to have been allowed at first only in such cases as insufficiency of fortune: hence, the ordonnance in 1181, which has given rise to these observations; and so in the old Costumier of Normandy, when speaking of judicial combats: Si n'est pas chevalier, ne il n'a point de fieu de hauberc, l'amende l'y doit estre par un roncin par un gambiex, par un chapel et par une lance. "If he be not a knight, and has not a fief de hauberk, he must make the amends by a hackney,[74] a gambiex, a chapel de fer, and a lance."

The wambais seems to have been made with sleeves, and to have reached to the middle of the thigh; hence, Albert de Argentin says:[75] Ubi manicas wambasii sui fractas cum novis peceis reparans. "Repairing with new pieces the sleeves of his wambais where torn." And from what he says further on, this garment appears to have been of a red colour: Quidam camifex episcopum super dextrario in rubea wambasia circumventum cuspide perforavit. "A certain butcher, riding on a war-horse, and protected by a red wambais, stabbed the bishop on his progress with a lance." It was also stitched down in parallel lines, which suffered the stuffed part, called, by Raymond de Agiles, culcitræ de gambasio, or "the cushions of the wambais," to appear convex. Hence, the Lord de Joinville, in his campaign of St. Louis, says: "he luckily found a gambeson of coarse cloth, which had belonged to a Saracen, and turning the furrowed part inward, lie made a sort of shield, which was of much service" to him.

The gamboised work is visible on the breeches of the earl of Oxford, Pl. XXII; below the termination of the hauberk of a knight of the Montford family, Pl. XXII; and on the sleeves of the knight, Pl. XXX.

---

[74] The roncin was a horse of inferior description, and hence, probably, was derived tbe name of Rosinante, which carded Don Quixote.

[75] P. 104.

Lord Lyttleton, in his Life of Henry II, says: "It is strange that the Irish, who had much intercourse with the Welsh before Henry the Second's time, should not have learnt from that nation, who greatly excelled in archery, that arrows were better weapons to annoy an enemy with than stones thrown by the hand without the help of slings, which, unless at a small distance, could have little or no elfect." He further observes, that "from many instances in the course of" Henry's wars with the Irish, "it appears that the English conquests in Ireland were principally owing to the use of the long-how in battle, which the Irish infantry wanted; and, therefore, Giraldus Cambrensis, in his chapter entitled Qualiter Hibernica gens sit expugnanda, advises, that in all engagements with that people archers should be intermingled with the heavy-armed troops."

The Turkish custom, originally prevalent in Egypt, of cutting off the heads of those who fall in battle, and placing them at the feet of the conqueror, continued in Ireland so late as the reign of Henry II,[76] which may be considered as one probability of their Asiatic origin, so earnestly contended for by General Vallancey.

---

[76] Girald. Top. Hib. c. 4,.

Richard the First.

1189.

SO extraordinary a military character as Richard Cœur de Lion demands our particular notice. His passion for war and warlike celebrity inflamed his bosom with heroic envy of the fame of Saladin. This renowned Mussulman, every where dreaded and execrated, but every where talked of with wonder, was the idol of the popular tongue; and Richard, though some thousand miles distant from the Saracen, yet resolved upon a personal competition. Abandoning, therefore, all the tempting objects of ambition that lay near him, he proceeded with the whole power of his kingdom to the encounter. He was valiant beyond the measure of human daring; inferior to no man in hardihood, strength, and agility; unparallelled in his feats of prowess; and his actions were so romantic that Gibbon, when recounting them, feels compelled to exclaim, "Am I writing the history of Orlando or Amadis!"[1] He had obtained the epithet of the British Lion before he began his reign;[2] and is extolled by Yinesauf, his companion in the Holy Land, for his flexible limbs, his strength, and length of arm, which was excelled by none in its power of wielding a sword, and of

[1] Decline of Rom. Empire, and observes that it is by his enemies such a character is given.

[2] Giraldo Top. Bib. 752.

striking with effect.[3]

Being attacked at Milete, in his way to the Holy Land, when he had strolled along attended by only one knight, by some rustics, who assailed them with clubs, stones, and knives, he disdained with true chivalric feeling to bathe his sword in ignoble blood, and therefore only struck at them with the flat of it; the sword, however, broke, and then he took up stones to defend himself.[4]

While in Sicily, previous to the crusade, he agreed to several judicious regulations with Philip Auguste King of France, for the peace and good government of their respective armies. Their followers were allowed to dispose at their deaths of their arms, horses, and clothes, and of half the property they had with them: the other half was to be applied to the expense of the crusade. None in the armies were to play for money, but knights and the clergy, and they were not to lose above twenty shillings in a day and night. Those serving might play in the king's mansion to that amount; but if elsewhere they were to be whipped naked through the army for three days. Mariners who gamed were to be dipped for the same space of time in the sea.[5]

We may learn the splendour of encampments in the time of Richard I from the following circumstance: He demanded from Tancred King of Sicily, as part of the dowry of his sister, a tent of silk, so large that 200 knights might dine under it.[6] This luxury had probably been derived from the preceding crusade, as, in the victory subsequent to the capture of Antioch, there was taken among the spoils a silken tent, gorgeously ornamented, and made to represent a fortified city with walls and towers, and capable of holding 2,000 men.[7] Richard also sent to Tancred a sword, that was believed to be the celebrated caleburno, the weapon of the famous Arthur, which so pleased that prince, that in return he gave the king of England the much more valuable present of four great ships, called ursers, and fifteen galleys.[8]

We discover the mode of attacking land forces by a fleet at this time, from what happened at Cyprus. The Cypriots formed on the shore, an undisciplined host, some with swords and lances, others with clubs and pilx;[9] and

---

[3] Iter Hierosol. in Gale's Script. Vol. II, p. 302.

[4] Rog. Hoved. 673.'

[5] Hoved. 675.

[6] .Ibid. 675.

[7] William of Tyre, 726.

[8] Hoveden, 688.

[9] My friend Mr. Douce conjectures, that pil is derived from pilum, a javelin. Villains', however, were not allowed the lance, so that this signification may be doubted. See pages 9 and 19.

placing the planks, benches, and chests, which had been shipwrecked, for their fortification, determined to await the king of England's attack. Richard called his knights to arms, and approached with his galleys, in which were ranged his bowmen. A shower of arrows cleared the shore, and an impetuous charge drove the Cypriot prince and his warlike array to flight.[10]

The royal fleets of France and England cast anchor in the bay of Acre, while the Christians in that country were besieging that town, and Saladin had just flown to its rescue. This timely arrival of 12,000 new adventurers saved the besiegers from annihilation. The attack and defence had been carried on with equal braveiy. Vast tow'ers of wood wrere erected to command the city. The besieged were as active in the invention of machines to withstand them. Repeatedly were the military contrivances on both sides consumed by flames. On both sides the projectile weapons incessantly hurled destruction on the combatants or their military engines. The Greek fire became lavishly used, especially from the city: individuals, machines, towns, and ships, were destroyed by it. Naval combats took place successively between other fleets of the contending powers, which became more terrible from the use of this fire, an inflammable composition, which water only aggravated, and which sand and vinegar only could subdue. One of these engagements took place with Richard's squadron, while in his course from Cyprus. He met a Saracen ship of uncommon size, well furnished with arms provisions, abundant phials of the Greek fire, and 200 combustible serpents, for the use of the besieged. Seven Turkish emirs were with it. Its magnitude and powerful engines deterred the English vessels, but Richard exclaimed: "Will you let it get away undamaged? Shame, shame ! after so many triumphs now to become cowardly! No one shall have safety while an enemy remains. Take her, or you shall all be crucified if she escapes." This vehemence compelled them to make a virtue of necessity, and the English sprang to board her. But the Turks, contending from a higher station, lopped off the arms and heads of those who took hold. Rage at this sight added new energies to the assailants; they rushed on with mingled fury and despair, and, after a bloody conflict, remained master of the prize, which soon sunk.[11] Bohadin, the secretary of Saladin, relates, that this vessel contained 650 strenuous warriors. Its captain, finding escape impossible, de-

---

10 Hoveden, 690; he calls the attendants of the king of Cyprus, Griffones. Strutt conjectures that it was from the falcastra, with which he supposes they were armed, which may be considered like eagles' bills: but there are many authorities to prove that by Griffones was meant the Greeks.

[11] Vinesauf, 329.

clared that the English should not profit by their victory: "Let us covet a glorious death," he exclaimed; and ordered the sides to be hewn with axes till the water rushed in.[12] Vinesauf states it to have been of that importance that, if it had reached Acre, the city could never have been taken.

As Richard approached Acre he beheld a spectacle of great military magnificence. Around the city spread the camps of the besiegers, a collection of warriors from every country in Europe, with their separate and appropriate standards. The walls of the place were manned by its resolute defenders, urging their active engines of warlike defence. Beyond, at a visible distance, the powerful army of Saladin appeared, covering the hills and plains; their tents radiating with the gorgeous colours so precious to Turkish taste, and their leaders watching to seize every favouring moment for a successful attack. The king of France, who had just before arrived, and all the nobles of the Christian army, advanced to meet Richard as he entered; and the acclamations of exulting thousands, anticipating relief and victory from his experienced prowess, completed the animating scene.[13]

Preparing for the attack, he planted his manganells, his stone-projecting machines and tower, against the gate of the city, which he resolved to force. A severe malady stopping his personal exertions, the king of France determined on an assault in the interval. The Turks within, by shouts, trumpets, and drums, gave the alarm to Saladin without: he hastened with his forces to attack the trenches, and the double conflict ended in the burning of the French engines by the Greek fire, and the failure of their attempts.[14] New machines were invented, called belfreys, cats, and cercleys, and these were again consumed; while Richard, confined to his bed by the fever, moaned heavily his restraint. His stone artillery was particularly distinguished for its activity and power, both in shaking the walls and destroying their defenders.[15] One of the stones it threw was taken to Saladin for his observation: it had killed twelve men.

Still disabled by his disease, yet impatient to partake the fray, having caused a strong walled edifice to be made and pushed to the trenches, within which his engineers might operate with some protection, Richard was carried thither upon a silken mattress, and from that pointed and discharged himself his own balista,[16] killing many Turks by the darts and arrows he sent

---

[12] P. 166.

[13] Vinesauf, 331; Bohadin, 165.

[14] Vinesauf, 332; Bohadin, 167.

[15] Vinesauf, 335.

[16] This was a cross-bow of the larger kind.

among them. His sappers were also at work under his eye. He stimulated the desperate exertions of his followers, by promising four pieces of gold for every stone which they could pull from the walls. Still the foremost himself, observing one of the Turks parading on the fortifications in the armour of a celebrated Christian knight, who had fallen, he aimed his own weapon with that strength and certainty, that the arrow it projected buried itself in his bosom.[17]

The fury of his assaults, seconded by the general ardour of all the besiegers, after nine months, compelled the surrender of the city, and Saladin, who had consented to it, made a truce with the Christian kings, and indignantly retired from its vicinity, meditating his future revenge.[18]

The particulars of this siege introduce to our notice several things worthy of remark, and requiring explanation. The first of these is the Greek fire.

This forerunner of gunpowder had its name from having been invented by a Greek, in the time of Constantine Barbatus Emperor of Constantinople. This was Callinicus, an architect, and a native of Heliopolis, in Syria.[19] Before this period the Greeks had used fireships, which they called κατάβοπῦρφόροι, and adopted for that purpose, vessels called χελανδία, whence the Parisians denominate a barge, chaland. The term καταβοπὺρφορος implies "carrying fire for the purpose of being ejected;" and sharp bolts of iron, covered with tow, well oiled and pitched, were thrown to set fire to engines. These vessels are mentioned as employed during the empire of Leo the Great. After the discovery of the Greek fire it was used at sea and on land. The vessels selected to carry it were called δρωμονες, and they had erected on their prows large tubes of copper, through which these fires were blown into the enemy's ships.[20] Anna Comnena[21] tells us, that on land the soldiers were supplied with copper tubes for a similar purpose: in this case it was made up in a cylindrical form, but at other times it was put into phials and pots, and fixed on the end of arrows and bolts; and from the walls of a city it was poured from large boilers, or launched in red hot balls of stone or iron. Its appearance we learn from the Lord de Joinville, who de-

---

[17] Vines auf, 338.

[18] Ibid. 341, 342; Bohad. 173, 179,.

[19] So says Theophanes, p. 295;- but Cedrenus, p.437, with more probability, intimates that he was a chemist, by assigning Heliopolis, in Egypt, as his native place.

[20] Leo's Tactics, c. 19. As these were fancifully shaped into the mouths of savage monsters, that seemed to vomit a stream of liquid and consuming fire, they gave origin to those tales, so current at the period of the crusades, of encounters with fiery dragons.

[21] Alexiad, lib. xiii.

scribes it as "resembling a long barrel, having a tail the length of a long spear. The noise which it made was like to thunder, and it seemed a great dragon of fire flying through the air; and giving so great a light with its flame, that we saw in our camp as clearly as, in broad day."[22]

Its composition, according to Anna Comnena, was pitch and other resins, mixed with sulphur, and the whole ground together. The author of the History of Jerusalem makes oil one of its component parts, as docs Abbo, in his Wars of Paris, who also adds wax. Procopius mentions this fire as used in the Gothic war, and says, that in its composition was naphtha, sulphur, and bitumen.[23] Jacques de Vitry speaks of a fountain in the East, ex cujus aquis ignis Græcus efficitur, quibusdam aliis admixtis, "from the waters of which, with some other ingredients, the Greek fire was formed." This was probably a spring of naphtha, by no means uncommon in Asia. It was found not to yield, like ordinary fire, to the extinguishing effects of water: hence, William of Newbury says, Mûris enim admotæ (machinæ) incende-bantur ab hostibus quodam ignis genere quam Græcum dicunt. Deniqué hoc genus arte confectum miræ esse potentiæ dicitur, nec contrario cedere elemento. "For the machines which were moved against the walls were burnt by the enemy with what was called the Greek fire. This kind of artificial combustible is said to possess an astonishing power, and not to yield to its contrary element." So Albert d'Aix remarks, hujus ignis genus aqua erat inextingui-bile, "this kind of fire is not extinguishable by water." Invention was therefore busy in searching for means for this purpose, as well as an antidote to its effects, and wliat these were we learn from Jacques de Vitry, who says, postquam vehementer fuerit accensus, vix aut nunquam potest extingui, nisi aceto, aut hominum urina et sabulo. "After the flame had acquired a degree of vehemence it could scarce ever be extinguished, unless by a mixture of vinegar or human urine with sand." He further informs us, that "to prevent its dreadful effects, ships were covered with cloths dipt in vinegar." Machines for attack were, for the same purpose, covered with boiled horse and bullock skins. The Roman de Garin says:

---

[22] See his Mémoires. According to this it must have greatly resembled the modern Congreve rockets. He brought home some of the moulds in which it was placed.

[23] We see, therefore, how near was the approach to the discovery of gunpowder, whose ingredients are merely saltpetre, sulphur, and charcoal. Naphtha is a light, tenacious, and inflammable oil,which oozes from the earth, and takes tire' as soon as it comes in contact with atmospheric ,air..

Le feu Grezois lors fet leans jalir,
Aux grans palez et h sales ferir,
Vente li venez, li palez est espris
N'iert m6s esteint par eve nes undis.

"The Greek fire then was made to spurt out from within,
To strike the great palisade and building:
Coming with smoke, the palisade is destroyed;
Nor will it be extinguished by clear water at all."

And again:

Lievent engins, sont perieres dreciees
A mangoniax le feu Grezois lor gietent.

"They raise engines, perieres are arranged
On the mangonels, is the Greek fire then cast."

The composition of this fire had long been kept a secret, and its use consequently confined to the Greeks themselves. It was concealed with the most jealous scruple, and the terror of enemies was increased and prolonged by their ignorance and surprise. At length, after having been confined by every precaution for above 400 years, it was either discovered by, or betrayed to, the Mahometans, who thereby acquired that superiority over the Franks the Greeks had once possessed over them.[24]

Robert de Brunne, in his Continuation of Peter Langtoff's Chronicle, says, that Richard I, in his wars against the Saracens—

In bargeis and galeis
He set mylnes to go,
The sailes as men sais
Some were blak and bio,

Some were rede and grenc,
The wynde about them blewe,
A selly sight to sene,
Fire the sailes threwe.

The stones were of Rynes,
The noyse dredfulle and grcte,
It affraied the Sarazins,
As leven the lire out scbete.

---

[24] A fuller account of the component parts of the Greek fire will be found under the 'reign of Edward III.

Which imports, that in his barges and galleys he had mills, that were turned by the wind, and by force of the sails threw fire, and stones which were got from the Rhine.

The use of the Greek, or, as it might now be called, of the Saracen fire, was continued to the middle, of the 14th century, when the discovery of gunpowder effected a new revolution in the art of war.

The next circumstance to notice is the account of military machines. The first of these mentioned is the mangana, or manganum, and its diminutive, the mangonel. William of Tyre, in his account of the first crusade,[25] says, Jaculatorias, quas vulgari appellatione mangana dicunt, et petrarias fabre fieri placuit, by which we learn, that the manganum was a machine for darting, and, as it would seem, was not the same as the petrary, which discharged stones. He again, in the following passage, distinguishes these engines, though he calls both jaculatory: Castella et machinas jaculatorias quas mangana et petrarias vocant.[26] The distinction, however, he appears inclined to place merely in the relative magnitude of the machines, as in another place he says:[27] Alii vero minoribus tormentis qua? mangana vocantur minores im-mittendo lapides. "But others, with the smaller instruments of attack, which are called mangana, for ejecting smaller stones." Thwrocz, in his account of Aba King of Hungary, says, Quosdam vero lapidibus obruentes, alios autem in manganis ferreis vastantes occiderunt. "While some attacked with stones, others threw them from mangana, made of iron, and killed great numbers." But Abbo[28] lets us somewhat more into the materials with which these machines were made: he says,

> Conficiunt longis aeque lignis, geminalis
> Mangana quae proprio vulgi libitu vocitantur,
> Saxa quibus jaciunt ingentia.

> "They constructed machines which, were twofold,
> of timber of equal lengths,
> Which, according to common consent, are called mangana,
> With which they cast immense stones."

Thus, then, we see as the result of all this, that the manganum was made

---

[25] Lib. III, c. 5.
[26] Lib. VIII, c. 6.
[27] Lib. VIII,. c. 9.
[28] Obsid. Lutetioe, Lib. I.

of wood and iron, projected great stones, but in general was of less size than the petrary.

The mangonel was a similar machine, but not so large as the manga-num; hence, Guillaume le Breton[29] tells us:

> Interea gross os pctraria mitlit ab intus
> Assidue lapides, mangonellusquc minores.

> "In the meantime the petrary rapidly discharges
> Immense stones, and the mangonel smaller ones."

William Guiart, under the year 1204, says:

> Cà et là, avant et arriérés
> Gietent mangoniaus et perieres
> La grosse pierre arrondie
> De maine à l'aller grand bondie. .

> "Here and there, before and behind,
> The mangonias and perieres cast
> The great stone, which was made round,
> Now destined to go with a great rebound"

Again—

> En ront mangoniaus et perieres
> Qui souvent tendent et destendent,
>   En destachant grans escrois rendent
> Pierres qui par l'air se rennie.

> "In a circle the mangonias and perieres
> Which are often stretched and distended
> By detaching great holds,t[30] cast
> Stones, which make resistance through the air."

The French, however, at a later period, called what was projected from the machines, mangoneaux. Hence, Froissart says, Et avoient les Brabançons de très grans engins devant la ville, qui jetoient pierres de faix et mangoni-aux jysques en la ville. "The Brabançons had very large engines before the town, which threw stones that had been shaped to a proper form, and man-gonias as far as the town."

---

[29] Philipp. lib, VII.
[30] Lacombe calls escroix, instrument à fendre les pierres.

The next thing to be noticed is the belfry, belfragium, or beffroi.

This was a warlike machine, in form of a square tower, made of wood, having different stories, each of which was filled with a proper number of soldiers, who shot from their bows and cross-bows over such part of the walls as were within their respective reach. These machines were generally moved on four wheels, and drawn near the walls for action.[31] Froissart[32] describes one at a later period thus: "The English had constructed two large towers of great beams of wood, three stories high:[33] each tower was placed on wheels, and covered over with prepared leather, to shelter those within from fire and from the arrows: in each story were 100 archers." In the Chronicle of Bertrand du Guesclin, written at the commencement of the 14th century, occurs the following passage:

> Un grant beffroy de bois orent fait charpenter
> Et le firent adonques à Arques apporter
> Jusques près des fossés ils le firent traisncr,
> Grande plenté de gent y pouvoit bien entrer.

> "They caused to be constructed a great belfry of wood,
> And had it transported to Arques;[34]
> Then they had it dragged quite close to the ditches:
> It would easily contain a great number of men."

William Brito, or le Breton,[35] names it belfragium, and gives of it the following description:

> Cratibus et lignis rydibus belfragia surgunt,
> Turribus alta magis et mœnibus, unde valerent
> Agmina missilibus, telisque quibuslibet uti
> Devexosque hostes facili prosternerc jactu.

> "With twigs and timber, from lumber arise the belfries,
> Having on their tops towers and walls, from whence
> The troops could throw their missiles, and use any kind of weapon,
> And easily overthrew, by such discharge, an enemy drawn towards them."

---

[31] See Pl. XXVI, Fig.I.

[32] Vol. I, c. 108.

[33] This is the height of one in the painted glass at St. Denis, depicting the second crusade.

[34] Caxton says, that the wooden tower which Richard I made use of at the siege of Messina, and. afterwards at Arces, was called mate-gryffons. Vide Polychron. lib. VII, c. 26. Does this imply a match for the Greeks?

[35] In the 2d book of his Philippiade.

And again, in his 7th book:

> Parte alia turres, quibus est belfragia nomen
> Roboribus crudis compactæ atque arbora multa
> Intactis dolabra ruditer, quibus ascia solos
> Absciderat ramos sic educantur, ut usque'
> Aëra sub medium longo volumine tendant
> Ut doleat murus illis depressior esse.

"In another part towers, known by the name of belfries,
Formed of rough oak, closely put together, and many trees,
Not shaped by the plane into an even form, but which, by the axe alone,
Had merely had their branches lopt off, (were seen) and so highly raised as even
To make resistance to the air, by being rolled on so far,
That the wall might regret to be depressed by them."
And easily overthrew, by such discharge, an enemy drawn towards them."

The Roman de Garin describes this machine without naming it:

> Un engin fet de tel parler n'oi,
> Qui ot de haut cent pi6s tos enterins
> Pres de la porte fist venir tels engins,
> A set estages tot droit de fust chesnin,
> Arbalestriers a mis jusqu'a vint,
> Bien fit clo6s couvert de cuir boli.

"An engine he made, such as I have never heard speak of,
Which was a hundred feet high to the full;
He had it moved close to the gate, as is done with such engines:
On seven stories quite erect, of chesnut wood,
Cross-bowmen were placed, about twenty:
Quite compact was it made, and covered with boiled leather."

But in another place this poem is more explicit, thus:

> La vcissies ces perrieres venir,
> Ces mangoniax et gater et llatir,
> Et les berfrois as cliastiax assaillir
> Et ces archers durement catir.

"There might you see come these perrieres;
These mangonias, which both destroy and hurl;
And the belfries on the cat-castles assail,
While the archers sorely press them."

William of Malmsbury[36] calls this machine berfreicl; his words are: Alteruin fuit pro lignorum penuria turris non magna, in modum ædificiorum facta, berfreid appellant, quod fastigium murorum sequaret. "There was another machine, which, from the scarcity of wood, could not have a large tower; it was in the form of an edifice, and called berfreid, because it squared with tlie summit of the walls." Simeon of Durham terms it, in 1123, berfreit; and Ordericus Vitalis, berfredus: Roloudin, in his Chronicle, bilfredus; and Wm. Heda, in 1190, verfredus.

The word beifroy, belfry, has since been applied to the highest towers of frontier towns, wherein a centinel is placed to watch for their security, and with a bell for him to strike on, to alarm the inhabitants and guards at the gates. This bell was subsequently employed to mark the hour for the retreat of the inhabitants to their houses, the garrisons to their quarters, and other public uses, whence it was denominated "campana vannalis;" and in the Statuta Gildæ Scotia, c. 28, we read Nullus regratarius emat pisces, foenum, avenas, ante pulsationem campanee in berefrido. "No retailer shall purchase fish, hay or straw, before the striking of the campana in the belfry."

The cats, according to Mr. Turner,[37] were so called, "because they clung to the walls like cats;" but, as they were covers for the sappers, who might be said to resemble the claws of that animal scratching, underneath, I am induced to derive the name from that circumstance. Anna Comnena calls it σῖόα, "a portico," which it exactly resembled, though, for the purpose of moving it, to the bases of four pillars were affixed a frame-work and wheels: yet I should mention, that when drawn up to the walls it was made fast to them. Guillaume le Breton says:[38]

Hue faciunt reptare catum, tectique sub illo
Suffodiunt murum.

"Hither they cause to be drawn the cat, and those covered by it
Undermine the wall."

The Monaclius Vallis Sarnasii[39] says, Machinam quandam parvani, quae lingua vulgari catus dicitur, faciebat duci ad sufFodiendum murum. "A certain small machine, which, in common parlance, is called a cat, he had brought forward in order to undermine the walls." Aimoinus goes a little

---

[36] Hist. Ang. lib. IV.
[37] Hist Eng. in Note. Vol. I, p. 318,
[38] Philipp. lib. VII,
[39] In bis Hist. Albig. c. 42.

further,[40] and mentions its composition: Erant carri vimineis cratibus tabulisque tecti ligneis, in quibus latentes milites fundamenta suifoderent murorum. "There were cars made with osier twigs and laths, and covered with wooden planks, within which the troops appointed for sapping the walls might lie concealed." William Guiart, speaking of the siege of Bovines, by Philippe Auguste, tells us:

> Devant Boves fit l'ost de France
> Qui contrc les Flamans contance
> Li mineur pas ne soumeiilent
> Un chat bon et fort appareillent.
> Tant euvrent dessous ct tant cavent
> Qu'une grant part du mur destravant.

> "Before Bovines came the army of France,
> Which against the Flemings made war,
> The miners were by no means asleep;
> A great and strong cat fitted up,
> They so much worked and excavated within,
> That a great part of
> the wall they destroyed."

Again, under the year 1205:

> Un chat font sus le pont atraire,
> Dont pieça mention feismes
> Qui fit de la roche meismes
> Li mineur desous se lancent
> Le fort mur a miner comruencent,
> Et font le chat si aombrer
> Que riens ne les peut encombrer.

> "They cause a cat to be drawn upon the bridge,
> Of which we have partly made mention,
> And which was upon the rock itself:
> The miners underneath darted onwards,
> And began to undermine the strong wall,
> And having made the cat completely to overshadow them,
> There was nothing which could incommode them."

They were sometimes used by the besieged themselves, and sent out to attack those in the belfries, while carrying on their operations against the

---

[40] Lib. III, c. 71, Hist,

city. Thus Radevicus:[41] Magnaque audacia super muros, et in suis machinis, quos cattas appellant, operiuntur, et cum admoverentur pontes, ipsi eos vel occuparent, vel dejicerent, murumque scalis ascendere nitentes vario modo deterrent. "With much boldness, on their walls and within their machines, which they call cats, they (the besieged) worked, and when those (who were attacking) moved to the walls their bridges (or their belfries) they either themselves took possession of them, or threw over those upon them, and by various means deterred such as were striving to scale the walls from their purpose."

They were further made use of to cover those who filled up the ditches preparatory to wheeling upon them the belfries,[42] and when used for this purpose were called by the French chats faux, "false cats;" and by the Italians catafalco.[43] From this and the last mentioned use of the cat was derived the French word eschafaux, "an elevated floor;" and, subsequently, the English word scaffold. The cercley is another machine noticed in this account; but I have not met with any description particularizing it.

There are many reasons for supposing that the balista, which Richard himself used in this siege, was in reality some kind of cross-bow. In the first place it did not discharge stones but weapons; in the next, as we shall see presently, the revival of this implement in Europe is attributed to that monarch; and last of all, the following words of Guillaume le Breton shew, that it often signified the arcubalista:

> Nee tamen interea cessat balista vel arcus,
> Quadrcllos hæ multiplica't, pluit ille sagittas.

> "Nor during this did cease the balista or the bow,
> The one multiplying quarrels, the other showering arrows."

The quarrel was the peculiar weapon in the shape of a short arrow and pyramidal head, that was ejected from the cross-bow. It is Brompton who says of Richard I of England, Siquidem hoc genus sagittandi, quod arcubalistarum dicitur, jam dudum sopitum, ut dicitur in usum revocaret unde et in eo peritus plures manu propria peremit. "Truly this kind of shooting,

---

[41] Hist. Fred. I[mi]. Vegetius bas given a similar description, lib. IV, c. 15.

[42] Muratori, Scrip. Ital.

[43] This, acoording to Vegetius, lib. IV, c. 16, was properly the use of the masculi of the antients. Angelo Portenari pella Felicita di Padua, lib. v, c. 5, p. 165, has given. an engraving of it.

which is called cross-bow shooting, already laid aside, according to report was revived by him, whence he became so skilful in its management, that he killed many people with his own hand." Thus far may be true, because the cross-bow had been used in England, at least on hunting excursions, in the time of Rufus, for Wace tells us, that Henry, going the same day to the New Forest, found the string of his cross-bow broken, and taking it to a villain to be mended, saw an old woman there, who told him he would be king. Odo, the cross-bowman, lived in the time of William the Conqueror.[44] Simeon of Durham speaks of it in the time of Henry I thus: Eminebat machina, unde sagitarii et albalistarii præliabantur. "He raised a machine from whence the archers and cross-bowmen might shoot." Their use was general in Italy in the year 1139, for at that time Pope Innocent II particularly forbad them. The German Emperor Conrad did the same, as we learn from William de Dole, who lived in the latter part of the 12th century, when he introduces Raoul de Hondane speaking thus:

> Par effort de lance et d'escu
> Conqueroit toz ses ennemis,
> Ja arbalestriers ni fu mis
> Por sa guerre en autoritez.
> Par avoir, et par mauvaistie
> Les tiennent ore li haut home
> Per demi le thresor de Rome
> Ne vosist-il n'a droit, n'a tort
> Qu'uns en eut un preud home mort.

> "By the effort of lance and shield
> Conquered he all his enemies:
> Then cross-bowmen were not put
> For his wars into authority,
> Through money and evil disposition,
> Keeping them in dread: the proud man
> For half the treasure of Rome,
> He would not, right or wrong,
> That any one should slay a man of prowess."

But though with much magnanimity the French held cross-bows and poisoned darts as too murderous for generous warfare, still to attribute the origin of the former to our Cœur de Lion is a wilful misrepresentation of

---

[44] See note, p. 15.

Brompton's words, displaying itself in a mean jealousy of England[45] In the first place William Guiart says:

> Nul ne savoit riens d'arbalestcs
> El terns dont je fais remembrance
> En tout le royame de France.

> "Cross-bows were quite unknown,
> Within the time which I record,
> Throughout the whole kingdom of France."

And Guillaume le Breton says, the French received them from Richard I.

> Venus estoit nouvellement
> Des arbalestes li usages,
> Richart qui de tiex fais iert sages
> Tout soit-il d'autre déporté L'ot issi ains en France aporte,
> Si corn les Croniques desquerrent.

> "Of modern origin
> Is the use of cross-bows.
> Richard, who of their service was well acquainted,
> Brought them from another country:[46]
> He also introduced them into France,
> According to what the Chronicles relate."

So again, while noticing the death of this monarch, he says:

> Ainsi fina par le quarel,
> Qu'Anglois tindrent a deshonneste,
> Li rois Richart, qui d'arbaleste
> Aporta premier l'us cn France,
> De son art ot male chevance.

> "Thus perished by the quarrel,
> Which the English account dishonourable,
> King Richard, who of the cross-bow
> First introduced the use in France:
> Of his art had he bad luck."

---

[45] It must be confessed, however, that Brompton, in the passage cited, goes on to say, Quo et ipse postmodum in terra propria inproemunitus, et inopinate interiit,

> Neque enim lex ulla.oequior est
> Quam necis artifices arte perire sua.

[46] An allusion seems here to be made to Greece.

In every action, however, of which we read in the histories of the second crusade, as well as the third, in which Richard participated, cross-bows as well as other bows are repeatedly noticed.

There is a very curious description, by Bohadin, the secretary of Saladin, of the march of Richard through Palestine, which shews that his talents as a general equalled his prowess as the soldier. The description is from an enemy, who witnessed and applauded it.[47] "The sixth day the Sultan rose at dawn, as usual, and heard from his brother that the enemy was in motion. They had slept that night in suitable places about Cesarea. They were now dressing, and taking their food. A second messenger announced that they had begun their march. Our brazen drum was sounded; all were alert. The sultan came out, and I accompanied him to their army. He surrounded them with chosen troops, and gave the signal for attack. The archers were drawn out, and a heavy shower of arrows on both sides descended. The enemy advanced, but hedged round by his infantry like a wall. They were covered with thick strong pieces of cloth, fastened together with rings, so as to resemble dense coats of mail.[48] Hence, though they were overwhelmed with our arrows, yet their progress was not impeded. I saw with mine own eyes several who had not one or two, but ten darts sticking in their backs, and yet marched on with a calm and cheerful step, without any trepidation. On their parts they darted a heavier species of weapon, which wounded both our men and horses. They had, besides, a division of infantry in reserve, to relieve and aid those who should be weary, and which, marching close to the sea-sliore, could not be molested. When the fighters were exhausted by fatigue or wounds this body advanced, and combated till the others were refreshed. Their cavalry, in the meantime, kept in the middle, and never moved beyond the infantry, unless when they rushed out to charge. In vain we tempted them to spread into the array of battle: they steadily restrained themselves and kept their close order, slowly cutting their way, and protecting their baggage with wonderful perseverance." This extract makes us acquainted with the species of armour worn by the infantry, which, from the Arab's description, seems to have been a kind of gambeson, that, for greater flexibility, was composed of several pieces held together by rings.

We cannot better conclude this notice of the third crusade than by relating one or two personal anecdotes of the king during his last encounters

---

[47] P. 190.

[48] These seem to have been borrowed from the Turks of Solyman's time, for the description exactly suits the painted glass in St. Denis, described p. 41.

in the Holy Land. One time, when a party of the knights templars were foraging, 4,000 Turkish cavalry surrounded them. The king, being at hand with a few knights, sent them to assist, while he armed himself, promising to follow. The vast superiority of the enemy put every one into the greatest personal peril. They fled, pursued by the Turks; and Richard was advised to escape. His countenance paled with anger at the counsel. "If I do not assist the dear friends I sent forward, with an assurance that I would join them, and they should perish, I will never usurp the name of a king again." He rushed on the Turks with that intrepidity and power that always distinguished him—now here, now there, wherever danger most pressed his sword was seen descending with unexampled rapidity. Heads, hands, and arms are described to have flown off as he struck. One of the most renowned emirs appeared before him, but perished like the rest. His astonishing bravery, or, what his secretary calls, his incredible victory, preserved both himself and his friends.[49]

Hearing that Jaffa had been surprised by Saladin during his absence, he sailed with some merchant vessels,[50] and leaped foremost on the beach: the castle was relieved by his presence, and 60,000 Turks and Saracens fled before his arms.[51] The discovery of the real weakness of his army encouraged them to attempt a surprise before day-break, and they found him carelessly encamped before the gates with only 17 knights and 300 archers. Richard was scarcely waked in time to escape being taken, but he soon armed himself, and collected enough about him to second his own extraordinary prowess, and check the panic that was spreading. The most perilous conflict took place that he had yet endured—a conflict remarkable for one trait of Saracen chivalry. As a strong proof of the Turkish estimation of Richard, Saphadin, the brother of Saladin, had sought and received knighthood from the king of England, for his son.[52] In this attack, meeting the king unhorsed, he gave him two fine coursers for his immediate service:[53] Richard gratefully received the important generosity, used them to rally his scattering troops, and restore the battle. Grasping his lance he rode furiously along

---

[49] See Mr. Turner's spirited account from Vinesauf.
[50] Bohadin, 244-251. This Arabian author says, he saw Richard's approach. "The first ship was the king's; it was all red, and was distinguished by its red sail." So that the fashion of emblazoning the sail with the armorial bearings of the chief of an expedition had not then been introduced.
[51] Vinesauf, 411-415.
[52] Vinesauf, 380.
[53] Ibid. 419.

the front of his enemies, from the right to the left wing, without meeting an adversary who dared encounter his career;[54] and yet so severe was this engagement, that he is described as appearing with his armour stuck full of lances,[55] and his horse's trappings with darts. His unexampled exertions at last repulsed the Turks and saved his army;[56] while the collective prowess he had shewn left a reputation among the Mahomedans which long survived himself.[57]

There is a letter of Richard's,[58] in which he relates the events of the battle of Gisors, and in which he tells us, that with one lance he prostrated and took prisoners three knights.

Camden, in his Remains,[59] has collected some of Richard's smart sayings, among which is the following anecdote. Having taken a bishop prisoner in a skirmish, and put him into fetters, the prelate complained to the pope, who desired Richard not to detain in prison his dear son in the faith. The king sent the pope the armour in which the bishop had been taken, with this message: "We found him in this dress; see whether it be your son's coat or not."

Bishops in early times often appeared in the field of battle: such was the case of Odo Bishop of Bayeux, at that of Hastings. But in Stephen's reign they went much further, for the author of the Gesta Stephani exclaims: "The bishops, the bishops themselves! I blush to say it; yet not all, but many, bound in iron, and completely furnished with arms, were accustomed to mount war-horses with the perverters of their country, to participate in their prey," &c.

Vinesauf, Richard's historian,[60] thus describes the French army as it appeared in the Holy Land: Inestimabilem, ibi, videres armatorum multitudinem armis decenter instructam, tot nitentes hamatas loricas, tot galeas rutilentes, &c. "There you might behold an inestimable multitude of armed men, properly furnished with arms, so many shining hooked loricæ,

---

[54] This is the evidence of Bohadin, his enemy, p. 249.

[55] This shews the utility of the gambeson under the surcoat; yet the load consequently borne by the knights accounts for their frequent faintings from fatigue.

[56] Vinesauf, 423.

[57] Mem. de Joinville. Mr. Turner observes, "that a Frenchman; whose sovereign was an unfortunate crusader, should relate this tradition of an English prince: is at least an indication that he believed it."

[58] Rymer's Foed. Vol. I, p. 96.

[59] P. 200.

[60] In his 3d book, c. 5, He details the siege of Tyre, p. 267-299. See the 2d vol. of Gale's Scriptores.

so many glittering ruddy helmets," &c. *Hamatas*, though a word used by the antients, in this author's meaning implies, probably, that the rings passed through, or were hooked into, the quilting; for though such an expression might be applied to the single mail, which was composed of the rings set edgewise, it seems more suitable to the rustred, in which part of the rings were absolutely hid. When he speaks of Richard's army[61] he seems to allude to the rings set edgewise, which must have very much rubbed against each other by any motion of the tunic on which they were sewn.

Rotantur loricæ ne rubigine squallescant, tractantur galea; mapulis, ne forte pallescant; liumore lainbente fulgorum gladium birris exterguntur mucrones, ne qua liumectatione claritudini inimica corrumpantur. "They whirled about their hauberks lest they might be foul from rust; they rubbed their helmets with cloths lest they might have become tarnished; the damp having dimmed the refulgence of their swords, they wiped the blades with their cloaks, that the hostile moisture might not spoil their brightness."

This extract introduces to our notice the large rough military cloak, called birrus. It was made of coarse woollen cloth, and intended solely as a defence against the inclemency of the weather, without any pretensions to ornament.[62] From the Romaunt de la Rose we learn, that rouge ou grisatre, "red or grey," were its general colours, but it is spoken of elsewhere as of a russet hue.

Richard I, in his first seal, appears in a hauberk of rings set edgewise, from under which falls the drapery of his tunic; in the second he has the same, but no drapery: in both he is represented as with cliausses; in the first wearing a conical helmet, but with its apex somewhat rounded; in the second with a cylindrical one, surmounted by some of the planta genista, whence he derived the name of Plantagenet, and having an aventadle, or plate, to protect the face. Thus he is represented in Plate XIII, which is not altered from the seal, excepting the substitution of a battle-axe for the sword. This ponderous axe is taken from one which was formerly preserved in the armoury at Chantilly, and is of tremendous weight, being here introduced to mark the favourite weapon of this monarch.

The aventadle has been noticed before, but this of Richard's clasps so much round his helmet as almost to meet behind. In a deed in Rymer's

---

[61] Lib. III, c.35.

[62] On the west front of Exeter cathedral, among the figures in the niches, is one of a knight sitting down, and wearing one of these cloaks. It appears to be of the time of Edward II.

PLATE XIII

RICHARD THE FIRST KING OF ENGLAND.

A.D. 1194.

Fœdera,[63] we find them thus noticed: has tredecim loricas, quinque aventa-
dles, quadraginta arcus, &c.; "these 13 hauberks, 5 aventailles, 40 bows, &c."
In time they were called merely ventailles; thus, in the Roman de Roncev-
eaux is the following line:

> L'escu au col, la ventaille fermée.

> "The shield suspended from the neck the ventaille closed."

Which was an appearance of being prepared for the fight. Again:

> Elmes lacier, et ventailles fermer.

> "Helmets made fast by the laces, and ventailles closed."

Philip Mouskes, in his Life of Charlemagne, has—

> La ventaille li ont ostée
> Si li ont la teste copée.

> "The ventaille they must remove,
> If they would cut off his head."

In later times the aventaille was of mail, and attached to the hood of the
hauberk.

The cylindrical helmet, therefore, came first into fashion in England
about the latter part of the reign of Richard I: though Charles the Good,
earl of Flanders, is represented in one on his seal so early as the year 1122;
but it may be doubted whether it be the work of that period.[64] The knights
templars, whose costume was appointed by Pope Eugenius, in 1186, are
represented on their official seal as wearing cylindrical helmets with aventailles, and they are perhaps the earliest who so did, Richard introducing it
after his return from Jerusalem. The seal of William Earl of Ferrers, in 1190,
exhibits him in one of these helmets, but without the aventaille. Guillaume
le Breton says, that, at the battle of Bovines, the earl of Boulogne, who was
very tall, wished to appear still more so than, he wras, and therefore added to his helmet horns made de côtes de baleine, which seems to be black
whalebone.

---

[63] Vol. VIII, p. 384.
[64] He was son of Canute King of Denmark. See Olivarius Vredius, page 11.

Cornua conus agit superasque eduxit in auras
E costis assumpta nigris quas fancis in antro
Branchia balcnae Britici colit incola ponti
Ut qui magnus erat magma super addita moli
Majorem faceret phantastica pompa vidcri.

"The cone of the helmet carried horns, and raised up its ears
From black pieces issuing from the sides, which, in the recess of their openings,
Contain a cubit measure of baleine, which is prepared by the inhabitants of Pont de Brique,
That he who was already great, from the immense added heap
Might appear more so with this fantastic parade."

Yet although this was greatly declaimed against, it was in later times, particularly in that of Edward I, a very prevalent fashion; stag's horns particularized Lord Hannak, and lunar ones the Connétable de Clisson.

Guillaume le Breton also speaks of the chapel de fer as worn, in his account of the skirmish, at Mante. Dreux de Mello, he tells us, having no other armour on his head was attacked by the Lord de Preaux, a vassal of the king of England, who, with a cut of his sword, beat down his chapel de fer and wounded his forehead.

Petrus fronte fcrit media Pratellicus ipsum
Qua male tectus erat retro labente galero.

"Peter de Preaux struck him on the centre of his forehead,
Which was imperfectly covered, by the chapel being beaten back."

But afterwards, being thus reminded by his wound, he returned to the combat with his helmet:

At Droco restricto jam vulnere casside rursus,
Induitur, &c.

"But Dreux, his wound being bound up, again
Put on his helmet," &c.

Armorial bearings on the shields were common in this reign; thus the earl of Ferrers is represented with his arms, with the bordure of horse-shoes on his seal; and the author last quoted mentions two instances of this kind, where he speaks of Richard I and the Lord Arundel, who was with him near Mante.

Ut comes erecta Guillclmus comminus hasta
Vidit hirundelæ velocior alite quæ dat
Hoc agnomen ei, fert cujus in ægide signum.

"As Earl William closes with his up-raised lance,
He sees swifter than the wing of the swallow, which gives him
This title, and which device he bears on his shield."

This supposes that Arundel is derived from hirondelle, a swallow.

Vinesauf's description of the French army has already in part been noticed; but besides describing the armour, he adds, tot equos nobiles hinnien-
tes, tot albi-cantia operimenta, tot milites electos, quot nunquam visi fuisse
æstimantur, tot satellites maximse probitatis et audacise, tot penuncellos,
tot banerias variorum operum. "So many noble snorting horses, white looking saddle-cloths, so many chosen knights, as never could have been supposed could have been seen. So many guards of the greatest prowess and
daring, so many penoncels, so many banners of various workman ship."

When Philippe Auguste was in the Holy Land, he found it necessary to
secure his person from the emissaries of a sheik, called the Old Man of the
Mountain, who bound themselves to assassinate whomsoever he assigned.
"When the king," says an antient chronicle, "heard of this, he began to re-
flect seriously, and took counsel how he might best guard his person. He
therefore instituted a guard of serjeants si maces, who, night and day, were
to be about his person in order to protect him."

These sergens a maces were afterwards called serjeants-at-arms, for Jean
Bou-teiller,[65] who lived in the time of Charles VI, that is, at the conclusion
of the 14th century, tells us: "The sergens d'armes are the mace-bearers that
the king has to perform his duty, and who carry maces before the king;
these are called sergeants-at-arms, because they are the sergeants for the
king's body."

It seems that they rendered great service to Philippe Auguste after his
return to France, for on a monument, composed of two stones, at the entrance of the church of St. Catherine, belonging to the regular canons of St.
Genevieve, is the following inscription: "At the prayer of the sergeants-at-
arms, M. Saint Louis founded this church, and laid the first stone, which
was done to commemorate the victory gained at the bridge of Bouvines, in
the year 1214, the sergeants-at-arms of that time having guarded the bridge;
and made a vow, that should God grant to them the victory, they would

---

[65] Somme rurale, lib. II.

found the church of Saint Catherine, and so they did." On the first stone is represented St. Louis, with two serjeants-at-arms; and in the second the Dominican confessor of this prince, with two other serjeants-at-arms.

These representations, however, prove, from the costume, that they were not made earlier than the commencement of the 15th century, about the close of our Henry IV. They have swords, and their maces are about as large as those borne by the beadles in the English universities. One thing, however, we learn by this representation, that the plate below the genouilliere, which hangs over the jamb, was not fastened to it, but held down by a strap, which went at the back over the upper part of the calf.[66]

The arms of the serjeants-at-arms were not only a mace, but, by a statute of Philippe le Bel, in 1285, a quiver full of quarrels, and consequently a cross-bow; and in 1388, they were further equipped with a lance. On the monument before noticed they are armed cap-a-pie, whence, Pere Daniel infers, they derived their name, reasoning from the analogy to gens d'armes.

Richard I of England soon imitated the conduct of the French king, but seems to have given to his corps of serjeants-at-arms a more extensive power. Not only were they to watch round the king's tent in complete armour, with a mace, a sword, a bow and arrows, but were occasionally to arrest traitors and other offenders about the court, for which the mace was deemed a sufficient authority: hence they came to be denominated "the valorous force of the king's errand, in the execution of justice." Their number was originally twenty-four. All persons of approved worth, and not under the degree of the son of a knight, were eligible; though, afterwards, the sons of gentlemen were admitted into the body. They held their places for life.

In the reign of Edward I the serjeants-at-arms were allowed two marks for their winter, and the same for their summer robes. Their pay in that of Edward II was twelvepence a day when they attended on horseback, and eightpence when they attended without a horse. In a manuscript account of Walter Wentwayt, treasurer of the household to Edward III, there is the following entry, in the 21st year of his reign: "Sergeauntes at armes with their retinew. Standard-bearers 4, Sergeauntes 67, Men-at-arms 3, Archers of horse[67] 7, Archers on foote 9."

According to the orders given by Thomas of Lancaster, constable at the

---

[66] The leg of one of these serjeants-at-arms is given at the foot of Plate xxxviii

[67] The initial letter to this reign has a Sagittarius, which may be regarded as representing the costume of the mounted archers soon after their introduction by King Stephen. It is taken from the capital of a column to the western door-way of Malmsbury abbey church, where it appears shooting at another, a tree being between them.

siege of Caen, September 3d, 1417, a serjeant-at-arms was to appear in the king's presence with his head bare, his body armed to the feet, with the arms of a knight riding,[68] wearing a gold chain with a medal bearing all the king's coats,[69] with a peon royal,[70] or mace of silver, in his right hand, and in his left a truncheon. In such manner is one represented in the presence of St. Louis on the sculptures at St. Catherine's before mentioned, and this date is very close to the costume there displayed.

We may contemplate in this corps the first attempt at establishing a standing army; and it was probably on this account, that in both countries there were views of ultimate policy in their continuance, beyond the pretext for their origin.

Richard I received his death wound from a quarrel, discharged at him from a cross-bow, when besieging the castle of Chaluz. Guillaume le Breton, while relating this event,[71] informs us, that the name of quarrel was given to the short arrow used for the cross-bow, from the iron at the end being four-sided:

> .... Quadrat cuspidis una
> Pendet arundo.

> ".......... With its four-sided pile
> Depends the reed."

From which, it should also seem, that the shaft of the quarrel was at this time a reed. In another place[72] he says:

> Qui non cessabant jaculis simul atque quadrellis
> Eminus et missis in cum sævirc sagittis.

> "Who did not cease, with darts and quarrels.
> And with missive arrows, to annoy him from a distance."

But it would appear, from the Roman de Garin, that the whole quarrel was of steel, for it is there said:

---

[68] With armour such as used by knights when they fought on horseback.

[69] On which all the king's armorial bearings were quartered.

[70] The peon, or pheon, was a barbed javelin: the heads of these are still heraldic bearings, and, from their figure, we find the barbs escalloped, or invecked, as the heralds term it, inside.

[71] Page 291.

[72] Page 264.

Il prend son arc d'aubor, et si le tendié
Met en la corde un grand carrcl d'acier
Le Comte avise de près, et si le fiert
De la sayete li met el corps plein pié.

"He takes his hazel cross-bow, and, if he stretches it,
Puts in the cord a great steel quarrel;
Is warne d that the count is near, if he strikes him
With the arrow, he will put it in his body point blank."

Alburnum, from which aubour is derived, signifies the white sapwood of trees next the bark: arc d'aubour, therefore, seems to imply, that the bow was made of hazel. In the Register of Philippe Auguste is Habet sagittam et arcum de aubour cum corda. "He has an arrow and hazle bow with its cord," so that it appears to have been the wood at this time used for the bow,[73] afterwards supplied by steel. From the Roman de Garin we further learn, that these quarrels were feathered:

Volent piles[74] plusque pluïe par pres
Et les saiettes et carriax empennes.

"Piles fly thicker than rain,
And arrows and feathered quarrels."

Nicephoras Gregoras frankly acknowledges, that the Greeks borrowed from the French the practice of tournaments; and not only history, but the genius of that people, authorize us in declaring that it must have originated with them. William of Newbury expressly says, that the English derived the usage from the French, and that it was first introduced to their knowledge in the reign of Stephen; cum per ejus indecentem mollitiein, nullus esset publice vigor disciplinæ; "when, through his reprehensible want of firmness, there was no vigour in the public discipline."

While government was weak and the police imperfect we find, from many instances, the importance of knight-adventurers. In Stephen's reign they were of the utmost service, for as he was considered an usurper, knights of all kinds flocked into the country, and especially from Flanders and

---

[73] See also the Mon. Ang. Vol. II, page 602.

74 This seems to countenance the opinion of my friend Mr. Douce, mentioned p. 70, that the piles were javelins, and if so, they were allowed to villains, while the lance was confined to freemen.

Bretagne, who distinguished themselves for their rapine[75] Even in John's time, we are told that all the castles in the country were the caves of robbers and the dens of thieves.[76] The counterpoise, therefore, to these lawless enterprises was found in the knights-errant, who conceived that they could not obtain higher renown than by travelling the country to release captives, assist terrified ladies, and to prevent or punish all other acts of violence.

Hence, a knight-errant, with a moderate portion of true chivalry and religious feeling, could easily contrive to unite his interest with his conscience, and relieve by his valour, with profit as well as credit to himself, the brave and the injured: on this account we read of their going in search of adventures; and our old satirist, Pierce Plowman, in the following words,[77] alludes to their roaming about for this purpose:

> .... Knyghtes shoulde
> Ryden and rappe adoune in remes aboute
> And to take trespassours, and tyen hem faste
> . . . .
> Trewely to take, and treweliche to fyghte
> Y s the profession, and the pure order that apendeth to knyghtes.

It was, therefore, to encourage the military disposition of knights-errant, and to enable them by practice efficiently to perform their task, that jousts and tournaments were first adopted; and as no persons were more benefited by their exertions than the female sex, their hands were destined to bestow the rewards of martial prowess.

The tournament, in its original institution, was a military conflict, in which the combatants engaged without any animosity merely to exhibit their strength and dexterity; but, at the same time, engaged in great numbers to represent a battle. The joust was the name given when two knights, and no more, were opposed to each other at the same time. The joust, as a military pastime, is mentioned by William of Malmsbury, as practised in the reign of Stephen,[78] and no doubt owing to the before-mentioned cause.

In the reign of Henry II, who, by succeeding Stephen, may be said to have allayed all doubt respecting the legitimacy of his sovereignty, William of Newbury says, Tyrones exercitiis in Angliâ prorsus inhibitis, qui forte annorum aifectantes gloriam exerceri volebant, transfretantes in terrarum ex-

---

[75] Malms. 179.
[76] Matt. Paris Ab. 118.
[77] In his Visions, Vis. I.
[78] Hist.·Novell. Coll. 106, sub. anno 1142.

ercebantur confiniis. "The English youths who had not yet attained knight-hood, and were, therefore, called tyrones, or pupils, (the military exercises being as yet prohibited in England,) wishing perchance, as they affected the glory of arms, to exercise themselves, crossed the Channel, and joined in these exercises on the confines of the Continent." Roger Hoveden and Brompton confirm this account.

The Roman Campus Martius was not the only one in which games were performed tending to give a military character, the Britons[79] and the Saxons had the same. In the reign of Henry II, therefore, martial exercises were by no means confined to the education of young noblemen; the sons of citizens and yeomen had also their sports resembling military combats: these consisted of various attacks and evolutions performed on horseback, the youths being armed with shields and pointless lances. This seems to have been derived from the Romans, resembling, as it did, the Ludus Trope, or Troy game, described by Virgil.[80] These amusements, according to Fitz-Stephen,[81] a cotemporary writer, were appropriated to the season of Lent; but at all times they exercised themselves with archery, fighting with clubs and bucklers, and running at the quintain. In winter, when the frost set in, they would go upon the ice, and run against each other with poles, in imitation of lances in a joust, and frequently one or both were beaten down, "not always without hurt, for some break their arms, and some their legs; but youth, emulous of glory, seeks these exercises preparatory against the time war shall demand their presence."

Although these games were the foundation of tournaments, that species of entertainment had not the royal authority for its introduction till the next reign. It was Richard who first encouraged the practice in England, for this illustrious prince, observing that the French tanto esse acriores, quanto exercitatiores atque instructiores, "were the more valiant the more they were exercised and instructed," sui quoque regni milites in propriis finibus exercere voluit, ut ex bello-rum solemni preludio verorum addiscer-ent artein usumque bellorum, nec insultarent Galli Anglis militibus, tan-quam rudibus et minus gnaris, "wished to have the knights of his kingdom exercised within their own country, that from the solemn prelude of real battle, they might learn the art and use of war; and that the French might

---

[79] For the Pedwar Camp ar Hugain, or four-and-twenty games practised by the descendants of the Britons, see the Introduction to my History of Cardiganshire.

[80] Æ. v.

[81] Description of London in the time of Henry II.

no longer insult the English knights as rude and ignorant." Matthew Paris relates the same circumstance, which he seems to date in 1194, the fifth year of his reign.

The joust was sometimes called the cane game, because hollow canes were then used instead of lances. This name and practice seems also to have been introduced by Richard I into England, and probably owing to the following circumstance, mentioned by Hoveden.[82] He tells us, that the English monarch being at Messina, the capital of Sicily, on his way to the Holy Land, went with his cavalcade one Sunday afternoon to see the popular sports exhibited without the walls of the city, and upon their return, they met in the street a rustic driving an ass loaded with arundinas quas cannas vocant, "reeds, which are called canes." The king and his attendants took each of them a cane, and began, by way of frolic, to tilt with them one against another. It so happened, that the king's opponent was William de Barres, a knight of high rank in the household of the French king. In the encounter they broke both their canes, and the monarch's hood was torn by the stroke he received, which made him angry, when, riding with great force against the knight, he thus occasioned his horse to stumble; but while he was attempting to cast him to the ground, his own saddle turned round, and he himself was overthrown. The king was soon, however, provided with another horse, stronger than the former, which he mounted, and again assaulted de Barres, endeavouring by violence to throw him from his horse, but he could not, because the knight clung fast to the horse's neck. Robert de Breteuil, newly created earl of Leicester, laid hold upon de Barres to assist the king; but Richard forbad him to interfere, desiring that they might be left to themselves. When they had contended a long time, adding threats to their actions, the king was much provoked, and commanded him to leave the place and appear no more before him, declaring, at the same time, that he would ever afterwards consider him as an enemy; but through the mediation of the king of France, a reconciliation was effected, and the knight was again restored to the favour of the monarch. This anecdote does not evince Richard's magnanimity.

The amusements of jousts and tournaments in the middle ages, which may properly enough be denominated the ages of chivalry, were in high repute among the nobility of Europe, and produced in reality much of the pomp and gallantry that we find recorded with poetical exaggeration in the legends of knight-errantry.

---

[82] Annal. sub. an. 1191.

In the romance of the "Three King's Sons and the King of Sicily,"[83] it is said the king, "to assaie a knight made justes and turnies, and no man did so well as he in runnyng, shotyng and castyng of the barre, ne found he his maister," so that we see these sports were ingrafted on the antient games. Hence in the romance, called "The Knight of the Swan," it is said of Ydain Duchess of Roulyon, that she caused the tutors of her three sons, "when they were somwhat comen to the age of strengthe to practyse them in shootinge with their bow, and arbaleste to playe with the sword and buckler, to runne, to just, to playe with a poll-axe, and to wrestle, and they began to bear barneys, to runne horses, and to approve them as desyringe to be good and faythful kniglites to susteyne the faith of God."

Tournaments and jousts were particularly exhibited at coronations, royal marriages, and other occasions of solemnity, where pomp and pageantry were deemed requisite. One great reason, perhaps, why the practice of these exercises gave such delight to the kings and nobility of the middle ages, is, that on such occasions they made their appearance with prodigious splendour, and had the opportunity of displaying their accomplishments to the greatest advantage. The ladies also were proud of seeing their professed champions engaged in these arduous conflicts; and, perhaps, a glove or ribbon from the hand of a favourite female might have inspired the receiver with as zealous a wish for conquest as the abstracted love of glory. This species of recreation lasted till the latter part of the reign of Queen Elizabeth, the death of Henry II, king of France, who was killed in a tournament, putting an end to the practice. Our historians, therefore, abound with details of these celebrated pastimes. Froissart, Hall, Hollinshed, Grafton, and Stow, with many others, are all very diffuse upon this subject.

The tournament, however, became a general name for several military exercises, and is, therefore, often used to signify the tilt and joust. Properly speaking, the tilt was a preparation for the joust and tournament, although that word is often used without discrimination. The tilt was generally performed at some inanimate substance, and this was called the quintain, a word for which it is difficult to find an etymon. By the Greeks, under the Roman Emperors, it was called κυντανος; and Joannes Meursius tells us,[84] it received its name from Quinctus, or Quintas, the inventor; but who he was, or when he lived, there is no information. Its Welsh name is gwyntyn, whence some would suppose it of British origin, and because it turned

---

[83] In the Har}l.Lib. at Brit. Mus. 326.
[84] De Ludis Græcorum in tit κοντᾶξ κνι'Ιανος.

round rapidly, and, consequently, excited the wind.[85] But this more complex contrivance was an improvement upon the original quintain, which was immovable; indeed it was at first nothing more than the trunk of a tree or post set up for the practice of the tyros in chivalry;[86] afterwards a staff or spear was fixed in the earth, and a shield being hung upon it was the mark to strike at. Thus Robert the Monk says,[87] terrae infixis sudibus scuta apponuntur—quintanæ ludus scilicet equestris exerceretur—in equis lusitari solitum appensis sudes in terrain impactas scutis. "Shields were affixed to staves stuck in the ground. The game of quintain was played by those who were mounted. It was a usual thing for those on horseback to strike the shields hung upon staves fixed in the ground." The dexterity of the performer consisted in smiting the shield in such a manner as to break the ligatures, and bear it to the ground.

The game itself was of remote origin, for Vegetius tells us, that the Roman military youths practised it twice in the day, at morning and at noon.[88] In the code of laws established by the Emperor Justinian,[89] the quintain is mentioned as a well-known sport, and permitted to be continued upon condition that κυνΊανον χονΊαξ κωρις της πυρπις, "it should be performed with pointless spears," contrary to the antient usage, which seems to have required them to have heads or points.

The first English writer who mentions the quintain is Fitz-Stephen, in the time of Henry II. He tells us, that this exercise was usually practised by the young Londoners, upon the water, during the Easter holidays. A pole or mast, says he, is fixed in the midst of the Thames, with a shield strongly attached to it; then a boat, which has been previously placed at some distance, is driven swiftly towards it by the force of oars and the violence of the tide, having a young man standing in the prow, who holds a lance in his hand with which he is to strike the shield, and if he be dexterous enough to break the lance against it and retain his place, his most sanguine wishes are satisfied: on the contrary, if the lance be not broken, he is sure to be thrown into the water, and the vessel goes away without him; but at the same time two other boats are stationed near to the shield, and furnished with many young persons, who are in readiness to rescue the champion from danger. It appears to have been a very popular pastime, for the bridge, the wharfs, and

---

[85] Gwynt implies "wind" in that language.
[86] Vegetius de re militari, lib. I, c. 11 and 14.
[87] Hist. Hierosol. lib. v.
[88] De re mil.
[89] Cod. de Aleatoribus, lib. III, tit. 43.

the houses near the river, were crowded with people on this occasion, who came, says the author, to see the sports and make themselves merry. There is a manuscript of the fourteenth century, in the royal library in the British Museum,[90] which contains an illumination, representing the water-quintain, in which a square piece of board is substituted for the shield.

It may be observed, that the rules of chivalry at this time, not permitting any person under the rank of an esquire, to enter the lists as a combatant at the jousts and tournaments, the burgesses and yeomen had recourse to the exercise of the quintain, which was not prohibited to any class of people. They performed this with their other exercises; hence, in the Roman de Jordain de Blaye, we read:

A la quintaine, et à l'escu jouster
Et courre as barre et liuitier et verser.

"To joust at the quintain and at the shield,
To run at the bar, to strike and overturn."

As, therefore, the performers were generally young men, whose finances would not at all times admit of much expense, the quintain was frequently nothing better than a stake fixed into the ground, with a flat piece of board made fast to the upper part of it, as a substitute for the shield that had been used in remote times; and such as could not procure horses contented themselves with running at this mark on foot. Conformable to this, in an illuminated manuscript in the Bodleian library at Oxford,[91] there is represented a lad mounted on a wooden horse with four wheels, and drawn by two of his comrades, tilting at an immovable quintain. Improvements, however, were afterwards made, which will be noticed in the subsequent reigns.

It is a generally received opinion, that the tournament originated from the Ludus Trojæ, or Troy-game, practised by the Roman youths, and so named, because it was said to have been derived from the Trojans, and first brought into Italy by Ascanius, the son of Æneas. Yirgil[92] has given us a description of this pastime, according to the manner it was exhibited at Rome in his time, from which it appears to have been nothing more than a variety of evolutions performed on horseback. He tells us, that each of the youths were armed with two little cornal spears headed with iron, Cornea bina

---

[90] Marked 2 B vii.
[91] Bod. marked 264.
[92] Æn. v.

ferunt prsefixa liastilia ferro, and having passed in review before their parents, upon a signal given they divided into three distinct companies, each company or troop consisting of twelve, exclusive of its leader. They then performed various modes of attack and retreat, endeavouring to imitate a combat, but it does not appear that they ever struck each other.

It was not, therefore, exclusively from the Troy game that the tournaments were derived, for they appear to have arisen by slow degrees from all the exercises practised by young warriors.

The following is an account of what seems to be the Troy game, as practised in England during the reign of Henry II. "Every Sunday in Lent, immediately after dinner it was customary for great crowds of young Londoners, mounted on war horses, well trained to perform the requisite turnings and evolutions, to ride into the fields in distinct bands, armed Avith shields and headless lances,[93] where they exhibited the representation of battles, and went through a variety of warlike exercises: at the same time many of the young noblemen, who had not received the honour of knighthood, came from the king's court and from the houses of the great barons, to make trial of their skill in arms, the hope of victory animating their minds. The youths being separated into opposite companies, encountered one another: in one place they fled, and others pursued without being able to overtake them; in another place one of the bands overtook and overturned the other."[94] According to Virgil, the youths presented their lances towards their opponents in a menacing position, but without striking them:[95] the young Londoners, however, having no iron heads to their weapons, probably went further, and actually tilted one against the other.

When Richard I permitted jousts and tournaments to be legally established within his territories, he imposed a tax, according to their quality, upon such as engaged in them: an earl was subjected to the fine of twenty marks for his privilege to enter the field as a combatant; a baron ten; a knight, having a landed estate, four; and one Avithout such possession tAvo; but all foreigners were particularly excluded. He appointed also five places for the holding of tournaments in England, namely, between Sarum and Wilton, between Warwick and Kenelworth, betAveen Stamford and Wallingford, between Brakely and Mixeberg, and between Blie and Tykehill. The act also specifies, that the peace should not be broken thereby, nor

---

[93] Hastilibus ferro adempto. In this they differed as we see from the Romans.
[94] Wm. Fitz-Stephen's Account of London.
[95] Nunc Spicula vertunt infensi, v,586.

justice hindered, nor damage done to the royal forests.[96]

In the troublesome reign of Stephen, as the rigour of Iuav Avas so much relaxed, tournaments, among other kinds of splendid dissipation, had been permitted, but they were immediately suppressed by Henry II; and by this act of Richard, their reestablishment was, it appears, under certain restrictions. They suited the growing temper of the times; and, therefore, as his father had prevented his practice at home, the young Prince Henry, son of Henry II, went every third year over the Channel, and spent vast sums of money in conflictibus Gallicis, "French combats," as they were termed.[97]

How long the imposts, which Richard had fixed, continued to be collected does not appear; but tournaments Avere occasionally exhibited Avith the utmost display of magnificence in the succeeding reigns, being not only sanctioned by royal authority, but frequently instituted at the royal command, until the conclusion of the sixteenth century: from that period they declined rapidly, and fifty years afterwards were entirely out of practice.

As notice has been taken of the royal hereditary arms of England; on concluding the observations in this reign it may be worth remarking, that it was Richard I who first assumed the hereditary motto of our kings, Dieu et mon Droit, "God and my right," probably at the same time that Philippe Auguste adopted the fleurs-de-lis for the arms of France, viz. on the crusade of 1190.

[96] MS .. Harl. lib. marked 69.
[97] Matt. Paris Hist. Ang. A.D. 1179.

John.

1199.

y the observations on jousts, tournaments, and tilting, in the last reign, it must have appeared how very attractive such kind of sports became to all ages, sexes, and classes. Persons of rank were taught in their childhood to relish exercises of a martial nature, and the very toys put into their hands as playthings were calculated to bias the mind in their favour. Hence, in an illuminated manuscript in the public library at Strasbourgli, written at the conclusion of the 12th century, is a drawing representing two puppets, equipped with hauberks and chausses of mail, conical helmets, large swords, and kite-shaped shields, upon a table. While these are put in motion by cords held in the hands of a figure on each side, two minstrels are blowing horns behind one, and two others perform on the harp and flute on the opposite side. The manuscript is entitled "Hortus Deliciarum of Herarde, Abbess of Landsberg."

The seal of this monarch affords the first example of an English king wearing a surcoat, and it is put over a hauberk of rings set edgewise. Previous to this the Italian knights had worn a garment over their armour, which was called armilausa, armilausia, annilcasia, and armigaisia, and which reached to just below the knees. The Emperor Maurice, in his Strategies, thus explains the and tells us it ἀρμελαὐσια, and tells us it ἐπάνω τῶν ὅπλω, put on over the armour. Isidorus says,[1] Armelausa vulgo vocatur, quod ante et retro divisa, atque aperta est, in armis tantum clausa, quasi armi-clausa, c, littera ablata. "It is commonly called armelausa, because it is divided before and behind, and left open, being closed only over the armour, as if it were called armiclausa, the letter c being omitted."

It probably originated among the Græco-Roman troops, for in the Mosaic of Ravenna, the soldiers of Justinian appear thus apparelled; and an old interpreter of Juvenal's Satires, explains Viridem thoracem,[2] by armilausiam prasinam, "a green armilausia." Paulinus, in his 7th Epistle, has: Sibi ergo ille habeat armilausam suam, et suas caligas, et suas buccas. "Therefore he may have for himself his armilausia, his boots, and his cheek-pieces."

It seems at first to have been almost the same as the paludamentum of the Romans, and as such was worn by the Goths and Saxons; hence, Anastatius tells us, that "Luitprand King of the Goths took off the clothes he wore, and placed before the body of the apostle his cloak, armilaisia, belt, long and short gilt swords." Here it seems to be a close garment, and worn under the cloak; but in a deed of the Anglo-Saxon King Ethelbert,[3] it is stated Missurum etiam argenteum, scapton aureum, item sellam cum freno aureo, et gemmis exornatam, speculum argenteum, armilaisia oloserica, camisiam ornatam pradicto monasterio gratanter obtuli. "To the aforesaid monastery I have gratefully made an offer of a silver dish, a golden vessel, also a saddle with a golden bridle, and adorned with jewels, a silver speculum, an armilaisia made wholly of silk, and an ornamented tunic." In the time of Justinian, however, it appears, from the Mosaic, to have been shaped much like the surcoat. It seems, nevertheless, to have been for some time disused before the latter was adopted. They differed in length, the surcoat generally reaching half way down the legs, and being either a loose garment not open at the sides, or else closed by a lace running down the whole length of them, though this seems to have been a later improvement: both were without sleeves.

Surcoats seem to have originated with the crusaders, for the purpose of distinguishing the many different nations serving under the banner of the cross, and to throw a veil over the iron armour, so apt to heat excessively when exposed to the direct rays of the sun. They were at first without any mark of distinction, and either simply of one colour or variegated.

---

[1] Orig. lib. XIX, c. 22.

[2] Sat.5.

[3] In the Monasticon Ang. Vol. I, p. 24.

PLATE XIV

ALEXANDER 2ᴺᴰ.	KING OF SCOTLAND.

A.D. 1214.

The Sicilian knights seem to have been forbidden to wear their surcoats on common occasions, for, in the Constitutions of Frederick King of Sicily,[4] we read: Volumus insuper quod liceat eisdem militibus habere, ultra prsedicta tria guarnimenta, syrcotum unum sine manicis cum cpio eomedant et morentur in domibus, quamdiu ibi steterint: sed eo extra domos aliquatenus non utantur sub pœna amissionis ejusdem syrcoti. "We will, moreover, that it be lawful for the same knights to have, besides the three aforesaid garments, one surcoat without sleeves, in which they may eat, and walk about in their dwellings as long as they remain there, but they shall never use it when away from home on pain of losing the said surcoat."Besides the surcoat the hauketon was a military garment in great esteem during this reign: thus, in a wardrobe account, dated 1212,[5] we find a pound of cotton was expended in stuffing an aketon belonging to King John, which cost twelvepence, and the quilting of the same was charged at twelvepence more.

John is represented with a cylindrical helmet, but without any covering over his face. The monument in the temple church, attributed to Geoffry Magnaville, and which appears to be about this period, has one very similar, except that in it the nasal is revived, and there are cheek-pieces, such as seem to be spoken of by Guillaume le Breton as worn by the Comte de Boulogne.[6]

The seal of Alexander II, king of Scotland, on the contrary, exhibits him with the aventaile upon his helmet, in mascled armour, and a surcoat. From this authority he has been represented in Plate XIV, though selected as affording the earliest specimen of plates for the elbows, which became common during the reign of Henry III.[7]

As the helmet was thus flattened at the top, so was the coif des mailles on which it was placed: many monumental effigies, therefore, after this period are so represented, though in some there is a little inclination towards a cone, for the more convenient support of a chapel de fer. To keep the coif in this state, however, the cap which was worn underneath[8] must have been made in the same form, and the object was probably to diminish the otherwise enormous weight on the head of the knight. The wooden monumental effigy at Gloucester cathedral, attributed to Robert Duke of Normandy, son of the Conqueror, cannot, therefore, be considered as earlier than the time

---

[4] C. 96.

[5] MS. in the Harleian lib. marked 4573.

[6] See it represented at tbe bottom of Pl. XIII.

[7] At the foot of this plate he again appears as on another impression of bis seal.

[8] There 'are authorities in the time of Edward I, to shew that at tbat period tbis under cap was of steel.

of John. He is represented with a coronet, perhaps the earliest specimen of this fashion, as, although the figures of monarchs when in their robes of state had this accompaniment, it never appears with their military costume. The seal of Richard I, as given by Speed and Sandford, indeed, shews us the coronet on the helmet, but in the more accurate engraving of it in the new edition of the Foedera it is wanting.

The monument attributed to Robert Duke of Normandy represents him in a hauberk and chausses of rings set edgewise, but it is very curious in its detail. In the first place, we learn from it the mode of fastening the hood or coif at this time. Except in the part which is made to fit on the cap, it is open in front, one edge descending along the right cheek; the other, after doing the same, projecting so as to wrap over the throat and run up the former, to which it is fixed by a leather strap, which is interlaced perpendicularly as far as the right temple, and then over the forehead till it reaches the other side. The surcoat is kept close to the body just above the hip by the sword-belt, which is fastened by a buckle in the front; over the right shoulder and under the left arm passes the guige, or belt for the shield, which was either hung at the back or the left hip, the latter being more particularly the fashion in France: hence, Phillippe Mouskes, in his Life of Robert, the king of that countiy, says:

La lance et l'escu en canticl.

"The lance and the shield on the left side."

Cantiel signifying the side on which footstools were placed. The former is alluded to in the Roman de Garin:

Au col ly pendant un cscu de cartier.

"From his neck was suspended a shield quartered."

And again:

Quant cop ly donne sur l'escu de cartier.

"When a blow is given him on his quartered shield."

There is also another peculiarity to be noticed in this monument, and that is the wearing of chaussons, or breeches, over the chausses:

they seem to be of some thick cloth, perhaps several folds of it, but not being stitched, cannot be said to be gamboised. Such breeches were not common till the reign of Edward I.

Each spur is fastened by a single leather, which passes through an aperture at the end of each shank, and buckles on the top of the instep. Those on the monument of King John himself are made in the same manner.

The seal of Saer de Quincy Earl of Winchester, who died in the year 1219, exhibits the earliest specimen of long flowing caparisons for the horse; it is at the same time covered with his armorial bearings, as is his short kite-shaped shield, and even his cylindrical helmet, the aventaile of which has merely small perforations, in lieu of the horizontal openings, for the sight. The caparison for the horse consists of two pieces, one of which goes over the head and neck of the animal, and then being divided falls over each fore leg, till it reaches almost to the fetlock joint and to the saddle; the other covering the hind legs and haunches, and is put on over the tail, reaching to the saddle, and being in length the same as the fore piece.

Dukes were at this period created, by girding on them the ducal sword: thus, Richard I, says Hove den,[9] accinctus est gladio ducatus Normannue, "was girt with the sword of the duchy of Normandy," or created a duke. Matthew Paris says the same of his brother John.

The earl was created in the same manner; thus Geoifry Fitz-Peter, on the day of King John's coronation, was girded with the sword of the earldom of Essex, and that day he served with others ad mensam regis accincti gladiis, "at the king's table girt with a sword."[10]

The pummel of John's sword on his monument is of the lozenge shape, that of Robert of a kind of foliage; the chape is also ornamented in a similar manner.

The initial letter to this reign is taken from the seal of Adam de Hereford, appended to a deed dated 1220, which represents him, however, in the military costume of Richard the First's time rather than at the commencement of Henry the Third's.

---

[9] P. 373.
[10] Hoveden, p. 451.

Henry the Third.

216.

ENRY'S seal affords us the earliest specimen of the ouvrage de pourpointerie, which came more into fashion towards the latter part of his reign. His hauberk and chausses are of this padded work stitched, which differs so little from what was termed gainboisee as not to be perceptible in delineation; the former, indeed, was only finer in its materials and more neat in its execution, but both were alike of stitched work. As the pourpoint arose in France in imitation of the wambais or gambeson of Germany, pourpointed or gamboised would differ only as the hauberk was made to represent the garment of one country or the other. Vine-sauf[1] relates, that during the march of Richard I to Jerusalem, such were the effects of the continual showers of rain and hail, that the weapons and armour of his men were covered with rust. It is probable, therefore, that it was such inconvenience frequently felt that suggested the use of gamboised or pourpointed armour, which continued to be used from the middle of this to the conclusion of the next century.

The helmets of John's time, though cylindrical, did not at the commencement of his reign come on the head lower than the ears, though the aventaile covered even the chin, but towards the latter part it reached to

[1] P. 363.

the neck, so that the front plate was not longer than the back piece. Henry the Third's first seal represents his helmet as with the visor or aperture for sight, not in the aventaile, but in the helmet itself, while the latter has merely perforations for the breath, and is therefore fixed at the lower part. His second seal exhibits him in a cylindrical helmet of a more perfect form, the aventaile, which contains both the before-mentioned conveniences, being apparently made to open and shut by means of hinges and a clasp. Such a one, with a crest on its top, which now came greatly into fashion, is given at the foot of Plate xvi, it being that of Roger de Quincy Earl of Winchester, and taken from his seal. In that of Richard Earl of Cornwall, that part of the aventaile intended for the breath consists of long apertures made by perpendicular bars.

The aventaile did not, however, secure the knight from injury in the head, as Matthew Paris[2] records the death of a nobleman in this reign, who was slain by the weapon being thrust through the sight or visor of his helmet into his brain. Per ocularium galeae caput ejus perforando, cerebrum effudit. Nor was there any subsequent invention to counteract so dreadful a wound, as Henry II of France was killed in a similar manner.

The seal of Henry III further represents him in his surcoat, and in spurs with rowels, being the earliest specimen of that compassionate invention.[3]

Plate xv, which has been taken from the monumental effigies of a knight in Malvern church, Worcestershire, exhibits a warrior in a hauberk, hood, and chausses of rings set edgewise; the hood laps over in the contrary direction from that attributed to Robert Duke of Normandy, reaching much further, as the fastening begins behind the left ear: it is also formed somewhat pyramidal, for the purpose of holding a chapel de fer. Suspended from his neck is a buckler instead of a shield, which he holds also in his left hand. The chain mail, as usual, covers his hands without dividing with the fingers, and the sleeves of the hauberk are held tight to the wrists by straps or bracelets. In his right hand is a martel de fer.

The Saxon convex shield, as was noticed, had been used so late as the reign of Stephen; the buckler succeeded it, which, though circular, was flat

---

[2] Sub anno 1217.

[3] It has been asserted that there are earlier specimens, but, unfortunately, the copyist has mistaken the round knob on the pryck-spur for rowels, and this particularly in the Bayeux tapestry, where that knob is made merely by a crossstitch. Indeed, I much suspect that these rowels on Henry's seal are the fancy of the engraver, and not in the original, as we do not find the rowel on sepulchral monuments before the time of Edward II.

PLATE XV

A KNIGHT ARMED 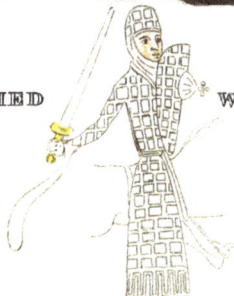 WITH A MARTEL,

A.D. 1220.

or nearly so. It is mentioned in the Consuetudines Brageraci:[4] Item armaturae, utpote enses, lanceie, scuta, boglaria, loricae, platee, pileus ferreus sive
capellus. "Also armour, as swords, lances, shields, bucklers, hauberks, plates,
steel hat, or chapel de fer." The plates here mentioned were what were used
as protections to the elbows.

The martellus, or martel de fer, differed from the maule, or mallet, in
having only one projection blunt, while the other was sharpened to an edge,
and at a subsequent period to a point. The grandfather of Charlemagne was
called Charles Martel, from having been probably the first to use this weapon. It seems to have come very much into fashion during the reign of Henry
III, for William Guiart makes the following allusions to it:[5]

> Mult fu fier le martelcis
> La noise et le cliqueteis.

> "Very fierce was the marteleis,
> The noise and the clatter."

And again:

> Et puis a fir marteleis
> Trebuchié le pont leveis.

> "And then with a fierce marteleis
> The raised drawbridge was beaten down."

That it was of steel we learn from the Chronicle of Bertrand du Guesclin,
though whether by that is meant merely the head, or the whole weapon,
as was sometimes the case at a later period, is not specified. The words are:

> Bertrand de Glajequin fu ou champ plenier
> Ou il assaut Anglois a un martel d'acier,
> Tout ainsy les ahat come fait le bouchier.

> "Bertrand de Glajequin was every where in the field,
> Where he assaulted the English with a martel of steel,
> And beat them down as a butcher would."

The mallet, or maule, a gothic weapon, and assigned by that people to Thor,

---

[4] C. XXVIII.

[5] Under the dates 1202 and 1205; but he, most probably, describes customs nearer
his own time.

PLATE XVI

WILL? LONGUESPEE ☰ EARL OF SALISBURY,

A.D. 1224.

their god of thunder, was still, however, in use, and is thus noticed by Guillaume le Breton, who was cotemporary with the French King Phillippe Auguste:

> Dum multiplied latus undique malleat ictu
> Hostilis rabies.

> "Whilst the hostile force strike with the maule
> Redoubled blows far and wide."

The plates for the elbows may be seen on the man at arms in Plate XVIII.

The next authority worthy of remark is the monumental effigy of William Longespee Earl of Salisbury, who died in the year 1224. It is the subject of Plate XVI. It differs not much from that last described: like it the hood fastens on the left side, and like it the strap merely encircles the head; but the mail is made to cover not only the chin but the mouth. The chausses seem to be composed of two parts, as it were breeches and stockings, as there are straps to fasten them together just below the knees, garter-fashion, but interlaced. The inside shank only of the spur has the aperture for the leather to pass through, it being nailed to the other and brought under the foot, buckling on the instep to another short one, also fixed: this was an improvement to prevent the spur slipping down from its proper place.[6]

Camden gives us the following account of the siege of Bedford castle in this reign, as transcribed from a cotemporary writer, and who was present on the occasion.[7]

"On the east side was one petrary, and two mangonels, daily playing upon the tower; and on the west two mangonels battering the old tower; as also one on the south, and another on the north part, which beat down two passages through the walls that were next them. Besides these, there were two machines contrived of wood, so as to be higher than the castle or the tower erected on purpose for the slingers and watchmen; they had also several machines where the balistarii and arcubalistarii lay in wait. There was moreover another machine, called cattus, under which the diggers, that were employed to undermine the castle, came in and went out." The mining instrument, we are informed by Matthew Paris, was called scrophus, or scrofus.[8] Camden goes on to tell us, that the castle was taken by four

---

[6] A circumstance complained of in the time of Edward I.

[7] See also the Chronicle of Dunstable in the British Museum, Harleian lib. 24, fol. 170.

[8] Scrofa ad suffodiendos muros.

assaults. "In the first was taken the barbacan." This was a breast-work before the outer ballium, and which secured the principal entrance, and stood on the opposite side of the ditch. Thus Mandatum est Johanni de Kilmyngton custodi castri regis et honoris de Pickering quoddam barbicanum ante por-taui castri regis prsedicti muro lapideo, et in eodem barbicano quandam portam cum ponte versatili de novo facere. "John de Kilmyngton, keeper of the king's castle and honour of Pickering, is commanded to repair a certain barbacan before the gate of the king's castle aforesaid, with a stone wall, and to make anew a certain gate with a drawbridge.[9] Camden goes on to say, that having secured the barbacan they recommenced the assault, and "in this second they got full possession of the outer ballium." This gave them free passage to the old tower, which appears to have contained the prin-cipal entrance into the castle-yard. "At the third attack the wall by the old tower was thrown down by the miners, where, by a dangerous effort, they possessed themselves of the inner ballium[10] through a breach. At the fourth assault the miners set fire to the chief tower on the keep, so that the smoke burst out, and the tower itself was so cloven to that degree, as to shew visibly some broad chinks: whereupon the enemy surrendered."

The mangonel seems to have been so formed, if such interpretation of the passage in Matthew Paris[11] be warranted, as to project half a dozen great stones at the same time. Speaking of their application to naval purposes, he says: Et lapides de mangonellis navalibus, cpii sic parabantur, ut quinque vel sex lapides simul de longo jacerent. "And stones from the naval mangonels, which were so prepared, that they cast five or six stones to a great distance at the same time." This same author,[12] who also gives an account of this siege of Bedford castle, by King Henry III, says, the walls were flanked by a large wooden tower, filled with crossbowmen, and that the king's troops destroyed with great loss two testudines, which, by the French, were called brutesclies.

These, which in the barbarous Latin of the times were termed bretacli-ise and brisegse, are, by different authors, denominated bertresc, bretescli, bretesques, bre-tagues, britesche, baltresch, and baldresh. They, however, differed from the testudo of the Romans, as that was formed by the troops covering themselves with their shields so as to resemble a tortoise-shell.

---

[9] Blount's Law Dictionary.
[10] Castle-yard.
[11] !list. p. 1091.
[12] Ibid. p. 321.

This was rather a covered tower of wood, with which camps and towns were at this time often fortified. Thus Guillaume le Breton de gestis Phillippi, under the year 1202, says, Fabricavit brestachias duplices per septem loca, castella videlicet lignea munitissima, a se proportionaliter distantia circumdata fossis duplicibus quadrangulis, pontibus versatilibus interjectis, imple-vitque hominibus armatis non solum castella ilia, immo interiorem omnem super -ficiem fossarum, et ita circumsessit obsessos. "He caused to be made double brestaches in seven different places: these were wooden castles, very highly fortified, surrounded with double quadrangular fosses at a proportionate distance from each, with drawbridges thrown across them, and he had not only these filled with armed men, but the interior surface of each foss, and thus he surrounded the besieged by his works." So William Guiart, in the year 1248, writes:

> Des haus creniaus et des breteches,
> Retraient quarriaus cours et Ions.

> "From the high turrets and from breteches
> Were shot quarrels, swift and to a distance."

In a copy of Matthew Paris, written in the time of Henry III, in Bennet College library, at Cambridge,[13] is a marginal drawing, representing the attack of a castle by water. The fortress consists of two towers, one within the other, and surrounded by a wall, within all of which appear archers, cross-bowmen, and those who hurled great stones on the besiegers. On the ship, at the stern, is erected a tower, which is filled with archers and slingers; in the mid-ships is an archer, and at the head a man armed with a flail, a weapon used so late as the time of the Emperor Maximilian I, as several men carrying them appear in his Triumph, by Hans Burgmair. This curious delineation is copied Pl. xxvi, Fig. 5.

The horse soldiers, at this time, consisted of the heavy cavalry, who were the knights, and completely covered with mail, or, as Matthew Paris expresses it,[14] ad unguem annatos, the face and left hand excepted. In a manuscript, entitled the Lives of the two Offas, written by Matthew Paris,[15] and of the time of Henry III, the knights appear generally in gamboised armour, with surcoats, and wearing shin-pieces, or greaves of steel. One, however, is in a hauberk, with hood and chausses of flat contiguous rings, and probably

---

[13] Marked C v, xvi.

[14] Hist. p. 204.

[15] Cotton lib. marked Nero, D. 1.

this is the latest example of such armour being worn. Some appear with visors, consisting of a convex plate of steel, on which is a cross, with perforations for the sight and punctures for the breath, which is tied upon the hood. Others have a nasal scullcap, though not the latest representation I have seen of this defence, and others the cylindrical helmet common to this period. The helmets of the kings are distinguished from the rest by a crown at top. They have all too those coverings for the knees called poleyns. This word is often erroneously confounded with poulaines, which were the long points at the toes of shoes, worn in Richard the Second's time, as well as anterior; but we learn from the following passage from Carolus Blessensis, in Lobineau's Hist. Bretagne,[16] that they were for the knees: Fecit sibi per Oliverium auferri a genibus polenas, et antebrachia a brachiis. "He caused Oliver to make for him poleyns for the knees, and vambraces for his arms."

The light-armed cavalry were the other kind of equestrian troops.

The foot soldiers were of three sorts: first, the men at arms, who were completely clothed in gamboised armour, with poleyns, covered with their surcoats, and wore on their heads the chapelles de fer: these supported the close battle when the armies came hand to hand, and were in fact dismounted knights.[17] The second were the spearmen, who bore oval shields, and were protected merely by pectorals, or tunicles of scales, which were thrown over their tunics; their heads were guarded by chapelles de fer: these gave and supported the charge on either side, when the armies began to join. The left hand figure[18] exhibits one of these.[19] A figure in pourpointed armour, with greaves, and ailettes on his shoulders, having his breast protected with a tegulated pectoral, may be seen in a MS. in the Sloanian library in the British Museum, entitled Liber Astronomiæ.[20] The book was pro bably written at the close of Edward the First's reign, and mention is made of the pectoral as armour for the chest, in the Stat. Riper.[21] The tunicle of scales is thus mentioned in the Chronicle of Flanders:

Un tournicle dessus aussi come d'escliaille.

"A tournicle thereupon also like scales."

---

[16] Vol. II, p. 566.

[17] See Pl. XVIII.

[18] Pl. XVIII.

[19] Taken from an illumination in a MS. in the Cotton library of the British Museum) marked Claud. D. II.

[20] Marked 3983. It has been introduced into the initial letter of the next reign.

[21] C. 12.

The third kind were the light-armed, and bore small round shields, and either light spears or oucins. One of these is represented in Pl. xvii.[22] The oucin was a weapon like a pickaxe, but with only one horn, which was fixed on a staff. It was used for striking between the rings or plates of the hauberks, and is thus noticed:

> Restitit uncino maculis lucrentc plicatis.

"He stood his ground tho' an oucin was sticking in the folding macles."

Round his head is wrapped the cargan, so called from the French carcan. In the MS. Statutes of Frejus, anno 1233, occurs: Peditum armatum intelligimus armatum scuto et propuncto, seu auspergoto et cofa, seu capello ferreo et cargan vel sine cargan, &c. "We understand by armed infantry those who are armed with shields and pourpoints, or auspergotes.[23] with coifs, or chapelles de fer, and cargans, or with out cargans," &c. The reference here, however, is to the heavy-anned foot. The province of the light-armed infantry was to gaul the enemy's horses with their long lances when they gave the charge, parrying with their small bucklers the points of the spears of the riders, and then retreating behind their own cavalry, leave them to support the second charge, constantly sallying out as they saw advantage.

The auspergote, or hauberg-coat, was in fact the hauberk, but the pourpoint requires some illustration.

This garment, which was called also prepoint, perpunctum, porpunctum, and propunctum, took its origin in France. It was formed on the models of the wambais and liauqueton, but probably not quite so thick and clumsy as the former, nor quite so stiff and inflexible as the latter: its principal distinction, however, arose from the elaborate stitching with which it was ornamented, and, as the name seems to import, on both sides. It resembled the liauqueton in being stuffed with wool, and the threads seem to have been knotted outside so as to form a kind of embroidery; for William Guiart, under the year 1304, says:

> Si comme de cotes faitices
> De coton à poins entailliez.

---

[22] Taken from an illumina'tion in a MS. in the Cotton library of the British Museum, marked Nero, D. i.

[23] That is, hauberk-coats, of which this word is a latinized corruption.

PLATE XVII

PETER EARL of RICHMOND and a SOLDIER.

A.D. 1248.

> "As with coats manufactured
> With cotton, with points embroidered."

Its facing or exterior covering was silk, but sometimes of that very fine and rich kind so highly esteemed in the middle ages, called cendal, or sandal, and which was purchased at a great price, for Odo de Rossilion, by his will, dated anno 1298, gives to the Lord Montancelin his porpoinctum de cendallo. The pourpoint was furnished with sleeves, for in letters remissory,[24] anno 1463, it is said, that "with a baston" icellui Jehan persa le manteau, et la manche du prepoint du suppliant, "that same John tore the cloak, and sleeve of the prepoint of the suppliant." William de Guilleville, in the Pèlerinage de l'Ame, MS., gives us the reason why it was confounded with the gambeson, thus:

> De pontures le gambison,
> Pourquoi pourpoint l'appelle-t-on.
>
> "A gambeson of punctures,
> Whence it was called pourpoint."

It was reckoned a species of armour, and, therefore, in the Liberties of Briançon, anno 1343, we read: Omnes de dieto numéro cum porpointis, gorgeriis, chirothecis ferreis, &c. "All of that number with pourpoints, gorgets, gauntlets," &c. And in the Chronicle of the Kings of Arragon, by Raimond Montanerio:[25] Eyo ab un bon cavall, que tenia mi terç de cavellers, armats ab lloriguesi et por-punts, &c. "Those who hold land by knights' fee shall perform service with a good horse, and armed with loricæ and pourpoints," &c.

It is thus distinguished from the gambeson in a charter of Philip the Fair, dated 1303: Et seront armez de porpoins et de liauberjons, ou de gambaison. "And they shall be armed with pourpoints and haubergeons, or gambesons." We meet with it so early as the twelfth century, for in a MS. History of the Siege of Acre, in 1191, occurs: Portantes ibidem lanceas, falcastra, cassides et loricas, tunica scammata, et perpunta, scuta cum clypeis, &c. "Carrying there lances, falcastra,[26] helmets, and loricæ, tunics of scale-work and pourpoints, shields and targets,"

Again, in the Registrum Homagiorum Nobilium Aquitaniæ, anno

---

[24] In Chartophy. Reg. Paris.

[25] C. 227.

[26] These were afterwards denominated bills.

1273: Ber-trandus de Podenssac domicellus dixit, quod ipse tenet à D. Duce Podensiarum, &c. débet facere personaliter exercitum cum gonjorie et perpuncto, si sit sanus, &c. "Bertrand de Podenssac, housekeeper, says, that he holds from the Lord Duke of Pódense, &c. and ought to perform personal service with a gonjo[27] and pourpoint, if in health," &c. And further on, "Geraldine de la Mote," &c. debet etiain D. Regis obsequium exercitiis de uno milite armato perpuncto et gonjone, "also owes military service by finding one knight armed with a pourpoint and gonjo." It seems, however, from the Statutes of Frejus, anno 1235, to have been worn by the cavalry with the hauberk, but by the infantry without, for there is this distinction made: Militem sine equo armato intelligimus armatum auspergoto et propuncto et scuto; peditum armatum intelligimus armatum scuto et propuncto seu aspergoto. "By a dismounted armed knight we understand one armed with an auspergote and pourpoint with a shield; and by an armed foot soldier, one bearing a shield, and clad in a pourpoint or an aspergote."

The same was the case in England in the time of Henry III, when the name seems to have been first introduced in this country, for Matthew Paris, detailing the king's ordonnances, says: Ad centum solidatas terræ unum purpunctum, capellum ferreum, gladium, &c. "Such as have a hundred shillings worth of land must come to the field armed with a pourpoint, a chapelle de fer, sword," &c.[28]

The use of the pourpoint seems greatly to have gained ground, and the military, in the delineations of this and the next reign, are almost constantly depicted in it. This garment was also called contrepoint.[29] Thus, in an inventory, dated anno 1296, in the Registry of the Royal Archives at Paris, occurs: Præterea inveni in dictis bonis, quinqué allierions et unum alberc et unum contrepointe. "Besides I found among the said goods five liaubergons, one hauberk, and one contrepointe." The making of these vestments was called ouvrages de pourpointerie, and there were several pourpointers in Paris and London.

Besides this threefold division of the infantry, there were the slingers, the archers, and the cross-bowmen.

The first of these do not appear to have had any kind of armour, being

---

[27] This was some kind of hauberk.

[28] A soldier thus habited appears in an illumination in a MS. in, the Cotton library, marked Claudius;D. 11, and is copied in Plate XVIII.

[29] In an inventory' of the hangings, &c. belonging to Charles I, at Windsor, in the possession of my friend Mr. Beard, dated 8th July, 1647, the counterpanes of the beds are called counterpointes,

generally formed of the poorest class in society, and carried merely their sling, which consisted of a thong fixed to the end of a stall, which they wielded with both hands, and from which they threw a very large stone. One of these, taken from a delineation of this period,[30] appears in Plate XVIII. Balistarii semper prseibant, "the slingers always preceded the army," says Matthew Paris,[31] beginning the battle with their slings. Next to these were the archers, both horse and foot, who, during this reign, were armed with scullcaps, hauberks of edge-ringed-work, with sleeves to the elbows, over which were placed leathern vests, each ornamented with four circular plates: they carried their arrows in a girdle. At this time, however, the vest was called cuirena, or cuirenia, from the French cuirie, for we meet with it in an account, dated 1239: Pro liernesio suo, videlicet baccis et cuireniis suis affecturis ix lib. v sol. Item Pro tribus baccis et tribus cuirenis at eosdem iv lib. iv sol. "For his harness, viz. for his breeches,[32] and the things appertaining to his cuiries, 9 liv. 5 sols. Also, for three pairs of breeches, and three cuiries for the same, 4 liv. 4 sols." So William Guiart, under the year 1268, has—

> Hyaumes, haubers, tacles, cuiries
> Fondent par Ies grans cops et fraignent.

> "Helms, hauberks, tags, cuiries,
> Are beat in by the great blows, and broken."

These scullcaps of the archers were called cerebrerium, for in Chron: Fransc: Pepini,[33] is, Quam comperisset se moriturum excogitavit novam capitis armaturam qsue vulgo cerebrerium sive cerebotarium appellatus qua jugiter caput munitum habebat. "Having ascertained which, and imagining he was going to die, his new armour for the head, which is commonly called cerebrerium, or cerebotarium, and by which he had continually guarded his head." It is to the mounted archers that Matthew Paris alludes, when he says, Viri autem sagittarii gentis Anglorum equi-tibus permixti. "But the English mixed their archers with the cavalry."

---

[30] A transcript of Mat. Paris, in Bennet College library, Cambridge, marked Cv, XVI.

[31] P. 248, Hist.

32 Bacoe, or baccoe, imply Iinks of a chain. Thus Gregory of Tours, in his Miracles of St. Martin, lib. I, c. 2, says: Omnes baccæ catenarum confractoe, ceciderunt. But as I find the word bache in an antient Latin and French Glossary, explained as femoralia, I have ventured to give the above translation.

[33] Lib. v, c. 50.

PLATE XVIII

A SPEARMAN, MAN AT ARMS, AND A SLINGER,

A.D. 1250.

The cross-bowmen shot from their cross-bows short arrows,[34] generally from the quadrangular shape of their piles, called quarrels, and, according to Matthew Paris,[35] wore hauberks: Et arcubalistarii circiter sexaginta lori-cati. "And about sixty loricated cross-bowmen."

Plate XIX exhibits an archer and an arbalister from delineations in the copy of Matthew Paris, at Bennet College, Cambridge, by which it may be seen, that the latter had nasal helmets, and were armed with short swords, called baselards. The archer appears with one of those arrows, which was headed with a phial full of quicklime,[36] and which is thus mentioned by Matthew Paris: Et phialas plenas calce, arcubus per parva liastilia ad modum sagittarum super hostes jaculandas; "and phials full of quicklime fixed on small darts, like arrows, were shot from the bows upon the enemy." But, besides these, it was not unusual for the archers to shoot arrows headed with some burning combustible matter, which were particularly used to destroy any wood-work either by land or sea. Matthew Paris calls them spicula ig-nita.[37]

It has been observed, that in the illuminations of this period, the archers are represented as having leathern vests over their hauberks of edge-ringed mail. These appear to have been the jack in its primary form, which origi-nated with the English,[38] and which afterwards assumed a shape so cumber-some. From the Chronicle of Bertrand du Guesclin, composed about the time of Richard II, we learn that it continued to be worn over the hauberk, for he says:

> S'avoit chascun un jacque par dessus son haubert.

> "Each had a jack above his hauberk."

This small vest was afterwards called jacket, and in the Latin of the time, jaquetanus, as was the jaque, jaquemardus, and jacobus. The monument of Eudo de Arsic, who died about the latter part of this reign, seems to repre-sent him in the jacque, and on that account it has been adopted for Plate XX. He is clad in mail, and wears this garment, which is made with sleeves, sits close to the body, is buttoned down the front, and has a puckered skirt

---

[34] Quidam arcubalista traxit sagittam. Rog. Hoveden Ann. p. 450.

[35] Hist. p. 591.

[36] This is taken from another delineation in the same MS.

[37] Misimus igitur super eos spicula ignita, p. 1090. One of them; from the transcript of Matt. Paris, at Bennet College, Cambridge, is given at the bottom of Plate XIX.

[38] Hence, called by the old French writers, jacque d'Anglois.

PLATE XIX

ARCHER AND CROSS BOWMAN.

A.D. 1250.

reaching to the knees. In later times it was generally of leather, for Coquil-
lart, an old French writer, sur les droits nouveaux, describes it as of shamois,
extending to the knees, and stuffed with flocks, so as to be a kind of pourpoint. He says:

> C'etoit un pourpoint de chamois
> Farci dc bourc sus ct sous
> Un grand vilain jaque d'Anglois
> Qui lui pendoit jusq'aux genous.

> "It was a pourpoint of shamois,
> Stuffed with wool, and stitched;
> A great villanous English jack.
> Which hung down to his knees."

In France the use of the arbalest seems to have been discountenanced
at this time, for though, by the charter of liberties granted to the town of
Vitry, by Theobald Earl of Champagne, in 1220, several of its inhabitants
were compelled to practice with the cross-bow,[39] yet it may have been with
this view that the following words were inserted in a royal charter, dated
1239: Domum nostram de Cheeigneio assiguravimus domino Comiti
Montisfortis tali modo, quod non possumus habere in eodem, archeriam,
nec arbalisteriam, neque crenelium neque scutum. "Our chateau de Chee-
ignee we have assigned to the earl of Montfort, in such wise that he is to
understand we cannot allow in it any perpendicular loop-hole for archers,
nor any cruciform loop-hole for cross-bowmen, any turret, nor any fortification shield."

What the aleors was is not so clear. Du Cange supposes it to be the
loop-hole. It occurs in a letter, dated 1213, apud Marten, thus: Concessi
quod possint facere murum sine fossatis et tornellis, et de archeriis et arba-
lestenis sine aleors. "I have granted them power to build walls, but without
ditches and drawbridges, with loopholes for archers and for cross-bowmen,
without aleors." As it cannot imply the loop-holes, I presume it is a corruption of the French word ailleurs, and that it would imply "without any thing
further."

Every leader had his own banner, on which was painted his device, a circumstance of which King Henry III took advantage to practise a stratagem.
Having but a small army to oppose to his enemy, he caused every baron

---

[39] Chascuns de la Commune de Vitré, qui aura vaillânt 20 livres, aura aubeleste en son
ostel, et quarriaux 50.

PLATE XX

EUDO DE ARSIC,

A.D. 1260.

and knight banneret to have two banners instead of one, which, making his troops appear double in number, had the effect of inducing the French to quit their post.[40]

The Emperor Frederick is said, by Sigonius, to have used a singular kind of standard: "he placed a castle," instar carrocii, "like a car, on the back of an elephant: this was decorated with ensigns at the angles, and the standard of the army in the centre, consigning the defence of it to the master of the elephants and the Saracens, who were placed within the castle."

From the circumstance of the standard-bearers in the Venetian army wearing tight hose, that kind of dress came to be called pantaloon. This word is a corruption of pianta leone, i. e. "plant the lion," the standard of the republic being the lion of St. Mark.

Matthew Paris speaks of the military cognizances when relating the conduct of the infidels at the approach of the Christian troops in the year 1250. Cum videret hostes Christi, armis, vexillis et cognitionibus picturatis, quas bene noverant cum derisionibus superbire. "When they saw the Christian hosts, with arms, banners, and painted cognizances, which they well knew, they disdainfully treated them with derision."

As the cognizance was that by which knights were known, it was not unfrequent for them to cast them away when it became necessary to favour their escape. Thus Ordericus Vitalis informs us,[41] that Petrus de Maulia, aliique nonnulli fugientium, cognitiones suas ne agnoscerentur projecerunt. "Peter de Mauley and some others, who were put to flight, cast from them their cognizances that they might not be known."

The consequence of neglecting to put on the sureoat became, at a later period, when the fashion of having them emblazoned had become more general, very serious. Thus[42] Moor relates, that in the battle of Bannockbourne, in the reign of Edward II, the earl of Gloucester would not have been killed, but that he went into the field without his toga propriæ arinaturæ, "emblazoned sureoat," and therefore was not recognised. It must, consequently, have been very serviceable to knights, and it is to be wondered at that the fashion did not become more suddenly prevalent. A very early specimen of the sureoat charged with armorial bearings occurs in an illumination in the British Museum.[43] The representations of Pierre de Courtenay, Simon, and

---

[40] Speed's Cbron. p. 577.
[41] Lib. XIII, p. 855.
[42] P. 594.
[43] Royal lib. marked 2 A XXII.

Amauri de Montfort, exhibit them in cylindrical helmets and pourpointed armour, with emblazoned shields, but plain surcoats.[44] The seal of Amaury de Montfort, and that of Henry de Metz, who carried the famous standard of France, called the oriflamme, represent them similarly habited, but with their armorial bearings on the caparisons of their horses as well as shields, but not on their surcoats.[45] So in an illuminated MS. written about the year, 1250,[46] the knights appear in the same manner.

That emblazoned surcoats were not, at this time, common, is confirmed by what we read in the Memoirs of Lord de Joinville. He says, that when "he was conversing with Philip the Fair, on the pomp and expense of dress, and on the embroidered emblazoned surcoats, now in fashion with the army, he observed, that, during the whole time he was beyond sea, in the army with St. Louis, he never once saw an embroidered coat or saddle either belonging to the king or any one else." He also speaks of forty knights, whom he had clothed in coats and surcoats simply of green; and tells us, that, at the time St. Louis was taken prisoner, his horse had merely a housing of silk.

In the Annales Colmarienses, A.D. 1298, we find not only this in its splendid state assigned to the knights, but two other garments. "Fecerat hoc anno ante festum S. Michaelis milites, quos omnes vestivit ad minus triplici vestimento, scilicet tunica pretiosa, surgotum . . . . . nobili vario, suchor-narn cum vario pretioso. "In that year, before Michaelmas-day, he created knights, all of whom he had clothed in three garments at least, viz.: a tunic of great value, a surcoat . . . . . beautifully embroidered, and a suchorne var-iegated in a precious manner." So also the Roman de Garin le Loheraus we read:

> La veissiis ces liaubers endosser
> Et ces enscignes de cendau venteler.

> "There you might see these hauberks
> And these devices of taffety blown by the wind."

With respect to the creation of knights, Matthew of Westminster[47] in-

---

[44] On painted glass in the church of Notre name de Chatres, given by Montfaucon in his Mon. Fr. Pl. LXXXVII and LXXXVIII. The seal of Walter Stuart, belonging to Sir R. Worsley, and engraved in the Ârchreologia, Vol. IV, p. 176, is of this period, and greatly resembles that of Roger de Quincybefore noticed.

[45] See Montf. Mon. Fr. Pl. LXXXVIII.

[46] Royal lib. Brit. Mus. marked 20 D I.

[47] P. 300.

forms us, that, after Henry III had made eighty new knights, the Prince Edward went with them to a tournament which had been proclaimed on the Continent, that each might try his strength, as is the custom with new knights. So also in 1253, the earl of Gloucester and another sailed across the Channel, principally to be at a marriage, but secondarily to prove their courage and strength and the swiftness of their horses, in a hastilude there proclaimed. They happened to be unfortunate, for they were thrown, spoiled, and sadly bruised, and required daily fomentations and bathing to be restored to health.[48]

St. Louis, desirous to begin his second crusade, invited Edward, son of Henry III, to join him. This prince, accompanied by his wife Eleanora, sailed to the coast of Africa, and, after having wintered in Sicily, took Acre. When he returned to England he found his father just expired.[49]

During the latter part of this reign the shape of the helmet underwent a partial change, taking the form of a truncated cone on the top of a cylinder; and as the apertures for the sight were horizontal, and pierced in the transverse part of a cross that ornamented the front, it was probably occasioned by this crusade. The monument of Huges Vidame de Chalon, in Champagne, in the abbey church of that place, who died in the year 1279, represents him in one of these, and wearing pourpointed armour;[50] and the helmet of Amaury de Montfort on his seal, which is given at the foot of Plate XVIII, is of this nature.

This change in the form of the helmet rendered necessary a corresponding one in that of the hood, and we consequently find them from this period taking the shape of the head. Capreville's helmet, which is engraved at the bottom of Pl. xx, is, indeed, the exact form of the hood, but this is by no means common. Peter Earl of Richmond adhered to the old fashion, as may be seen in Pl. xvii, taken from his monumental effigy. But he is introduced to the notice of the reader principally because his hauberk, hood, and cliausses, which have the rings set edgewise, have them all inclined one way,[51] whereas, in general, they were sewn on so that one row might lie to the left and one to the right alternately.

In the Temple church is a monument attributed to William Marshall Earl of Pembroke. He, however, died in 1219, and, therefore, if the effigy

[48] Mat. West. 252.

[49] W. Rishanger's Continuation of Mat. Paris, p. 1006.

[50] See Montfaucon's Mon. Fr. Pl. xci, Fig. 5.

[51] This is more clearly shewn at the bottom of the plate. The armour of the knights on Mr. Douce's curious ivory casket is the same, though of a somewhat later period.

was intended to commemorate him, it could not have been done before the latter part of this reign. Henry III, indeed, owed his crown, and the English their emancipation from a foreign sovereign, to the wisdom and exertion of this great man, who had been appointed regent of the kingdom;[52] hut if this was the grateful return it came very late. In proof of this observation it will be necessary to examine the armour on the figure. It may, however, be remarked, by the way, that the manufacture of armour, at the commencement of this reign, must have greatly improved, for when Louis the Dauphin, in 1216, contended for the crown of England against the claims of Henry III, the city of London sent him 600 knights, and 60,000 coats of mail:[53] the quantity must have been the result of its cheapness.

The effigy above mentioned,[54] as well as that of Sir Hugh Mauveyson, has cliaucons, or breeches, on which were sometimes fastened the poleyns. It has, indeed, the armour of rings set edgewise, turning one row to the right and another to the left. In both the monuments the hood is hemispherical; and both are placed cross-legged, which has been supposed to be a mark of having been, or, at any rate, made a vow to go, to the Holy Land in a crusade.[55]

But the crusade in this reign seems to have introduced a new and most ingenious species of armour, probably of Asiatic discovery, and still worn by those nations at the present day. This was the interlaced rings, which rendered unnecessary garments to hold them. The earliest specimen I have met with is the monumental effigy of De L'Isle, in Rampton church, Cambridgeshire, which exhibits him in the flat coif worn during the greater part of this reign, but made, as well as his hauberk and chausses, of interlaced chain. The shape of his shield, however, is that of the close of it, and, with his surcoat, is emblazoned with his armorial bearings. His sword and shield-belt are both highly ornamented, and the outer shanks of his spurs are nailed on the leathers which pass through the apertures made in the others. This armour is made by four rings joining a fifth, all of which are fastened with rivets. One row, indeed, on the hood, seems to double the number which would authorize the term double chain mail; but as all the rest are as above described, the armour must be considered as the single

---

[52] Mat. Paris, p. 304, who also mentions tbat he was buried in the Temple church.

[53] Ibid. p. 293.

[54] That of William de Goldington, in Rusbton cburch, Northamptonshire, exactly resembles tbis, and the date attributed to it is 1240; but it appears à. little later.

[55] The hand in tbe attitude of the sheathing the sword has also, with much probability, been supposed to shew that the vow had been performed.

chain mail. Yet mention is made in the Chronicle of Flanders of double chain mail, thus:

Un hauberk clavez de double maille.

"A hauberk of rivetted double mail."[56]

Matthew Paris speaks of two pieces of armour worn during this reign, one of which was termed alcato and the other collarium, both intended for the throat. The first was of Arabic origin, and derived from the crusaders; the latter, though thus early mentioned, I have not seen represented any where so soon as this period. The passage in which he speaks of it is under the year 1252: Carens collario, says he, lethaliter vulnerabatur. "Being without his collar he was mortally wounded." That part of the capuchon or hood, which covered the throat, had been called collare, during the reign of Richard I, for Guillaume le Breton writes:

Qua ligno junctum est, ferri transcgit acumen
Per collare triplex et per thoraca trilicem.

"The sharp-pointed blade, down to where it is fixed on the wood,
Was driven through bis threefold collar and bis trellissed broigne."

Evidently made of three folds of cloth, which hung over the trellissed armour as in Plate xi. So again the Archbishop Thomas[57] says: Venitque ictus inter cassidem et collarium, dejecitque caput ejus multum a corpore. "There came a blow between his helmet and collar, which struck off his head to a great distance from his body." Now in Leo's Tactics[58] it is called περὶ Ἰραχήλια σιδηρά, a "collar of steel." If such, therefore, was worn at this time, it must have been under the capuchon.

The chapel de fer continued to be used in this reign, as has been ob-

---

[56] Mr. Bullock had in his museum a piece, brought from Lancaster castle, and said to have belonged to John of Gaunt, which was made of ten instead of five rings interlaced. This he has disposed of, but promised to recover for me, though, after shewing him the collar of an Asiatic shirt of mail, he has acknowledged the resemblance. The rings are probably only flatter, and with smaller apertures, so as to be held more closely together. In my son's collection, however, are four gussets of double chain mail, whieh are made by each upper ring passing through two lower ones. These are of German manufacture, and came from Nuremberg.

[57] Hist. Salonist. c. 28.

[58] Compiled in the ninth century.

served; hence, Joinville says, "that the king[59] raised the helmet from his head, on which I gave him my chapel de fer, which was much lighter, that he might have more air."He further tells us, that this helmet of the king's was gilt. So also in a charter, dated 1263:[60] Item XVI cappillinae cum vii balistis de ligno fractis. "Also sixteen chapels de fer, with seven broken wooden cross-bows."

Joinville observes, that when the knights were wounded it became impossible very often, from the weight, &c. to put on their defensive armour so early as the following day. He further mentions, that a Saracen gave him such a thrust between the shoulders as drove him on his horse's neck, and held him there so tightly that he could not draw his sword, which was girted round him, on which account he was forced to draw another sword that was at the pummel of his saddle. This is, perhaps, the earliest instance of having the stabbing or arming sword, as well as the long one.

This stabbing sword, which was of French origin, and called épée à l'estoc, occurs in an arret of the parliament of Paris, in the year 1268: Sufficienter inventum est quod dictus Boso dictum Ademarum percussit cum ense à estoc in dextro latero propria manu, et de ipso ictu cecidit dictus Ademarus. "It is sufficiently discovered that the said Boso stabbed the said Aymer with an épée à l'estoc, with his own hand, in the right side, and that by that blow killed the said Aymer,"&c.

St. Louis, according to Joinville, used a German sword. These were extremely large, as we learn from William Guiart, in his Life of Philippe Auguste. He says:

> A grans espées d'Allemagne
> Leur tranchent souvent les poins outre.

> "With great German swords
> They cut them often, without the reach of their points."

Again, of their daggers:

> Alemans uns coutiaus avoient
> Dont aus François se combatoient
> Grailles et ague à trois quieres
> L'en en peut ferir sus pierres.

---

[59] St. Louis.
[60] Apud Muratori.

"The Germans had knives,
With which they fought the French,
Tapering and sharp, with three edges,
So that they could strike one even under stones."

But though at Bovines he thus arms them with short weapons, in another place he assigns long two-handed swords to them:

Car les deux mains en haut levées
Gietent d'une longues espées
Souef tranchans à longes meures.

"For with two hands raised on high
They struck with their long swords
Instantaneous cuts to great depths."

These two-handed swords were still in use in the German army so late as the time of Maximilian I, but seem to have been revived about the early part of the fifteenth century, having been previously confined to the Swiss.

The Emperor Nicephoros Phocas reproaches the Germans for their long swords; and in some old ordinances of the town of Paris, mention is made of the swords of Lubec. But large swords were the general fashion of this period.

Though the lance and the sword were confined to freemen in France as well as England, yet, in the reign of St. Louis, we find from an anonymous poem, entitled l'Outillement du Villain, that they were also permitted to the serfs; not that they were allowed to carry them on ordinary occasions, but merely on joining the army, their weapons by right being only bows and arrows, mallets or maules, clubs, and such like. The poet,[61] therefore, says:

Si Ie convient armer
For la terre garder
Coterel et haunct
Massue et guibet
Arc et lance enfumée
Qu'il n'ait soin de mesliée
Avec luy ayt couchiée
L'Espee cnrouilliec
Puis ayt son vieil escu
A la paroy pendu
A son col doit pendre
Por la terre deffendre

[61] Lacombe calls him La Forestier.

Quand il vient est bannie.

> "If it should be agreed on to arm,
> For the defence of the land,
> With long knife and haunct,[62]
> Mace and guibet,[63]
> Bow and smoked lance,
> That he need not dread the close fight,
> Let him have with him, couched,
> The sword cased in its scabbard,
> Then taking his old shield That hangs on the wall,
> Which ought to be suspended from his neck,
> To defend the land
> When the assembled army appears."

It is, therefore, that he says the lance is covered with smoke, and the sword concealed in its sheath, because they hung up, to be used only on such particular occasions. Guillaume le Breton, in his History of Philippe Auguste, alludes to this particular permission, thus:

> At famuli, quorum est gladio pugnare vel hastis
> Officium.

> "But the serf, whose duty is to fight with
> The sword or lance."

The weapons used in that author's time are enumerated in the following lines:

> Nunc contus nunc clava, nunc vero bipcnnis
> Excercbrat, sed nec bisacuta, sudisve vel basta
> Otia vel gladius ducit,
> Quadrellos hie multiplicat, pluit ilia sagittas
> Funda breves fundit Iapides, glandesque rotundas.

> "Now the javelin, now the mace, now the double-axe,
> Break open skulls; but neither besagiic, spear, or lance,
> Or sword, is suffered to be idle:
> Quarrels in successive numbers fly here, there showers of arrows;
> Slings pour forth swift stones and round bullets."

---

[62] Lacombe says it is a kind of lance.

[63] A broad-bladed weapon resembling a pointed spade, probably the .same as the anelas.

To these may be added, in the time of Henry III, the faussar, a small curved sword with its edge inside, like those at present used by the Albanians. In the manuscript Chronicle of Alberic, in the year 1214, where mention is made of the battle of Bovines, it is said: Ante occulos ipsius regis occiditur Stephanus de Longo Campo, in capite percussus longo gracili trialemello quern falsarium nominant. "Before the king's eyes was killed Stephen de Longchamp, who was struck on the head by a long thin three-edged weapon, called a faussar."The Roman de Roncevaux also speaks of it thus:

> Et grans juizarmes et faussars acerez.

> "And great gisarmes and sharp faussars."

The Roman of Guillaume au Court-nez does the same:

> Et arbalestes, javelos et faussars.

> "And cross-bows, javelins, and faussars."

Matthew Paris seems to allude to this by the word sicas, unless by that is meant the hand-gisarme. Gestabant autem, says he, gladios, bipennes, gæsa, sicas, et anelacios. "They were armed with swords, double-axes, gæsa, sicæ, and anelacii."The gæsum, according to Hesychius, was a dart wholly of iron. Γαισὸς ἐμβόλιον ὀλοσίδηρον are his words. Such are still used in India for tiger-liunting, but I am inclined to believe it a blade-weapon, derived from that used by the antient Gauls. An old Latin glossary says it is the same as the gisarme, adding maniere de glaive: it was probably its prototype. Guillaume le Breton[64] makes mention of it:

> Clavam cum jaculo, venabula, gesa, bipennem.

> "A mace with a dart, hunting spears, gesa, double-axe."

And Matthew Paris, in 125G, couples it with the Danish axe: cum jaculis, Danis que securibus et gesis. "With darts, Danish axes, and gesa."

The anelacius, Du Cange considers to be a short knife. It was called in English anelas, and had a very broad blade tapering to a point. The misericorde, which Geoffry Vociensis, in his Chronicle, calls a Burgundian sword, was used at this period, and, indeed, is mentioned in the Roman de la Rose.

[64] Lib. v, Phillip.

It was forbidden by a charter,[65] dated 1211, together with pointed knives, &c. It has been generally supposed, that this weapon took its name from the knights obliging their antagonists to call for mercy after having prostrated them with their swords or lances, holding it over them in a threatening manner; but, as it appears to be of earlier use than the time when knights wore both swords and daggers, I am inclined to doubt this opinion.

A superb ornament was introduced during this reign—the cointise, which was a scarf worn by the knights. It is noticed by Matthew Paris, under the year 1252: Mille enim milites et amplius vestiti serico, ut vulgariter loquamur cointises, in nuptiis, ex parte regis apparuerunt. "For upwards of a thousand knights attended the nuptials on the part of the king, clad in silk scarves, which are commonly called cointises."It took its name from the French word cointe, which signifies elegance.[66] The military figure introduced into the initial letter to this reign is adorned with one, being copied from an illuminated MS. in the Bodleian library.[67]

The tents seem to have been veiy splendid at this time, for Joinville mentions, that "St. Louis sent to the Cham of Tartary a tent in the form of a chapel: it was of fine scarlet cloth, very rich and handsomely made, embroidered with the annunciation of the angel Gabriel, the nativity, the baptism of our Lord, the ascension, and the descent of the Holy Ghost."

In a parchment roll,[68] of the time of Henry III, is a curious drawing in red ink, which represents the duel fought between Walter Blowebenne and Hamon le Stare, in consequence of a trial by wager of battle. The combatants are in their tunics, with their heads and feet bare, and armed merely with besagiies, or comuted staves, and semicylindrical shields, which are held by the hand in the cavity of the umbo.

The duel, which signifies a contest between two persons, was not, as at present, the private satisfaction demanded and granted by individuals. This modern duel arose from a precedent set by Francis I King of France, who challenged the Emperor Charles V, [69] and indeed for a century after was punishable in France by the penalty of death. But the antient duel was a combat fought according to legal forms: these were sometimes on foot and sometimes on horseback. The arms used in pedestrial duels are thus

---

[65] Charta Comm. Atrèbat.

[66] Hence Contoier means to adorn. So in the statutes of St. Louis, lib l, we read: et son lit, et sa robe à contoier.

[67] Marked 86. Arch. B.

[68] In the Queen's treasury of the records in the Tower of London.

[69] Robertson's Charles V.

described, in the Speculum Saxonicum.[70] Judex cuique duos præbere debet,
qui videant quod secundum consuetudinem præparentur. Quandum voluerint de corio et lineo induant, dummodo frontes, id est, capita atque pedes
permaneant enudati. In manibus non nisi simplices habeant chirothecas:
nudum in manu quilibet liabeat gladium et cum uno vel pluribus secundum
cujusque arbitrium præcingatur. Clypeum ligneum corio tectum, et non
nisi umbonem ferreum in manu ferant, et unicam tunicam induant, cujus
manicæ usque ad cubitum se extendant. "To the judge it belongs to produce the two combatants, who shall take care that they are armed according
to custom. With respect to leather and linen they may wear as much they
please, provided that their fronts, that is, their heads and feet, remain naked. On their hands they shall have merely gloves. If any one prefers it he
may have in his hand a naked sword, and one or more girded upon him.
They shall each have a buckler of wood covered with leather, and merely a
convex iron umbo; and they shall wear a single tunic, the sleeves of which
extend to the elbows."

The arms of those who fought on horseback we learn from the Assisiae Hiero-solymitanæ:[71] Et se ils sont chevaliers, ils doivent venir à cheval
en l'hotel dou seignor pour eaus offrir, et doivent avoir les cliauces de fer
chaucies, et lor espa-lieres vestués, et doivent faire amener les clievaus couverts de fer, et de toutes autres choses appareillées ainsçy coin por entrer en
champ, et faire apporter lor autres armures, dequoy ils doivent estre armés
el champs, de haubert, et de cliauces et de heaumes et visieres, et que chacun
ait cote à armer et gambison, se veaut, et se il ne veaut gambison, il peut
mettre devant son ventre une contrecurée de télé, ou de coton, ou de boure
de sec télé, et si fort coin il vodra; et doit avoir un escu et une lance et deux
espées, et que les lances soient d'un long, et que les fers des lances et des
espées des chevaliers qui se combattent en champ guagécs de bataille, et
doivent estre de tel façon coin il vodront; mais que ils ne soient pas tels, que
ils puissant passer par les mailles dou haubert sans tailler ou rompre maill, et
doit avoir en l'oreille dou heaume tout autour orles de fer, tels corn il vodra,
ou rasors. Et en l'escu doit avoir deux broches de fer l'une emmi l'escu, et
l'autre au pié de soute, et doivent estre de tel grosse, corne il vodront, et
tel longour jusques à un pié, et neent plus. Et entour l'escu tant de broches
de fer corn ils vodront, agues ou rasours. Et le cheval doit estre couvert de
couverture de fer, et avoir une testiere de fer, et emmi la testiere une broche

---

[70] Lib. I. Art. 63.
[71] C. 99:

de fer telle corne celle de l'escu: et peut mettre chascun en ses couvertures de fer d'entour cliene si lone come il vodra pour les jarés, et les jambes de son cheval couvrir et garder, et chascun doit avoir l'une de ses espées attachée à l'arcon de la selle devant et l'autre doit avoir ceinte, et la feure taillé jusques à renges, et peut avoir se il veaut, un ou deux fourreaux plein de ce que il vodront; mais que de chose que il puisse nuire son aversaire ne gregier, et peuvent couvrir leurs clievaus d'autres couvertures sur celles de fer, telles corne il vodront. "And if they be knights they ought to come to the hotel of their lord to offer themselves, and ought to have chausses of mail drawn upon them and their shoulder-plates[72] put on; and their horses they should have led, covered with mail, and in every other respect fully caparisoned in such manner as proper for entering the field. And they should cause to be brought their other armour, with which they should be armed in the field, that is to say, hauberks, chausses, and lielines with visors; and each should have an arming coat, and gam-beson, if he chooses; but if he does not like a gambeson he must put before his belly a contre-cuirass of hemp or cotton, or tow of dry flax, and as strong as he chooses. And he ought to have a shield, a lance, and two swords,[73] and the length of the lances as well as their blades, and those of the swords of the knights combattant, should be such as they please, and in whatever fashion: but they must not be such that they may pass through the mailles of the hauberk without cutting or breaking the mail. And they ought to have at that part of the helmet, just above the ears, all round, a circle[74] of iron, ornamented according to their fancy, or smooth. And in the shield they ought to have two spikes of iron, one in the middle of the shield, the other at the foot of the soute[75], and they ought to be of whatever thickness they choose, and whatever length, provided they do not exceed one foot; and on the circumference of the shield as many iron spikes as they please, sharp-pointed or smooth. And the horse ought to be covered with a housing of mail, and have a testiere[76] of iron, and in the

---

[72] The epauliere was a collection of plates placed upon the shoulder.

[73] Here is another, though not quite so early an instance of the use of two swords on horseback,

[74] The orle was a chaplet or border,

[75] The supplementary or lower part of the shield.

76 The testiere, or head-piece, was for a crest, that was fixed on the head of the horse between his ears, though here intended for a chanfron. It was not worn before the reign of Edward I, nor the chausses, generally speaking, later than the commencement of Edward the Third's time, plate having been introduced before. I presume that the MS. from which this is copied was written in the time of Edward III.

centre of the testiere an iron spike,[77] such as that on the shield. Each having been put in a housing of mail, they may be girded as low as they please, to cover and guard the houghs and legs of the horse. And each ought to have one of the swords attached to the bow of the saddle in front, and the other to his girdle, and the scabbard-belt cut just at his loins, and may have, if he chooses, one or two leathern cases full of what he chooses, but not of what might injure his adversary, nor charm him. And they may cover their horses with other housings over the iron ones according to their fancies."So also in the Roman Partonopex.

> Rois Sorncgur est bien armez
> Bien sai comment or m'escoutez:
> En chauccs est de soie faites
> Beles, bones, et Iegeretes
> Si a un bon hauberc vestu
> Et a un bon double cscu
> Et bon heaume el chief lacié
> Et en son poing un bon espié,
> S'a une espee longue et dure
> Et bien molue à sa mesure
> Une autre à son arçon pendue,
> D'autrepart une besagüe
> Et sa miséricorde à ceinte
> De fres entouchement entainte;
> Et un alesnas bien poignant
> Moult s'en pooit faire à tant.
> Et est sor un moult gran cheval,
> Qui bien covient à tel vassal
> Bien est couvert de coutures
> De fer tenant com pieres dures.
> Partonopex rest bien armez,
> Et il loi de Frans adobez.
> Chauces de fer a bien tailliées
> Et bien de soie appareilliées
> Heaume et escu et fort espié
> Et bon hauberc meme maillié;
> Mais il n'a c'une sole espée
> Cela à son arçon noée
> Et siet sur le bon cheval noir
> Bon le cuide à son oes avoir
> Et culiere et bone cropiere

---

[77] This expression seems as if a chanfron was intended, a piece of horse armour, that I have not met with in representation before the time of Richard II, who, on his seal, appears in chausses.

Aate de fer et legiere
N'a cure de miséricorde
Ne d'alesnas pas ne le borde
Ne cure pas de besagüe
Ja n'en est pas lui esmolue.

"The king Sornegur was well-armed,
I well know how: Listen:
He was in chausses of silk, made
Handsome, good and light,
Also he was clad in a good hauberk,
And had a good double shield,[78]
And a good helmet laced at top,
And in his clenched hand a good lance.
Also he has a long and strong sword,
And well sharpened its whole length,
Another hung at his saddle bow,
With a besague[79] at the other side,
And his miséricorde at his girdle,
But lately prepared for its purpose,
And an alesnas,[80] sharp-pointed,
Much could he do with so much:
And being seated on a very great horse,
Quite suitable to such service,
Well covered with housing
Of iron, resisting with the strength of stone,
Partonopex remains well armed,
Who was knighted according to the law of France,

Chausscs of iron, well shaped
And apparelled with plenty of silk,.
Helme and shield, and strong sword,
And a good hauberk itself mailed,
But he has but one single sword
That is attached to his saddle-bow,
And lie sits on a black horse
Good, he thinks, to have his will;
And a culiere[81] and good croupiere
A defiance[82] of iron and light,
He cares not for misericorde,

---

[78] I have not met with any account of the double shield, nor what was its peculiarity.
[79] I'he besagüe was not so frequently used as the mace, or battle-axe.
[80] Probably a contraction of anelacius.
[81] The part of the croupiere made round to hold the tail.
[82] From aatir, to defy; armour worn in front.

Nor an anclas without its sheath,[83]
Nor cares for a besagiie
As yet none is sharpened for him."

The duel seems to have been originally a Danish institution, and antiently called campwig, from kampf, a battle; and viig, manslaughter. Thus,
in a decree of Tassilio,[84] we read: Qui supra diette pugnæ, quod camswic
dicimus, peracto judicio,&c. "Who of the above-mentioned fight, which
we call camswic, judgment having been pronounced."In England, by the
Anglo-Danes, it was called a kemp-fight. Such being the origin of its name
we shall not wonder at finding that the combatants were called campiones,
or champions. These were sometimes knights, and sometimes persons of
inferior rank: for the champions were not necessarily those who were parties in the suit at law, but very often hired to fight their battles.[85] Thus, in
the Assisiae Hieros:[86] Toutes manieres de gens, autreque chevaliers, pour
quelque quarelle que se soit, se doivent combattre a pied en bleaut, ou en
cotes rouges, et chauces a estrier, et braies et braier, tel com est use, que
champion a pied les ont, et estre rongnez a la reonde, et avoir chanevas,
et bastons de champions, et qui avoir ne les peut, si ait autres bastons, qui
soient d'un Ion. "All kind of people other than knights, for whatever quarrel
it may be, ought to fight on foot in blue or in red coats, and in chausses that
are made to come under the foot,[87] and breeches, and a steel bandage[88] such
as are used, and worn by champions on foot, and have their hair cropped
close, and have canvas and champions' batons, but which they need not
have if they have others of full size."The clipping of the hair was an antient
ordinance, for we find in the old municipal law of Normandy,[89] Chascun
doit avoir les cheveux rongnez par dessus les oreilles. "Each should have his
hair cut above his ears."

The arms of champions were at first merely a club or staff and a shield;

---

[83] Literally"lodgment."

[84] Dux. Bajwar, c. 2, s. 6.

[85] So an anonymous writer on the genealogy of some citizens of Padua, cited by Muratori, says: Talis enim erat antiquorum consuetudo. Si duo nobiles aut potentes homines inter
se homicidium commississent, utraque pars inveniebat sibi unum campionem prétio, &c.

[86] MS. c. 101.

[87] Stirrup-fashioned.

[88] Lacombe explains brayer by bandage d'acier: whether right or wrong, it was attached
to the breeches, which are themselves termed brayer in a MS. of the time of Edward I.

[89] C. 68.

hence, we read:[90] Eligantur duo ex ipsis, id est, ex utraque parte unus, qui scutis et fustibus in campo decertent. "They shall choose two of them, that is, one from each side, who shall contend with shields and clubs." So also, in the law of the Lombards:[91] Et illi duo decertent cum scutis et fustibus. "And those two shall contend with shields and clubs." Indeed, the besagiies were interdicted by the constitutions of Sicily.[92] Statuimus præterea ut a modo campiones habebant clavas æquales, non spinosas nec cum aguzonibus, nec habentes cornua, nec ex parte fustis ad modus unguis. "Moreover we decree, that the champions, from henceforth, have staves of equal thickness throughout, not knotty nor with sharp points, nor have horns, nor in the nature of a club made in the form of a claw." The contrary, however, was the case in England, for Britton[93] says: Puis voisent combattre armés sans fer et sans longe arme, à testes découvertes et à mains nues et piés, ovesque deux basions cornut d'un longueur, et chascun de eux d'un escu de quatre corners sauns autre arme, dont nul ne puisse autre griever. "Then they are seen to fight anned without iron or any long weapon, with their heads uncovered and their hands and feet naked, with two cornuted staves of the same length, and each of them with a quadrangular shield, without any other arm, with which the one might injure the other." Philippe Auguste King of France thought it necessary to restrict the size of the staves. Thus, in a deed, dated 1215: Nos consilio bonorum virorum et pro commuai omnium utilitate statuimus, quod campiones non pugnent de cætero cum baculis qui excedant longitudinem trium pedum ad pedem manus, sed cum baculis trium pedum . . . . . vel minoris longitudinis, liceat eis pugnare, si voluerint, &c. "We, by the advice of our council of good men, and for the common advantage of all, have decreed, that champions should not for the future fight with staves which exceed the length of three feet, of feet measured by the hand; but with staves of three feet or shorter we allow them to fight, if they choose," &c.

The old Coustumier of Normandy describes the combat thus:[94] Au jour

---

[90] Capitula Ludovici Imp. ad legem Salicam,
[91] Lib. II. Tit. 51, s. 10.
[92] Lib. ir, Tit. 37, s. 1.
[93] De Jure Angl. fol. 41.
94 C. 68. In the same manner the Leges Normann. apud Ludewig say: Ad diem autem duelli assignatam debent se pugiles in euriâ justiciario offerre, antequam horâ meridiei sit transacta, apparati in corietis vel tunicis consuetis, et cum scutis et baculis cornutis armati. The corietum was the same as the corium, being made of overlapping flaps of leather as in Plate XXIV.

qui est assis à faire la bataille, se doivent les champions offrir à la justice ains que midy soit passée tous appareillez en leur cuirées, ou en leur cotes, avec leur escus, et leur basions cornus, armez si comme mestier sera de drap de cuir, de laine, et d'estoupes. Es escus, ne es batons, ne es armures des jambes ne doit avoir fors fust ou cuir, ou ce cpii est pardevant dit: ne il ne peuvent avoir autre instrument à grever l'un l'autre fors l'escu et le baton. "On the day appointed for the battle, the champions ought to oiler themselves for the purpose of justice, immediately after twelve at noon, completely appar-elled in their cuirees,[95] or in their coats, with their shields and their cornut-ed batons, armed according to their rank, either in cloth, leather, woollen, or stuff. Except their shields they ought to have neither batons, nor armour for their legs, unless it be of leather, or of the materials aforesaid, nor ought they to have any other instrument by which they might injure one another, except the shield and baton."

The knights, it has been observed, were permitted to fight on horse-back; but this did not extend to causes of murder, homicide, or theft. When accused of these the knight was obliged to clear himself by duel on foot, and go into the field, tonsus pariter ad instar campionis, "shorn like a champion thus, in the Assisiæ Hieros: Les chevalier qui se combate por murtre ou por homicide, se doive combattre à pié, et sans coiffe, et estre roignés à la reonde. "The knight who fights on account of murder or homicide, ought to combat on foot, and without his hood, being shorn all round."

The punishment for being overcome in a duel was various. In the capit-ulum of St. Louis[96] it is decreed, that "the champion who is overcome on account of his previous perjury should lose his right hand."The Lombard laws enact the same. But in capital crimes the champions were hung after being defeated, as well as the party for whom they fought. Thus in the As-sisiæ Hieros[97] Si la bataille est de chose qu'on à mort deservie et le garant est vaincu, il et celui pour qui il fait la bataille, seront pendus, et se le garant est tel, que il puisse mettre champion pour soi, et son champion est vain-cus, il seront tous trois pendus. Et se feme fait l'apeau et son garent et son champion est vaincu, elle sera arse, et le garant se combat, et est vaincu, sera pendus, et se il met champion pour soi, et il est vaincu, il seront tous deux pendus, et la feme arse. Et se la bataille est pour la quarele tel que l'on ne doit mort recevoir, qui en sera attaint, celui ou celle, pour qui il combat de

---

[95] Leathern vests.
[96] Ad Legem Salicam,
[97] C. 37.

qui le champion est vaincu pert la quarelle, et vois et répons en court, et le champion doit estre pendus. "If the battle be for a thing deserving of death, and the guarantee is vanquished, he and the person for whom he fought shall be hanged; and if the guarantee be of such a rank that he can have a champion to fight for him, and his champion is vanquished, they shall be all three hanged. And if a woman makes the appeal, and her guarantee and her champion be vanquished, she shall be burnt; and the guarantee, if he fights and is vanquished, he shall be hung; and if he substitutes a champion for himself, and he is overcome, they shall both be hung and the woman burnt. And if the battle be for a complaint not deserving death, whoever shall be attainted, this or that person for whom he fights, and whose champion is conquered, he shall lose his suit, and all voice and answer in court, while the champion shall be hung."

They were also forbidden the rights of sepulture.

Cydwely castle, in Caermarthenshire, which was built during this reign, affords a good specimen of the improvement in military architecture.

Edward the First.

1272.

ONSIDERABLE improvements were made in Armour during the reigns of the first three Edwards. The ordinance for arms in the time of this monarch, according to an old MS. of the period, cited by-Strutt,[1] ran thus: Comaunde per le rey, que chekun homme eyt en sa mesoun pour se armur, pour la pes garder, selon le auncien assise; ces est asavour, que chekune homme entre 15 auns et 60 seyent assis et jures, as armes selon la quantité de lur teres, et de leur chateus; ceo est asavour, a 15 livers de tere, et de chateus de 40 marc, habergeun, chapel de fer, espeye, cotel et chyval; et 10 liveres de tere, et chateus de 20 marc, habergeun, chapel, espeye, et cotel; et cent soudes de tere, purpoynt, chapel, espeye, cotel; et 40 soudes de tere, et de plus dekes a cent soudes des teres, espeye, ark, cotel, et setes, e que ad meyns des chateus de 40 soudes, seyt iuree as, faus, gysarmes, coteaux et autres menus armes, et tous les autres qui povut, ave ark, et setes hors de foreste, et en foreste ark et piles. "It is

---

[1] Manners and Customs of the English, Vol. II, p. 4:3. But in his Sports and Pastimes Ile seems to allude to this ordinance, though he there calls it Stat. temp. Ed. ii apud Winton. It is, however, the celebrated statute of Winchester, which passed in the 13th of Edward I, A.D. 1285. That copy of it in the new edition of the Statutes of the Realm ,differs merely in the orthography.

commanded by the king, that every man should have in his house where-
with to arm himself, and for keeping the peace according to the an tient assize; that is to say: that every man between the ages of fifteen and sixty shall
be assigned and sworn to arm himself according to the quantity of his land
and chattels, that is to say, those avIio have 15 pounds in land, and chattels
to the value of 40 marks, shall have a habergeon, chapel de fer, sword, knife,[2]
and horse; and of 10 pounds of land, and 20 marks of chattels, a habergeon,
chapel, sword, and knife; and 100 shillings of land, a pourpoint, chapel,
sword, and knife; and 40 shillings of land, a sword, bow, knife, and arrows;
and those who at least have chattels to the value of 40 pence, shall be sworn
to have faus,[3] gisarmes, knives, and other ordinary arms; and all others who
are able, shall have a bow and arrows, on living out of the forest; and in the
forest a bow and piles.[4]

It was also further ordered, that constables and proper officers should
make search in every house, to see that the aims were kept in due order, and
ready for service; and these officers made their report accordingly, to the
justices who were ordained for that purpose.

The iron ferrule that covered the arrow was called the pile, so that it might
be thought those persons living out of the forest were not compelled to have
their arrows thus strengthened. The little execution, however, that could be
done with arrows merely pointed with wood against troops in armour, must
occasion the rejection of such an idea. Pile also signified a club, and seems to
have been the weapon used by the archers before they were enjoined to carry the mallet, or maule. It was often called pilette and pilote. Thus William
Guiart, speaking of a transaction in the year 1214, says:

---

[2] The cultellus, or coutel, serveu as both knife and dagger. One, of the 15th century, is
in the armoury of Llewelyn Meyrick, Esq.

[3] In later times called bills.

[4] The pile is an heraldic bearing, and is drawn in the form of an inverted isosceles.
triangle. Strutt, however, says: "The word pile, I believe, is derived from the Latin pila, a
ball; and, I suppose, these arrows were used to prevent the owners from killing the king's
deer, from which, it seems, Strutt imagined that the pile was an arrow, with a ball at the
end instead of a sharp point. Archers at this day continue to call the iron ferrules of their
arrows blunt piles, and when with projecting pieces barbed piles. Still the people, by this
ordinance, are called on.for arms to be used against an enemy, and, therefore, blunt arrows
would be of no service. Had the cross-bow been ordered the piles might have been the
balls. cast by one species of them. But why may not piles signify darts, as conjectured by my
friend Mr. Douce, and mentioned under a former reign? The word bow implies that and
arrows for it likewise.

Ribaces que de l'ost se partent
Par les ehams ça et la s'cpartent
Li uns une pilote porte
L'autre croc, ou maque torte.

"Ribalds who separate themselves from the army,
Scatter them here and there over the field;
Some carry a pilote,
Others a crook, or curved mace."

The croc was somewhat like the oucin, but more bent down in the form of a shepherd's crook.

Further on, the same author says:

Maçes levées el piletes
Se firent parmi les vilettcs.

"Maces raised and piletes
Are seen amongst the villages."

Edward I intermixed his archers with his cavalry at the battle fought against Llewelyn, the last of the Welsh princes, near Orewyn bridge, and thus did great execution.[5] The same was done by the earl of Warwick, in another battle with the Welsh forces, in the 23d year of this king's reign, which Nicholas Trivet thus describes:[6] "They, on the earl's approach, had set their men at arms fronting his army, with exceeding long spears, which, being placed on the earth, the points were suddenly turned towards the earl and his company, to break the force of the English cavalry. But the earl had well provided against them; for, between every two horsemen, he placed an archer, so that, by their missive weapons, those who held the lances were put to the rout."

Indeed, this arrangement seems to have been in high esteem during this reign, for three years after, at the battle of Falkirk, says Hollinshed,[7] "the Scotts divided their battles into four scliiltrons, as they termed them, or as we may say, round battailes, in forme of a circle, in the which stoode their people that carried long staves or speares, which they crossed joyntly together one within another, betwixt which skiltrons, or round battailes, were

---

[5] Hen. de Knyghton, p. 2464. These may, however, have been mounted, for such, as appears in the next page, served in Wales.

[6] Annales, fol. 282.

[7] P. 833. See also Robert de Brunne's Chrono p. 304.

certain spaces left, the which wer filled wytli theyr archers and bowmen; and behinde all these were theyr horsemen placed: they had also prudently chosen a ground, somewhat sideling on the side of a hill."

The first statute of Westminster,[8] which was passed in the third year of the reign of this monarch, A.D. 1275, determines the sum to be paid for what was called Aids for Knighthood. It is as follows:

Purceo q avaunt ces lires ne fut unkes resonable aide a fere fiuz chivalers, ou à filles marier, mise en certein ne q^nt ele devoit estre prise, ne quel houre, par quei les uns levèrent outraiouse aide plus tost q ne sembloit mest, dont le pople se senti grevee; Purveu est q desoremes de fee de chivalier entier solement seient donez vint souz, e de vint liveres de tere tenues par socage vint souz, et de pls plus, e de meins meins solum le afferaunt; e q nul ne puisse lever tiel aide de fere son fiuz chivalier, taunt q son fiz seit de age de quinze aunz, ne a sa fille marier tant q ele seit de age de set aunz: Et de ceo serra fet mención en la brief le rey forme sur ceo q^nt il le veille demaunder. "Forasmuch as before this time, reasonable aid to make one's son a knight, or to marry his daughter, was never put in certainty, nor how much should be taken, nor at what time, whereby some levied unreasonable aid, and more often than seemed necessary, whereby the people were sore grieved: It is provided, that from henceforth of a whole knight's fee there be taken but twenty shillings; and of twenty pounds worth of land, holden in soccage, twenty shillings; and of more, more; and of less, less, after this rate. And none shall levy such aid to make his son a knight until his son be fifteen years of age: nor to marry his daughter until she be of the age of seven years. And of that there shall be made mention in the king's writ, formed on the same, when any null demand it."Among the records in the Tower of London is a roll of expenses of king Edward I, at Rhuddlan castle, in North Wales, in the tenth and eleventh years of his reign, which arose in the following manner. In the first of these, which was the year 1281, Llewelyn ah Grufydd, the last of the Welsh princes, endeavoured to throw off the English yoke, and commenced his revolt by seizing the castle of Hawarden, in Flintshire, and laying siege to those of Flint and Rhuddlan. On the Gth of April, the king being then at Devizes, in Wiltshire, summoned his barons and other military tenants to attend him at Worcester, on Whitsunday following,[9] in order to proceed against the Welsh; and afterwards, by a second summons, dated from Hartlebury, near Worcester, called upon them in greater num-

[8] See.36.
[9] Rot. Wallire in Turr. Lond. m. 10. in dorso.

bers to attend him, properly equipped, at Rothelan,[10] on Sunday, on the morrow of the feast of St. Peter ad Vincula.[11] Rhuddlan castle appears to have been the head quarters of the king during this expedition; and most of his orders, entered on the Rotuli Walliee of the 10th and 11th years of his reign, are thence dated. This roll of expenses contains the particulars of sums paid to the carpenters, masons, smiths, and other workmen, employed at the castle, which, no doubt, had great additions made to it on this occasion. But it is the wages of the cross-bowmen and archers at this period which has any thing to do with the subject of these volumes, and, therefore, such only have been extracted.

Archers mounted (Sagittarii).

	£.	s.	d.
Saturday next after the feast of the assumption of the blessed Mary, at Rothelan, paid to Geoffry le Chamberlin, for the wages of twelve cross-bowmen, thirteen archers, for 24 days, viz. from the day of the assumption of the blessed Mary to the vigil of her nativity, each day being reckoned, each cross-bowman eceiving by the day 4d, and each archer 2d	7	8	0
Thursday 27th of August, paid to Robert Giifard, for the wages of eight constables of cavalry, each receiving per diem 12d, and of eight hundred and fifty-seven archers, each receiving by the day 2d, and of then· forty-three captains of twenties, each receiving 4d per diem, from Tuesday the 25th day of August, for the seven following days	55	6	0
Sum	£62	14	0

Archers on Foot.

	£.	s.	d.
To Master R. Giffard, for the wages of six archers, newly come, from Friday 27th day of August, for the six following days	0	6	0
Thursday 3d day of September, paid to Guillemyn and his companion, cross-bowmen, for their wages from Thursday 20th day of August to Wednesday the 2d day of September each day being reckoned, each receiving *6d* a day	0	13	0
To Master R. Giffard, for the wages of eight constables and eight hundred and twenty-six archers, with forty-one captains of twenties, from Wednesday the 2d day of September to the	62	4	0

[10] Rhuddlan.
[11] Rot. Wall. in Turr. Lond. m. 7. in dorso,

	£.	s.	d.

Wednesday next after the feast of the nativity of the blessed Mary, for seven days   53   7   6

Friday next after the feast of the nativity of the blessed Mary, paid to Master R. Giffard, for the wages of one thousand and forty archers, and ten constables, and fifty-two captain of twenties, from the Thursday next after the feast of the nativity of the blessed Mary to the Wednesday next after the feast of the exaltation of the Holy Cross, each day being reckoned   67   4   0

Friday next after the feast of the exaltation of the Holy-Cross, for the wages of a thousand and sixty archers, with fifty-three captains of twenties, from the Thursday next after the feast of the exaltation of the Holy Cross to Wednesday next after the feast of St. Matthew the Apostle, each day being reckoned, for seven days, with the wages of ten constables of cavalry   68   8   6

Sum £189   19   0

Archers.

	£.	s.	d.

Friday after the feast of St. Matthew the Apostle paid to Master R. Giffard for the wages of a thousand and twenty archers, with fifty-one captains of twenties, from Thursday next after the feast of St. Matthew the Apostle to Wednesday next after the feast of St. Michael, for seven days following, each day being reckoned, with ten constables of cavalry   68   18   6

To Guillemine and his companion, cross-bowmen, for their wages from Wednesday 2d day of September to Wednesday next after the feast of St. Matthew the Apostle, for twenty-one days, at 2*d* per diem   1   1   0

Wednesday next after the feast of St. Michael paid to eight constables and one hundred archers, being in the fortification of the castle of Flint, for their wages, from Tuesday on the feast of St. Michael to the Monday next following, for the seven days ensuing, by the hands of Master William Pyforer   6   9   6

To Master R. Giffard, for the wages of the same archers, from the Tuesday next after the feast of St. Michael to the Monday next following, for seven days, by the hands of Master William Pyforer   6   9   6

To Master R. Giffard, for the wages of a thousand archers, from Thursday next after the feast of St. Michael to the Wednesday on the morrow of St. Faith, each day being reckoned, for seven days, reckoning the constable and captains of twenties   63   15   0

	£.	s.	d.

Monday 25th day of October, atRothelan, paid to Master R. Giffard, for the wages for four constables, four hundred archers, from Sunday 24th day of October to Wednesday the 4th day of November, for eleven days 40 14 6

To Master William de Audeley, for the wages of five constables, five hundred and forty archers, with twenty-seven captains of twenties, from Saturday next after the feast of St. Luke to Thursday on the morrow of the Apostles Simon and Jude, for six days 29 17 0

To Master R. Giffard, for the wages of three hundred and fifty-eight archers, with seventeen captains of twenties, or constables, from the Friday next after the feast of the Apostles Simon and Jude, for three days, to Sunday on the morrow of All Saints   9   7 6

Sum £223 12 0

Archers.

	£.	s.	d.

To Master R. Giffard, for the wages of one constable of foot, receiving 6*d* per diem, and of fifty-three archers, with two captains of twenties, from Monday on the feast of All Souls to the Wednesday following, for three days   1   9 0

Thursday the 14th of January, paid to Master R. Giffard, for the wages of five constables, five hundred and twenty archers, with twenty-six captains of twenties, from Thursday aforesaid to Wednesday next after the feast of the conversion of St. Paul, for the fourteen days following   67   4 0

To Master William le Botiller, for the wages of one constable, two hundred and six archers, with ten captains of twenties, from Saturday 16th day of January to Wednesday 27th day of the same month, for twelve days   22   4 0

Tuesday next after the feast of the Ascension of our Lord, paid to Master R. Giffard, for the wages of two hundred archers, with two constables and ten captains of twenties, from Sunday on the feast of St. Benedict to Saturday the 15th day of May, for fifty-six days 103 12 0

Sunday on the feast of Pentecost, paid to Master R. Giffard, for the wages of one constable and one bundled archers, from the said Sunday 16th day of May to Saturday next after the octaves of the Holy Trinity, for twenty-one days   1   8 6

St. John Baptist's day, paid to Richard de Estham, for the wages of fifty-seven archers, with three captains of twenties, from the Sunday next after the feast of St. John Baptist to the Saturday next following, for seven days 3 10 0

	£.	s.	d.
Sunday on the feast of the translation of St. Martin, paid to Master R. Giffard, for the wages of fifty archers and one constable of cavalry, with three captains of twenties, from the said Sunday to Saturday the 10th day of July, for seven days	3	8	10
Sunday on the feast of the translation of St. Benedict, paid to the same, for the wages of fifty archers, from the said Sunday to Saturday on the vigil of St. James, each day being reckoned, for sixteen days	6	5	0
Saturday the 4th day of September, at Chester, paid to Richard de Daneport, receiving 12d per diem, for his wages, and of sixty archers, conducting David de Rothelan to Chester, for two days ..	2	3	0
For the wages of R., clerk of Master R. Giffard, from Friday next before the feast of St. Bartholomew to Wednesday on the morrow of St. Faith, each day being reckoned, for forty-nine days, at 4d per diem, the lord bishop of Bath being voucher	0	16	4
Sum	£230	12	0

Knights.

	£.	s.	d.
Saturday the 5th day of January, paid to the Lord Engolrane, serving with the Lord John de Deynile, and his four esquires, for their wages, from the 1st day of April to the 4th day of June, for sixty-five days	19	10	0
To the same, for the pay of his fifth esquire, from the 12th day of May to the 4th day of June, for twenty-four days	1	4	0
To the said five esquires, for their pay, for fifteen days following the 4th of June	3	15	0
To Master Richard de Brus, on account of his wages, by the hands of Robert de Edenliam, by order of Master William de Luda	10	0	0
Tuesday on the feast of the nativity of the blessed Mary, paid to Master G. de Picheford, in advance of his pay	2	0	0
Monday on the feast of the conversion of St. Paul, paid to Master John Weston, on account of his pay, by order of the treasurer ...	6	0	0
Sum	£42	9	5

Esquires.

	£.	s.	d.
To Robert de Cantelu, for his wages	1	0	0
To Peter de Welles, for his wages	1	0	0
To Henry de Qwetel, for his wages	0	16	8
To William Fitz Clay, for his wages	1	0	0

Esquires.   £. s. d.

To William de Wyndedore, for his wages 1 14 0
To Roderick of Spain, for his wages   1   0 0
To Robert le Despencer, for his wages   2   0 0
To John de Silvestrod, for his wages 2 10 0
To Matthew of the Exchequer, for his wages 0 17 0
To Symon de Chiltenliam, for his wages 0 10 0
To Richard de Burgh, for his wages   0   2 6
To Master J. de Clifford, for his wages   0   4 8
                                                          Sum £12 15 4

From the wardrobe account of this king we also learn the expense attending the fabrication of armour as far as a tailor could be concerned, as lining, surcoat, &c. The following is therefore extracted:

Expens' Roberti cissoris Regis.   £. s. d.

Robinetto cissori, prò expensori's sui prò 181 dies, inorando London' prò armaturis Domini Edwardi filii Regis, et Joliis de Lancastr', &c.   3   7 10
Waltero de Compston de dono Regis ad unum haketon, et unum gambeson' sibi emend, &c   5   0 0
Domino Radulpho de Stokes, clerico, emptori et liberatori magne garderobe regis, prò diversis operibus factis per Robinettum cissorem regis, videlt factura robarum, etc\ factura diversorum armorum, vexillorum, et penocellorum, prò Domino Alio Regis, et Johé de Lancastr jamberis, poleynis, platis, uno capello ferri, una cresta cum clavis argenti prò eodem capello, coffris, saccis, bahudis et forelhs, empt' prò diversis armaturis imponendis.

"Expenses of Robert the King's Tailor.   £. s. d.

"To Robinett the tailor, for his expenses, for 181 days residence in London, for furnishing the armour of our Lord Edward the king's son, and John of Lancaster, &c   3   7 10
"To Walter de Compston, by the gift of the king, for a haketon and gambeson, bought for him, &c   5   0 0
"To Mr. Ralph de Stokes, clerk, purchaser and dispenser of the great wardrobe of the king, for different work done by Robinett the king's tailor, namely, for the making of robes, &c., and for the

making of different arms, banners, and penoncells, for our Lord Edward the king's son and John of Lancaster, for jambs, poleyns, elbow-plates, a chapel de fer, a crest with silver nails for the said chapel de fer, for coffers, sacks, boxes, and cases, purchased to contain the differents kinds and parts of the armour."

The jambs were shin-pieces or greaves, at first made of leather or quilted linen, on which were placed the flat contiguous rings, as appears in the figure of a kneeling knight in an illuminated Latin Psalter of this time, in the Royal library in the British Museum;[12] but, as there was no necessity for this additional guard to be flexible, the adoption of a piece of steel soon superseded this invention.

The original idea was probably borrowed from the statues of the antient Greeks, for the earliest specimen with which I am acquainted occurs on the seal of Baldwin Earl of Flanders and Emperor of Constantinople. They do not appear in any illuminations prior to the year 1250, but occur in the manuscript of Matthew Paris, in Bonnet College library, so that they seem to have been generally introduced into Europe in consequence of the crusade of St. Louis.

These guards were also called bainbergs or bembergs, from the German beinbergen, i. e. shin-guards. They do not seem to be the same as the Emperor Leo, in his Tactics, calls ποδοψελλα σιδρα, "iron feet-guards and yet, in the illumination before noticed, where they are composed of flat rings, the guards are not only in front of the legs but cover the whole of the feet. In the will of St. Everard Due de Frejus, we meet with the bequest of Bruniam unam, cum halsberga, et manicam unam, bemivergas duas, See. "A broigne with a hauberk, and one muffler, (or glove not divided into fingers,) two bainbergs,"&c. And in another place: Bruniam unam, hel-mum I, et mani-cam I, ad ipsum opus bembergas, &c. "A broigne, one helmet, and one muffler, to the same work bembergs,"&c. The Lex Ripuar[13] estimates baim-bergas bonas pro vi sol. tribuat, "good baimbergs at threepence value." These shin-pieces were generally worn with the poleyns,[14] and in this manner we find a knight of the Barri family accoutred in the monumental effigy engraved in Sir Richard Hoare's edition of Giraldus Cambrensis,[15] as well as in other sepulchral remains.

The great advantages of compactness and pliability afforded by the in-

---

[12] Marked 2 A xxii.

[13] C.36. s. 11.

[14] So on the figure in the initial of this reign, before noticed at p. 110.

[15] Vol. II. From the monument at Manorbir church, Pembrokeshire.

genious invention of the chain mail rendered its use almost universal. There are, how ever, a few exceptions in regard to the rings set edgewise, which shew how difficult it is to eradicate established prejudices. Such is the fact with regard to that monumental effigy at Dublin, which has been attributed to Strong-bow, but which appears, from the shape of the shield and the general form of the costume, to be the workmanship of this period. To find the less convenient fashion retained in so distant a country is not however so surprising as to meet with it in France, where it appears on some of the monuments of the Bourbon family[16] of this time.

The monument of Telim O'Connor, nephew of the unfortunate Roderick and king of Munster, who died in the year 1265, affords us a representation of two galloglasses, as the Irish infantry were then called, and it is curious to find these with sliin-pieces: yet they were of leather only, and retained ever since their introduction to that island by the Danes.[17] The armour of these troops consists of a helmet of a somewhat conical shape, a tunic with short sleeves, and a gorget which just covers the shoulders. These last are either quilted or merely plaids, the crosslines upon them not clearly indicating which. One of these soldiers has in his hand a battle-axe, the other a sword suspended at his left hip by a belt which passes over his right shoulder.

The monument of Thomas Berkeley, grandson of Robert Fitzharding, who died in the year 1243, is the earliest specimen of the camail attached by a cord to the round scullcap. This was introduced probably from the Asiatic fashion, which continues even to this day, and is of the highest antiquity. The camail was the hood deprived of its coif, and had this name from its resemblance to a kind of tippet formed of cancel's hair, and stiled by the Greeks of Constantinople καμελαύκιον. The scullcap from its being thus made in the form of the coif de mailles, was called coiffe de fer. Thus, in the will of Bartholomew de Lega, is the following clause: Item W. Bordel loricam suam cum coifa ferrea. "Also to W. Bordel his chemise de maille[18] and coif de fer." By the Italians it was called eervelliera, derived from the word cervella, "the scull," and it is explained to be capelleto de ferro per difesa del capo, "a chapel de fer for the defence of the head." Its invention is thus spoken of in the Chronicon Nonantulanum, in the time of the Emperor

<hr/>

[16] Very neat etchings of these have been made by the Rev. Mr. Kerrioh, of Cambridge.

[17] See Introd. p. lxix.

[18] The word loricula implies the smaller kind of hauberk, which was called also camisia ferrea, or shirt of mail.

Frederic II. "At this time flourished Michael Scott,[19] the domestic astrologer of the Emperor Frederic, who invented the use of that armour for the head which is called cervelliere. Imagining that he should die in consequence of a wound on his head which caused to grow upon it a stone about three ounces in weight, he had a cap made for his head of a plate of iron, which he generally wore. When, however, he was in the church, and the host was lifted up at the altar, he raised this cap from his head in token of reverence for Christ, then the little stone of two ounces weight fell from his pole, which hurt the skin a little. He doubting how heavy it was had it weighed, and found that it was two ounces. Being then certain of death he made a disposition of his effects and died."

William Guiart frequently mentions the cervelliere. Thus, in 1264, he says:

> Le chaple commence auz espées
> Dont la a de maintes manieres
> Sus hyaumes, sus cervelieres,
> Preunent plommées a descendre
> Et liachetes par tout pour fendre.

"The battle began with swords,
Of which there were many kinds,
On helmes, on cervelieres,
They took leaden maces to strike,
And axes every where to defend themselves."

Again, under the year 1298:

> Aucuns d'entre eus testes desnuent
> De hyaumes et de cervelieres,
> Et plantent aleñas es ciñeres.

"Some among them denuded heads
Of helmets and cerveliers,
And planted their aleñases in the faces of their enemies."

So also, in 1298:

> Mes hauberjons et cervelieres
> Gantelets, tacles et gorgieres.

---

[19] This Michael Scott wrote a book on Physiognomy.

> "But hauberjons and cervelieres,
> Gauntlets, tags,[20] and gorgets."

Thomas Berkley is also represented with beinbergs, poleyns, and elbow-plates: he also wears a dagger with a very wide blade which tapers to a point, instead of a sword, and which may be the alesnas, or, as sometimes called anelas.[21] Gilbert de Clare is represented in painted glass with one of these scullcaps, from the top of which depends a bunch of horse-hair.[22] The coif of the figure attributed to Strong-bow has an excavation at top apparently for the same purpose.

Previous to this invention the warrior was obliged to slip his head through the aperture for his face, and thus let the capuchon hang on his shoulders. A monument in the Temple church, attributed to one of the Ros or Rous family, but evidently of Edward the First's time, is carved in this manner, and is represented in Plate XXI. He is in a hauberk and chausses of chain mail, with poleyns on his knees; bears in one hand the large axe, such as used by the infantry, and in the other his shield, which is formed at top by a line nearly straight, the kite-shape not occurring later than the time of Henry III; his surcoat is very long, and has sleeves reaching almost to his wrists.

The cross-bar of the swords in this reign were often made to bend down on each side: this we see in the seal of William de Capreville, in the monuments of Scotch chieftains in the monastery of St. Ilay, and many others. An antient dagger was, however, lately found among a quantity of old iron in a smith's shop in Durham, the hilt of which is composed of parallel pieces perforated:[23] it is all of iron, of very rude workmanship, but has inscribed on its blade, "Anton: Eps. Dunolm by which it clearly appears to have belonged to Anthony Beck, bishop of Durham, in 1283, or to some of his military attendants. The length of the hilt is five inches, of the blade sixteen, and its breadth one and a half; the length of the guard is three inches, and the width of the pommel two.

The men at arms were at this period called arinati, and are thus described in the Chronicon Colmariense, under the year 1298: Habuit secuin

---

[20] Lacombe renders the word "bucklers," but it would appear from the context to be a part of the body armour. See observations on this in the Glossary.

[21] Several of these, of Italian workmanship and beautifully engraved, with inscriptions on them, made at the commencement of the sixteenth century, are in the armoury of Llewelyn Meyrick, Esq.

[22] He is in a broigne, with a javelin in one hand and a large shield in the other.

[23] It is represented in the Arcbæol. Vol. XII, Pl. XLI, Fig. 4

Australes, qui armis ferreis utebantur. Igitur Rex Adolphus contra Ducem Austrian cum magna multitudine venientem, in occursuin currit cum hominum armata multitudine copiosa. Armati reputabantur, qui galeas ferreas in capitibus liabebant, et qui wambasia, id est tunicam spissam ex lino et stuppa, vel veteribus pannis con-sutam, et desuper camisiam ferream, id est vestem ex cireulis ferreis contextam, per quae nulla sagitta arcus poterat liominem vulnerare. Ex his armatis centum inennes mille kedi potuerunt, liabebant et multos qui liabebant dextrarios; id est equos magnos, qui inter equos communes quasi Bucephalus Alexandra, inter alios eminebat. Hi equi cooperti fuerunt coopertoriis ferreis, id est veste ex cireulis ferreis contexta. Assessores dextrariorum liabebant loricas ferreas, liabebant et caligas, manipulos ferreos, et in capitibus galeas ferreas splendidas et ornatas, et alia multa, quae me taeduit enarrare. "He had with him natives of the South, who used armour manufactured from iron. King Adolphus, therefore, marched against the duke of Austria, who was coming with a large army, with an immense body of men at arms. Those were called men at arms who wore on their heads steel helmets, and who were also clad in the wambais, that is, a tunic wadded with wool, tow, or old cloth, and stitched; and upon it an iron shirt, that is, a garment formed of iron rings interlaced, through which it is impossible for any bow to send an arrow so as to wound a man. A hundred of these men at arms could injure a thousand unarmed; and there were many who had destriers,[24] those are, great horses, which excelled the rest as much as Alexander's Bucephalus did ordinary ones. Those horses were caparisoned in iron housings, that is, in a garment made with iron rings interlaced. The riders of these destriers had iron hauberks, they had also leg-coverings, being a band of iron-clad men; and they wore on their heads steel helmets splendid and adorned, with many other things which it would be tiresome to enumerate."

The beautiful Asiatic armour of interlaced chain was used for horses as well as men, and, therefore, was adopted for both purposes by the Europeans. Thus the anonymous author of the Asiatic Expedition of Frederic I tells us, that the Germans, gentem ferream in equis ferreis ad venire, "marched forward an iron race on iron horses."Thus too, in a roll, in the chamber of accounts at Paris, the title of which is—Compte du Voyage qui fu l'an 1294 et 1295, pour les gages de Monsieur Bertran Massole retenu aux gages accoutumez pour lui et deux ecuyers, occurs: Et estoit luy et autre a chevaux couverts, et un autre sans cheval couvert. "And he with one of the others

---

[24] War-horses, so called because the pages led them by the fight hand.

PLATE XXI

ROBERT ROUSE.

A.D. 1270.

shall have armed horses, and the other an unarmed horse."And further on: Onze ecuyers a chevaux couverts, a chacun sept sols six deniers par jour, et pour deux qui n'ont point chevaux couvert, chacun cinq sols. "Eleven squires on armed horses, threepence three farthings each per day; and for two who have not armed horses, twopence halfpenny."From this it appears, that the horses in housings of chain mail were not confined to the knights, but were permitted also to the esquires. Horses thus protected were used also in the English army, for we learn from W. Hemingford, that when Edward I prepared to attack the renowned Scottish chieftain Wallace, he had three thousand select knights on horses that were mailed, and four thousand on unarmed steeds: over this was worn the caparison which had on it the armorial bearings of the rider, and both may be discerned in the seals of Edward and some of his cotemporaries.

Jeoffry Malaterre[25] thus speaks of the interlaced chain-mail: Clamucium quo indutus erat, nullis armis poterat violari, nisi ab imo in superius impingendo inter duo ferrea, qiue per juncturas catenata sint, ingenio potius quam vi vitiaretur.""When once the clamucium is put on, the wearer cannot be injured by any weapons unless a blow is struck from below upwards, where one part of the chain-mail laps over the other, so that a wound must be given by skill rather than force."The clamucium seems to he the same as camusiam, which is a corrruption of cami-siain, the chemise de maille. It was also called a corset of mail.

We meet with mention of a kind of dagger-knife about this period, which was called canipulus, probably from the French canif. Thus Radulph. de Diceto, under the year 1275, tells us: Ne quis viator canipulum deferret, vel arcum. "No traveller shall carry with him a caniple nor bow,"which Matthew Paris, in 1276, thus notices: Prohibuit ne quis gladium ferret viator vel arcum. "He prohibited all travellers from carrying swords or bows."

What were considered full arms, or a complete equipment, at this period, we learn from the will of Odo de Rossilion, dated in 1298: Item do, et lego Domino Petro de Monte Ancelini prædicto, centum libras turonenses, et unam integram armaturam de armaturis meis, videlicet, meuin heaume à visiere, meum bassignetum, meum porpoinctum de cendallo, meum godbertum, meum gorgretam, meas buculas, meum gaudiclietum, meas trumulieres d'acier, meos cuissellos, meos chausones, meum magnum cultellum, et meam parvam ensem. "Also I give and bequeath to the Lord Peter de Montancelin aforesaid, a hundred livres tournois, and one entire suit of

25 Lib. II, c.35.

armour out of my collection, viz. my visored helmet, my basinet, my pour-point of cendal silk, my godbert, my gorget, my buckles, my gaudichet, my steel greaves, my thigh-coverings and chausses, my great coutel, and my little sword."

The little sword was the estoc, and not that usually worn with the coutel, or military knife. The godbert, i.e. good protection, was another name for the hauberk, and probably the gaudichet was nearly similar to the hauketon. A French MS. Chronicle thus distinguishes the basinet from the helmet: "The king (speaking of Ph. de Valois) appeared in his tent habited in a tunic adorned with the arms of France, and upon his head he wore a basinet covered with white leather; behind him stood an officer, who bore his helmet encircled with a crown, and surmounted with a fleur de lis; and before him was another officer who held his shield and his spear."[26] That it was worn under the helmet is clear from a metrical romance in the Cotton library in the British Museum,[27] entitled Ly Beaus desconus. A warrior is therein represented striking so severe a blow with his sword, that he cut through the helmet and the basinet of his antagonist, and wounded him upon the crown of his head. Sometimes, however, visors were affixed to the basinets, and they then served as helmets. Such a one is engraved at the foot of Pl. xxi.

There can be no doubt but that jousts and tournaments arose by degrees from the exercises appointed for the instruction of the military tyros in using their arms, but which of the two had the preeminence in point of antiquity cannot so easily be determined. We know that both of them were in existence at the time the Troy game was practised by the citizens of London, and also that they were not then permitted to be exercised in this kingdom.

In the middle ages, when the tournaments were in their splendour, the Troy game was still continued, though in a state of improvement, and distinguished by a different denomination. It was then called in Latin, behordium; and in French, bohourt or behourt, which name it derived from the mock lances that were used on the occasion. These were called bouliourz, from burdis or bordis, a jest or playful joke. It was a kind of hastiludium, or lance game, in which the young nobility exercised themselves, to acquire address and prove their strength, and at the same time considered as harmless. In a letter remissory, dated 1393, occurs: le premier dimanche de quaresme, appelle les brandons ou behourdiz, &c.; "the first Sunday of Lent, called the

---

[26] In the Cotton library, marked 20. C. vi.

[27] Marked Caligula, A. 2.

brandons or behourdiz,"from which we learn that particular days were set aside for the entertainment; and the place where it was held was generally a field without the town, thence denominated bourdoire. The lances were of wood, however, according to another letter, dated 1476, which states, that the suppliant print une perche de bois, nommée behou, et frappa ung cop seulement Jehannin Mousnier, "the suppliant took a perch of wood called behou, and struck Jehannin Mousnier only one blow."The kind of wood of which they were made appears in another letter, dated 1375, thus: Iceulx Jehan et Girant prinrent chascun d'eulx un blanc petit tilleul pelé, pour en behourder l'un à l'autre, et en eulx ainsi esbatant, et bouhourdant, brisèrent pluseurs tilleux l'un contre l'autre. "The same John and Gerard took each of them a little white linden branch peeled, in order to behour at one another, and in thus engaging and bouhourding, they broke several linden boughs against each other."

The word behordium will, however, admit of a more enlarged significa-tion; and from the Roman d'Aubrey, a MS. we find it was occasionally used for running at the Quintain:

> Emmi le pre ot quintaine levee
> Le jouvencel behordent par la prée.

> "They raised a quintain in the middle of a meadow,
> And the youth behorded at it iu the meadow."

The derivation of the French word tourney from the Latin troja, how-ever the exercise itself may have originated, is not consistent with reason-able analogy. The opinion of Fauchet, wlio thinks it came from the practice of the knights running par tour "by turns"at the quintain, and wheeling about successively in a circle to repeat their course, is adopted by Cotgrave, who says, "our word tournament signifies to turn or wheel about in a circu-lar manner."This derivation is probably the right one; and Fauchet[28] adds, in process of time they improved on this pastime, and attacked each other with spears, clubs, and maces. In one of these encounters Robert Earl of Clere-mont, son of St. Louis, and head of the house of Bourbon, was so severely bruised by the blows he received from his antagonist, that he was never well afterwards. It was very common for some of the combatants to be beat or thrown from their horses, trampled upon and killed upon the spot, or hurt

---

[28] This celebrated antiquary lived in the time of Henry II of France, and was a cotem-porary of our Oamden.

most grievously,[29] on which account these entertainments were interdicted by ecclesiastical decrees. Indeed, a tournament at this period was rarely finished without some disastrous accident: and it was an established law, that if any of the combatants killed or wounded another he should be indemnified, which made them less careful respecting the consequences, especially when any advantage gave them an opportunity of securing the conquest.[30]

The prevalence of the taste for these exercises at this period may be gathered from a passage in a satirical poem,[31] written in the 13th century, which may be thus rendered in English:

> "If wealth, sir knight, perchance be thine,
> In tournaments you're bound to shine:
> Refuse—and all the world will swear
> You are not worth a rotten pcar."[32]

The following quotation from an antient romance, entitled Ipomydon,[33] plainly indicates that the tournament was held in an open field; and also that great numbers of the combatants were engaged at one time, promiscuously encountering each other We further learn from it, that the champion who remained unhorsed at the conclusion of the sports, besides the honour he attained, sometimes received a pecuniaiy reward:

> The kyng bis sonne a knyght gan make,
> And many another for his sake:[34]
> Justes were cryed ladyes to see,
> Thedyr came lordes grete plente.
> Tournamentis atyred in the felde,
> A thousand armed with spere and shelde;
> Knyghtis began togedre to ryde,
> Some were unhorsyd on every side
> Ipomydon that daye was victorius;
> And there he gaff many a cours;

---

[29] So in this reign, Roger Bigod, earl of Nor folk and marshal of England, had his limbs dislocated in a tournament.

[30] On this account, those who were slain in such encounters were by the church canons, according to Camden, denied Christian burial; and Henry III, by the advice of Parliament, enacted, that all who, without leave, should keep a tournament, should forfeit their estates, and their children be disinherited.

[31] In the Harleian library, marked 2253, fol. 108.

[32] Or rather apple, "purry poume."

[33] MS. Harleian library, marked 2252, fol. 61.

[34] It was usual to honour the creation of the king's son by making many other knights at the same time. This was the case when the Black Prince was knighted.

For there was none that he mette,
But he hys spere on hym woulde sette:
Then after within a lytell stounde[35]
Horse and man both went to grounde.
The Heraudes[36] gaff the child the gree:[37]
A thousand poun he had to fee:
Mynstrcllys had giftes of golde,
And fourty dayes this fest was holde.

In some instances the champions depended upon their military skill and horsemanship, and frequently upon their bodily strength; but at all times it was highly disgraceful to be unhorsed, by whatever exertion it might be effected. Thomas Walsingham[38] relates, that when Edward I returned from Palestine to England, and was on his passage through Savoy, the Earl of Chabloun[39] invited him to a tournament, in which himself and many other knights were engaged. The king with his followers, amounting to one thousand, accepted the challenge, although fatigued by the length of them journey, and only half the number of their antagonists. On the day appointed both parties met, some on foot, others on horseback, and being armed with swords the engagement commenced. The earl, a most athletic man, singled out the king, and on his approach, throwing away his sword, cast his arms about the neck of the monarch, and used his utmost endeavour to pull him from his horse. Edward, on the other hand, finding the earl would not quit his hold, put spurs to his horse, and drew him from his saddle hanging upon his neck, and then shaking him violently, threw him to the ground. The earl having recovered himself, and being remounted, attacked the king a second time, but finding himself disabled, gave up the contest, acknowledging him to be the conqueror. The knights of the earl's party were enraged when they saw their leader drawn from his horse, and run upon the English with so much violence, that the pastime assumed the tumultuous appearance of a real battle. The English on their side repelled force by force: and Edward's archers drove their opponents from the field, mixed among the knights, and sometimes cutting the girths of the saddles or ripping up the bowels of their horses, brought their riders to the ground,

---

[35] A small space of time.

[36] The heralds, whose office it was to superintend the ceremonious parts of the tournaments.

[37] What had been agreed, i. e. the reward.

[38] Hist.Ang.. fol. 3, A.D. 1274. See also W. Hemingford, 592; Matt. West, 402; and Trivet, 261.

[39] The Count de Chalons.

and secured them as prisoners. Had not the resignation of the earl put an end to the conflict in all probability the consequences would have been very serious.

In the Record Office at the Tower, is a roll, containing an account of a great variety of articles provided for a tournament, held in Windsor Park, in the month of July, the sixth year of the reign of King Edward I. It is entitled Emptiones facte per inanum Adinetti cissoris, et visu Albini et Roberti de Dorset contra[40] torniamen-tum de parco de Windsore, nono die Julii anno sexto. "Articles purchased by the hands of Adinett the tailor, and under the inspection of Aubyn and Robert De Dorset, against a tournament in the park of Windsor, on the 9th day of July, in the sixth year."In the account of armour to be provided appear the following names of the several knights, thirty-eight in number, twelve of whom are styled "digniores The Earl of Cornwall with a companion, the Earl of Gloucester, the Earl of Warren, the Earl of Lincoln, William de Valence, the Lord Robert Tibetot, Roger de Clifford, Hugh Fitz-Otho, William de Monte Reuelli,[41] Pagan and Patricius de Cadurcis,[42] —— de Pontist, Giles de Fenes, Walter de la Hide, John de Wanlope, John de Britannia, Amadis de Sabaudia with two companions, —— Bonfillard, Gerard de St. Laurence, Walter Beck, Roger de Trumpington, Berth, de Breanzon, William de Goneville, W. Ernaldi, W. de Hauteresliam, Walter Garcelini, Walter de St. Martin, Rob. Johannis, G. de Picheford, Geoffry Gopil, Andrew de Rat, and Peter Picot. Several of these appear to have been foreigners. Of the English, the greater part were of high rank and distinguished for their martial exploits, and several of them nearly allied to the king. Edmund Earl of Cornwall was the king's cousin, son of his uncle Richard King of the Romans, and at this time must have been about thirty years of age, having received knighthood in the fifty-fifth year of Henry III, when he was of age. Gilbert de Clare Earl of Gloucester was one of the most powerful barons of his time, and a distinguished warrior, who, a few years afterwards, married Joan of Acres, the king's daughter. John Earl of Warren was nearly allied to the king, having married Alice, sister by the mother's side to King Henry III, being her daughter by the Earl of March, her second husband. William de Valence Earl of Pembroke was the king's uncle, being the son of his grandmother Queen Isabella, by her second husband.

---

[40] The use of *contra* is whimsically curious.
[41] Montreuil.
[42] Payne and Patrick de Chaworth.

Three of these knights, namely, the Earl of Gloucester, the Earl of Lincoln, and William de Valence, in conjunction with the king's eldest son, Prince Edward, and his brother Edmund Earl of Lancaster, seem to have had, a few years afterwards, tlie chief superintendence of tournaments; for in the Statuta de Armis, (which will be found in a subsequent page,) it is said, that if any earl, or baron, or other knight, should go against that statute, such knight, by assent of all the baronage, should lose horse and harness, and abide in prison at the pleasure of our lord Sir Edward, the king's son, and Sir Edmund, the king's brother, Sir William de Valence, Sir Gilbert de Clare, and the Earl of Lincoln.

Many knights, whose names appear on this roll, had been with King Edward in the crusade. Pain de Chaworth,[43] who possessed the barony of Kempsford, in Gloucestershire, was signed with the cross in the 54th year of King Henry III, together with his brother Patrick, whose name also appears on this roll, and accompanied Prince Edward to the Holy Land, as no doubt did Roger de Trumpington, who is represented cross-legged on his grave-stone in Trumpington church, Cambridgeshire. Robert de Tibetot was a faithful servant to king Edward I for many years, and attended him in the crusade: he was much employed in military affairs till the time of his death, which happened in the 26th year of that king. It appears also by the clause roll 54th Henry III, that Roger de Clifford attended Prince Edward to the Holy Land. John de Britannia, or Bretagne, was, no doubt, the earl of Richmond and duke of Brittany, who had license from the king to go to the Holy Land the year following,[44]

Armour, called hemesium de armis, is by this roll provided for all the knights. It appears to have been of leather gilt, and various sums, from 7s to 25s were paid for making, stuffing,[45] and gilding each suit, to the three persons employed, Cosmo the tailor, Salvag' the tailor, and Reymunde de Burdieus.[46] At the end of this item of the account there is a memorandum, stating that each suit of armour consisted of a tunic of arms, which was, in fact, the surcoat with the arms emblazoned thereon; two pairs of chaussetons, or chastons, as they are called, and a hauberk, (coopertorium,) with a pair of ailettes, (par'allet) so called from the French ailette, a little wing.

---

[43] He led one division of the English army on the conquest of Wales.

[44] In the various royal grants to him, entered on the patent and other rolls, he is sometimes styled Johannes de Britannia, Comes Richemundioe, sometimes Dux Britannioe and Comes Richemundire , and sometimes simply as on this roll, Johannes de Britannia.

[45] Item ad trussand' dem hnes xx ulii canoh'.

[46] Savage the tailor, and Raymond of Bourdeaux.

These are those singular pieces fixed on the shoulders, of various shapes, which appear on most representations of warriors at this period.[47] Besides these are two[48] crests, one emblazoned shield, a helmet of leather, and a sword of balon, that is of whalebone, and then covered with parchment. This tournament was not, therefore, to be a hastiludium; as no spears are provided, the attack and defence was merely to be with the sword, and as that was rendered harmless, armour of leather would be sufficient protection from bruises.

The sum of 3s was paid for the carriage of the armour from London.

The shields were of wood, and provided by Stephen the joiner, at 5d each. Peter the furbisher, fabricated the thirty-eight swords made of balon and parchment, at 7d a piece, and was paid 25s for silvering them,[49] and 3s 6d for gilding the pommels and hilts with pure gold: he also furnished thirty-eight pairs of brachias or brassarts of parchment. Ralph de la Hay received 12s for gilding with pure gold twelve helmets for the knights of the highest rank; and for silvering the remainder 17s 4d, being after the rate of 8d each.

Milo the currier furnished the thirty-eight head-pieces of leather made to fit on (de similitudine) the horses' heads,[50] at 2s each; and the thirty-eight pahs of ailettes, at 8d the pair.

Richard Paternoster provided eight hundred little bells,[51] sixteen skins for making bridles, and half a horse's skin for cruppers, and twelve dozen silken cords for tying on the ailettes, seventy-six calf-skins were provided for making the crests; and Henry de Hoppedemery supplied seventy-six pairs of chastonsat 3d each, being two to each knight. These last were the breeches usually of mail, and may be seen, worn by a knight of this period, in Strutt's Habits of England, PI. LXVI. The word is a diminutive of chausses.[52] He also provided the same number of pairs of clauons, which seem to be shin-pieces, or greaves of cloth, which also appear in that plate of Strutt's. The sum total for the articles provided in England, was fourscore pounds

---

[47] See Plate XXVII.
[48] One was intended to he placed on the horse's head.
[49] The silvering the parchment was to give it the appearance of steel.
[50] This is the most early notice of chanfrons I have met with.
[51] From the tournament roll of Henry VIII in the College of Arms, we learn that these little bells were hung round the neck, on the bridle, and other trapping's of the horse; the number gives one and twenty to each.
[52] Du Cange met with it misspelt chanton, and was therefore unable to give any explanation of it.

eleven shillings and eightpence.[53]

The Statuta de Armis, or Statutum Annorum in Torniamentis, as it is variously called, is very interesting to the investigation of antient armour. The date of it has been considered as wholly uncertain, yet there are grounds for assigning to it that of the year 1295, the names mentioned in it, of Edward the king's son and Edmund his brother, might have served for the reign of king Edward III, and so might those of Gilbert de Clare and the Earl of Lincoln; but William de Valence Earl of Pembroke, who died in 1296, was the last of his family of that name, and as the earl of Gloucester died in 1295, and Edmund Croucliback Earl of Lancaster in 1296, the statute could not have been of a later date than 1295. By this statute it is provided that no knight or esquire serving at the tournament should bear a sword pointed, or dagger pointed, or baton, or mace, but only a broad-sword for turneying: and all that bear banners should be armed with mustilers[54] and cuishes, with shoulderplates and a sculleap, without more. But, as the whole statute is interesting, it is here inserted.

THE STATUTA ARMORUM.

Incipiunt Statuta Armor[m].   *Here begins the Statues of Arms.*

A la requeste de contes e de barons e de la chivalrie de Engletere, ordine est, e pr nostre Seignr le Rey comaunde, q^e nul ne seit si hardi desoremes, conte ne baron ne autre cliivaler, q^e al torney voysent de aver plus q^e treys esquiers armez pur li svir al turney; e q^e chescun esquier porte cliapel des armes son Seigneur q^e il svira a la jornee pur enseygne.

At the request of the earls and barons and of the chivalry of England, it is ordained, and by our lord the king commanded, that from henceforth none be so hardy, whether earl, baron, or other knight, who shall go to the tournament, as to have more than three esquires in arms to serve him at the tournament, and that every esquire do bear a cap of the arms of his lord who he shall serve that day, for ensign.

Number, &c. of esquies at tournaments

---

[53] After this exposition of the contents of this roll it would be superfluous to insert it, written as it is entirely in . contractions, but those who are curious will find it in the 17th Vol. of the Archoeologia, p. 302.

[54] The mustiler is evidently the armour for the body, and so called from the particular kind of cloth of which it was made. See the Glossary.

E q^e nul clir ne esquier q^e sert al turney ne porte espeie a point, ne eotel a point, ne bastoun ne mace, fors espee large pur turneer. E q^e tuz les baneors, q^e baners portent, seent armez de mustilers, e de quisers, e de espaulers, e de bacyn sanz plus.

E sil avent q^e nul conte ou baron, ou autre chivaler, voyse encontre sra trove en forfetaunt en nul poynt encontre le estatut, seyt encurru cele peyne, q^e il perde cliival e armes, e demeorge en p'son a la volunte de avantdiz Sire Edward, Sire Eumond, e le autres. E q^e le esquier qAe serra trove fesaunt encontre le estatut, q^e issi est devise, en acun poynt perde cliival e lierneys e seyt iij aunz en la prison. E q^e nul sake chivaler a terre, fors ceus q^eserrunt armez pur lur Seignr servir, q^e le chivaler pusse recovir son cheval, e cely soit en la forfeture des esq^ers avant diz.

E q^e nul fiz de graunt seignur, ceo est asaver de conte ou de

And no knight or esquire serving at a tournament shall bear a sword pointed, nor a dagger pointed, nor staff, nor mace, but only a broadsword for turneying. And that all the baneors who bear banners shall be armed with mustilers, and cuishes, and shoulder-plates, and a basinet, without more.

And if it happen that any earl, or baron, or other knight, do go against this statute, that such knight by assent or command of our Lord Sir Edward son of the king, and Sir Edmund brother of the king, and Sir Wm. de Valence, and Sir Gilbert de Clare, and the Count de Nichole,˙ who shall be found to have forfeited in any point contrary to this statute, shall incur this penalty, that he shall lose horse and arms, and abide in prison at the pleasure of our Lord Sir Edward the king's son, and Sir Edmund his brother, and the others. And the esquire who shall be found oifending against the statute here devised, in any point, shall lose horse and harness, and be imprisoned three years. And if any man shall cast a knight to the ground, except they who are armed for their Lord's service, the knight shall have his horse, and the offender shall be punished as the esquires aforesaid.

And no son of a great lord, that is to say, of an earl or bar-

Armour at tournaments

Penalty on transgressing the staute.

Armour of noblemen's sons.

˙ Earl of Lincoln.

baron, ne seit arme fors de must-ilers e de quisers, e de espaulers, e de bacynet, saunz plus, e q^e ne aporte cutel a poynte, ne espeye, ne mace, fors espee large. E si nul seit t°ve q^e, en ascun de ceos poynz, alast encontre le estatut, q^e il perde son cliival le quel il serra munte a la jornee, e seit en la prison un an.

on, shall have other armour than mustilers, and cuisses, and shoulder-plates, and a basinet, without more; and shall not bear a dagger, nor sword point-ed, nor mace, but only a broad sword. And if any one be found who, in either of these points, shall offend against the statute, he shall lose his horse whereon he is mounted that day, and be imprisoned for one year.

E q^e ceus q^e vendrunt pur veer le tumëmt ne seent armez de nule mañe de armure, ne q^e il ne portent ne espee, ne cutel, ne bastun, ne mace, ne perre, sur la forfet'e des esq^ers avañt diz. E q^e nul gar-son, ne home a apee ne porte espee, ne cutel, ne bastón, ne perrer; e si il seent trovez enforfetaunt q^e il seyent emp'sonez vij aunz.

And they who shall come to see the tournament shall not be armed with any manner of ar-mour; and shall bear no sword, or dagger, or staff, or mace, or sling, upon such forfeiture as in the case of esquires aforesaid. And no groom or footman shall bear sword, or dagger, or staff, or sling; and if they be found of-fending they shall be imprisoned for seven years. `Spectators shall not be armed.`

E si acun grañt Seignr ou autre, teygne mangie, q^e nul es-quier ne ameyne eynz fors ceus q^e tren-cliernt devant lur seig-nurs.

And if any great lord or oth-er keep a table, none shall bring thither any esquire but those who are wont to mess in their lord's presence. `Guests at feasts.`

E qe nul roy des haraunz ne menestrals portent privez armez, ne autres forz lur espees sañz poynte. E q^e le reys des harraunz eyent lur huces des armes saunz pluz, &c.

And no king at arms or min-strels shall bear secret arms, nor any other besides their swords without points. And the kings of arms shall have their mantles of arms without more, `Arms of heralds.`

&c.

In an illuminated romance in the British Museum,[55] entitled St. Graal, written about this period, is a representation of the manner in which the

---

[55] Royal library, marked 14, E. III. The word is Welsh, and implies"a mythological collection; "whence also the land of spirits was termed Gwlad y grëal.

chief barons entered the field at the commencement of a tournament. The
king at arms standing in the midst, holds the banner of one knight and the
guidon of the other, with his arms extended. A little in front of him are two
knights in gamboised armour, with ailettes and lambrequins,[56] not cointises, hanging from the tops of their helmets. They both have their surcoats
on, hut one has his shield and ailettes emblazoned. Their horses are fully
caparisoned. As they have not received their weapons, but are stretching
forth their right arms with open hands, they are probably in the act of ap-
pealing to heaven in proof of their having no charm to protect them, and
no inclination to make use of any unlawful means to secure the conquest.
Behind them are the minstrels, whose instruments are adorned with the
blazonry of their arms, &c.

I have not been able precisely to ascertain what was the peculiarity of
the mustiler. It is evident from the context, that some kind of body-armour
is implied, and thus named in all probability from the material of which
it was composed. In the Paston Letters, written in the time of Henry VI,
are the following expressions: "a musterdevelers gown,"and "a fyn gowne
of must 'dewylersand Elmham, in his Life of Henry V, mentions a French
town of similar name as near Harfleur, but whether or not mustiler is the
contraction of these I am not certain. The armour for the tournament at the
close of this reign, and how it was to be put on, are more fully set forth in
a MS. in the British Museum,[57] which contains regulations for this kind of
information. It proceeds to explain

"How a knyt suld be arinyt and tournay.

"Ffyrst, a harness of gampes (leg-armour) corvet w^t ledd and sowet
w pōntes (points) the bouth (bend) of the gambe (leg) to ye kne, and ij
ataches larges for to atach ym in to his brayer (the waistband of the braie or
breeches, but here put for the breeches themselves). Itm cuisses and poul-
lanis armyt w^t ledd^r. Itm hosn of mail above the harnes of gambes atached
to the brayer, as said is, above ye cuisses. And a payr of gylt spurrs quliiche
salbe knet w^t a small cord about the gambes, because ye spur turn not und^r
ye fute. Item unes actione et unes espaullieres. Item paur de manclies q^{che}
salbe knete to the curie, (leathern cuirass, used instead of the mustiler);
and ye curie w^t all his aggrapes (hooks and eyes) sur les espaulles; et une
soureilleur apone ye foit (ear-coverings on the neck) befor. Item bratheres
knet to ye sliuldre of the cuyrie. Item basynet a tout he liousson (with all

---

[56] So called from lambres, a strap or shred.
[57] Harl. lib; 6146. fol. 46.

its housings or appendages) and an escusson of balayn (whalebone) apone the nek, corvit w^t ledd^r, w^t the coureres (leather straps) for to knete-to ye brayer or the cuyrie. And apun ye basynet a coife of mail and a fair offroy (jewel) befor on ye front qūh a will, and a wyn brod, (broad vane or flag) to put in ye knyt's liande. Item a lieaume and ye tymbre (crest) sic as he will. Item ij thengeis knet to the brest of ye cuyrie, one for the suord, the toyr for the bastone (short staff mentioned in the last cited statute), and ij visiones (lateral cords) for to festyn the heauine.

"How a squyar suld be armyt.

"The abillemēt of ye squyar salbe sum lik as ye knyt's excepte that he suld have na lioife (coife) of maill, na corsette (gorget) of mail apone his basynet but he suld have a cliaplette of Montaubien (Montauban liat,) and he suld have no bratheres, and of uther things may arm him as a knyt, and suld have na sautour (stirrup) at his sadill."

The joust, or jouste, as before observed, differed materially from the tournament, but was often included in it, taking place when the grand tournamental conflict was finished. This hastilude derives its name from the French jouster, or jouer, to play; or from the Latin jocare, because it was a sportive combat. It was, however, perfectly consistent with the rules of chivalry, for the jousts to be held separately, but as it was accounted inferior to the tournament, a knight who had paid the fees for admission to that was priviliged to joust also; whereas, if he had only given those due for permission to joust, he would be charged some in addition for the tournament. The joust too was at first distinguished from the tournament on account of the weapons used, the sword being appropriated to the tournament, while the lance was for the joust. Hence, in an old manuscript treatise on tournaments, it is said: Item pour les nobles qui tournoient s'ils n'ont autrefois tournoie, donnent leurs heaumes aux officiers d'armes, ores qu'ils ont autrefois jouste; car la lance ne peut, affranciir l'espee, et l'espee affranciit la lance. Mais il est a noter, si un noble homme tournoie, et qu'il ait paye son lieaume il est affranchi du heaume de la jouste, mais le heaume de la jouste ne peut affranciir celui du tournoy. "Also for nobles who tourney: if it be their first appearance at the tournament, their helmets are claimed by the heralds, notwithstanding their having jousted before, because the lance cannot give the freedom of the sword, which the sword can do of the lance, for it is to be observed, that he who has paid his helmet at the tournament, is freed from the payment of a second helmet at the joust; but the helmet paid at jousting does not exclude the claim of the heralds when a knight first enters the tournament."

During the government of Henry III the joust had assumed, as observed, the appellation of the round table game; and in the eighth year of Edward I, Roger de Mortimer, a nobleman of great opulence, established a round table at Kenelworth, for the encouragement of military pastimes. At this a hundred knights with as many ladies were entertained at his expense. The fame of this institution occasioned, we are told, a great influx of foreigners, who came either to initiate themselves, or give some public proof of their prowess.[58]

In the jousts the combatants most commonly used spears, at first, without heads of iron, and the excellence of the performance consisted in striking the opponent upon the front of his helmet, so as to push him backwards from his horse, or break his spear. The lances were, however, subsequently supplied with heads, and in the illuminated MS. entitled St. Graal, before alluded to, there is a representation of the joust, where two knights appear in the act of tilting at each other with spears, having monies placed on them instead of blades. These monies consist of three diverging rays or points of iron, which form together what is called the coronel, or little crown, but they are much longer than what were used at a subsequent period. There are no vamplates to the lances, nor any swell to protect the hand. The combatants are in gamboised armour, with square ailettes, pryck-spurs, and tilting-helmets: they wear their surcoats, but the horses, different from those in the preparation for the tournament, are quite uncovered.

Jousting was not only performed on horseback, but also in boats on the water.

In a manuscript in the British Museum,[59] of this period, is an illumination representing two boats rowing against one another, in each of which is a knight in gamboised armour wearing a surcoat. One has a shield, the other a roundel, and instead of helmets they appear simply in their cervelieres. They are in the act of pushing against each other with pointless lances. The conqueror at these jousts was the champion who could dexterously turn aside the blow of his antagonist with his shield, and at the instant strike him with his lance in such a manner as to overthrow him into the water, he himself remaining unmoved from his station, the rowers at the same time performing their part as dexterously.

A delineation in a beautiful manuscript book of prayers, written about

---

[58] Walsingham, Hist, Ang. sub. an. 1280, fol. 8.
[59] Royal library, marked 1, B. vii.

the same time, and in the possession of F. Douce, Esq. strongly indicates
how early was the inclination to join in these sports. It represents two boys
riding upon long sticks to supply the place of horses, and each holding another in the manner of a tilting-lance, with which he is about to push his
antagonist.

Sometimes at the jousts the knights were armed and unarmed by the ladies, which, however, was a peculiar mark of their favour, and only granted
upon particular occasions, as when the heroes undertook an achievement
on their behalf, or combated in defence of their beauty or honour. This is
represented in a beautiful illuminated missal,[60] where Sir John Lutterel, in
the armour of this period, and on his charger, is receiving from one lady his
helmet, and from another his lance. So too, in a MS. Life of Thomas a Becket,[61] written apparently in this reign, a knight resuscitated by the Virgin
Mary, as he rises from the grave, is depicted as receiving from her and her
attendant ladies his gamboised hauberk, his helmet, and his lance.

There was another kind of hastilude called cembelluin, cembel, and
chenbele, which appears to have preceded the tournament,[62] but afterwards
continued with it. It is mentioned as early as the year 1080, at a council at
Lillebone; and Robert Wace, in the Roman de Rou, says:

> Ni a qui lor ost faire, ne assaut ne ccmbel.

"Nor was tberc any thing for their army to do, neither assault nor cembel."

From which it appears to have been a kind of attack; but the Roman des
Miracles du Chevalier unites it with the tournament.

> Ne tornoie ne chenbele.

"Neither tournay nor chenbele."

And in another place:

> Li chevaliers qui moult ert biaux
> Mains poigneis, ct mains chcnbiaus,
> Mainte joute, mainte encontrée,
> Faisoit de li par la contrée.

---

[60] In the possession of —— Weld, Esq. of Lulworth castle, Dorsetshire.
[61] In the Royal library, marked 2, B. vii.
[62] It seems to have been at first a kind of war-dance:

"The knights, who were very eminent
In many a combat, and many a chenbele,
In many a joust, and many encounters,
Caused much hilarity throughout the country."

And in the Roman dc Partonopcx it is said:

Hermans est issus du chastel
Qui fu abatus au cenbel.

"Hermans is gone forth from the castle,
Who was defeated in the cenbel."

The romance of Arthur, king of Little Britain, which was written during this reign, affords some lively pictures of the manners of the age. The following tend to throw much light on the tournaments, arms, and armour of the period. In the wager of battle between Governar and Sir Aunsel the fight is thus described. In the first onset they drew "aparté fro other, and dressed their speres to the restes, and dashed theyr sporres to the horses sydes, and met togider so rudely, that they frusshed their speres to tlieyr listes like hardye kniglites and ful of great valure. How be it Syr Aunselle's valure was not to be compared with Governar; for Governar had been a man greatly to be redoubted. And after the breking of theyr speres, they past by, and in the retorninge they set theyr handes to theyr swerdes. And Governar stroke Syr Aunsell so rudely, that he did ryve his shelde to the bocle, and brake a great part of his harneys; so that the swerde entred depe into the flesshe. And Syr Aunsel stroke again Governar on the helme, and broke with the stroke many barres[63] thereof; and the stroke glanced downe on the lifte syde, and share away a great parte of his harneys to the bare sadell, but God kept him that it entred not into the fleshe. Than Governar florysshed agayne his swerde, and stroke Syr Aunsell on the heyght on his helme, and cut it to the harde sercle of stele,[64] and the stroke glanced downe by the shelde so rudely that he clave it to the middes. And with the same stroke the swerde did lighte on the necke of the horse, wherewyth the horse was so sore wounded that he fell downe to the erthe. And when Syr Aunsell felte his horse fallen under hym, he lept on his feet with his swerde in hys hande; wherfore he was of some greatly praysed: and some other dyd

---

[63] See the seals of the three first Edwards and Richard II.

[64] This circle is very manifest on a helmet of this period, engraved at the foot of Pl. XXII, from a MS. in the Royal library of the Brit. Mus. 2. A. xxii.

greatlye prayse the stroke of Governar. And when Governar saw him on the erthe, he thought that he would not renne on his enemy with his horse, he being on fote. Therfore incontinent he dyd a lyght downe on fote, and putte his shelde before hym, and wente sekynge his enemy; and gave hym such a stroke; that he strake a waye parte of his cheke; and the stroke dyscended to his sholder and wounded him to the harde bones; wherwith Syr Aunsel was constrayned to knele, and right nere to have fallen. Than al the lordes sayd that theyr was non coude longe endure the strokes of Governar. Therewith Arthur laughed with a good herte, so that Governar harde hym, wherby his herte douwbled in courage. And whan Syr Aunsel felt hymself thus hardly bestad, he sware in his mynde that he wolde be avenged of that stroke, and therwith lyfte up hys swerd to have stricken Governar: but when he sawe the stroke coming, he put his shelde before hym, and advysed wel how that Syr Aunsell had his arme up a loft, and with a backe stroke he stroke at Syr Aunsell under the armour so rudely, that the arme and swerde and all flew into the felde: weerof Syr Aunsel had so much payne, that he fel to the erth in a traunce. And then Governar lept to hym, to have stryken of hys head: but he cryed for God's sake mercy."

We further learn from this romance, that it was the custom to place a spear upright outside the tent of a knight,[65] probably by that means to designate the rank of the owner.

Jousting at a shield, a kind of quintain that has been already noticed, is also spoken of in this antient tale;[66] and we are informed: "then Hector caused a fayre quintayne to be pyght up in the myddes of the cyte, and thereat ran these yonge knyghtes, brekynge and sheveringe of theyr speres."[67]

It is further said of Arthur, that "none ever abode hym but he avoyded the arson of hys sadel and fell to the erthe," and that "he unbarred helmes, clave asunder sheldes, and unmayled hauberks." We read too,[68] that "Arthur took his mase of stele hanging at hys sadel bow, and strake so fiersly therwyth rounde aboute hym in every place, that he brake the prese, and bet downe knyghtes." There is also the expression holding hatches (haches) and mases of stele;[69] and flails are likewise spoken of as military weapons.

In the combat between Arthur and Sir Isembarte, it is said: "and whan Syr Isembarte felt hymselfe wounded he strake Arthur on the helme, so that

[65] C. 34.
[66] C. 42.
[67] C. 112.
[68] C. 29.
[69] C. 43.

PLATE XXII

DE VERE EARL  OF OXFORD.

A.D. 1280.

it entred till it came to the coyfe of stele."[70] From this paragraph we gain an acquaintance with the mode in which the armour was worn, which is again more fully detailed in another passage, where Arthur is said to have struck "through the shielde, hauberk, doublet, and shirt;"and that "a lion put his paw on his helmet, and the claws entered to the bokle of his harness."

The circumstance of ladies appareling the knight for the tournament has been already mentioned; and in this romance we are told,[71] that "the ladyes and damoysells dydde sende them chaplettes and streamers to set on their helmes and speres."

In these observations on the several amusements comprehended under the general name of tournament, the gambison or wambais and the pourpoint often occur. Several seals, illuminations, and monuments, afford us specimens of this armour at this period. Thus the seal of Roger de Percival represents him in gam-boised chausons or breeches over his hose, and the monument of the Scottish chieftain before noticed, in the monastery of St. Ilay, appears to shew him in the gambison, his tunic being marked with parallel perpendicular lines. But the gamboised breeches are very manifest in the monument intended for one of the De Veres Earls of Oxford, but evidently of the time of Edward I, in Hatfield Broadoak church, and as it has the poleyns fastened upon them, it has been selected for Pl. XXII. A brass plate in Chatham church, of one of the Septuan, or Harflete family, exhibits a specimen of the hauketon first at the wrists, the mail-glove being thrown off, and again below the hauberk. The sleeve is plain, but this bottom part appears stitched. His poleyns are highly ornamented. He wears the ailettes, and his hood of mail is thrown off his head and left hanging on his shoulders, as in the monument of Robert Ros.

That it was usual for the knights to throw back their hoods in this manner we learn from Fauchet, for in his Annals of France, where he speaks of Regnault Comte dc Dammartin fighting at the battle of Bovines, he mentions that "he had a hood, or coif de mailles, besides his hauberk, in which he put his head; which capuchon he threw back, after he as a knight had taken off his helmet, in order to refresh himself."

The ailettes which are worn by this knight have, as well as his surcoat, his armorial bearings and are put behind his shoulders. This is also the case in the brass plate of Sir Hugh Trumpington, and both have the belt to gird the surcoat, and a very large belt to hold the sword, and on the scabbards

---

[70] C. 65.
[71] C .75.

PLATE XXIII

A KNIGHT OF THE MONTFORD FAMILY,

A.D. 1256.

of each are several little shields of arms; on all which accounts these monuments should be assigned to the latter part of this reign. The sword-slieatli thus ornamented may be seen in Pl. XXIII, which represents a knight of the Montford family.[72] The gambeson may be observed just below his hauberk. In this specimen we find the cerveliere worn under the coif, and it not only appears just below it on the forehead, but in a broad open space above. The strap which fastens up the right side of the hood is not interwoven, as in former specimens, but passes outside the rings on the forehead. This monument is so curious on this account, as well as probably affording the latest representation of the rings set edgewise, that it has been made the subject of Plate XXIII.

The helmet of Roger de Percival before-mentioned, seems to be an approach from the convex one of Wm. de Capreville, given at the foot of Pl. XX, to that of Theobald de Verdun, at the bottom of Pl. XXIII, which appears to have been the prototype of the conical helmets introduced in this reign. The caparison of Sir Roger's horse is singular from being cut into what are now called two large vandykes, with tassels at their ends, in front, and four behind. Of the conical helmet, that on the seal of Sir Henry de Percy affords an early specimen, having in front the grating which generally occurs on the cylindrical helmets.[73] It has on its top a crest to resemble red feathers, round which is tied a ribbon in the manner of the cointisse, or lady's scarf, which succeeded it. The helmets of Edmund Earl of Cornwall in 1296, and Thomas Earl of Lancaster in 1280, seem to combine the cylinder and cone in their forms, while those on the seals of King Edward himself are wholly cylindrical.

In the hand of the figure in Pl. XXIII is a mace, but in the monument it is a dagger, which he clasps just below the pommel.

This is the earliest specimen I have met with of that weapon being worn with the sword, though, as we have seen, there are literary authorities for it still earlier. It is pendant from the right side, being attached to the sword-belt by a strap. The word dagger occurs as early as the time of William the Lion, king of Scotland, who was cotemporary with our Coeur de Lion. Thus, in one of his statutes,[74] are the words: Habeat equum, habergeon, capitium e ferro, ensem et cultellum, qui dicitur dagger. "He shall have a

---

[72] On his surcoat is the blazon of Wellesbourne, viz.: guo a griffon segreant devouring a child or, a chiefchecquy or and az, over all a bend ermine; but on his shield are the arms' of Montford, viz.: arg. a lion devouring a childwithin an orle of cross-crossletts sa.

[73] At the foot of Pl. XXIV

[74] C. 23.

horse, an habergeon, a scullcap of iron, a sword, and a knife, which is called dagger."Again: Habeat arcum et sagittas, et daggarium et cultellum. "He must have a bow and arrows, a dagger, and a knife."Our historian Walsingham speaks in the same way:[75] Mox extracto cultello, quern dagger vulgo dicimus, ictum militi minabitur. "Immediately drawing the knife, which we commonly call dagger, he threatened to stab the knight."St. Gelais, in Viridario Honoris, speaks of them as worn with the sword thus:

> A son costé cbascun la courte dague.

> "At his side each has the short dagger."

Again:

> A leur costé l'espee longue et large,
> La courte dague pour son homme aborder.

> "At their sides the long and broad sword,
> And the short dagger to deprive their antagonist of life."

The council of Pisa limited the length of the dagger-blade to one palm.

The gambeson, in the last cited specimens, was worn under the armour, which was often the case, as well as by itself. An anonymous writer de Rebus bellicis Notitiæ Imperii subjectum, observes, that hoc induta primum, lorica vel clibanus aut his similia, fragilitatem corporis ponderis asperitate non læderunt, "it was put on before the hauberk or clibanus,[76] or such like armour, that, being so ponderous, they might not injure the more delicate body."The softness of this garment must at the same time occasion it to be very hot, for in an account of expenses in the year 1268,[77] one of the items is: Expense pro cendatis, bourra ad gambesones, tapetis, See. "Expenses for taffety, tow for gambesons, with tapes,"&c. When worn without the armour they were frequently called cotes gamboisiées. Thus, in the statutes of the armourers and coustepointiers of Paris they are thus particularly described. Item se Ton fait cotes gamboisiées, que elles soient coucouchées deuë-ment, sur neufves estoffes et pointées, enfermées, faites à deux fois bien et nette-

---

[75] P. 252.

[76] This may be the interlaced chain-mail, so called from its resemblance to filagree work, but by the Romans the word was applied to the scale-armour. See my paper on the lorica catena, in the 19th vol. of the Archreologia.

[77] Entitled Comptus Baillivorum Franciæ. The cushions of a gamboised gauntlet of leather in my son's collection, engraved at the foot of Pl. LXXVII, are an incb in diameter.

ment emplies de bonnes estoffes, soient de cotton, ou d'autres estoffes, &c. "If any one makes gamboised coats they must be duly embedded within new stuffs and stitches, closed together, and each side finished separately, well and neatly filled with good stuffs, whether of cotton or other stuffs," &c. The stitching of those gambesons, which were worn without the armour, was made more ornamental than when intended to be put under it, and gave rise to the pourpoint. Indeed, they became so greatly assimilated, that the difference between them and even the liauketon was scarcely perceptible. Thus, in the Roman de Percival, is the following passage:

> Puis il font vestir un gambes
> De soie, et d'auqueton porpoint
> Qu'il i ont un aubère vestii
> Si fort, &c.

> "Then they clothed him in a gambes
> Of silk, pourpointed like a hauketon,
> So that he was clad in a hauberk,
> So strong," &c.

The kniglit, PI. xxiv, appears in one of those gamboised coats, which answers for a strong hauberk, and his chausses are the same. This is taken from an illuminated manuscript in the Sloane library,[78] and alfords the earliest specimen of gloves with separate fingers, and covering the wrists, which may be considered as the prototype of gauntlets. His basinet too has an aventadle moveable on pivots. It is here represented open, but at the foot of Plate xxi is one closed. He has the elbow-plates.

There are other statutes of the year 1296 for the pourpointiers, one of which runs thus: Item que nul doresenavant ne puist faire cote gamboisiée, ou il n'ait 3 livres de coton tout net, si elles ne sont faites en freines, et au dessous soient faites entremains, et que il y ait un ply de vieil linge, enprez l'endroit de demie aulne et demy quartier devant, et autant derrière. "Also that no one henceforward shall make a gamboised coat which has not in it three entire pounds of cotton, if they are not made in frames, and underneath worked between the hands, and that there be a fold of old linen about the place, of half an ell and an eighth before, and the same behind."

The soldier in Plate xxiv wears a hood and sleeves of rings set edgewise, but his body is protected by a corium, the leathern flaps of which are of different colours. On his legs are chausses of trellissed work, from the

---

[78] Marked 346.

PLATE XXIV

A SOLDIER AND KNIGHT,

A.D. 1295.

colouring of which the studs appear of steel, and the bandages of leather.[79] The illuminated MS. from which this is taken, contains also the figure
of a knight in a hauberk of mail, and chausses thus made, except that the
bandages are not again crossed by others. He has, wrapped round his body
and passing over his right shoulder, the cointisse, which, from its position,
gave such picturesque folds to the drapery, as well as the scarf itself being of
delicate materials, that it received this name, which implies "elegance."[80] It
had been at first worn by the ladies, and afterwards adopted by the military.
Hence Matthew Paris, in the year 1252, tells us, that Mille enirn milites et
amplius vestiti sérico, ut vulgariter vocamur cointises, in nuptiis ex parte
regis apparuerunt. "For there were a thousand knights and more clad in
silk garments, which we commonly call cointisses, who appeared at those
nuptials on the part of the king."

The cointisse, or scarf of his lady, was often worn by the knight on his
helmet, just at the bottom of the crest, and the seals of St. John Lord Hannak and Lord Monthermer afford us representations of this custom. It is
thus referred to by William Guiart, in his Histoire de France:

> La ot tante enseigne orfresee
> Du loue dcs rens en l'air assise,
> Tant liyaume brun, tante cointisse
> De soie parfaite et tissue.

> "There were so many glittering gold and silvered ensigns,
> Held from the belly up into the air;
> So many brown helmets, so many cointisses
> Of perfect silk and tissued."

The gamboised and pourpointed work not only formed armour for
men but also for their horses. Thus, in a letter of Philippe le Bel, king of
France, dated 20th of January, 1303, to the bailli of Orleans, we find orders given that those who had 500 livres of revenue in lands within the
kingdom should give aid in time of war, by a gentleman well armed, and
mounted on a horse worth 50 livres tournois, and covered de couverture de

---

[79] This is copied from an illuminated MS. inthe Bodleian library at Oxford, marked
86, Arch. B.

[80] In a MS. entitled Le Livre des Moralitez, it is even put among the Virtues: thus
Honesté est departie en 4 choses, en cointise, en forche, en droiture, en atempranche.
Cointise est une vertue qui fait connoistre les bonnes choses des mauvaises, et enseigne à
departir les unes des autres. This very figure has been introduced into the initial letter of
the last reign.

fer, ou de couverture pourpointe, with a housing of interlaced rings, or one pourpointed. So also in an inventory of arms belonging to Louis X, king of France, and taken in the year 1316, two years after his accession, we meet with a couverture de gamboisons.

The seal of John le Baliol, king of Scotland, represents him in a hauberk, with gamboised sleeves and hood; and the monument of William de Valence exhibits him in hauberk, hood, and chausses, of ouvrage de pourpointerie, or pourpointed work. An illumination in a missal, belonging to F. Douce, Esq. shews Edmund Croueliback, earl of Lancaster and St. George, in gamboised armour, having ailettes; but this earl in his monument has chain-mail instead: in other respects they are alike. The effigy of William de Valence, moreover, affords us a specimen of the French mode of wearing the shield, which is at the left hip just over the sword, and which may have given the idea in after times of hooking the buckler on the sword-hilt.

The extreme elegance in point of workmanship of the seal of Robert, fifth baron Fitzwalter, which was struck at the close of the reign of Edward I,[81] is accounted for by the following curious historical circumstance. He was possessed of Baynard's castle, near Paul's wharf, in the city of London, which was then called the Castle of London, and as constable of the same enjoyed several privileges. One of these was, "that he and his heirs should be banner-bearers of the city of London by inheritance, as belonging to Baynard castle, and in time of war should serve the city in manner following, viz.: To ride upon a light horse, with twenty men at arms on horseback, their horses covered with cloth or harness, unto the great door of St. Paul's church, with the banner of his arms carried before him; and being come in that manner thither, the mayor of London, together with the sheriffs and aldermen, to issue armed out of the church unto the same door on foot, with a banner in his hand, having the figure of St. Paul depicted with gold thereon, but the feet, hands, and head, of silver, holding a silver sword in his hand. And as soon as he shall see the mayor, sheriffs, and aldermen, come on foot out of the church, carrying such a banner, he is to alight from his horse, and salute him as his companion, saying, 'Sir Mayor, I am obliged to come hither to do my service which I owe to this city.' To whom the mayor, sheriffs, and aldermen, are to answer: 'We give you, as our banner-bearer of the city, this banner, to bear and carry to the honour and profit thereof to your power,' Whereupon the said Robert and his heirs shall receive it into their hands; and the mayor and sheriffs shall follow him to the door,

---

[81] 27th Edward I, A.D. 1299.

and bring him an horse worth twenty pounds: which horse shall be saddled with a saddle of his arms, and covered with silk, depicted likewise with the same arms: and they shall take twenty pounds sterling, and deliver it to the chamberlain of the said Robert, for his expenses that day."[82]

The seal seems to perpetuate this circumstance.[83] The horse is elegantly engraved, and covered with trappings of his arms, which are represented as almost transparent in order to resemble silk; and, what is a rare instance, his arms are carved on the rest behind his saddle.

Of a period cotemporary with the monument of Edmund Crouchback are those very curious paintings lately discovered on the walls of the painted chamber at Westminster.[84] These represent female figures in armour to personate the Virtues, and several battles, &c. intended to be illustrative of the Old Testament. The female figures are curious as exhibiting the hauberk not covered by the camail, so that its termination at the neck is quite visible. It appears to come nearly close to it, but to be without any collar. It reaches not quite to the wrist, so that in some instances the red sleeve of the hauketon is seen below it, and in others a mail-glove unites with it. Another curious fact derivable from other figures is, that the cerveliere is worn with the coif de maille, as noticed in p. 161, but over it, which is made visible by the former being put more over the forehead, otherwise as the coif is detached from the camail, and exactly of the same size and shape as the cerveliere, it would have been hid by it completely. The next remarkable circumstance is, that the cerveliere, like that in the MS. of Matthew Paris before noticed, has the nasal, and there are conical helmets with nasals very much like those worn in the time of Henry I. This is the last specimen I have met with; but in the following quotation from Egidius de Roya, the name seems to have been applied to the visor in the year 1371: Dux Geldriæ habita liac victoria, dum nasale cassidis suae pro respi-ratione levaret, incaute, volante sagitta occubuit apud Beziers. "The duke of Gelders having obtained this victory, incautiously lifted up the nasal of his helmet in order to breathe more freely, when he was struck by a random arrow, and died at Beziers."But the nasal in its more correct sense is thus mentioned in the Roman of Girard de Vienne, MS.

---

[82] MS. of Robert Glover, Som. Herald in the reign of Elizabeth, and printed in Dugdale, &c.

[83] See it engraved in the Archseologla, Vol;.V, PI. X VII.

[84] This is evidenced by the borders and ornaments of one of these figures representing the Virtues, which, together with the mode ôf introducing the royal arms, are precisely like those in the monument.

El Due Rolland ne n'ot que corroçer,
Quand de son elme vit le nasel trancher
Et son aubert desrot et desmaille.

"The Duke Rolland could not suppress bis anger
When he saw the nasal cut off from his helmet,
And his hauberk torn and deprived of its mail."

The armour of all the figures in these paintings is that of the rings set edgewise, each row taking the contrary direction, and all the knights are in their cliausses. One figure only has ailettes. The surcoats have all sleeves reaching nearly to. the elbows like that of Robert de Ros, in Plate XXI, and their being emblazoned forms the only distinction between the knights and esquires. The horses are mailed like the figures, and in some instances covered with emblazoned housings. Where those are not on, the coverture of mail is fully displayed first covering head and neck, and the fore part of the horse, then put over the hinder part, and a piece between these under the saddle; being therefore altogether exactly the shape of the housings, and perhaps the finest specimen in existence. There are broad-bladed swords, the backs of which are straight while the edges are curved, and curved swords, probably the earliest examples, as well as straight ones. The shields are not only like those of this time, but some of the kite shape, similar to those used in the middle of Henry the Third's reign. There are also flat circular shields or bucklers, and one of these, held by a female figure, has not only the general mark of the cross, but four passant lions, so as greatly to resemble the noble, which was coined in this reign. Besides the swords, there are spears, bills, pole-axes, maces, and bows and arrows. The first of these have but small heads; the bills are like those used in the time of Edward IV, and indeed so late as Henry VIII; the pole-axes are formed of a broad axe blade on the end of a pole; and a spike jutting out on the opposite side, and the maces have their heads projecting but very little.

The weapons of this period may also be seen on the eastern gate of the cathedral of St. Denis, in the hands of different figures: among these are two varieties of the glaive, and two of the battle-axe, one being the ordinary one, and the other long-bladed.

The attack of the pel, a word corrupted from the Latin palus, was when the post-quintain was used for infantry to acquire strength, and learn skilfully how to assault an enemy with swords and battle-axes. In a manuscript, written at the commencement of the fourteenth century, entitled Les Etab-

lissmentz des Chevalrie,[85] the attack of the pel is particularly recommended. The author, who appears to have been a man of science in the military
tactics of the times, tells us, that the pel ought to be six feet in height above
the ground, and so firmly fixed therein as not to be moved by the strokes
that are laid upon it. The practitioner was then to assail the pel, armed with
a sword and shield, in the same manner as he would an adversary, aiming
his blows as if at the head, the face, the arms, the legs, the thighs, and the
sides, taking care at all times to keep himself so completely covered with his
shield, as not to give any advantage, supposing he had a real enemy to cope
with. Prefixed to this treatise is a neat little painting representing the pel,
with a young soldier performing this exercise, which is copied, with scarce
any deviation in point of drawing, on Plate xxv.[86]

The post appears to be notched in several places to point out the vul-
nerable parts, and whither the blows should be aimed. The warrior is armed
with a hauberk and capuchon, with chausses of gamboised work, protected
by genouilieres or knee-caps, and, what I have no where else observed, with
convex plates to cover the calves of his legs; over his hauberk are two tunics,
and above all a surcoat of leaf-like scales, with sleeves reaching to his elbows.
On his head is a chapel de fer, and he is represented protecting it by his
shield, which he holds up with his left hand, while with the right he makes
a cut at the pel with liis sword.

In the Cotton library[87] is a curious poem, written early in the fifteenth
century, and which appears to be a translation, or rather a paraphrase, upon
the last-men tioned treatise. It is entitled "Knyghthode and Batayle,"and the
author describes the attack of the pel in the following curious manner:

"Of fight the disciplyne and exercise,
Was this. To have a pale or pile upright
Of mannys light, thus writeth olde and wise,   .
Therewith a hacheler, or a yong knyght,
Shal first be taught to stonde and lerne to fight
And fanne of double wight tak him his shelde,[88]
Of double wight a mace of tre to welde."

---

[85] In the Royal library, marked 20, B. xi.
[86] Underneath it is a moveable quintain.
[87] Marked Titus, A. xxxiii, fol. 6 and 7.

88 This fan was to be used instead of a shield, and to be double, the weight of his own
shield; and, as we learn' from the next line, the wooden mace was to be the same. The shape
öf the fan, as appears in a drawing of the time of Henry VIII, in my son's possession, was
oblong, with a handle projecting at each end.

PLATE XXV

THE ATTACK  OF THE PEL,

A.D.1500.

Both the treatises recommend the use of arms of double weight upon these occasions, in order to acquire strength, and give the warrior greater facility in wielding the weapons of the ordinary size; to which the poet adds, at page 9:

> "And sixty pounds of wight 'tis good to bear."

The poem proceeds—

> "This fanne and mace whiclie cither doubil wight
> Of shelde, and swayed in conflicte, or bataile,
> Shal exercise as well swordmen, as knyglhtes.
> And noe man, as they sayn, is seyn prevaile,
> In field, or in castell, thoughc he assayle,
> That with the pile, nathe[89] first grete exercise,
> Thus writeth werrouris[90] olde and wyse.

> "Have eche his pile or pale upfixed fast,
> And as it were uppon his mortal foe;
> With mightynesse and weapon most be cast
> To fight strongc, that he nc skape him fro.
> On hym with shield, and sword avised so,
> That thou be cloos, and preste[91] thy foe to smyte,
> Lest of thyne own dethe thou be to wite.

> "Empeche[92] his head, his face, have at his gorge[93]
> Beare at the brest, or sperne him one the side,
> With myghte knyghtly poost,[94] ene as
> Seynt George Lepe o thy foe; looke if he dare abide:
> Will he not flee ? woundc him; make woundis wide,
> Ilcw of his houde, his legge, his theys, his armys,
> It is the Turk, though he be sleyn noon harm is."

The last lines evidently allude to the quintain in the form of a Turk or Saracen, which was sometimes used upon this occasion. Hence it was called by the Italians, running at the armed man, or at the Saracen.[95]

The pel was also set up as a mark at which to cast spears, as the same

---

[89] Ne hath, or hath not.

[90] Warriors.

[91] Ready.

[92] From, the French, to withstand, here to àttack.

[93] Throat.

[94] Power.

[95] Traité des Tournois, Joustes, &c., par Claude Fran. Menestrier, p. 264

poet thus informs us:

> "A dart of more wight than is mestcr[96]
> Take hym in honde and teche him it to stere,
> And cast it at the pile as at his foo,
> So that it conte and right uppon him go."

And likewise for the practice of archery:

> "Set hert and eye uppon the pile or pale,
> Shoot nyghe or onne; and if so be thou ride
> On horse, is eck the bowis bigge by hale,
> Smyte in the face, or breste, or back or side,
> Compelle to fie, or falle, yf that he bide."

The sword-dance, or a combat with swords and circular shields, regulated by the music of their gleemen, was practised by the Anglo-Saxons. This amusement continued after the Conquest, the performers being called joculatores, or jugglers, and even gladiators by our early historians,[97] from their supposed resemblance to those of antient Rome. It also appears that they instituted schools for teaching the art of defence with sword and buckler in various parts of the kingdom, and especially in the city of London. The conduct, however, of the masters and scholars became so outrageous, that it was necessary for the legislature to interfere; and in the 14th Edward I, A.D. 128G, an edict was published by royal authority, which prohibited the keeping of such schools, and the public exercise of swords and bucklers, therein called "eskirmer au bokeler,"which had been practised by day and by night, to the great annoyance of the peaceable inhabitants of the city: the offenders were subjected to the punishment of imprisonment for forty days, to which was afterwards added a mulct of forty marks.

An illumination in a MS. in the Royal library at the British Museum,[98] represents this kind of combat. The performers have gloves in the manner of gauntlets, or like the military ones of the heavy cavalry of the present day, being of white leather. The bucklers are flat, with a convexity in the centre for the purpose of admitting the hand, which lays hold of a bar that reaches quite across the diameter, and appears to be about one foot.[99] The blades

---

[96] "Mete in time of real action.

[97] John of Salisbury de Nugis Cur. lib. I, c. 8.

[98] Marked 14, E. iii.

[99] One of these, but rather larger, of the time of Edward IV, is in the armoury of Llewelyn Meyrick, Esq.

of the swords are broad near the guard, and apparently cut and thrust, for in this representation one combatant seems about to strike while the other is on his guard. Behind them is a bagpiper. There is also an illumination in a manuscript about the same date, in the Royal library,[100] which gives a similar representation, except that one of the fighters is about to thrust, and the other to parry, while the performance is carried into execution with the assistance of a minstrel.

In the romance of Arthur, king of Little Britain, before cited, it is said that Arthur and his companions met with "a messenger with a javelyn in his hande, and scochen of arms on his breste."[101] There is a MS. in the Harleian library, not much earlier in point of date, that has a delineation of a messenger, where he is depicted with a small shield blazoned with arms, fastened to the left side, but not carrying any weapon.[102] These are the earliest representation and notice of the habiliments of a messenger I have met with. In the 14th century the herald carried the blazoned shield behind him, and was armed with a spear.[103] In a copy of the Roman de la Rose, of the ensuing century,[104] the messenger has his master's arms on his breast, but is without any weapon. At this period the small escutcheon of arms was discontinued, and the tabard, the modem state garb of a herald, substituted. Fauchet, however, says, that messengers wore the arms of their employers on their breasts or left shoulders so late as the end of the 16th century.

From the romance of Arthur, king of Little Britain, it may be inferred, that it was usual to let the banner fall when its lord was taken prisoner.[105]

My worthy friend Mr. Douce possesses a curious ivory chest on which are several carvings. One of these represents the attack of a fortified place, and from it has been taken the figure of the trepied, given in Plate XXVI, Fig. 3. This has been called by Grose, a trebuchet, but that name appears to apply to a military engine that ejects its ammunition from a trap-door, trab-occlieto. This has evidently a large sling at one end of a beam, supported on three legs; at the other end of the beam is a great weight, which, falling by the instrument being suddenly released, must eject the stones with considerable force. Maundrell, in his Travels, tells us,[106] that he saw at Damascus,

---

[100] Marked 20, D. vi.

[101] C. 25.

[102] Marked 1528.

[103] This appears in a MS. in the Royal library of the Brit. Mus. marked 16, G. VI. See also Strutt's Habits, Pl. LXXXIII.

[104] Harl. lib. in Brit. Mus. marked 4425.

[105] C. 35.

[106] P. 126.

in the castle, what he calls an old Roman balista, but he has no where described it. The Baron De Tott says, in his Memoirs, that he found a catapult in the arsenal of Constantinople. Camden speaks of the warwolf and the bricole, but does not particularize them. He, however, supposes the first is that alluded to by Hollinshed,[107] where he says Edward I, at the siege of Strively castle, "caused certain engins of wood to be raised up against the castell, which shot oif stones of two or three hundred weight." There is a MS. in the Royal library at the British Museum,[108] dated 1270, but probably by some mistake ten or twelve years too early, which is peculiarly embellished with antient military engines. In it is a ballista on this construction, but more simple, the beam resting merely on a forked tree. There is also a hand ballista, or large handle sling. From this manuscript is taken the onager, Plate XXVI, Fig. 4, of which machine a very ample account has been given by Grose, though he never saw any antient representation of one. The large beam performs the office of a spring by being put between twisted ropes always inclined to recoil, and therefore having the same effect as the weight to the ballista. There are also in this work different representations of wooden towers for attacking castles.

King Edward I, according to Stowe, when he had taken the manors of Markes and Hay, the enemy being still near them, made use of hogsheads filled with stones, to act as a protecting rampart to defend the workmen who were building the walls of forts and castles; a resource still of service at the present day.

The same MS. has also a sketch of a chas-chateil, or cat-castle, which was a gallery under which the miners worked, tearing up the ground like the claws of a cat. This is also represented in Plate xxvi, Fig. 5. The text of the manuscript underneath it states: Ces engins ci estoient fais en la maniers de chars couvers de gins establissements de gros fus, et des clois pardessus, dedans estoient les minaours. "These engines were thus made in the manner of covered cars of great planks of large beach, and spaces underneath, in which were the miners." Joinville, speaking of such engines in the crusade of St. Louis, says: "the king determined to have a causeway made to enable him to pass over to the Saracens; and to guard those employed on it, he had built two beffrois, called clias-chateils. There were two towers in front of these beffrois, and two sheds in their rear to receive the things the Saracens threw from their machines, of which they had sixteen that did wohders."

---

[107] Chrono p. 839.
[108] Marked 16, G. VI.

PLATE XXVI

Fig. 1.

Fig. 3.

Fig. 4.

Fig. 2.

Fig. 5.

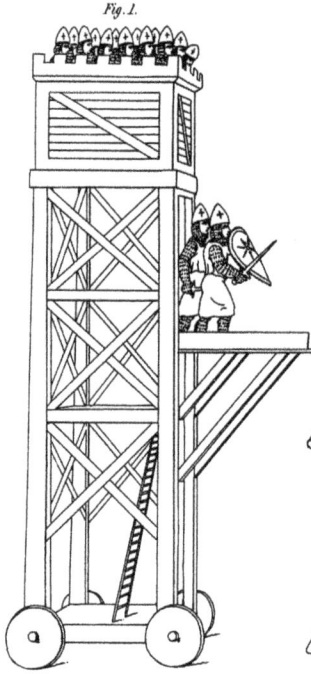

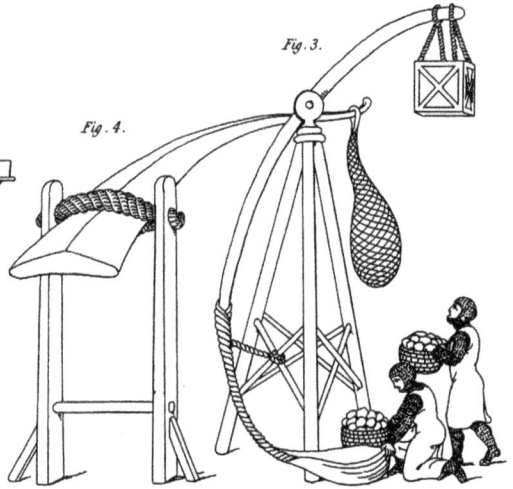

Drawn by S. R. Meyrick.

Etched by R. B.

MACHINES AND ENGINES OF WAR.

Edward the Second.

1307.

RESPECTING the armour of this period it is proper to premise, that it is of a mixed cha, being neither altogether mail nor wholly plate. When, therefore, the French authors use the term armures de fer, it must not be considered as applying exclusively to the plate before the close of this reign, though after that it became the distinctive term. The expression had been used in an indefinite sense in a treaty dated 1294,[1] between Philippe le Bel, and Jacques de Chastillon, lord of Leuse and Conde, by which this nobleman engages to furnish him, for a certain sum of money, cent armures de fer, "a hundred suits of iron armour," which had belonged to bannerets and knights who had been taken in Hainault. So again in a roll, dated 1317, under Philippe the Tall, it is noticed that the Dauphin de Vienne brought him three hundred men "en armures de fer "in iron armour."

The Florentine annals, however, consider the year 1315 as remarkable for a new regulation in armour, by which every horseman who wrent to battle was to have his helmet, breastplate, gauntlets, cuisses, and jambes, all of iron; a precaution which was taken on account of the disadvantages their

---

[1] See Du Tillet's Collection of Treaties.

cavalry had suffered from their light armour at the battle of Catino.[2] But this usage did not find its wray into general practice in Europe for at least ten years after.

In the return made to Parliament of the losses sustained by Hugh le Despencer and his father, from the conduct of the confederate barons, occurs, for the elder, "arms and armour for 200 men," and the same number for the younger, a fact that enables us to form some idea of the proportion kept at the castles of the principal nobility.

Perhaps the earliest specimen of this reign occurs in the monument of Sir Robert du Bois, in Forsfield church, Norfolk. He has a conical scullcap with camail attached, a hauberk with plates put over its sleeves, and these as well as the scullcap covered with silk, drawn tight over, and emblazoned with his arms. The gauntlets are painted to correspond, but his elbow-pieces left plain. On his legs are cliausses, and he wears the pryck-spur. He has on a surcoat with his arms emblazoned thereon, which was usual at this time, as Moor mentions,[3] that at the battle of Bannockbourne, the earl of Gloucester would not have been killed, but that he went into the field without his toga prop rise armaturae, "emblazoned surcoat," and therefore was not recognised. It is clasped by the military girdle, which became under this reign highly ornamented with silver or precious stones. These plates of metal were called plateinnes, as we learn from an account in the Chamber at Paris, where there is the following: Item plateinnes d'argent a mettre dessoubz clous de ceintures. "Plateinnes of silver to place underneath the rivets of the girdle." The mode too of covering the armour with silk, as occurs on the basinet and sleeves of this figure, is by no means singular, though, perhaps, this is an early specimen, for it is mentioned in an inventory of arms, belonging to Louis X, king of France, dated 1316, thus: Item unes plates neuves couvertes de sarnit vermeil. Item deux paires de plates autres couvertes de samit vermeil. Item un estivau de plates garnit de sainit. "Also a new plate covered with vermilion samit. Also two pairs of other plates covered with vermilion samit. Also an estival of plate garnished with samit." The estival was light armour for the legs. Thus in a deed, dated 1399,[4] occurs: Et aura pour ses chaimbres stivelez de plates garnis de teles et de fer. "And he shall have for his legs stivels[5] of plates furnished with linen and iron."

Plate xxvii represents a king and his mace-bearer, which is taken from a

---

[2] Modern Part of the Universal History, Vol. XIII. Folio edition, London, 1763.

[3] P. 594.

[4] In Lobineau's Hist. Bret.

[5] The word is still retained in the German language, stiefel, a boot.

PLATE XXVII

A KING AND HIS MACE-BEARER,

A.D. 1510.

MS. in the British Museum, in the Royal library.[6] Here, instead of the arms, the legs are covered with plate. The mace-bearer is entirely in mail, but his right hand gauntlet, which is visible, appears to be of cloth, and studded, being of a red colour, and therefore may be what was termed garni de teles et de fer. In his right hand is a mace, and in his left a buckler. Just such a buckler is in the hand of the figure at the bottom of this plate,[7] which has also a scymitar, a weapon that had been bor rowed from the Turks. It has also the ailettes, which are observable on the shoulders of the king.

The seal of Edward Prince of Wales, afterwards King Edward III, represents him with ailettes, on which are his arms, in the same manner as Edmund Croueliback is exhibited in Westminster Abbey, and in a missal belonging to F. Douce, Esq.[8] What is curious in this is the early representation of the mamelieres, or pieces put on the breast, from which depended chains, one of which was attached to the sword-hilt, and the other to the scabbard, which will be more fully explained hereafter.

The armour at the close of this reign may be seen in the initial letter, which is exactly copied from an original grant of Edward II, constituting his brother, Thomas de Brotherton, marshal of England.[9]

In the year 1313, being the seventh of this king, a statute passed, which seems to shew civilization advanced, and confidence more fully established, forbidding all persons coming to Parliament with arms or in armour.

The cavalry of the European armies consisted at this time of knights, who were called, when embodied, men at arms, and of liobilers. The former derived the appellation from being completely covered with armour de cap-a-pied "from head to foot," and were composed of the tenants in capite holding by military service, or their substitutes, sometimes styled servientes. The hobilers were so called from their riding on little horses termed hobbies, and were the light cavalry calculated for the purposes of reconnoitring, carrying intelligence, harassing troops on a march, intercepting convoys, and pursuing a routed army; the smallness of their horses rendering them unfit to stand the shock of a charge. The name has been derived by some from the dress of the troops, as they are supposed to have worn the hobile, a kind of French tunic; but Johnson and others say, that the small Irish horses were called hobbies, and that their appellation was thence derived. Hobilers

---

[6] Marked 16, G. VI.

[7] Taken from a glazed tile found at Margam Abbey, Glamorgansbire.

[8] See Pl. XLIV, Vol. XII, of the Archreologia, where St. George is represented in the same manner, with a visored basinet, very like that of the mace-bearer just described.

[9] In the Cotton library, marked Nero, D. VI.

PLATE XXVIII

ARCHERS AND 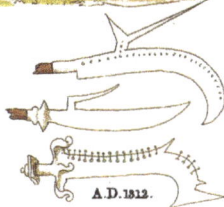 CROSS-BOW-MAN.

A.D. 1312.

are mentioned as part of the British army that attended king Edward II into Scotland in the year 1322. A MS. which formerly belonged to Thomas Astle, Esq. on this subject, has the following words: Titulus de denariis solutis diversis comitibus, baronibus et aliis, pro vadiis suis, et hominum suorum ad anna et liobelarioruin tam in guerra Scotiæ quam in munitionibus castrorum in marchia Scotiæ et Angliæ a priino die Mail anno quintodechno, usque ad septimum diem Julii anno regni ejusdem sexto decimo finiente tempore Rogeri de Waltham tunc custodis, et Roberti de Baldok tunc constarobulatoris garderoba? "Minute of money paid to divers earls, barons, and others, for their expeditions, together with their men at arms and liobilers, as well during the war in Scotland as for placing forces in the castles situated in the marches of Scotland and England, from the first day of May, in the fifteenth year, to the seventh of July, in the sixteenth year of the same reign, terminating during the time Roger de Waltham was keeper, and Robert de Baldok was constable, of the wardrobe."

Notwithstanding the hobilers rode on small horses, still we find mares were not allowed in their ranks, for in a writ to the Bishop of Durham, A.D. 1324, the 18th Edward II,[10] directing him to raise within his diocese the greatest possible number and most valiant men at arms, liobilers and infantry, he can find, there is the following exception: Des hobelars convenablement apparaillez, monter a chivaux autre qe jumentz. "Of hobilers suitably accoutred, mounted on horses but not mares."

The infantry at this time were armed with spears, bills, gisarmes, and poleaxes; besides which were the cross-bowmen and archers.

Plate XXVIII represents an archer, a mounted archer, and a cross-bowman, of this period. From this it will be perceived that their costume was uniform; that they wore hauberks and chausses of gamboised work, with surcoats over them; and conical helmets, with visors affixed, and made each of a perforated plate. These are taken from a MS. in the British Museum, entitled Livre des Histoire,[11] and from some other illuminations which it contains, we perceive that the conical helmets were held fast upon the head by something like platted ropes, such as sailors would call points, and which, as observed p. 155, were termed visiones.

From the wardrobe account of Edward II we learn, that the arrows were sometimes winged with peacocks' feathers. Thus Pro duodecim flecchiis cum pennis de pavonae emptis pro rege, 12 den. "For twelve arrows with

[10] Rymer's Fœd,
[11] Royal lib. marked 20, D. I.

peacock's feathers, bought for the king, 12 pence."[12]

The archer is represented in the act of stringing his bow, the cross-bow-man in that of shooting.

The custom of using the foot in bending the arbalest, if we may judge from the following circumstance, mentioned by Pitiscus, appears to be very antient. "In the district of Alexis, in Burgundy, were lately found two silver seals, one apparently of a legionary soldier, at least clad as such, with a beard, arcubalistam ad pedem tendere conantis, endeavouring to bend the cross-bow with his foot; the other of a beardless youth stringing a bow. Both were found in a glass-urn that was under ground." We have less questionable authority, however, in Guillaume le Breton, who wrote his Philippics at the close of the 12th century. He asserts this practice in the following line:

> Ballista duplici tensa pcde missa sagitta.

> "The two-liorned arbalest, being bent by aid of the foot, arrows were sent."

Yet neither of these authorities are sufficient to prove that a stirrup was attached to the bow, and then used for that purpose. Hence in the illuminations of Edward the Second's time,[13] we may perceive the foot merely put upon the bow, the ring at the end of the stock serving only as a rest.

But we have, nevertheless, undoubted proof of the invention of this appendage at the close of the thirteenth century, mention being made in a charter, dated 1299, of the ballista grossa ad stapham. Besides this, in the year 1294, mention is made of turni balisterii, which were the same as the arbaleste à tour, which Caseneuve, in his Origines de la Langue Françoise, says, was so called, parce qu'elle étoit bandée avec un tour, "because it was drawn up by a turn." That seems to imply something like the moulinet, but there is no appearance of such in illuminations of this time.

And yet, in the year 1320, we meet with balista grossa de molinellis, which determines its existence, and also the balista de precorio.

The balista grossa de arganellis was that which was furnished with tubes for ejecting the Greek fire.

Respecting the mercenary troops employed during this reign, there exist several orders in Rymer's Foedera. In 1308 there is one to the constable of Burgundy, to pay the arrears due to divers officers, particularly to Elias de Ponte and William Alarde, for their wages, and those of their followers. In

---

[12] MS. Cotto lib. Nero, C. VIII, p. 53.
[13] See one in a MS. in the Roy. lib. marked 2. B. VII.

1310 an allowance is directed to be made to Walter de Scudamore, sheriff of Dorset, for £25 5s, paid by the king's order to four men at arms, four cross-bows, and four archers, of the guard of the castle of Shireburn, for one hundred and one days' wages.[14] We also find cross-bows, banders, and quarrels, purchased for the garrison of Sherborn castle, each arbalest at 3s 8d; each bander or apparatus, with leather thongs for bending the bow, at 1s 6d and every hundred of quarrels at 1s 6d. A.D. 1322, the seneschal of Gascony was directed to raise two hundred crossbowmen, and two hundred lance-men, both foot, and bring them over, so that they might be at New-castle-upon-Tyne in October, to go against the Scots. Ray-munde de Mille Sactis was made commander of the whole.[15]

The mell, maule, or mallet of arms, as it was called, was a weapon partic-ularly used at this time both by the Scotch and English. In the memorable combat fought in Bretagne, in the year 1316, between thirty champions on the part of the English, and the like number on that of the French, one of the English champions, named Billefort,[16] was armed with a leaden mallet, weighing 25 lbs.[17]

Aylmer de Valence is represented, in Plate XXIX, in the mixed armour of this period, with the crest and cointisse on his helmet. Underneath he is in his chapelle de fer, which has also the cointisse, and his legs merely defended by greaves.[18]

We learn the method of degrading knights during this reign from an old MS. Chronicle of Douglass,[19] monk of Glastonbury. He tells us, that Sir Andrew Harclay, knight, earl of Carlisle, being accused of treason in the time of Edward II, "was ladde to the barre in the manner of an erle, rially araiedde, with a swerde gorde,[20] and liozedde and sporedde; and thenne Sir Antonye Lucye seide in this maner, Sir Andrew the king recordeth on yow for the worthinesse thatte he gaff to you, making yow erle of Cardoille; and ye as a treitour have ladde the folke off this countre bi Sopelande, and bi the erldom off Lancaster, werefor the Scottes have discomfited us, by yowre tresonne, atte the Abbey of Bekelonde; for iff ye hadde come thinder by

---

[14] Rymer's Fœd. Vol. III. p. 211.

[15] Ibid. p. 946.

[16] Probably from the strength he had displayed in using the bill.

[17] Hist. de Bretagne, par Dagentré, Iiv. VI, p. 393.

[18] Both these are taken from his monument in Westminster Abbey. The greaves are put over chausses of mail.

[19] MS. in the Harl. lib. N°. 4690, fol. 64.

[20] Girded on.

PLATE XXIV

AYLMER DE VALENCE   EARL OF PEMBROKE.

A.D. 1515.

resonnabell tyme, the king hadde liadde the victorie: and thatte tresonne ye dide, for the grete somine off money thate ye receivedde off Sir James Dowglas, the kingges onemy; and therefor the king wolle thate the order of knighthode, by which ye received your worschippe, be in your parsonne broughte to noughte, thatte all other knightes, of simpell blode as ye bene, in alle Englande, nowe take ensample by you, to serve the king the more trewly. Thanne he made a knave to hewe off his sporees, with an axe from his helis;[21] and after thatte he made the same knave to breke his swerde on his owne hede[22] the whyche the king hadde geve to hym, ther with to defende his londe, when he made him erle of Cardoile; and than he made a knave to do off his clothes, bothe gowne and hode, gurdell and cote, and then the foreseide Antony seide: Andrewe nowgh arte thee no knighte, but thow arte a knave; and for thi tresonne, the king wille thatte thow be drawe, and hongedde, and behededde, disbowelde, and thi bowelles brennedde, thy body quartredde; and thi liede sclialle be sente to London, an there itte sclialle be sette on the brigge, and the 4 quarters sclialle be sende to 4 townes of Englonde, thatte by the alie other such mowghte be chastized. And so itte was do in alie pointes, the laste day of Octobre, the year of oure Lorde 1322."

Edward II was the first prince of Wales of the English line, but whether the mode of creating a prince of Wales, which has been since practised, was then first formed does not appear on record. At the present time "he is presented to the king in princely robes, who putteth about his neck a sword bend wise,"[23] &c.

In the chancel of Ash church, Kent, is the monumental effigy of a knight, which has formed the subject of Plate xxx. It exhibits a still further progress towards plate-armour, and is therefore extremely curious. The basinet takes the shape of the head in the manner of the cerveliere, and is very highly ornamented; the camail is attached to it above the ears, the basinet forming ornamental flaps below. Instead of a mail hauberk several successive hoops of steel are riveted on a tunic of cloth, which reaches nearly to the knees. On the top of the shoulder are two or three sliding plates, and,

---

[21] This does not seem to agree with the time of Edward II, nor any period before that of Henry V, as the spurs were not screwed to the armour earlier than that reign, if so early. See Pl. xlv of Charles VII of France, where they are so fixed. But they may have been thus cut off at tbe heels though there seems no reason for it; and tbis is further asserted by Walsinghamto have been done.

[22] Probably over it.

[23] Analysis of Honor, Tit. Prince.

PLATE XXX

A  KNIGHT.

A.D. 1320.

instead of ailettes, large lions' heads are carved so as to form circular pieces. The armpits are protected by small plates, riveted on the shirt of plate; the arms above the elbows and to a short distance below have semicylindrical plates buckled upon them. Half way between the elbows and wrists appear the sleeves of the hauketon, which garment is again visible below the shirt of plate, placed over another tunic. The gauntlets are composed of several small plates riveted on cloth, and have been engraved from the monument at the foot of the plate to exhibit them more clearly. The warrior's feet are covered in much the same manner, but his legs are protected by jambes of steel, and he wears highly ornamented knee-caps. This effigy also affords an early specimen of the shortened surcoat, the prototype of the cyclas, which was used at the commencement of the next reign. The manner in which it was laced at the right side only, beginning just under the right arm and going down to the end, is also worthy of remark. The narrow girdle too, put round the hips, and buckled in front, to keep down the surcoat and allow the broad ornamented military belt to hold the sword and dagger, is worth notice. This knight has his shield suspended from his right shoulder, and his armour seems to be that described by William Guiart in the following lines, under the year 1296:

> Les mains couvertes de balainest[24]
> Et de gans de plates clouées
> En plusieurs parties trouvées.
>
> "The hands covered by stuffings of wool
> In gloves, on which plates are riveted,
> Perceptible in various parts."

Again, in 1304:

> Gans de plates et de balaine[25]
> Lances roides, juisarmes saines.
>
> "Gloves of plate and stuffed with wool
> Stiff lances, sound gisarmes."

And:

---

[24] This word is derived from the Breton word baIen, latinized balinja.
[25] Derived also from baIen.

Qui les mains garnies de plates
Les épaules d'armes fretees
Et les targes sur eus getees.

"Who have their hands furnished with plates,
Their shoulders with overlapping pieces,[26]
And their targets thrown over them."

What the name of this kind of hauberk is I have not been able satisfactorily to discover. The expression "a pair of plates" occurs in the next reign, but I think cannot be here applied, because should the dress be divided into a back and front, so as to be considered a pair, some such expression as "cloths of plate" would probably occur. Du Cange says, the armour ex laminis confecta was called placca, and this word occurs in a will, dated 1349: Placcas, corellum, gurgeriam, barbutam, &c. "Laminated hauberks, a thigh-piece, gorget, head-piece," &c. The panzeria might come in for its claim, for Jac. Hemricurtus[27] has this expression: Mais à présent cascun est armeis d'une cotte de fier appellée panchire sor petits clievax, et ont vestu en jupon de festaine à la deseur, &c. "But now-a-days every one is armed in a coat of iron called panchire, on small horses, and clad in a fustian jupon after the manner above mentioned." But this kind of hauberk is mentioned so early as the year 1211, and seems more like the gambeson in its make. The word colectum, if that be a corruption of collectum, implying aggregate, might also be selected. It occurs in the Vita B. Cocci thus: Corpus suum jejuniis multis casti-gabat, assidue portans pro camisia nudam panseriam vel colectum. "He inflicted on his body many tortures, assiduously wearing, instead of a shirt, a naked panseria or colectum." Probably, however, the proper name is placca, before noticed, but be that as it may, it seems to have been the prototype of the jazerant work, which became after this period very general.

In the year 1316 an inventory of the arms and armour of Louis le Grand, king of France, was taken, which is so curious as to merit being here inserted at full length. It is entitled: C'est d'Tnventoire des Armeures, et premièrement de celles que Doublet a rendus aux Exécuteurs.

Premièrement 33 hautes gorgieres double de chamli. Item uns pans et uns bras de jazeran d'acier. Item uns pans et uns bras de roondes mailles de haute cloüeure. Item uns pans et un bras d'acier plus fort de mailles roondes de haute cloiieure. Item uns pans et uns bras d'acier et le camail de mesme. Item 3 coloretes Pizanes de jazeran d'acier. Item une barbiere de haute

---

[26] Armes frettees are so called from frète which is an iron hoop or band.
27 De Bello Leod. c. 41.

cloüeure de cliambli. Item un jazeran d'acier. Item un haubergon d'acier à manicles. Item une couverture de jazeran de fer. Item une couverture de mailles rondes demy cloées. Item une testiere de haute cloüeure de maille ronde. Item un haubert entier de Lombardie. Item 2 autres liaubergons de Lombardie. Item 3 paires de cliauces de fer. Item 8 paires de chauçons et un chauçons par dessus. Item unes plates neuves couvertes de samit vermeil. Item un couteau à manche de fust et de fer, qui fu S. Louys, si corne l'en dit. Item 3 paires de grèves, et 3 paires de pouloins d'acier. Item 6 autres paires de grèves d'acier, et 2 paires de pouloins. Item 2 heaumes d'acier. Item 5 autres heaumes dont li uns est dorez, et 5 chapeauroons, dont les 2 sont dorez. Item 2 cors d'acier. Item 2 bacinez roons. Item 4 espées garnies d'argens, dont les 2 sont garnit de samit, et les deux de cuir. Item une espée à parer garnit d'argent, le pommel et le poing esmaille. Item 8 espées de Toulouz, et deux miséricordes. Item 17 espées de Bray. Item une espée de Jean d'Orgeret, et 2 espées, et une miséricorde de Verzi. Item 15 espées de commun. Item 15 coutiaus de commun et 7 fers de glaives de Toulouze. Item 2 de commun et le bon fer de glaive de le Roy. Item 2 clianfrains dorez, et un de euh·. Item une fleur de lys d'argent doré, de mauvese preure à mettre sus le heaume le roy. Item uns gantelez couvers de velveil vermeil. Item 13 bannières batues des armes le roy. Item 16 banniers consues des armes le roy. Item 18 pennonciaux batus des armes le roy. Item unes couvertures, une flanchieres, une picieres et une tunicle de velveil, les fleurs de lys d'or de Chipre. Item une cote gamboisée de cendal blanc. Item 2 houces et 2 tunicles des armes de France, et le chapiau de meismes. Item 2 tunicles et un gamboison de bordure des armes de France. Item 2 tunicles batués des armes de France. Item 2 manches broudées. Item 3 paires de braciere en cuir des armes de France. Item 2 paires de resnes de fer. Item 4 paires d'espérons garnis de soye, et 2 paires garnies de cuir. Item une testiere, et une crouppière garnie des armes de France. Item un estuiaus de plates garny de samit. Item 2 chapiaus de fer couvers. Item 3 escus pains des armes le roy, et un d'acier. Item 16 paires de couvertures batuës, et une non per des armes le roy. Item 5 cotes batués des armes le roy fourrés, et une défourrés. Item 3 cottes battues défourrées des armes le roy. Item 22 penonciaux batués les armes le roy. Item une couverture de gamboisons broudées des armes le roy. Item 3 paires de couvertures gamboisées des armes le roy, et unes Indes jazeqnenées. Item 2 paires de couvertures batués, et une eolière des armes le roy. Item une quantité d'aiguillettes et las à armer. Item G bacinetz. Item une paire d'estamine à couvrir chevaux. Item un cuissiaux gamboisez, et uns esquivelans de cuir. Item une tunique et une liouce de drap des armes de France, et de Navarre, d'or de Chipre, les fleurs broudées de pelles. Item une houce et une tunique de drap simple des armes de France et de Navarre. Item un vieil jupel des armes de France à fleurs broudées Item cote, bracieres, houce d'escu, et chapel de veluyau, et couvertures à cheval des armes du roy, les fleurs de lys d'or de Chypre, broudées de pelles. Item picieres et flancliieres de samit des armes le roy, les fleurs de lys d'or de Chypre. Item uns cuissiaus sans pouloins des armes de France. Item une cote gamboisée à arbroissiaus d'or broudées à chardonereus. Item 18 bannières batués des armes de France et de Navarre, et 4 de couture. Item 51 penonciaux batus de France et de Navarre. Item unes couvertures à cheval batués de France et de Navarre. Item unes couvertures gamboisées de France et de Navarre. Item flancieres et picieres de France et de Navarre. Item un escu et 2 targes de France et de Navarre; et un escu Ynde à lettres d'or, et un chappiau de drap de France et de Navarre. Item unes couvertures d'estamines.

"This is the Inventory of the Armour, and first of all of that which Doublet has rendered into the hands of the Executors.

"First: Thirty-three high double gorgets of chambli. Item a breast-piece and an arm of steel jazerant. Item a breast-piece and an arm of ring mail of superior riveting. Item a breast-piece and an arm of steel much stronger, of ring mail of superior rivetting. Item a breast-piece and an arm of steel with a camail of the same. Item three Pizan collars of steel jazerant. Item a barbiere[28] of superior riveting of cambli. Item a jazerant of steel. Item a steel haubergeon with hand coverings. Item a housing of iron jazerant. Item a housing of ring-mail half riveted. Item a testiere[29] of ring mail of superior riveting. Item an entire hauberk from Lombardy. Item two other haubergeons from Lombardy. Item three pairs of chausses of iron. Item eight pairs of chauçons and one chauçon besides. Item a new plate covered with vermilion samit. Item a sleeve knife of wood and iron, which belonged, as it is said, to Saint Louis. Item three pairs of greaves and three pairs of steel poulaines. Item six other pairs of steel greaves, and two pairs of poulaines. Item two steel helmets. Item five other helmets, of which one is gilt; and five chaperons, of which two are gilt. Item two bodies of steel. Item two round basinets. Item four swords ornamented with silver, of which two are orna mented with samit, and two with leather. Item a parrying-sword ornamented with silver, the pommel and hilt enamelled. Item eight swords of Toulouse and two mi-

---

[28] Headpiece, whence a person wearing armour was said to be "barbed."
[29] That part of a horse's covering which was placed over his head.

sericordes. Item seventeen swords of Bray. Item a sword of John d'Orgeret, and two swords and one misericorde of Verzi. Item fifteen ordinary swords. Item fifteen ordinary knives and seven glaive blades of Toulouse. Item two ordinary ones, and the excellent blade which belonged to the king's glaive. Item two gilt chanfrains[30] and one of leather. Item a silver fleur-de-lys gilt, not of standard value, to place on the king's helmet. Item a gauntlet covered with vermilion velvet.[31] Item thirteen banners with the arms of the king stamped thereon. Item sixteen banners with the king's arms worked thereon. Item eighteen penoncels with the king's arms stamped thereon. Item one housing, one flanchiere,[32] one pieiere,[33] and one tunicle of velvet, the fleurs-de-lys of Cyprus gold. Item a gamboised coat of white sandal. Item twro pairs of hose and two tunicles of the arms of France, and the chapeau[34] of the same. Item two tunicles and one gainbeson, each with a border of the arms of France. Item two tunicles with the arms of France stamped thereon. Item two embroidered sleeves. Item three pairs of bracers [35]of leather of the arms of France. Item two pairs of iron bridles. Item four pairs of spurs furnished with silk, and two pairs furnished with leather. Item one testiere and one crouppiere[36] ornamented with the arms of France. Item an envelope of plates[37] ornamented with samit. Item two chapel de fers covered. Item three wooden shields with the arms of the king, and one of steel. Item sixteen pairs of housings with the kings arms stamped thereon, and one without. Item five coats with the king's arms stamped thereon furred, and one not furred. Item three coats without their fur, with the king's arms stamped thereon. Item twenty-two penoncels with the king's arms stamped thereon. Item a housing of gamboised work, embroidered with the arms of the king. Item three pairs of gamboised housings having thereon the king's arms, and an Indian one made in the manner of a jazerant.[38] Item two pairs of housings stamped, and a collar of the king's arms. Item a quantity of tags and laces for arming. Item six basinets. Item a pair of woollen cloths for covering

---

[30] This shews that the cbanfrain and testiere were considered distinct.
[31] See tbe mace-bearer in Plate XXVII.
[32] The piecewhich covered tbe horse's flanks.
[33] A breast-piece for a horse,
[34] The knigbt's cap.
[35] Coverings for tbe arms, probably for archers.
[36] The covering which went over tbe borse's tail and binder parts.
[37] This seems to express the kind of armour worn by tbe knigbt in Plate xxx.
[38] Tbis mode of forming tbem still continues in India and Persia, as well for the elephants as the horses, and is another proof that the jazeran consisted of small overlapping"plates.

horses. Item a gamboised thigh-piece and two esquivalents[39] of leather. Item a tunic and hose of cloth with the arms of France and Navarre The covering which went over tbe borse's tail and binder parts. of Cyprus gold, the embroidered flowers worn off. Item hose and a tunic of mere cloth with the arms of France and Navarre. Item an old jupel[40] with the arms of France, the flowers embroidered on it. Item a coat, bracers, hose, and shield, and chapel covered with velvet, and horse-covering with the king's arms thereon, the fleurs-de-lys of Cyprus gold, embroidered on skins. Item picieres and flanchieres of samit, having on them the king's arms, the fleurs-de-lys being of Cyprus gold. Item a thigh-piece without its poulaine, with the arms of France. Item a gamboised coat with a rough surface[41] of gold embroidered on the nap of the cloth. Item eighteen banners with the arms of France and Navarre stamped thereon, and four stitched. Item fifty-one penoncels with the arms of France and Navarre stamped thereon. Item a covering for a horse, the arms of France and Navarre stamped thereon. Item a gamboised housing with the arms of France and Navarre. Item flanciers and picieres of France and Navarre. Item one shield and two targets of France and Navarre, and one Indian shield lettered with gold, and a chappeau of cloth of France and Navarre. Item a housing of woollen cloth." With respect to the gorget we learn, from an old ehartulary,[42] that its value was not very great, the expression being la gorgerette doit un denier. William Guiart, under the year 1285, says:

Hyaumes fondent, targes deffacent,
Mailles chieent de gorgeretes,
Tabour tentisscnt ct trompetes.

"Helmets beat in, targets defaced,
Mails fall from gorgets,
Tabours strike up, and trumpets."

Again, under 1297:

Hyaumes mis, gorgieres lacies.

"Helmets put on, gorgets laced."

Further, under 1304:

---

[39] The same as estival, armour for the legs.
[40] A short surcoat.
[41] Like a thicket.
[42] Peron e chartul. 21, Carl. fol. 341.

Bacinez fondent, boucliers faillent,
Haubers et gorgieres desmaillent.

"Basinets beat in, bucklers,
Hauberks, and gorgets, dismailed."

The previous extract contains the earliest notice, with the exception of that at p. 151, I have met with of the use of the chanfron or champfrein, which was a plate of steel or leather to cover the horse's face, and I have not been able to discover any delineation of it before the reign of Richard II: however, we have here a clear proof that it was known at this time, and was distinct from the testiere, which was a covering for the whole head, generally of mail.[43] As we have seen, it was formed either of metal gilt or boiled leather, but in later times the nobility piqued themselves on the magnificence they displayed in this part of the armour.

The testiere is spoken of in a charter of the earl of March, in 1269: Mandamus vobis quatinus duo paria turnicliarum, et duo paria cuissetorum, duas testerias ad equos, apportari faciatis vobiscum. "We command you hereby to cause to be brought with you two pairs of tunicles, two pairs of cuissettes, and two testieres for horses."

In Tewkesbury church, Gloucestershire, are painted in glass several figures intended to represent the earls of Clare. These differ very little from each other, but afford good specimens of the armour on the knight in Plate xxx. The helmet is the same, but the camail is composed of several plates fastened on it with rivets. Under this name it was called a gorget. Thus, among the stores of the Castrum Carcasson., of which an account was taken in the year 1294, are enumerated gorgeriic ferri de Lombardia, "gorgets of iron from Lombardy," where they probably originated. In an inquisition, taken in the year 1323, it is ordered: Item quod idem castellanus praecepit quod haberent centum gorgerias ferri, et dictas centum gorgerias misit qiuesitum. "Also that the said castellan should take care that they have a hundred gorgets of iron, and that the said hundred gorgets be sent on being demanded." The camail seems also to have been called goceon at this period. Thus in an instrument, dated in 1309,[44] is goceons suffesans de mailles de haubert, "sufficient goceons of hauberk-mail." The cuffs and fingers of the gauntlets are made in the same manner as is the upper part of the thigh-coverings. The

[43] Subsequently the testiere implied the plate between the ears, which was affixed to the cbanfron by means of hinges.

[44] See Hist. de Bret. Tom. I, col. 1222.

arms, legs, and feet, are completely covered with plate-armour, so that below the shoulder-piece we have the complete brassart, and below the elbow the entire avant-bras or vambrace. On the shoulders of each knight are his ailettes, at his left thigh his large sword, and in his right hand a short spear with a lozenge-shaped head.

On the wall of the hall at Tamworth castle, in Warwickshire, was, within memory of the old people there, a rude painting, intended to represent Sir Lancelot du Lac and Sir Tarquin, drawn in gigantic size, and jousting together.[45] This was probably done in the time of Edward II, as was evidently that on glass formerly in the church at Tamworth, representing the gift of this castle by William the Conqueror to Robert de Marmion.[46]

That curious ivory carving, engraved in the Archæologia,[47] and taken from some romance, is of this period. It represents several knights in their surcoats scaling the walls of a castle, where they are received by ladies. On entering they oiler their swords holding them by the points, and at the same time take off their helmets, on the top of which are cointisses. They have also ailettes on their shoulders.

The hauberk of plates, as represented in Plate xxx, seems noticed in the Con-suetudo Brageriaci,[48] in the following enumeration: Item annatura, utpote enses, lancese, scuta, boglaria, loricse platee, pileus ferreus sive capellus, perponcha sive gambaycho, guisarma nec alia genera armorum necessaria ad tuitionem corporis pro ullo debitu pignorenter. "Also no armour, as swords, lances, shields, bucklers, hauberks of plates, iron hats or chapelles de fer, pourpoints or gambesons, gui-sarines, nor any kind of arms necessary for the defence of the body shall be pledged for any debt."

This quotation also shews that the pourpoint and gambeson were both worn at this period. So in a deed of Philip the Fair, king of France, dated 1303,[49] it is said: Et seront annez de porpoins et de hauberjons ou de gambaisons. "And they shall be armed with pourpoints and haubergeons or gambesons." This seems to indicate that the pourpoint was nearly the same as that gambeson which was worn without the coat of mail, and was what the French called cote gamboisee. Thus William Guiart, under the year 1298, says:

Que seul des cotes gambesies Pouvoit-on emplir maintes jaillcs.

---

[45] Warton's note on Spencer's Faëry Queene, Vol. I, p. 43.
[46] Engraved in Dugdale's Hist. of Warwickshire.
[47] Vol. XVI, Pl. xlix.
[48] Art. 28.
[49] In the Royal Registry at Paris, number 115.

"Which of gamboised coats alone Might fill many jars."[50]

And, in 1304:

Espces d'estos et dc taille
Cotes gambesies, ventailles.

"Estoc swords, and well shaped,
Gamboised coats, ventailles."

Gamboisié seems to have been used to imply stitched and padded work generally, for in an account of Robert de Sevis,[51] occurs: Une selle de la taille d'Alle-maigne, et se siege de cendail vermeil gamboisie et pourfillee d'or. "A saddle of German shape, with its seat of vermilion sandal, padded, and stitched with gold." The hauketon was also much worn during this reign: thus, when the bishop of Exeter was taken in arms against his king, "he had on a coat of defence called aketon."In the wardrobe account of wages paid the army raised to go against the Scots in 1322,[52] are the following entries: De Com. Norf. Ricardo Warin, Johanni Dacre, Henrico de Norton, et Johanni Plaice centenariis pro vadiis suis 436 pedites, cum aketon et bacinet, &c. De Com. Suff. Willo de Ryshall et Henrico Poer centenariis pro vadiis suis et 240 peditum cum akton et bacinet, &c. "For the county of Norfolk, to Richard Warin, John Dacre, Henry de Norton, and John Plaice, commanders of hundreds, for their expeditions, having furnished 436 foot soldiers, with aketons and basinets, &c. For the county of Suffolk, to William de Ryhall and Henry Poer, commanders of hundreds, for their expeditions with 240 foot soldiers with aktons and basinets," &c.

Such men as wanted hauketons or the like were called naked foot, and received inferior pay. Thus in the same account we read: Com. Lincoln, Jordano de Blacke-neye ductori peditum de Kestevene, in comitatn Lincoln, pro vadiis 100 peditum nudorum, &c. De Com. Norlfpt. Edmundo de Lokenote, Stepliano Scott, Thome de la Husse, et Johanni Jewel, centenariis pro vadiis suis et 440 peditum nudorum de comitatu Northampt. &c. "For the county of Lincoln, to Jordan de Blackeneye, commander of the infantry of Kestevene, in the county of Lincoln, for the service marching of 100 naked foot, &c. For the county of Northampton, to Edmund de

---

[50] Or puncheons, in which they were probably packed.
[51] Reg. 5. Chartoph, reg. fol. 5. 1.
[52] The Iôth Edward II.

Lokenote, Stephen Scott, Thomas de la Husse, and John Jewel, commanders of hundreds, for their expeditions with 440 naked foot of the county of Northampton," &c. It was used as armour also by the Scotch, for it is said in the statutes of Robert Bruce: Quilibet habeat in defensione regni, unum sufficientem actonem, unum basinetum, et chirothecas de guerra, See. Qui non habuerit actonem et basinetum, habeat unum bonum habergellum, et unum capitium de ferro. "Whoever prefers it, may have for the defence of the kingdom one sufficient acton, one basinet, and gauntlets, &c. He who shall not, however, possess an acton and basinet, must have a good haubergel and a chapelle de fer." By this a preference seems in Scotland to have been given to the hauketon before the haubergeon. Among the Rotuli Scotiae of the 10th Edward II, is one dated York, 4th Sepr, 1317, "for raising men between the ages of 16 and 60, in different counties, and the kind of armour they are to have." From this we learn, that Quilibet liabens quindecim libratas terre per annum et catalla ad valentiam quadriginta marcarum, aketonum, loricam, capellum ferreum et equum competentem. Alius quilibet habens decern libratas terre per annum et catalla ad valentiam viginti marcas, aketonum, loricam et alia anna competentia sibi provi-deat. Qui plus[53] terræ et catallorum habuerit competentius sibi provident de equis et armis juxta facilitates suas. "Every one having £15 of land per annum, and chattels to the value of 40 marks, shall provide himself with an aketon, a hauberk, a chappelle de fer, and a sufficient horse. Whoso has only £10 of land per annum, and chattels to the value of 20 marks, shall have an aketon, a hauberk, and other sufficient arms. He who has not so much land and chattels, shall sufficiently provide himself with horse and arms as well as he is able."

Lance was the word used at this time for the peculiar weapon of the cavalry, for William Guiart, noticing the death of Walter Lord of Vaucouleur in 1304, says:

Qui s'alla emmi eus laucier
Sus la chaucie et il l'occirent.

"Who went among them to lance
On the high-road, and they killed him."

The usual pay of knights bannerets was 20 sols tournois a day; that of knights batchelors and esquires banneret 10 sols each, that of simple esquires 5 sols; of gentlemen on foot 2 sols; of serjeants on foot 12 deniers,

[53] Probably a mistake for minus.

and of cross-bows 15 deniers.

Bannerets had the privilege of a war-cry, called crie d'annes, that particularly attached to them, to the exclusion of all knights batchelors; from having the right of leading their vassals to war, and from being chiefs of a large body of men at arms. Hence the origin of mottos.[54]

Troops were generally drawn up by a kind of field-marshal, called arraiour.[55] Thus in a letter of Edward II, written in the year 1322, he says: Assignavimus ipsum comitem capitalem custodem comitatuum et superiorem arraiatorem, et ducem tarn hominum ad anna, quam peditum. "We have assigned to the said earl the chief custody of the county, and appointed him cliief-aiTaiour and commander, as well of the men at arms as the infantry." In another letter of the same king, dated in 1326, is: Le roy as tous arraiours et mesnours des gens d'annes et de pie, &c. "The king to all arraiours and leaders of men at arms and infantry," See. The manner in which the troops were drawn up was also called arramentum, arrayement, arroy, and array. In the Chronicle of Flanders it is said: Puis feit le roy de France son arroy, et prit avec lui tous ses liauts hommes. "Then the king of France made his array, and took with him all his principal men."

The helmet on the seal of Edward II is of a cylindrical fonn, with a grated or pierced aventaille and visor attached. The clasp which fastens this on the right side is very visible, and it is probable that on the other it was retained by hinges.

The basinet at first was worn, as being lighter than a helmet, when the knight did not expect an attack, but wished to be prepared. When visors were made to them they, for a time, superseded the use of the helmet, as is evident in the statute of Robert I of Scotland, already cited. Under the year 1214, William Guiart has:

> Penonccaux et bannières bruire
> Li yaumes et bacinez reluire.

> "To display penoncels and banners,
> And exhibit the glittering of helmes and basinets."

But under that of 1270 he says:

> Et clers bacinez à visieres.

---

[54] Several of those now in existence may be traced to this source, but it may be sufficient to notice that of the earl of Kildare, Crom-aboe, bellum exultare, "buzza, for war!"

[55] That is, he who placed in array.

"And shining basinets with visors."

And in 1304:

> Shields, basinets with visors."
> And lower down he speaks of:

> Bacinez brunis à visieres.
> "Burnished basinets with visors."

The coif de fer or hood was still used during this reign. Hence William Guiart, under the year 1301, says:

> Boucliers és poins, coifes lacices,
> Et blanches espées sachiées.

> "Hand-bucklers[56] and laced coifs,
> And fair swords in their sheaths."

Again, under the year 1304:

> Armées de cotes à leur tailles,
> Et de bons hauberjons à mailles,
> De fors gans,de coiffes serrées,
> De gorgieres, d'espées.

> "Armed in coats fitted to their shape,
> And with good haubergeons of mail,
> With strong gloves, and riveted coifs,
> With gorgets and swords."

It was very much the custom during this reign to wear over the armour the cointisse. Thus William Guiart, under the year 1304, says:

> Cil escuier ot le jour mise
> Sur ses armes une cointisse
> De gueules, sans ouvres tremées,
> Fors molettes d'argent semées.

> "This esquire had that day put
> Over his armour a cointisse
> Of gules, without any mixture of work,

---

[56] Such as were held by the hand, and not put on the arm.

Except being semée of mullets argent."

When describing the French naval armament before Ziriez, he says:

> Couleur jaunes, Indes ct rouges,
> Vers vermeilles et desguisées,
> Peuvent ilenc estre avisées,
> Et cointises qui leur apendent.

"Yellow colours, Indian and red,
Almost vermilion, and resembling it,
Might there be observed;
And cointisscs which were hung round them."

In another place he says:

> Qu'en aj oignant des bords assises
> De tuniques et de cointises, &c.

"The ship breaks, galleys are tossed about,
So that in striking their sides where persons are
Sitting in tunics and cointisses," &c.

Under the year 1268 he writes:

> La veissiez cointises bruire,
> Et aval le vent freteler.

"There might you see cointisses blown about,
And the wind playing among them."

But he gives the following full description when relating a battle in 1304:

> Les atours de divers guises,
> Les paremens et les cointises,
> Dont li flos d'eus est assené,
> Ne deviseroit homme né
> Comment que il i entendist,
> Le pais huist et resplendist,
> Aussi clercment comme espars
> De gens armez de toutes pars.
> Car le soleil s'est embatus
> Es garnemens à or batus,

Que cil ont sur leur armeures
A beles entrelaceures,
Si très gentes que c'est merveille,
De soie Inde, blanche, vermeill
Jaune, vert, sore, ardent et perse,
Netoiée de tache terse,
Et n'est pas mise par monciaus,
Qui bien prend garde aux lionciaus,
Aux oiselez, aux besteletes,
Qui d'euvres polies et netes,
Sont là par diverses couleurs,
Ne li souvient des ses douleurs.
Or fin, qui tant est agréable,
Rose, sinople, argent et sable,
Vermillon et azur et mine.
Que les biaus atours cnlamine,
Reflamboient par estancelles,
En riches escus et seles,
En çaintures et en tissous,
Sur ceus qui sont aux chams issus.

"The arrangements made, of different kinds,
The preparations, and the cointisses,
The folds of which are exactly placed.
No man born can devise
How it can be in any way intended
To proclaim peace with this glitter,
As clear as he can, he sees the splendour
Of men armed at all points.
For if the sun has set,
The furniture of stamped gold
Which they have upon their armour,
With its beautiful interlacings,
Is of such superior kind as to be astonishing:
Of Indian silk, white, vermilion,
Yellow, green, reddish yellow, light, and blue,
Free from spot or blemish;
And which is not put on in heaps,
But great care taken of the little lions,
The little birds, and little beasts,
Which in neat and polished work
Appear there in different colours,
Such things cannot be called to mind without griefs.
In short, which is so agreeable,
Rose, ruddy, argent, and sable,
Vermilion, azure, and metal,

Which these fine arrangements set in order.
Shining forth with attraction,
In rich shields and saddles,
In girdles and in tissues,
On those who issue from the field,"

The ceinture or military girdle is here mentioned, the conferring of which was the mode of investiture on the creation of a knight. Thus in a deed of Philip King of France to Peter Du Chenin, his valet, dated in the year 1313, is: Quern hac instanti die Dominica ordinavimus, disponente Deo militari cingulo decorare. "Whom on this very Sunday we have designed, God willing, to decorate with the military girdle."

The gonjo was a military habiliment worn at this period. Thus in a charter, dated 1312,[57] occurs: Cum armis discopertis, videlicet lanceis, capellinis ferreis, gonjonibus, &c. "With naked arms, namely lances, chapelles de fer, gonjos," &c. This word seems to imply the gorget, and was probably a corruption of goceon.

There is another garment, called gonnus or gown, spoken of. Thus, in a charter of the same year, it is said, that Guillelmus de Stapo bajulus civitatis Albiæ cum multitudine hominum armatorum, equitum et peditum, portantium arma discoperta, videlicet lanceas, balistas, cadrellos, scuta, gasarnias, gonnos, et perpontis more liostili. "William de Stapho, bailiff of the town of Albia, with a multitude of armed men, both horse and foot, carrying naked arms, namely, lances, cross-bows, quarrels, shields, gisarmes, gowns, and pourpoints, in a hostile manner."

The following armour, as being at Norham castle, occurs in an inventory taken in the year 1314: 87 pair de trappes, 9 targes, 88 chapeus de fere, 136 arblastes, 103 baudries, 9 pair de quisseus, 19 actons, 20 haubergeons, and 62 morrns (or lance-heads for jousting).

The French at this period seem to have used short swords, for William Guiart says:

Li François cspées reportent
Courtes et roides dont ils taillent.

"The French carried swords
Short and inflexible, with which they cut."

---

[57] In the Royal library at Paris.

And under the year 1301.

> Espees viennent aus servises
> Et sont de diverse semblance,
> Mes François, qui d'accoustumance
> Les ont courtes assez légieres,
> Gietent aus Flamens vers les chieres.

> "Swords come into use,
> And are of different kinds;
> But the French, who, from custom,
> Have them short and sufficiently light,
> Struck at the faces of the Flemings."

The thin-bladed dagger, called miséricorde, was also much used at this time, being more easily inserted into the interstices of the armour. Thus William Guiart, under the year 1302, says:

> Plusieurs piétons François ala,
> Qui pour prisonnier n'ont pas cordes,
> Mais coutiaus et miséricordes,
> Dont on doit servir en tiex fester.

> "Many French foot-soldiers go,
> Who had not cords to make prisoners.
> But knives and miséricordes,
> Which they used in such extremities."

And under the year 1303:

> Fauchons tranchans, espées cleres,
> Godendas, lances csmoluës,
> Coutiaus, miséricordes nues.

> "Cutting faulchions,[58] sharpened swords,
> Godendas, sharp lances,
> Knives, and naked miséricordes."

What the godenda or godendac was we learn from the same author, who informs us it was a Flemish weapon, in these words:

> A grans bastons pesans, ferrez

---

[58] This term, in moderntimes used to signify a large sword, was originally either the bill, or a sword on its principle.

A un long fer agü devant,
Vont, ceux de France recevant:
Tiex baston, qu'il portent en guerre,
Out nom godendac en la terre.
Godendac, c'est, bon jour, à dire,
Qui en François le veut descrire.
Cil baston sont long et traitis,
Pour ferir a deux mains faitis,
Et quant l'en en faut au descendre,
Se cil qui fiert, y veut entendre,
Et il en sache bien ouvrer,
Tantost peut son cop recouvrer,
Et ferir sans s'aller mocquant
Du bout devant en estoquant
Son ennemi parmi le ventre,
Et Ii fers et agus qui entre
Legierement de plaine assiete
Par tous les lieus où l'en en giete,
Sarmeures ne le détiennent,
Cil qui les grans godendac tiennent,
Qui l'ont ù deus poins empoignez,
Sont un poi des rancs esloignez
De bien ferir ne sont point lasches.

"With great heavy ironed staves,
Having a long sharp iron projecting from them,
They go; the French receiving them.
Such a staff, which they carry in war,
Is named godendac in their country.
Godendac implies 'Good day,'
Which in French would be thus expressed.
This baton is long and tapering,
Made for striking with two hands,
And when on the point of descending,
If he who strikes wishes to understand it,
And knows well how to work with it,
As soon as he can recover his blow,
And strike, without going to imitate it again,
From the projecting end let him thrust
His enemy in the belly;
For the iron is sharp, that enters
Lightly when well directed
Into all places in which it may be thrust.
If armour only resists him
Who wields the great godendac,
And has it in his two clenched hands,

He should draw back a little from the ranks
To strike well where there is no armour."[59]

From this description it seems to have been a kind of pole-axe, with a spike at its end. The Danish axe was somewhat of this kind, except that, instead of the spike, there was a hook, to which a horse might be fastened when it was driven into the ground, there being a pointed ferrule at the lower end. William Guiart also speaks of them, under the year 1304, they being used in England and France, and indeed pretty generally in Europe.

The javelin, under the names of javrelot, gavrelot, gavelot, and gaveloce. Thus the Statuta Senescal. Bellicad. of the year 1320, decree respecting Quicunque por-taverit lanceas, gaverlotos, tela, ballistas, et hujusmodi anna mortífera. "Whosoever shall carry lances, javelins, darts, cross-bows, and such kind of deadly weapons." This could have differed very little from the dart, unless by being without feathers. Of this latter William Guiart speaks in 1302:

> La veissiéz au remuer
> Lances brandir et dars ruer
> Qui traper§ent coton etbourre.

> "There might you see in commotion
> Lances brandished and darts hurled,
> Which pierced cotton and wool."

Alluding to their effect on the hauketons and gambesons.

The small mace, called mazara, and by the French mazuete, was also a weapon in vogue at this time, for the same author, under the year 1304, has:

> En se main une mácete,
> Le lance en cele reverete.

> "In his hand a masuete,
> The lance in the opposite one."

By the English it was termed masuelle. Thus in a charter, dated 1319,[60] it is ordained: Ne quis per civitatem gladium, masuellam, vel alia arma, ex quibus contumelias preesumatur oriri posse, &c. deferet in civitate preedictá. "That no one in the aforesaid state should be allowed to carry through the

---

[59] Lacombe says, laches is a cuirass, or sort· of military vest.
[60] In Rymer's Fœdera,

state a sword, masuelle, or other weapon, which may give rise to quarrels," &e. The mace, though excepted in this particular instance, was nevertheless still used, for in the words of William Guiart, under the year 1305, we have:

> La oist-on aus coups donner
> Diverses armes raisouner,
> Et tcnlir espées ct maces.

> "There might you hear blows given,
> And different arms resound,
> Swords and maces tried."

The following very curious description of the art of war, with the arms and machines used in the northern parts of Europe, is translated from a manuscript in Latin, entitled Speculum Regale, and supposed to have been written in the fourteenth century, and in the nature of a dialogue:[61]—

"If your companions are desirous of leaving the palace for awhile, and going to exercise themselves, or on a convivial party, the king's leave being obtained, make use of the following mode of amusement which I shall point out to you.

"If you shall be in a fit place for riding, and you have a horse, mount him, having first put on your heavy armour, and exercise yourself in acquiring a safe and handsome seat; exercise your feet also, so that your legs being extended they may stand fast in the stirrups, the heel a little lower than the toes,[62] not to be in fear of an adverse blow, when with closed thighs you may hold yourselves firm and immoveable, covering your breast and other parts of your body with your shield. Accustom yourself to hold your reins and the handles of your shield with the left hand, bearing your dart with your right, either to throw it at a certain mark or to brandish it, assisting your motions with the upper part of your body. Teach your horse to run circularly at his full speed, keep him clean from dirt, properly shod, with splendid trappings firmly put on.

---

[61] This translation is extracted from the 4th Volume of the Antiquarian Repertory: but it is. to be regretted, that neither is the original Latin given, nor any reference to where it may be found.

[62] It is curious, that in the times of Henry VI and Edward IV the warriors are always represented with their toes pointing down when in the stirrup; indeed, from the Conquest to the close of Richard the Third's reign, the fashion was to ride with the toes down, after which period the heel was dropped and the toe up, a curious fact that seems, if the translation be correct, to throw some doubt OІІ this extract having the early date assigned to it: I am, however, more inclined to doubt the translation.

"If you are in a market town, where you cannot take your horse or use him for amusement, adopt this recreation: Go home and put on your heavy armour, then seek for one of your companions, whether inmate or dwelling elsewhere, who will play with you, and whom you know to be skilful in fencing or sword play, either with the greater or less shield. Being always fully armed, even with your iron lorica,[63] enter the sham field, bearing in your hand either a shield of proof or the larger sword. In this play you will learn how to give the proper and necessary, strokes, and also how to evade them; as likewise how to cover yourself with your shield against all sorts of blows when in real action with an enemy.

"If you are desirous of becoming expert in this art, if possible exercise yourself in this sham fight every day, never letting a day pass in which you do not repair to the field, unless it prove a holiday. This is an art not less becoming than necessary for a courtier. If you leave off from this exercise tired and thirsty, drink gently and frequently, lest you be overcome by thirst, taking care that whilst you indulge yourself with this diversion you do not intoxicate yourself with too much wine.

"If you are desirous of other amusements there are others which may be used in the open air, if they give greater pleasure. Prepare yourself a staff to use instead of your spear, than which let it be larger, and set up a mark against the butts, by which you may know how far and with what degree of exactness you can conveniently throw your spear. It is a famous art, which also yields amusement, to go into the jaculatory field among others, and to shoot arrows with a bow.

"Nor is it less pleasant than useful in an army, to throw stones with precision to a great distance from a sling, whether held in the hand or fixed to a staff; also to throw the war-stone with exactness.

"It was once a received maxim among those desirous of being perfect in this art, and skilled in the foot and horse exercises, to accustom themselves to bear arms equally in each hand when they met the enemy, which you should imitate if you are able, for those who are ambidexter are used to excel in the art of war, and are extremely hurtful to the enemy.

"Abstain from all kinds of homicide, unless it be for the legal punishment of crimes, or committed in open war. For in war, or if you have the just commands of your prince, you are not more to abstain from slaughter than from any other act you know to be good and lawful.

"In war shew yourself bold and spirited, cutting and thrusting like a

---

[63] The hauberk.

gentleman, whose mind is somewhat excited to anger, fighting according to the rules you have formerly learned.

"Never strike rashly nor at an uncertainty, nor, as is the custom of cowards, throw your dart at random, but rather watch and improve by the dexterity of others.

"In war be always patient of labour, neither precipitate nor boastful, rather choose that others may give you a good character. Never boast of your great actions, lest in the course of years revenge may be taken for the death of a beloved person, by some provoked to it by your boasting.

"If in a foot engagement you are placed at the point of the wedge,[64] you must know it is material not to be overthrown at the first shock, nor to give room for the destruction of the tortoise.[65] Take care lest you entangle your shield; take care likewise lest your spear be snatched from you, unless you have two, for in an engagement on foot one spear is better than two swords.

"In a naval engagement provide yourself with two spears, which you must not lose in throwing: let one of them be a long one, capable of reaching out of one vessel to another;[66] the other with a shorter handle, so that you may be able to use it conveniently in boarding an enemy. Divers darts are to be used in a sea-fight, as well heavy spears fenced with iron, as the lighter ones, and headed like a dart.

"When you assault any one with a spear armed with iron, strike his shield; if his shield be moved then attack him with the lighter javelin, or with darts, if you cannot strike him with the long-handle spear.

"At land, so on ship-board, you must fight with an undaunted mind and wary strokes, nor cast away your arms in an inconsiderate manner.

"Many arms may be conveniently used in a sea-fight that cannot be used on shore, unless in a city or castle.

"In sea-fights, scythes firmly fixed to very long spears,[67] axes with broad blades and fixed to long handles, boat-hooks, slings fixed to a staff,

---

[64] In which troops were at this period frequently drawn up.

[65] The covering formed by placing the edge of one shield close to that of another, so as to resemble the shell of that animal.

[66] In many antient representations of sea-fights the warriors appear thus armed.

[67] From these originated the bills, but at this time called falcastra. Indeed that word .occurs in the MS. Hist, Excidium Acconis, A.D. 1291, but the original document would shew whether:by this expression the gnisarme be not in reality intended.

catajæ[68] and others of that kind, stones, the bow, and the rest of the missive weapons; but of these, bituminous sea-coal mixed with sulphur holds
the first place.

"Nor are galtraps,[69] made heavy with lead, and sharp battle-axes, to be
contemned. Towers are also good, from which you may use the arms here
enumerated. Also a lever or bar, its four sides armed with iron nails.[70]

"In sea-fights, a boar[71] armed with iron may be advantageously used,
pushed forwards with oars. From this, as such a variety of arms may be
used in a sea-fight, it is necessary that before you engage in a naval war,
you should accustom yourself to use those kind of arms, thereby becoming expert for a sea-fight.

"As you will not know before-hand at what hour, or what kind of arms
are to be used, therefore take care to collect a variety of arms before you
want them, it being esteemed honourable to possess good arms, which,
when wanted, are the best of treasures.

"For the defence of a ship the following apparatus is highly necessary.
A fence of beams, erected at the side of the vessel prepared for war, carried
up so high that there may be formed four doors sufficiently large for the
passage of two men in complete armour, these to be fixed to both sides
of the main deck so firmly, that in jumping on the floor it may not totter.
Broad shields and armour of all kinds may be advantageously used in defending a ship. But a very useful instrument[72] for those defending a vessel,
is a body-covering, made of soft and blacked linen sewed together;[73] also,

---

[68] Littleton says, that the catajoe were barbed darts or spears, each having a string at
the end to recover them.

[69] These were formed with four iron spikes in such a manner that, when thrown in the
way of the enemy's cavalry, one in each was sure to point upwards and wound the horses in
their hoofs. There is a specimen in the armoury of Llewelyn Meyrick, Esq, Yet I strongly
suspect this to be a wrong translation, and rather think that the maule with .spikes in it was
intended, as it is associated with battle-axes. Such occur in some (If the illuminations to
Froissart, done in the time of Edward IV, and such a one is in my son's collection.

[70] A short mace upon this principle, but being cylindrical instead of four-sided, is in
the before-mentioned armoury.

[71] Aper, a boar's head with projecting iron tusks, was placed at the heads of vessels, that
when impelled they might destroy those they happened to strike. Ships of this description
may be seen in the illuminations of the thirteenth century.

[72] Instrumentum.

[73] Ex linteri mollihus et atratri consutoe, It seems to he the wambais tbat is here described; .and in illuminations it has a black or steel-like colour.

with the helmets, the pendulous protection for the head, made of iron.[74] Many other arms might be used in sea-fights, but it does not seem necessary to enumerate them.

"As our discourse just now turned on the means of defending oneself and attacking an enemy, it seems requisite to lay down in a few words the best manner of conducting a land war, as well respecting an engagement of cavalry as the attack and defence of towns. If you will explain these things I shall listen attentively.

"To combat on horseback, as we before observed, it is necessary to be a good horseman, and the horse must be equipped with the following apparatus: First, let him be provided with shoes firmly fixed, a saddle with girths and the rest of the apparatus: let him have also a strong, a lasting leather breast-piece, a girth passing over the middle of the saddle: let him likewise be provided with strong housings; and that the horse may be defended from wounds, both before and behind the saddle let him have a strong covering, to answer the purpose of armour, made of soft blacked linen.[75] But chiefly against all sorts of arms, a phylactery or charm, then a firm breastplate. With these defences let the head, loins, belly, breast, in a word, the Avhole horse, be armed, that no one may be able secretly to wound him.

"Let the horse have a strong bridle, whose reins are sufficiently strong to check his impetuosity: and if necessary to raise him, or oblige him to run circularly, let his head, bridle, and neck, quite to the saddle, be rolled up in linen for armour, that no one may fraudulently seize the bridle or horse.

"For the rider the following accoutrements are necessary: Coverings for his legs, made of well blacked soft linen sewed, which should extend to the kneeband of his chauçons or breeches;[76] over these steel shin-pieces, so high as to be fastened with a double band. The horseman is to put on linen drawers, such as I have pointed out, and over these steel coverings for the knees.[77]

"The upper part of his body should be covered with a linen body-armour[78] reaching down to the middle of his thighs. Over that a breastplate of iron, extending from the breasts to the band of the chaiçons; then a strong

---

[74] It is to be regretted tbat tbe translator bas not given us the Latin for this passage, as I conceive what be calls "pendulous" headpiece is the coif de maille worn under the helmet.

[75] This is called couverture de gamboisons in the Inventory of Arms of Louis le Grand, A.D. 1316, already cited; and gambaiseure in a letter of John, king of France, in the year 1353.

[76] These were gamboised hosen, which the reader will better understand by referring

[77] The genouillieres. See them on the gamboised chauçons in Pl. XVIII and XXII.

[78] The hauketon.

firm hauberk, succeeded by a body-covering of linen without sleeves.[79]

"Let him have two swords, one of which let him wear in his belt, the other let him hang at his saddle-bow; a dagger or war knife.[80] A steel helmet on his head, with an entire covering for his face. Let him carry on his neck a solid shield hung by a strong thong. Lastly, a sharp javelin of steel firmly fixed on its handle.

"There seems no need of treating further of the appointments of cavalry, nevertheless there are many more arms that might be used by horsemen, particularly the slighter bow,[81] which may be easily bent on horseback, and the rest of that kind.

"As you seem to have mentioned all the different sorts of arms that may be conveniently used in either equestrian or naval combats, I must now beg you to point out in a few words those with which castles are besieged and defended.

"Those arms which I have mentioned, as proper for naval and equestrian fights, and many others, may commodiously be used in the attack and defence of castles. He who is desirous of taking a castle with the arms already recited, must add to them the balista and catapulta, and of these the most powerful; as by the stones thrown from them, and their violent strokes, the walls and works may be beaten down. The weaker kind of these machines will be sufficient to throw darts on the walls of houses, or for slaying the men in castles or on board of the ships. If the balista should prove insufficient to throw down or shake the walls, these machines may be used with certainty: the ram, with a head shod with iron, to the impetuosity of which few walls are able to resist. But if this machine should fail to shake or throw down the wall or work, the sow, or moveable towers placed on wheels, may be used, which must always be higher than the walls to which they are opposed, for the higher they are the more proper for demolishing of castles; nor would it be at all superfluous if they exceeded the opposed walls the height of seven ells.

"To this machine they add ladders placed on wheels, with planks strongly fixed to them, so that they may be moved from one place to another by means of ropes dependent from each side. In short, I conceive that all

---

[79] The cyclas is perhaps that alluded to, at least it is the garment for this purpose in Edward the Second's time.

[80] The dagger was not in general use till the reign of Edward III; but there are instances as early as Edward I.

[81] We are here made acquainted with a fact which must have been conjectured, that the mounted archers were obliged, to use bows of less size than those on foot.

sorts of arms may be used in the attack of castles; and that it is necessary for those employed in the sieges of towns to know, on all occasions, what kind of arms are most fit for the time and occasion.

"Moreover, those who are to defend a castle may make use of most of the arms I have mentioned, with many others, such as balistae, great and small; slings, whether held by the hand or fixed to a staff; hand-bows of all sorts: spears and long poles capped with iron, some heavy and some light; with the other kinds of missive weapons.

"For eluding the effects of the balistæ, sows, and rams, the wall should be strongly propped up with oaken posts on the inside, or rather by heaping up against it earth and potters' clay, if any is at hand. The defenders of castles may hang out hurdles or baskets made with oaken twigs, and those triple or fivefold thick, filled with fat and bituminous clay, thereby endeavouring to keep their walls entire. Against the shock of the ram, large bags of hay, closely stuffed, and let down by iron chains opposite that part of the wall to which the force of the ram is directed; nor does it unfrequently happen, that the castle is so overwhelmed by showers of arrows, that the guards are not able to remain on the ramparts, (or place opposite the crenelles in the battlements); in such case it is necessary that hanging ports should be suspended by light laths, two ells higher and three lower than the embrasures, and so remote from the walls, that all kinds of weapons may have room to be thrown downwards in the interval between the wall and these pensile ports. These ports should be fixed to long beams, that they may be thrust outwards and retracted at pleasure.

"The prickly cat[82] is one of the best kind of arms, and most useful for the defenders of castles, which, being made of great and heavy beams, and bristled with oaken teeth, hung at every embrasure, may, if the enemy approaches near the works, be thrown down upon him.

"Likewise a beam or great piece of timber fashioned with long poles, having well sharpened oaken teeth, were used to be erected near the battlements, that they also might be thrown on the enemy if they came under the walls.

"Among the best kind of arms is also the war rammer,[83] fitted with curved steel nails and hooks, which, when it is let down on the enemy, is fixed with chains armed with curved nails, that the enemy can neither seize nor cut it. At the end of the chain is a rope sufficiently strong to draw it up;

---

[82] Felis echinata.
[83] Fistuca bellica.

this serves to take and bring into the walls one or more of the enemy, as often as a body of the besiegers come within its reach.

"Nor among the defensive machines is the missive wheel to be despised. It is formed of two mill-stones joined by an oaken axis, and is thrown down upon the enemy by means of a plank sloping from the embrasure.

"The missive chariot may also be effectually used, formed like an ordinary chariot, with two or four wheels, and so formed that it may be loaded at will with either hot or cold stones: on both sides are strong chains, which serve to stop it when it has run a sufficient distance, and to keep the wheels from deviating when it runs from a declining plank in the embrasure. This, when the chains check its course, will cast its load among the enemy, which, from its weight, will fly in all directions.

"Some more prudent men than ordinary used to incrust fragments of stones in potters' clay, which would bear throwing, and when they arrived at their destined mark separated into the smallest particles, and could not be thrown back again.[84] For the destruction of dry walls great flints were used. If a castle defended by a wall would demolish by batteries a castle of wood, ambulatory towers, ladders, sows, and other machines fixed on wheels, your success will be greater in proportion as the stones used are large and hard.

"Hot water, glass, or melted lead, may be very useful in the defence of a castle. If a sow or any other machine is brought near a castle which cannot be hurt by hot water, but are lower than the walls of a castle, the use of long poles shod with iron, to which sharp and hot ploughshares are fixed, will greatly conduce to the destruction of these kind of machines, by throwing those poles with the ploughshares on the wooden engines, and the ploughshares being left, the poles may be drawn back. Sometimes burning pitch and sulphur may be thrown on them.

"Pits round about a castle are reckoned among the methods of defence; these, the more numerous and deep they are, the more they tend to the defence of the fortress. First, if the enemy attempts to move any machine fixed on wheels over these pits against the place, they ought to be prepared that they have many and small apertures, but all so artfully covered that no traces of them may appear: then let the pits be filled with brushwood, and other things of that kind, such as easily take fire: at night, when the enemy from his wooden castle, ladders, or other wdieeled machine, attacks the castle, some man may steal secretly out, and set fire to the pits.

"If it should so happen that the enemy batters the castle so vehement-

_____
[84] The prototype of grape-shot.

ly with stones, that the garrison cannot keep their posts without doors, or defend the castle, strong oaken columns must be erected, upon which large beams are to be laid, sustaining holm planks, earth heaped up in the manner of a wall three or four ells thick, for covering them from the stones thrown. The same to be done against a wooden tower for besieging a fortification of stone: the columns must be very stable and firm, and somewhat higher than the wooden tower.

"But of all the arms and machines we have enumerated, the most excellent is the curved giant of shields vomiting poisoned flames.[85] In a word, in the defence of any castle the same kind of arms may be made use of that may be thrown, stricken, or pierced with, and every species of arms used for defence or offence."

I have met with nothing that can at all throw a light on what is here called the "curved giant of shields," but suppose it must have been something much larger than a pavaise made to curve over the heads of those it was intended to protect, and furnished with several tubes, through which the Greek fire might be thrown."Tournaments remained in the same degree of estimation during this reign as in the last, and were conducted in a similar manner. Piers Gaveston distinguished himself particularly on such occasions, and his celebrity could not fail, as it wounded the pride of the nobility, to augment their jealousy of that favourite. In different encounters he unhorsed the earls of Leicester, Hereford, Pembroke, and Warenne.[86]

In this reign were abolished the Knights' Templars, who had become affluent, dissolute, and sensual, and whose order was no longer of service.

All warlike machines were called artillaria or artillery, whence the French term artiller, to fortify. This word is so used in the Roman du Chevalier du Barisel, MS.

> Avoit fait son chastel fermer,
> Qui moult estoit bien batilliés
> Si fort est, et si bien artilliés,
> K'il ne cremoit ne roy ne comté.

> "He had caused his castle to be closed,
> Which was well built,
> So strong is it, and so well furnished with weapons,
> That he feared not king nor count."

---

[85] Omnium autem quoe enumeravimus armorum et machinarum, præstantissimus est incurvus clypeorum gigas, flammas venenatas eructans.

[86] Trokelowe's Annals, p. 5, 6.

So William Guiart, under the year 1304, speaking of the battle of Maiden's-mount, says:

> Nul ne pense ore à leoherie:
> Plusieurs vont à l'artillerie,
> Qui fut sans que ce truste lise,
> Près des tentes le roy assise.
> Artillerie est le charroi,
> Qui par duc, par comté ou par roy,
> Ou par aucun seigneur de terre,
> Est chargie de quarriaus de guerre
> D'arbalestes, de dars, de lances,
> Et de targes d'unes semblances,
> De tiex harnois lit prendre seulent,
> Li desgarni, qui prendre en veulent
> Cil qui Ies delivrent, en baillent
> A ceus & qui tiex choses faillent.

> "Not any think of lechery:
> Many go to the artillery,
> Which was without this trusty list,
> Placed near the king's tents.
> Artillery is the waggon
> Which, by a duke, earl, or king,
> Or by any territorial lord,
> Is loaded with quarrels for war,
> With cross-bows, darts, lances,
> And with uniform targets,
> Also such harness as they were accustomed to take there:
> The unarmed, who wished to take
> That which was delivered to them, distributed them
> To those who wanted such things."

The root of the word, however, is ars, which was the barbarous Latin term for a machine. In the same manner the fabricator of such warlike implements was called artillator. Thus, in the Statute of Edward II, on the office of seneschall of Aquitaine, we read: Item ordinatum est quod sit unus artillator, qui faciat balistas, carellos, arcus, sagittas, lanceas, spiculas et alia arma necessaria pro garnizionibus castrorum. "Moreover it is ordained, that there be one artillator to make balistse, quarrels, bows, arrows, lances, darts, and other arms, requisite for furnishing castles."

William Guiart speaks frequently of these quarrels, which were called cadrelli, quarriaus, and garrotz. Thus, under the year 1304, he says:

Quarriaus traient au cliqueter
Et font l'espringalle geter;
Li garros qui lors de la ist
Les plus viguereus eshabist.

"Quarrels arc discharged resounding,
And the espringalle is made to cast them;
The quarrels that thence issue
Terrify the most vigorous."

And again:

Et font gfeter leur espringalles,
Ca et la sonnent li clairain;
Li garrot empané d'arain
Lassent leur lieux de ce me vent
Plutost que tcmpeste ne vent.

"And make their espringalles work:
Here and there the clarions sound;
The quarrels, feathered[87] with copper,
Quit their places, and with such discharges come upon me
Quicker than tempests or wind."

Again:

Espringalles font leur service,
Dont li garrot en main lieu saillent.

"Espringalles perform their service,
From which the quarrels in hand quit their places."

These quarrels were so called from their square heads, so that, properly speaking, the garrot was the complete weapon, and the quadrille its head. Thus in a decree of the French parliament, on the 9th May, 1321, it is said: Item ad reddendum et restituendum tres magnos guarros cum cadrilis pertinentibus ad eosdem. "Also to render and restore three great garrots with the quadrilles belonging to them."From which we gather that those used for the espringalles were termed "great quarrels."

The Chronicon Leodiense, under the year 1313, enumerates many

---

[87] The expression, "feathered with wood,"&c. is very frequent in old inventories of armour; and though I have seen nonè feathered with copper, there are in the collection of Llewelyn Meyrick, Esq. some quarrels feathered with leather and others with wood as well as geese feathers.

kinds of warlike machines used at this period: Mangondia seu fructibula, sive tribuceta vel aries, vel sues, vineas, biblias, petrarias, sive cattos versitales. "Mangonds or fructi-bules, or tribuchets, rams, sows, besiegers' coverings, biblia, petraries or versatile cats."Of the tribuchet[88] I have seen no ant. ient, delineation, but of the trepied we have a representation which, though more strictly of this period, has been noticed before at page 170. It is in the ivory carving on a chest belonging to F Douce, Esq. which exhibits an attack of a castle.[89] It is given Fig. 5 of Plate XXVI, from which it will be seen to have been in the nature of a sling affixed to one of the arms of a balance, and that it derives its effects from the sudden falling of a weight at the other end. The biblia seems to be the same as the blida, called by the Danes blie, and by the Welsh bliv, but its distinctive character I have not been as yet able to trace. From a poem, however, which the bard Iolo addresses to King Edward III, we learn that this machine was for projecting stones purposely selected, which were called maeneu bliv; thus he says:

> Curaw it bliv, ddyliv ddelw,
> Ceryg Caer Verwig vur welw.

> "Battering with the bliv, like a torrent,
> The stones against the gloomy walls of Berwick."

And that it was a powerful instrument Tudor Aled bears testimony in his Sonnet to his Bow, of which he says:

> Hi a davlai o'i deuvlacn
> Ergyd bliv ar goed o'i blaen.

> "It would impel from its two horns[90] the shaft
> Forward with the force of a bliv."

Besides stones, balls of earth (probably baked) called pelotes, and corruptedly bullets, were ejected from these, as we learn from a deed, dated 1319.[91] Lapides ac pelotes terreas ad hoc aptas, et alia nocira emittunt per

---

[88] Of this mention has before been made, and of its Italian origin.

[89] See Carter's Specimens of Antient Sculpture. This same chest exhibits a knight sleeping on his arms, from which we learn that the helmet was taken off the head, and then in its open state placed over it, so that the knight was protected from a sudden attack, while he had plenty of air. He covers himself also with his shield.

[90] Deuvlaen implies "two projections,"and if designating the bow, must be its two horns; but if the shaft, then it would signify the nock.

[91] Rymer's Fœd.

halistas et arcus supra-dictos, per vicos et venellas in civitate. "Stones and earthen bullets made to fit, with other noxious missiles, are shot from the balistæ and bows aforesaid, in the villages and avenues of the city."

The catti versitales, or versatile cats, were those furnished with draw-bridges, in the same manner as moveable towers generally were, to enable those upon them the more easily to get into a besieged place. It is evident, therefore, that the kind of cat here alluded to must have been the chat-faulx.

Fordun, in his Scoti-chronicon,[92] describing the result of the battle of Bannockburn, says all the English provisions fell into the hands of the Scots, cum petrariis et ligonibus, trabiculis, et mangonellis, scalis et ingeniis, pavilionibus et canopeis, fundis et bombardis, cæterisque bellicis machinis,[93] "with their petraries and shovels, rafters and mangonels, ladders and engines, pavilions and bell-tents, slings and bombards, and other machines of war." Scala not only signifies a ladder, but like the present military term eschelle, a division of troops. Indeed it seems to imply both the larger and smaller sections of armies. Thus in the MS. Roman de Turpin, it evidently means what were called batailles: Charlemagne fit trois eschelles, la premiere fu de chevaliers, la seconde de gent de pié, la troisième de sergent à cheval. "Charlemagne made three eschelles, the first was of knights, the second of infantry, the third of mounted sergeants." The nature of these troops shews that not the divisions of one line, but three distinct lines themselves, are intended by the expression. The Chronicle of Bertrand du Guesclin uses the word apparently in the same sense:

> Son escliielle conduit par compas bellement
> Vers l'eschielle Bertrand, qui moult ot hardement, &c.

> "He conducts his eschiellc to wheel finely round
> On the eschielle of Bertrand, who had very boldly," &c.

And William Guiart, under the year 1214:

> D'entre cux ont dcus eschieles faites,
> Cele oh sont les plus honorables;
> Conduit Gauchier li connestables.

> "Between them are two eschielles made:
> That composed of the most honourable
> Were led by Gauchier the constable."

---

[92] Lib. XII, c. 21.
[93] Other MSS. add tribuchetis et arietibus,

Guillaume le Breton cites it in the other sense in the following passage:

> Disposuitque acies par scalas, perque cohortes,
> Ordine compositas recto.

> "And he disposed his line in eschelles, and by cohorts,
> Drawn up in straight ranks."

Again:

> .... Ut subsit qæsque tribuno
> Scala suo.

> .... As each eschelle is assigned
> To its officer."

And:

> .... Scalasque suorum
> Quisque magistrorum densant.

> .... And their eschelles
> Each of their commanders deepen."

So in Wace's Roman de Rou:

> Sa bataille ordena, ses eschielles parti.

> "Arranges his line, and separates his eschielles."

This account of the art of war during the time of Edward II, cannot be better terminated than by a description of the military arrangements at the battle of Bannockburn, in 1313.

Bruce, whom even his enemies praise, says Mr. Turner, met the peril like a consummate general. He could not hope to beat the English cavalry, and therefore did not attempt it.[94] He dismounted all his own horse, and formed his forces into an army of foot.[95] They were about 40,000 men. He divided them into three bodies. Each man wore light armour, which a sword

---

[94] Trokelowe says, the battle of Falkirk had taught the Scotch the inferiority of their horse, p. 25.

[95] The Scala Chronica observes, that the recent victory of the Flemings 0v:er the French at Courtray, bad given Bruce an example, that cavalry might be defeated by infantry, 2 LeI. 547.

could not easily pierce;[96] battle axes were at their sides,[97] and lances in their hands. He compacted them into a thick mass, forming as it were a bristled hedge,[98] and to secure them from the English cavalry, employed the night in digging trenches along his front, three feet deep and sufficiently broad, which he covered with hurdles and strewed with turf.[99] These were strong enough for his infantry to pass over, but would not sustain the weight of the English cavalry loaded with heavy armour. Bruce was himself on foot that his example might prevent any one from thinking of flight.[100]

The English were formed in three lines, the first of which consisted of their knights, from which it would appear that on their charge much reliance was placed; the second was composed of the infantry and archers, and the third had with it the king and clergy. The English cavalry began the attack, but while in full speed to charge the Scots their horses stumbled on the treacherous turf, and threw their riders on the Scottish lances. The second line increased the evil, for seeing the enemy rush on they discharged their arrows, which fell on the unprotected back parts of the struggling English knights; so that, alarmed at the confusion, Edward was advised to quit the field. Moor[101] blames the English cavalry for beginning the struggle while the sun was shining on their gilt shields and burnished helms, instead of waiting till noon. Be this at it may, at the sight of the royal banner quitting the field, the army dispersed in panic. The knights, throwing off their armour, fled half naked over the country, so that no defeat could be more disgraceful. Bruce, however, by this brilliant success, completed the independence of Scotland, and the security of his hard-earned throne.[102]

END OF VOL I.

---

[96] From the ordinances of this king, before quoted, we learn that this was the hauketon, while the result of this battle confirms the prefernece there given to it.

[97] One of these Scotch axes, but probably of a later date, is in the possession of Llewelyn Meyrick, Esq.

[98] Malm. 149. Trok. 29.

[99] This agrees with the advice at p. 200, which, however, shews that this was no uncommon deception at that period.

[100] Trok. 26.

[101] P. 594.

[102] Trokelowe, 28.

www.ingramcontent.com/pod-product-compliance
Lightning Source LLC
Chambersburg PA
CBHW040412110426
42812CB00033B/3364/J

*9 7 8 1 9 8 9 4 3 4 0 0 0 *